Your Career in MARKETING

second edition

John A. Beaumont
Formerly Director of the
Distributive Education Branch
U.S. Office of Education

Kathleen H. Langan
Educational Consultant and Writer

Louise H. Taylor, Ed.D.
Chairperson of Student Affairs
College of Business Administration
Chicago State University

Gregg Division/McGraw-Hill Book Company
New York St. Louis Dallas San Francisco Auckland Düsseldorf
Johannesburg Kuala Lumpur London Mexico Montreal New Delhi
Panama Paris São Paulo Singapore Sydney Tokyo Toronto

ST. PHILIPS COLLEGE LIBRARY

658.87002
B379y2

senior editor/**Mary Alice McGarry**
editing manager/**Sylvia L. Weber**
editing supervisors/**Carole Chatfield, Susan Berkowitz**
production supervisors/**Phyllis D. Lemkowitz, Iris Levy**
designer/**Charles A. Carson**
art supervisor/**George T. Resch**
illustrator/**Emmanuel Stallman**
cover photos courtesy Dennis Rizzuto Associates, Action Vista, Men's Fashion Association of America, and J. P. Stevens & Co., Inc.
This book was set in Times Roman by Progressive Typographers.
It was printed and bound by Kingsport Press.

Library of Congress Cataloging in Publication Data

Beaumont, John Appleton, (date)
    Your career in marketing.

  First ed. published in 1968 under title: Your job in distribution.
    Includes index.
    1. Marketing. 2. Marketing—Vocational guidance. 3. Distributive education. I. Langan, Kathleen H., joint author. II. Taylor, Louise H., joint author. III. Title.
HF5415.B38   1976   658.8'7'0023   75-31984
ISBN 0-07-004245-4

YOUR CAREER IN MARKETING second edition

Copyright © 1976 by McGraw-Hill, Inc. All Rights Reserved.
First Edition published under title *Your Job in Distribution*
by John A. Beaumont and Kathleen H. Langan. Copyright ©
1968 by McGraw-Hill, Inc. All Rights Reserved.
Printed in the United States of America.
No part of this publication may be reproduced,
stored in a retrieval system, or transmitted,
in any form or by any means, electronic, mechanical, photocopying,
recording, or otherwise, without prior written permission of
the publisher.

  34567890 KPKP 78543210987

CONTENTS

Preface v
Unit 1 Marketing: What It's All About viii

Part 1 What Marketing Means to You **2**
Part 2 Marketing in Action **10**
Part 3 The Marketing Activities **20**
Part 4 The Background for Marketing **30**
Part 5 What You Can Do for Marketing **42**

Unit 2 You and a Marketing Career **54**

Part 6 Thinking About Careers **56**
Part 7 Understanding Basic Human Needs **66**
Part 8 Understanding Why You Are Unique **77**
Part 9 Getting to Know the Real You **87**
Part 10 Thinking About What's Important to You **97**
Part 11 Making Decisions **107**
Part 12 Putting It All Together **119**

Unit 3 Preparing for a Career in Marketing **132**

Part 13 Distributive Education: An Opportunity **134**
Part 14 The Basic and Social Skills **144**
Part 15 The Economic Facts of Life **154**
Part 16 General Business Organization **164**
Part 17 Marketing Management **175**
Part 18 Marketing Skills **187**
Part 19 Cooperative Education **197**

Unit 4 Careers in Marketing Goods **208**

Part 20 Food Stores **210**
Part 21 Food Wholesaling **225**
Part 22 Apparel and Accessories **239**
Part 23 Home Furnishings **256**
Part 24 Products for Health and Beauty **273**
Part 25 Leisure-Time Goods **284**
Part 26 Automotive Products **294**
Part 27 Farm and Garden Supplies and Floristry **309**
Part 28 Hardware and Building Supplies **322**

Unit 5 Careers in Marketing Services 336

Part 29 Food Services **338**
Part 30 Hotels and Motels **351**
Part 31 Personal Services **362**
Part 32 Business Services **373**
Part 33 Recreation Services and Tourism **385**
Part 34 Transportation Services **398**
Part 35 Finance and Credit **414**
Part 36 Insurance and Real Estate **427**

Unit 6 Starting Your Education and Experience 444

Part 37 Broadening Your Horizons **446**
Part 38 Developing a Personal Career Plan **456**

Index 465

PREFACE

Your Job in Distribution was first published in 1968 to answer the need for a textbook that would introduce students from every possible background to the field of marketing and to the broad range of opportunities that it offers for building personally satisfying careers. Today the need for such an introductory book is even greater. Many schools have found that it is unrealistic to expect students to commit themselves to the distributive education program without first giving them the information that will make their decision valid in terms of their own needs, values, goals, personal characteristics, and desired life style.

The opportunity to assess marketing as a possible career area is important, because marketing is frequently not understood in the students' homes and little reference is made to it in the average school curriculum. By offering an introductory course, the school can help those students who might not otherwise have thought of the DE program. At the same time, an introductory course can make some students realize, with a minimum cost in time and effort, that DE is not the right program for them. These students will have made a decision that will help them with their final career choice, and they will also be better prepared for their life-long role of consumer.

Careful research about exactly how such an introductory course should be presented has led to this revision of *Your Job in Distribution*. The change of title to *Your Career in Marketing* reflects first the feeling of most DE educators that "marketing" is a more readily understood and more descriptive term than "distribution." The choice of the word "career" to replace "job" is even more significant, representing as it does a deep commitment to the purposes and objectives of career education. Furthermore, in this edition, even more effort has been made to make the book relevant to each individual student, regardless of race, color, creed, sex, or economic background. This is readily apparent in the text itself, as well as in the illustrations.

ORGANIZATION OF THE TEXT
While this book is technically a revision, in actual fact the material in it is almost entirely new. It has been carefully organized into six units, with a total of 38 parts, to give the students everything that they will need to make an informed, rational decision about whether to continue their study of marketing.

To begin, the students have to understand the three key ideas in the title: *you, career,* and *marketing.* Thus the first two units are devoted to clarifying these ideas. Unit 1 is a basic introduction to the world of marketing, giving the students an idea of its scope and variety and showing how it fits into the modified free enterprise system. The emphasis here is on the relevance of marketing to the students' own lives, not only as possible workers, but also as citizens and consumers. Unit 2 then turns the students' attention to the significance of careers, the importance of careful career selection, and the necessity for intensive self-knowledge in order to make valid career decisions. The students are encouraged to try to understand how and why they are unique and to develop a positive view of their own individuality. Goal and values clarification and decision making are important ingredients here.

Unit 3 provides the students a summary of the DE program, indicating its scope, relevance, and significance for them. The authors firmly believe that making this kind of information available to students in advance will result in much more highly motivated DE classes.

In Units 4 and 5, the students have the opportunity to look at marketing more intensively by studying the businesses that market specific kinds of goods and services. In each case, the method is to present a general description of the business and to show the possibilities for entry-, career-, and management-level jobs. Both the advantages of and the requirements for the jobs are discussed so that the students can see whether they are suited to the field and what they would have to do to prepare for it. The students learn about the possibilities for lattice- as well as ladder-type moves, because the flexibility of marketing is stressed throughout.

The specific businesses discussed follow the standard DE taxonomy,[1] with two exceptions. General merchandise, rather than being treated separately, is covered in each of the specific businesses, thus giving the students an awareness of the full scope of the general merchandise category and the various ways of entering the field. Also, advertising is presented as just one of the many business services that offer career opportunities. Since spending for business services has increased in recent years even more than for personal services, the authors believe that stressing advertising over the other business services is no longer valid.

As the final part of the book, Unit 6 turns the students' attention back to themselves, to try to help them understand where they want to go next and how they can get there. Here a theme that has run throughout the book is reiterated: that the "right" answer is the answer that is right for the individual student.

AIDS FOR TEACHING AND LEARNING

In an attempt to make the teaching and learning processes as easy as possible, the authors have built the material in this book on the foundation of what the students already know. This is true of the examples

---

[1] Standard Terminology for Curriculum and Instruction in Local and State School Systems, edited by John F. Putnam and W. Dale Chismore, *State Educational Records and Report Series: Handbook VI*, U.S. Dept. of Health, Education, and Welfare, 1970, Washington, D.C.

that are used and it is also true of how the material is presented. For example, the detailed discussion of marketing businesses in Units 4 and 5 begins with a study of food stores. The assumption is that every student has at some point been in a food store and can therefore relate to this material in a personal way. By starting with such common experiences, the students can be carried along comfortably to new situations. Also, the vocabulary and style are straightforward and on the students' level. Words and concepts that are new to the students are defined in everyday terms.

As another kind of aid to teaching and learning, goals are presented at the beginning of each unit and part so that both teacher and student know what kind of performance will be expected. Questions related to the goals are included at the end of each unit and part so that performance can be measured. Additional activities give the students many opportunities to relate the material directly to themselves. The end-of-part activities include a vocabulary drill, to emphasize the terms which are in boldface type in the text, and a section that indicates whether the student has understood the material. A third section asks the student to relate the materials to everyday marketing situations. In many instances, these activities and the end-of-unit activities bring marketers into the classroom and take the students out to where marketing is happening. These activities serve as a way of emphasizing that marketing is not just something to read about, but a real subject for real people living in a real world.

SUPPLEMENTARY MATERIALS

This book is accompanied by a Job Activity Guide containing some of the end-of-part and end-of-unit material, as well as additional material that emphasizes training in the basic and social skills. Also available is a teacher's manual and key, which gives the teacher many ideas for enriching the material. The teacher's manual contains a final exam in the form of an objective test ready to be duplicated, with a key.

ACKNOWLEDGMENTS

The authors wish to thank the many trade associations and marketing companies that provided research materials and photographs for this book. There are also many people, including teachers, executive directors of trade associations, and marketing executives, who have reviewed portions of the manuscript and given invaluable suggestions. Unfortunately, the list of people who have provided assistance is much too long to print, but their help has contributed immeasurably to the authors' efforts to present accurate, up-to-date material.

John A. Beaumont
Kathleen H. Langan
Louise H. Taylor

After completing this unit, you will have developed an understanding of the role played by marketing in our society and how marketing affects your life.

This book is about three very important subjects. First of all, it is about *you*. By giving you the opportunity to think in new ways about all the special qualities that make you an individual, this book can help you make career plans that are exactly right for you.

The second subject of this book is *careers*, a word that brings to mind the world of work. It is important for you to begin now to think about how you are going to earn your living, because the question is such a complex one. It is not just a matter of how you are going to spend 35 or 40 hours a week for the largest portion of your life. Although that in itself is a lot to consider, much more is involved, such as the kind of life that you want for yourself. Because the work that you do will directly affect the way that you live, leaving the choice of a career to chance is not a good idea. There is a big difference between just falling into a job and planning for a career that is right for you.

Finally, this book is about *marketing*, a major career area for you to consider when making your future plans. The special importance of this field is that it has room for so many different kinds of people. Therefore, you might be able to work in this field in the way that suits you best. This first unit is an introduction to marketing, which will help you understand what it is all about and how it relates to you.

Marketing: What It's All About

What Marketing Means to You

After reading Part 1, you will be able—
- To identify the marketing activities in a given list of business activities.
- To distinguish between goods and services.
- To define the word "marketing."

Marketing is a word that you may have only vague ideas about, and yet you are part of it every day of your life. Every time you buy something—a pizza, magazine, or movie ticket—you are playing a role in the marketing process. The same thing is true whenever you sell something—an outgrown bicycle or your services baby-sitting.

You are going to be doing more and more buying and selling as you grow older. The only way to be sure that you are buying and selling wisely is to understand what marketing is all about. That is a good reason all by itself for studying marketing, but there is an even more important reason. Marketing is such a broad field that roughly one out of every four workers in the United States today is employed in marketing. There is one word that summarizes all those marketing jobs: *opportunities*. It's a word that is hard to ignore when you are thinking about yourself and possible careers.

MARKETING: AS OLD AND AS NEW AS PEOPLE

Having to study a subject that seems to have nothing at all to do with your life can be very difficult. But marketing is definitely not that kind of subject. It is concerned with what is going on around you every day. It can't help but be interesting because it's all about people. It is done by people for people, and it's as exciting and challenging and as full of variety and surprises as people are.

The Beginnings of Marketing

We cannot say exactly when marketing began, anymore than we can say exactly when the wheel was invented. We can imagine, though, that one day two early cave dwellers sat down to eat together. One had an extra supply of meat, and the other had too many berries and nuts. One of them got the bright idea that they should trade their extras, and at that very moment marketing was on its way.

This, of course, is only a guess, but we do know from the records of such early peoples as the Egyptians, Greeks, and Romans that marketing was a very real part of their lives. We also know that marketing has often been the cause of historical events. For example, one important reason for the discovery of America was that Columbus was trying to find a better route to the Far East, the source of spices and other goods that the Europeans wanted to buy.

The Effect of the Industrial Revolution

Although marketing is older than written history, it did not begin to assume its present importance until the time of the Industrial Revolution. This was a period in history that drastically changed the way that people lived. The Industrial Revolution began in England in the last part of the 1700s, first with the invention of machines to spin thread and weave cloth and soon after with the invention of the steam engine. More and more machines were invented in rapid order, and suddenly life was so different that "revolution" is the only word strong enough to describe this period of change.

Before the Industrial Revolution, people had generally produced goods to fill their everyday needs right in their own homes or had purchased goods from individual craftspeople. These craftspeople, using only hand tools, had to work many hours to produce relatively little. By contrast, the new machines were fast and efficient and could

Before the Industrial Revolution, even such things as barrels and buckets had to be made by hand. A craftsperson working only with hand tools spent many hours making one wooden barrel. (*Courtesy Old Sturbridge Village*)

PART 1 • WHAT MARKETING MEANS TO YOU • 3

produce so many goods that a new term had to be added to the language. That term is **mass production,** which refers to the process of producing goods by machine in great quantities.

Once the new machines were invented, people became much more dependent on each other than they had been before. The people who were hired to run the machines in the large factories could no longer grow their own food or make their own clothing. However, they could use their wages to buy the things they needed from other people. At the same time, the farmers and the miners were also enjoying the benefits of new and better machines. They could use the money that they earned from selling their surpluses to buy the things that the factories were turning out.

Mass production brought with it a new problem. On the one hand, there were **producers,** people who make, mine, and grow things. On the other hand, there were **consumers,** people who use, or consume, things. The producers wanted to be able to sell their products, and the consumers wanted to be able to buy them. But there was a problem in getting them together. It was no longer a question of neighbors dealing with neighbors. The producers and consumers were spread over a wide area. So how could they find each other?

There had to be some kind of bridge that would make it possible for the producers and consumers to reach each other. That is exactly what marketing is, a bridge over which the tremendous output of farms, factories, and mines can roll smoothly along the way to the consumers. Without this bridge, mass production could not work.

Marketing is the bridge that links producers and consumers. Without marketing the tremendous number of goods and services produced today could not reach the people who want to buy them.

The Age of Marketing

Now that we are almost in the twenty-first century, the marketing bridge is being asked to carry greater weight than ever before. There are many people who think that strengthening this bridge is the most important challenge of our time. Certainly it is true that if the marketing bridge were to break down, business life everywhere would break down with it. This is because the producers cannot go on and on making new products that cannot be moved along to the consumer. Let us now take a closer look at the reasons why people speak of our present time as the age of marketing.

INCREASED PRODUCTION OF GOODS. Production in the United States and many other countries of the world has become a highly developed process. We have reached the age when machines are so efficient that many of them are run by computers rather than by people. Today's complex machines are turning out such a variety of goods that we cannot even begin to list them—goods that range from the simplest necessities of life to the most ultramodern luxuries.

Not only are there many different products, but there are many varieties of the same product. As an example of this variety, think about all the different kinds of television sets that are available today. There are miniature sets that can be carried around, table models in many sizes and shapes, and cabinet models in styles to suit every taste. This same kind of thing is true of many other products, from automobiles to breakfast cereals.

Mass production has obviously become very important in today's world. Production on such a massive scale can only work when there is a very strong system of marketing to go along with it.

A NEW EMPHASIS ON SERVICES. So far, we have been talking only about the production of goods. **Goods** are material things. Because they have size and shape and can be seen and touched, they are called "tangible products." But the sale of goods is only part of the marketing picture. The complete picture must include the sale of services, which are known as "intangibles" because they cannot be seen or touched. When you buy a service, you are paying to have someone do something for you, rather than paying someone to give you an actual thing. For example, when you take a bus ride, your fare is your payment to the bus company for its services in getting you where you want to go. When you have your clothes cleaned or your television set repaired, you pay for the services you are receiving.

Sometimes services are offered to you in connection with the product you are buying. For example, let's say that your family buys a new refrigerator that must be delivered to your home. One store, especially one that is known for its low prices, might charge you an extra sum of money for the delivery service. In another store, the delivery service would appear to be free in that you do not have to pay anything for it over and above the price of the refrigerator. Actually you are still paying for the delivery service, but in this case the cost of the service has been included in the price of the refrigerator. In either case, you are buying both a product and a service.

Services can be defined as benefits or satisfactions offered for sale or provided in connection with the sale of goods. Services are not a new part of the marketing picture. What is new, however, is the tremendous variety of services that are available today and the willingness of people to buy them. Life has become so complex that people cannot do everything for themselves anymore than they can make everything for themselves. Because services make people's lives easier and more comfortable, they are becoming more important every day.

CONSUMERS BY THE BILLIONS. The large number of goods and services for sale is one explanation for the importance of marketing today. But it is only part of the story. Other reasons are the great number of people who want to buy these goods and services and the vast geographical area that they occupy. The population of the United States alone is roughly 220 million people, living all the way from Alaska and Hawaii to Maine and the Virgin Islands. The modern-day marketing system has to be good enough to reach all these people. It also has to reach the many people in other countries who want to buy American products and to sell their products to Americans. Today's marketplace is the whole world.

WHEN ARE GOODS AND SERVICES USABLE?

Your school probably has a candy machine that you have used. Perhaps you even bought a candy bar at lunch today. You can learn a lot about marketing by thinking about how that candy bar came to be where you could buy it when you wanted it.

The candy bar was made in a factory that may be many miles from your school. After it was made, it had to be wrapped in a specially designed wrapper, partly to keep it fresh and partly to make it attractive to you. Then the bar was packed with other bars in a box, and that box was packed with other boxes into a larger carton. The carton was stored for a while, and when an order came in, the carton was sent to the warehouse of a vending machine company in your area. From there it was picked up by the person whose job it is to keep the candy machine in your school filled. The candy was then placed in the machine so that you could buy it when you wanted a snack.

This is only the simplest explanation of how the candy bar got to you. The full story would have to include much more—the papers that had to be filled out; the money that had to be exchanged; the trucks that had to carry the cartons, first to the warehouse and then to your school; and, above all, the people who had to carry out all these activities. It is obvious that the marketing of even the simplest product is a very complex process.

It is also obvious that marketing serves you in a very special way. The shoes you are wearing may have come from a factory on the outskirts of St. Louis, Missouri. When you bought them, you probably wanted them right away, either for a special event or because yours were worn out. The fact that there were shoes sitting at the factory would have been of no help to you at all. The only way you could use the shoes was to have them right there in a shoe store that you could get to easily. Goods and services are useful to the consumer only when they are *in the right place at the right time.* By adding this time and place value to the original value of goods and services, marketing is helping producers to sell their goods and consumers to enjoy them.

MARKETING IS A CIRCLE

Another interesting fact to think about in connection with the candy bar is that the company producing it was also a consumer. The company had to buy all sorts of goods and services in order to make the candy. First of all, the company had to borrow money from a bank to get the factory started. Then it was necessary to buy the chocolate, sugar, nuts, butter, and other ingredients needed for the candy, plus machines for making the bars, wrapping paper and packing boxes, and equipment for the factory's office. The company also had to buy services from the telephone, electric, and water companies, and insurance, in case someone got hurt or there was a fire. The services of an advertising agency were also needed to let people know about the candy bars.

As the producer of the candy bars, this company was very dependent on a good marketing system to sell the product to the consumers. At the same time, the company was equally dependent on a good marketing system to buy the goods and services needed to produce the candy bars. Remember too that the people who sold their goods and services to the candy bar company also had the same problem of buying supplies for their own businesses. It is because marketing goes around like this that it is such an interesting field to work in.

A WORKING DEFINITION OF MARKETING

This has been only a brief introduction to the exciting story of marketing. Yet we have already touched upon many of the different activities that are included in marketing, such as buying and selling, storage,

Marketing is a circle. The people who work to produce goods and services are themselves also consumers of goods and services.

recordkeeping, package design, transportation, banking, insurance, and advertising. If our definition of marketing is going to allow for this range of activities, it obviously has to be very broad. Thus, **marketing** is all the activities that make it possible to get goods and services from the producers to the consumers.

Included in that one-sentence definition are more than 30 million jobs. Perhaps your future is also included.

- **BUILDING YOUR MARKETING VOCABULARY**

Define each of the following terms and then use each one in a sentence.

consumer	mass production
goods	producer
marketing	services

- **UNDERSTANDING WHAT YOU HAVE READ**
  1. How long has marketing been in existence?
  2. What effect did the Industrial Revolution have on the production of goods?
  3. Why can marketing be compared to a bridge?
  4. Give five examples of goods and five examples of services that you either have bought recently or would like to buy.
  5. Give three reasons why marketing has become so important today.
  6. What do we mean when we say that marketing adds time and place value to goods? How does this help the consumer?

- **APPLYING WHAT YOU HAVE LEARNED**
  1. On a separate sheet of paper, rule a form like the one below. In the left-hand column, list the following business activities: (a) mining gold, (b) storing wheat, (c) delivering furniture, (d) producing candy bars, (e) growing cotton, (f) fishing for salmon, (g) selling shoes in a store, (h) advertising new automobiles, (i) buying insurance, (j) filling out a sales slip. Indicate whether the activity is a marketing activity or a nonmarketing activity by putting a check mark in the appropriate column.

BUSINESS ACTIVITY	MARKETING	NONMARKETING
Example: Borrowing money from a bank	✔	

  2. On a separate sheet of paper, list the following producers and state one way in which each would also be a consumer: (a) candy manufacturer, (b) clothing manufacturer, (c) coal mine operator, (d) tailor, (e) wheat farmer, (f) restaurant owner.
  3. Mass production and marketing have worked together to make our lives very different from the lives of people living at the turn of the century. Make a list of five products that can be purchased today that were not available in 1900. Choose one of the five products and be prepared to discuss with the class whether that product has added to or taken away from what is called the "quality of life."

Marketing in Action

After reading Part 2, you will be able—
- To explain the difference between direct and indirect marketing.
- To state whether each customer in a given list would buy from wholesaling or retailing middlemen.
- To distinguish between industrial and consumer products.
- To explain why it is sometimes difficult to separate the jobs of producing and marketing a service.

The best way to show how exciting a field marketing can be is to take a closer look at how it actually works. We have said that about a quarter of the entire labor force of the United States works in marketing. What do all those people do? Is the process of getting goods and services from producers to consumers really complicated enough to keep all those people busy?

In this part and in the following one, we will begin answering those questions. The emphasis here is on the word *begin,* because the longer you study and work in marketing, the more answers you will find. Even experts who have spent their lives in marketing learn new things every day. When you are studying marketing, you are really studying people, and people are always changing. Like people, marketing is always in action.

GETTING GOODS TO THE ULTIMATE CONSUMER

In the early days of mass production, any producer who was making a good product could count on selling it. But today the picture is quite different. With so many kinds of goods being produced—and so many varieties of the same goods—today's producer has to compete with many other producers for the consumer's dollar. In this kind of competitive climate, producers know that they will lose out unless they make sure that their products are easily and readily available to anyone who wants to buy them. In other words, the producers must be certain that their products are moved along in such a way that they will be in the right place at the right time.

10 • UNIT 1 • MARKETING: WHAT IT'S ALL ABOUT

The official marketing term for the ways in which goods are moved from producer to consumer is the "channels of distribution." (**Distribution** is a word that explains one part of the total marketing picture: the process of moving, handling, and storing goods on their way from producers to consumers.) Every producer must understand how each of these channels works in order to choose the one that is right for a particular product.

As an introduction to this subject, let's look at the four basic ways of moving goods from the producer to the **ultimate consumer,** that is, the person who will finally use the goods. Since ultimate consumers are the people who buy food to eat, clothes to wear, and cars to drive, they are the most important people in marketing. The four ways of moving goods to these consumers are (1) marketing directly, (2) marketing through a retailer, (3) marketing through a wholesaler, and (4) adding another wholesaling step.

Marketing Directly

Suppose that you have become expert at some craft—candlemaking, for example. Your friends and neighbors see some of the candles you have produced and ask if they can buy them. Or suppose that a farmer

Many craftspeople use direct marketing to get their craft products to the consumer.
(Stanford Daily/ College Newsphoto Alliance)

PART 2 • MARKETING IN ACTION • 11

sets up a small roadside stand in order to sell fresh eggs, fruits, and vegetables to passers-by. The term that is used to describe both these cases is **direct marketing,** the process whereby a producer sells directly to the consumer.

These two examples might lead you to think that it is only the small producer who markets directly. But such large manufacturers as Avon Products (cosmetics and toiletries), the Fuller Brush Company (brushes, household cleaning supplies, and toiletries), and the Electrolux Corporation (vacuum cleaners) have become famous because they send their own sales representatives directly to people's homes.

Other producers find customers by sending out some kind of catalog. The people who want to buy the products can then order them by mail directly from the producers. Still another direct marketing method is for producers to sell their products through stores that are under their own control. Good examples of this are the stores run by the Singer Company (sewing machines) and by Fanny Farmer candy shops.

It is important to realize that those producers who sell directly to consumers are not bypassing marketing problems. They are simply taking them all on themselves. This means that they must be able to handle such problems as selling, recordkeeping, storage, transportation, and advertising on their own. If they are not willing or able to do this, they will have to use one of the other channels of distribution to get the help that they need.

Marketing Through a Retailer

Let's think now about a pants manufacturer in California who makes many thousands of pants every year, in many different styles, colors, and sizes. This producer finds that taking on all the marketing problems would take too much time away from running the factory. For this producer, the best idea is to sell the pants to the owners of stores all around the country, who can then resell the pants to their own customers.

These store owners, called "retailers," save the producer time, effort, and therefore money. To see what this means, look at what happens when 50 stores sell 200 pairs of pants apiece. If the producer tried to sell each pair of pants individually, there would be 10,000 (50 × 200) completely separate sales transactions. But by selling to the stores, the producer has only 50 sales to make. The producer also has only 50 orders to process, 50 bills to send out, 50 payments to collect, record, and put in the bank, and 50 shipments to pack and send. Since, by using this method, the problems of marketing are greatly reduced, the producer can concentrate on producing pants.

To understand how the retailer serves the consumer, you have only to think about the person in Seattle, Philadelphia, or San Antonio who can go to a store right near home to buy a pair of pants. Probably the store's selection will include pants made by several manufacturers, so the customer will have a large choice. While in the store, the person can also buy a shirt and sweater to go with the new pants.

This convenience is possible because retailers are marketing experts. They are called **middlemen,** meaning that they are marketers who do their work in the middle, with the producers on one side of them and the consumers on the other. Retailers know where to find the producers who are making the things their customers want to buy. They also know when to buy the goods and how much to buy, so that their customers can always buy what they want when they want it.

Marketing Through a Wholesaler

The distribution channel that goes from producer to retailer to ultimate consumer works well for many kinds of products. But think about the things you buy in a hardware store. Nails, nuts, bolts, screws, hinges, locks, sandpaper, tools of all kinds, paint—the list goes on and on through thousands of items made by hundreds of producers. How could the people who own the hardware stores—or the owners of stationery, drug, or food stores—find all the producers and deal with each one individually? It would take all their time just to do the buying, with no time left for running the stores. And the producers too would find it very hard to go on producing at top speed if they had to deal with thousands of stores all over the country.

To solve the selling problems of the producers and the buying problems of the retailers, there is another group of middlemen called **merchant wholesalers,** usually referred to simply as "wholesalers." These are middlemen who buy large quantities of goods from many producers, store the goods in their own warehouses, and then divide the goods up for resale among many retailers. Merchant wholesalers simplify a process that would be enormously complicated if they were not in the picture.

Adding Another Wholesaling Step

The merchant wholesaler is only one of the wholesaling middlemen whose work takes the confusion, snarls, and delays out of the marketing process. To give another example, there are the wholesaling middlemen called "assemblers," who do what their name implies: assemble the goods of many small producers. The assembler might gather together all the potatoes produced on a number of small farms or all the

For potatoes and other produce, the function of the wholesaling middleman may involve not only assembling but also washing, sorting, and bagging. (*Courtesy Idaho Potato Commission*)

fish caught by a fleet of small boats. The whole collection would then be sold to just a few wholesalers, saving both the producers and the wholesalers a lot of work. This example shows that it is possible for a channel of distribution to go from producer to wholesaling middleman to merchant wholesaler to retailer to ultimate consumer.

IDENTIFYING MIDDLEMEN BY THEIR CUSTOMERS

The process whereby a producer does not market directly to the consumer but uses the services of a middleman is called **indirect marketing**. Because the greatest majority of goods in this country are sold indirectly, it is important for you to know about the middlemen who do this work. Even if you are not going to go on studying about marketing, this information will be useful to you for the rest of your life as a consumer.

It is especially important for you to understand the difference between retailing and wholesaling middlemen. The surest way to do this is to think about who their customers are. When a middleman's customer is the ultimate consumer, then you know that the middleman is engaged in retailing and can properly be called a **retailing middleman**. For example, let's say that you go into a music store to buy some records. In this case, the owners of the music store are clearly retailing middlemen because they are selling goods to you, the ultimate consumer. Wholesaling is different from retailing in that it does not have this direct connection with the ultimate consumer. Because the ultimate consumers never see the wholesaling process, many of them are not aware of just how important it is.

Can you explain the three channels of distribution represented here?

PART 2 • MARKETING IN ACTION • 15

The customers in wholesaling fall into two groups. The first group includes anyone who is going to resell the goods: retailers, wholesalers, or other wholesaling middlemen. These people who resell the goods are not considered to be consumers, because they just pass the products along and do not use them in any way. The second group of customers in wholesaling are considered to be consumers, but they are not ultimate consumers. They do use the products that they buy, but not to satisfy their own needs.

Because these consumers use the products to make new goods and services that the ultimate consumer will use, they are called **industrial consumers.** The raw material and supplies that they buy to make into new goods and services are called **industrial products** (versus **consumer products,** which are goods and services used by ultimate consumers). Also, the wholesalers who sell to this group are given the special name of "industrial distributors" or "wholesaler distributors." Industrial consumers include manufacturers; business people (including storekeepers, who need supplies to run their stores); hotels, restaurants, beauty salons, and all other businesses that sell services; and institutions, such as hospitals, schools, and churches.

To show how wholesaling takes care of all its customers, let's think about the customers who buy light bulbs. These customers might include the people who run an office building, factory, hotel, restaurant, hospital, school, or hardware store. In each of these cases, the people buying the light bulbs would be industrial consumers because they would be using the bulbs to help them produce other goods and services for the ultimate consumer. However, the hardware store might also buy the light bulbs for resale, and in that case it would be acting not as an industrial consumer but as a retailer.

This information about the customers in wholesaling can be used to form a definition of **wholesaling middlemen.** They are middlemen whose customers are buying either for resale or for some kind of business use.

THE MARKETING OF SERVICES

The main difference between the marketing of goods and the marketing of services is that services are produced as they are needed, when people are ready to buy them. This fact makes it hard to separate the two jobs of producing and marketing the service. As an example of this, think about the people who repair television sets right in their customers' homes. They perform the repair service on the spot, so they are producers. At the same time, they are marketing the service directly to the ultimate consumers. Thus, these repairers are in the same position as any direct marketing producers and have the same basic marketing problems.

Which customer is considered an industrial consumer—the manufacturer who buys fabrics to make clothing, or the owner of a fabric store who buys the same goods for resale? (TOP *courtesy ILGWU* Justice; BOTTOM *courtesy The Singer Company*)

The people who repair television sets obviously do not have to store the service itself. But they do need a place to keep all the supplies and equipment that are necessary for their work. They also have to think of some way for their customers to contact them. If a business is small, it may be possible to work with just a truck and a telephone. However, when a business is large, it is necessary to maintain a shop. This kind of shop may be compared to the Fanny Farmer Candy Shops and the Singer Company's stores, where the producer

A dog-walking service could be produced and marketed with only a telephone and a solid pair of walking shoes. *(Bruce Davidson/Magnum)*

also markets directly. Another example of a producer who markets a service directly is the person who operates a small hand laundry where the customer brings in clothing to be washed and ironed.

It is also possible for services to be sold through middlemen. For example, customers take their film to a camera store to be developed. The store does not do this work but sends it out. In this case, the producer of the film developing service sells the service to the retailer, who in turn sells it to the ultimate consumer. Also, if your family buys automobile or life insurance from an independent insurance agent, that agent is acting as a retailing middleman for the insurance company he or she works for.

Services are also an important part of the wholesaling picture. We have already seen that industrial consumers need light bulbs and other tangible products to run their businesses. By the same token, they also have to buy banking, insurance, advertising, and many other services.

Services are like goods in that they must be marketed. To be successful, the producers of services must plan for the marketing of their services as carefully as they plan for the production of them.

- **BUILDING YOUR MARKETING VOCABULARY**

  Define each of the following terms and then use each one in a sentence.

  consumer product
  direct marketing
  distribution
  indirect marketing
  industrial consumer
  industrial product
  merchant wholesaler
  middleman
  retailing middleman
  ultimate consumer
  wholesaling middleman

- **UNDERSTANDING WHAT YOU HAVE READ**

  1. What are the four basic ways of moving goods from the producer to the ultimate consumer?
  2. Suppose that Bonnie and Robert, two children who live on your block, make a batch of lemonade to sell at a stand they have set up on the sidewalk. Which channel of distribution would they be using?
  3. Name four kinds of customers that are considered to be industrial consumers.
  4. Give an example of a product that a clothing store might buy as a retailer and one that it might buy as an industrial consumer.
  5. Why is it sometimes difficult to separate the jobs of producing and marketing a service?
  6. Name three kinds of services that might be purchased by industrial consumers.

- **APPLYING WHAT YOU HAVE LEARNED**

  1. If you were a producer of handmade leather goods, would you try to market directly to the consumer or would you prefer to market through a retailer? Write a short paragraph explaining the reasons for your choice.
  2. List the following consumers and state whether each one would buy from a wholesaling middleman or a retailing middleman: (a) homemaker, (b) restaurant, (c) hospital, (d) home gardener, (e) service station, (f) sporting-goods factory, (g) school, (h) student.
  3. Rule a form like the one below. In the left-hand column, list the following products: (a) ice cream, (b) toy truck, (c) locomotive, (d) ballpoint pen, (e) ticket to the movies, (f) textbook, (g) bag of potato chips, (h) lawn mower, (i) bathroom sink, (j) baseball. Indicate whether the product is an industrial product, a consumer product, or both by putting a check mark in the appropriate column.

PRODUCT	INDUSTRIAL	CONSUMER	BOTH
Example: Typewriter			✔

The Marketing Activities

After reading Part 3, you will be able—
- To give an example of how each of the ten marketing activities applies to a specific business.
- To distinguish between personal and nonpersonal selling.
- To name the marketing activities necessary to move a specific product from the producer to the consumer.

Another way of approaching the question of how marketing actually works is to take a closer look at the marketing activities. If we think of marketing as a bridge between producers and consumers, then the marketing activities are the upright beams that support the bridge. Just as each beam bears its share of the weight, each marketing activity plays its specific part in the movement of goods and services from producers to consumers. Each one does its share in making the total marketing process work.

There are ten of these activities for you to learn about: (1) buying, (2) selling, (3) promoting sales, (4) transporting goods and people, (5) storing goods for future use, (6) providing money for marketing, (7) keeping records, (8) identifying the product, (9) installing and servicing goods, and (10) researching the market. Each one of these activities has something different to offer in terms of jobs. This means that you don't have to be a certain "type" to be successful in marketing. Because the marketing activities are so varied, there is room in marketing for people from widely different backgrounds, with widely different personal characteristics.

BUYING

As the owners of a toy and hobby store, Cynthia and Richard Garcia must be very selective about what they buy. If they have **merchandise** (which is another word for goods) left on their shelves that nobody wants, they will lose money. So they have to think carefully about what kinds of things they can sell to their particular customers and what the quality of those things should be. The Garcias also have to

Buyers must use great care and good judgment when selecting the merchandise that will be sold in retail stores. (*Courtesy Levi Strauss & Co.*)

think about quantity when they are ordering goods—how much of each item to order—and about where to buy. They want to be sure that the companies they buy from will send them exactly what they have ordered, in perfect condition, on time, and for the lowest possible price.

The Garcias have to be just as careful when they are buying the many goods and services that they need to run their store, ranging all the way from paper and string for wrapping customers' purchases to trash removal service. Whenever they buy something they don't need or pay a higher price than they have to, they are losing money. This is equally true for the bowling alley, hot dog stand, department store, food wholesaler, and motorcycle factory. A sure knowledge of the ins and outs of wise buying is essential to the success of every marketing business.

SELLING

When it comes to selling the goods they have so carefully bought, there are many things for the Garcias to think about. First of all, they need customers, and so they must choose a location for their store that is easy for people to get to. Then they must try to make the store look as attractive and inviting as possible. They also have to set prices for their goods that are in line with the prices of other stores in the area. The competition from these stores is something that the Garcias have to be constantly aware of.

PART 3 • THE MARKETING ACTIVITIES • 21

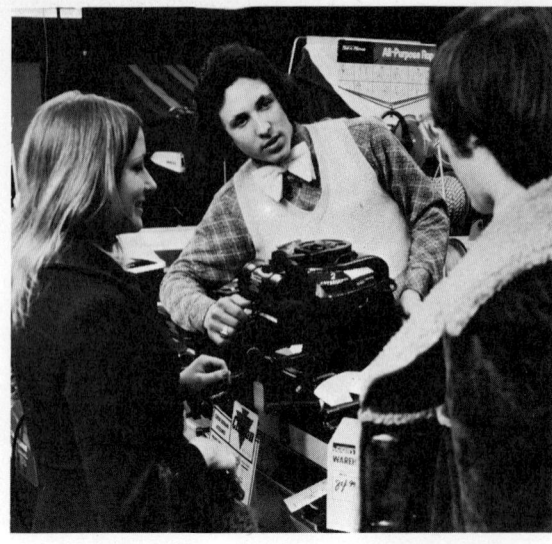

This salesworker needs to know all about the outboard motors he sells if he is to help his customers decide which motor is right for their needs. (*Courtesy Montgomery Ward*)

They also have to know a lot about the art of personal selling. There are many times during the day, such as when a customer comes in for some small item, when all Cynthia or Richard has to do is ring up the sale on the cash register and give the customer the change. But there are also many times when the sale would be lost unless they knew how to sell the item actively to the customer.

To do this, the Garcias need a pleasant personality—the kind of personality that says to people, "I'd like to help you." They also have to know a lot about people—what they are like, why they act the way they do, and what makes them decide to buy. It is also important for them to know all about the products in their store—what they are made of, what they will and will not do, and how they compare with other products on the market. This kind of personal selling ability is so important that people who are skilled in it are very much in demand at all levels of marketing.

PROMOTING SALES

It is the job of the salesworker to sell a product or service to a customer in a personal, face-to-face situation. To support the task of personal selling, there are marketing activities that, in a nonpersonal way, encourage possible customers to want to buy a product or service. Because marketing is so highly competitive, this nonpersonal selling is very important throughout the marketing process. It is widely used by producers, wholesalers, and retailers to get people in a buying mood.

The nonpersonal selling activity that you are probably most aware of is advertising, which follows you all through the day—on radio and television, in newspapers and magazines, on billboards and posters, and through the mail. **Advertising** is a selling activity whose purpose is to persuade a large group of people to buy the goods, services, or ideas of the sponsor. This sponsor, who is the person or company paying for the advertisement, wants to catch and hold people's attention so that they will get the right message. So, when advertisements are being prepared, a great deal of effort is put into trying to understand why people buy and into making the ads attractive and appealing.

There is another area of nonpersonal selling with which you are probably also familiar, especially if you have done any window-shopping. This is **display,** which is a way of persuading people to buy by appealing to their visual sense. Those mannequins in the clothing store window, all dressed up in the latest fashions, and the sample photographs in the camera shop window, all have the same purpose. The idea is to make you want to go into the store and see more of what is

Can you identify the types of nonpersonal selling represented here?

PART 3 • THE MARKETING ACTIVITIES • 23

for sale there. Once inside, there will be more displays that will make the store's products seem even more desirable. Some of these store displays may have been provided by the producers or wholesalers, who make this effort because they know how much an attractive display can help the personal salesworker.

Still another nonpersonal way of making people want to buy is **public relations,** which is the effort to make the public think well of the company and therefore to want to do business with it. The public relations staff tries to get favorable stories about the company into the newspapers and on radio and television. The public relations staff also helps the company to be a good neighbor. For example, a large store might put on a fashion show in the local high school, allowing the student organization to make money on the sale of tickets. In this case, the store will be rewarded for its efforts with the goodwill of the community. People will want to buy at the store as a way of saying thanks.

TRANSPORTING GOODS AND PEOPLE

To get some idea of the enormous role that transportation plays in marketing, you have only to go into the food store where your family shops. You'll see sugar from Louisiana, cereal from Minnesota, oranges from Florida, potatoes from Idaho, cheese from Wisconsin, and many products that come from other countries. These goods probably were moved more than once on their way from producer to wholesaler to food store. They may have been moved by train, plane, boat, or truck, or by a combination of these methods. But the most important fact is that the transportation job was done quickly, safely, and inexpensively.

Now let's look at the picture from another angle and figure out what would happen if the transportation system didn't work so well. Factories would have to close down because they could not get raw materials. Service businesses could not operate either if their supplies were not delivered. In fact, business on every level would come to a halt because people would not be able to get to their jobs. And if people could not travel for pleasure, the hotels and eating places that they use when they are away from home would have to close their doors.

The importance of the transportation system cannot be overestimated. Without transportation, there would be no marketing as we know it today.

STORING GOODS FOR FUTURE USE

The part that storage plays in the marketing process is shown by the fact that you can buy flour every day of the year, even though wheat is not harvested every day. The reason for this convenience is that the

Transportation and storage are essential parts of marketing. Without them most of the fruits and vegetables we buy regularly would not be available.

wheat is stored until the mill is ready to grind it into flour. Then the flour itself is stored until it is needed.

What happens with wheat and flour happens to all kinds of products. Strawberries are frozen when they are picked and then put into cold storage. They can then be sold to stores all year long, so that there is nothing unusual about eating strawberries when there is snow on the ground. A company making football uniforms, for example, which are sold mostly in early fall, can keep its factory going at a steady pace all year long and then store the uniforms until people are ready to buy them. If the uniforms could not be stored, the producer would have to close down the factory for part of the year and then work overtime to meet the demands of the football season.

Consumers take for granted the steady flow of goods that the storage activity makes possible, but actually it represents the efforts of many people.

PROVIDING MONEY FOR MARKETING

When people are planning to open marketing businesses, they usually need more money than they have saved to get started. And later on, if they want to expand their businesses, they will need still more money. This money that keeps businesses alive and well is borrowed from banks. Banks also lend money to consumers so that they can buy homes and other goods and services. When a bank lends someone the money to buy a new car, the bank is obviously helping the car manufacturer and the car dealer, as well as the buyer. Banks also help people by keeping their money safe for them until they need it. Banks offer many other services too, such as checking accounts that let people pay their bills easily and safe deposit boxes where valuables other than money can be safely stored.

Another activity that helps to finance marketing is insurance. Suppose that a wholesaler's warehouse burns down. The wholesaler had many thousands of dollars worth of goods stored in this warehouse, and nothing was saved. The wholesaler would be ruined and all the warehouse employees would be out of jobs if it were not for the fact that the warehouse was insured.

Besides this fire insurance, the business person can buy insurance against death, property loss, and the willful mischief that is called "vandalism." There is insurance that will take care of anyone who suffers an accident on the business person's property. There is also health and life insurance for the company's employees. These same kinds of insurance are also available to the ultimate consumer.

KEEPING RECORDS

You can imagine how much paper work is involved in marketing. It is necessary to keep exact accounts of what comes in and goes out of the warehouse or store, what bills must be paid and collected, how much pay each employee should receive, what taxes are due, and how much money is in the bank. In recent years, it has become possible to do much of this work on computers and other large business machines. This change from manual work to machine operations has made some jobs unnecessary. But it has also opened up a whole new area of jobs requiring special knowledge about how machines work and how to get the most out of them.

IDENTIFYING THE PRODUCT

Because customers like to know exactly what they are buying, there is a group of marketing activities that identify the product. The first of these is **grading,** which means giving the customer information about the relative quality of the product. Many food products are graded according to quality standards set by the Department of Agriculture. For example, meat is graded as to whether it is prime, choice, or good. Some stores also grade some of the products that they sell. For example, towels might be graded as good, better, or best quality.

The identifying activity known as sorting goes along with grading. **Sorting** means putting all the goods that are the same grade or size together. You can see an example of this when you buy eggs. Food stores sell eggs in boxes by the dozen. The eggs in each box have been sorted so that they are all the same size, either small, medium, large, or extra large. This helps the retailer to price the eggs, since larger eggs cost more than smaller ones. It also makes it possible for the consumers to buy the size eggs that will best meet their needs.

Another identifying activity is **standardizing,** which means making the quality the same for each item. This allows the customer to count on getting the same quality with each purchase. A national hamburger chain standardizes the ingredients for its products, so that a hamburger bought in Maryland tastes the same as a hamburger bought in Oregon. Building this kind of customer confidence is also the reason for using **brand names.** These are names that are given to products, sometimes by producers and sometimes by wholesalers or retailers, to indicate clearly to the public what company stands behind the product. When consumers see Nabisco on boxes of cookies and crackers, for example, they know that all the know-how of the National Biscuit Company is in those boxes.

Clothing labels that tell what the garment is made of and give instructions for proper care are very important to the consumer.

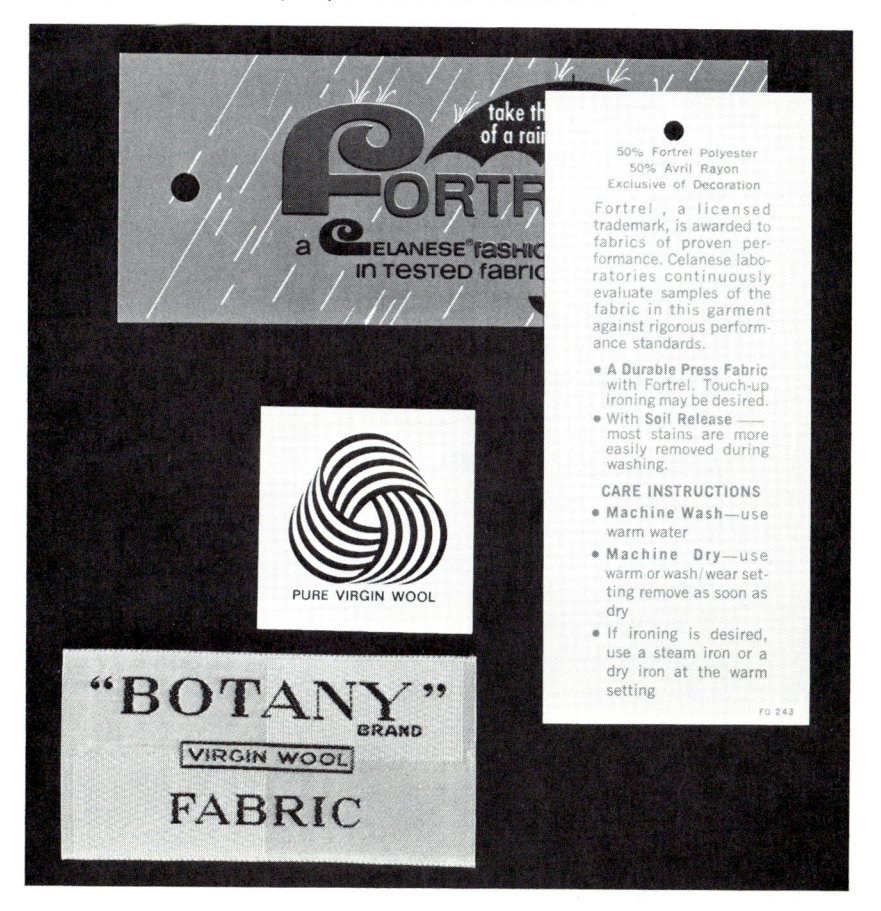

PART 3 · THE MARKETING ACTIVITIES · 27

The customer also appreciates the identifying activity that takes the mystery out of shopping by **labeling** the goods, which means marking the items so that they can be identified easily. Labeling may be very simple, as when the Sunkist brand name is stamped on oranges. It can also be more elaborate, as when a printed label is attached to a garment, which states exactly what it is made of and how it should be cared for.

Often the label for the goods is part of the package, which is still another means of identifying the product. **Packaging** means putting goods into containers or wrapping them. So many goods must be packaged before they can be sold that packaging has become a $1-billion-a-year business. Packaging keeps the product in good condition and also makes it look attractive, so that the customer will want to buy it. The people who design packages have to think about what colors, shapes, and materials will make their packages stand out.

INSTALLING AND SERVICING GOODS

A couple buys a washing machine that has to be hooked up to the plumbing and wiring in their home. They would not buy the washer if they had to hook it up themselves because they don't know how to do this. But the store will send a person who has been trained to do this installation job. Later, if the machine breaks down, the couple can call a repairer to come to their house to fix it.

There are many other products that have to be installed or serviced: refrigerators, clothes dryers, television sets, air conditioners, and large business machines, to name just a few. Because there are so many products that need extra attention after they have been sold, there are many job opportunities in this marketing activity.

RESEARCHING THE MARKET

Very few producers these days make a product first and then see whether they can sell it. With costs so high and competition so intense, today's producers want to know whether a new product will sell or not *before* spending money on it. To find this out, sample groups of people will be asked for their opinions about what kinds of goods and services they like and dislike and what they want to buy. The process of gathering, writing down, and thinking through information about marketing problems is called **marketing research.**

Besides helping with product planning, marketing research can do many other things for marketers. For example, it can test whether an advertising program is hitting its mark. It can also tell marketers how they stand in relation to their competitors. Because it takes the hit-or-miss quality out of planning, marketing research is becoming more important every day.

- **BUILDING YOUR MARKETING VOCABULARY**

  Define each of the following terms and then use each one in a sentence.

  advertising
  brand name
  display
  grading
  labeling
  marketing research
  merchandise
  packaging
  public relations
  sorting
  standardizing

- **UNDERSTANDING WHAT YOU HAVE READ**

  1. List five things that storekeepers have to think about when buying goods for resale.
  2. Explain the difference between personal and nonpersonal selling.
  3. Explain the following sentence: "Without transportation, there would be no marketing as we know it today."
  4. How does the storage activity benefit both producers and consumers?
  5. Name two activities that help to finance marketing. State two specific ways in which each one helps.

- **APPLYING WHAT YOU HAVE LEARNED**

  1. Suppose that you own a store that sells radios, phonographs, stereo equipment, and television sets. Give one example of how each of the ten marketing activities would apply to your business.
  2. Choose one product that you use every day and make a list of the marketing activities that were necessary to get that product from the producer to you.
  3. Bring to class an example of a package or label and be prepared to explain how it identifies the product for the consumer.

part 4: The Background for Marketing

After reading Part 4, you will be able—
- To distinguish between controlled, free enterprise, and modified free-enterprise economic systems.
- To identify the checks and balances that are built into a modified free-enterprise system.
- To identify the purpose of a given list of governmental activities relating to business.
- To state one way in which a given list of decisions made by individual marketers as a way of winning out over their competitors has benefited the public.

When we talk about a country's **economy,** we're talking about the way in which the country makes decisions about the production and distribution of goods and services. The country has to decide what kinds of goods and services will be produced and how many of them. It also has to decide how they will be produced and who will get to use them. Some countries have a **controlled economy.** This is a system in which the country's government makes all the economic decisions. The government owns the factories, farms, and other means of production. The government also sets prices and decides how much the workers should be paid, and even where people should work.

This is not the way that the economy is run in a democracy such as the one we live in. Our economic system is based on the idea that people should have as much freedom as possible. Our government was set up to be a government of, by, and for the people. This principle applies to our economic life as well as our political life. Let's see now how this economic freedom actually works and how it affects the field of marketing.

HOW MODIFIED FREE ENTERPRISE WORKS

The economic system that is in direct contrast to a controlled economy is **free enterprise.** This is a system in which all economic decisions are made by the people themselves. Businesses are owned and managed by private individuals, rather than by the government. And all individuals are free to work where they want. They can change jobs whenever they want. And they can go into business for themselves, selling whatever they choose at their own price to anyone who will buy from them.

Free enterprise is the basis for the economic system that we have in this country. But we do have some laws that state what business may and may not do. These laws can be compared to traffic laws, which tell people how to drive in a way that protects the safety of others. Likewise, our economic laws are designed to keep one individual or group from taking away any of the rights of the other people in the country. Because of these laws, we call our economic system **modified free enterprise.** This is a system in which the people make most of the economic decisions, but the government modifies (changes or limits) some decisions. This includes not just the federal government but also state and local governments.

Modified free enterprise gives you, as an individual, a large measure of economic freedom. Instead of being part of a "master plan," as you would be in a controlled economy, you are largely free to chart your own course. How can so much individual freedom be possible in a country with more than 220 million people? To answer this question, let's look at the ways in which a modified free-enterprise system regulates itself and at the role government plays in regulating business.

Built-in Checks and Balances

You might think that so much economic freedom would lead to a mixed-up situation, where too many people were in one kind of business and not enough in other kinds. For example, a small town might find itself with ten bookstores and no food stores. Or you might have a thousand producers making paper flowers and none making paper bags. Also, why shouldn't people set their prices very high, regardless of the quality of what they are selling? If people are free to make their own decisions, what is to prevent such things from happening?

The answer to these questions is that our economic system has within it a system of checks and balances, just as our political system does, so that things cannot go too far in one direction. The three factors that provide a natural method of regulating a modified free-enterprise system are (1) the profit motive, (2) the laws of supply and demand, and (3) competition.

THE PROFIT MOTIVE. Profit can be defined as the amount of money that is left over after all the expenses of running a business have been paid. In the countries that have a controlled economy, all profits go to the government. But, under our system, individual business people are allowed to keep their own profits. There are some people who think that anyone who makes a profit is doing something dishonest. But this is far from the truth. Profits represent a way of rewarding owners for their know-how in starting and running their businesses. This is hard work, and they have the right to be paid for it, just as other workers have the right to be paid for their efforts. Profits are also a way of paying owners back for the risks they are taking. It takes money to get a business started, and more money to keep it going. There is always the risk that the business will not do well and the money will be lost. Profits represent the other side of that coin—the return that the owner gets if the business does do well.

Before business people open new businesses, they must think about what their chances for making a profit are. If the field they are interested in is already overcrowded, they will not want to risk failure. They will look instead for a business that is needed.

THE LAWS OF SUPPLY AND DEMAND. There are two economic rules that sound very complicated, but you have seen them in operation many times. First is the **law of supply,** which says that when a lot of goods are available for sale, the price goes down. The second is the **law**

Did the owners of this new business make a wise decision when they chose to open a plant store in this shopping area?

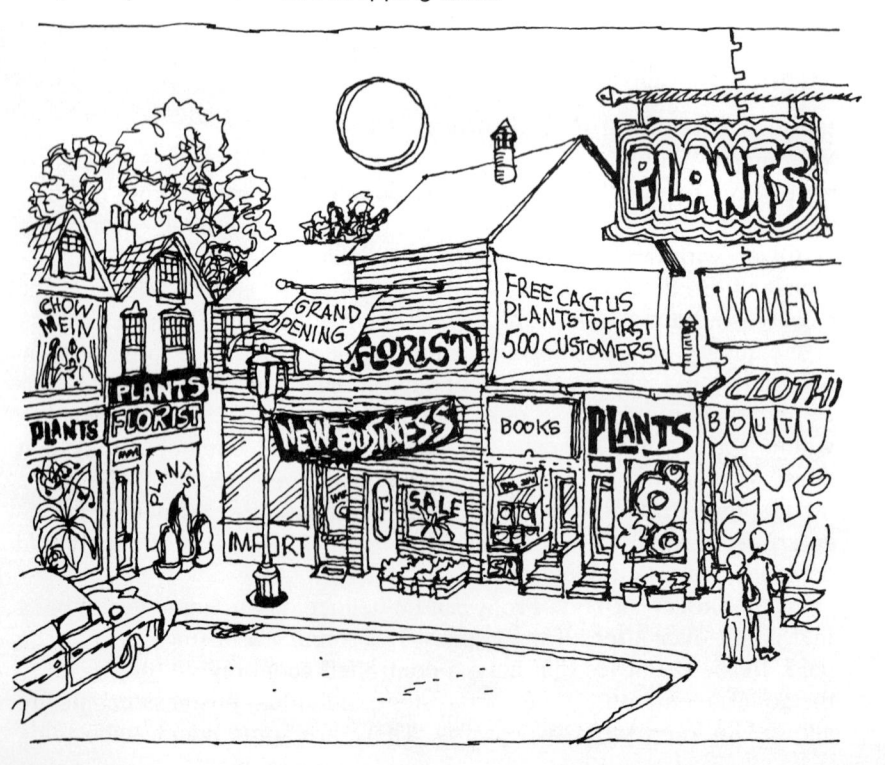

32 • UNIT 1 • MARKETING: WHAT IT'S ALL ABOUT

of demand, which says that when goods are scarce and a lot of people want to buy them, the price goes up. When oil products were plentiful, the price was low. But when there were not enough oil products to go around, the price went up. You have also seen this happen with food products.

The effect of the laws of supply and demand is to move things back toward the middle. When the supply is too great and prices too low, producers are discouraged from making any more of that product until the supply levels off. And when the demand is high and prices are up, producers find it worth their while to try to produce as much as they possibly can. As soon as gasoline began to be in short supply, the demand for large cars went down. At the same time, the demand for smaller cars went up. As a result, the automobile manufacturers began making fewer large cars and more small ones.

It is the principle of supply and demand that prevents ten people from opening bookstores in one small town. Supply and demand also affect the careers that people choose. For example, there have been times when the supply of teachers or engineers has been greater than the demand. These times have been followed by a slowdown in the number of people training for those careers, until the supply has leveled off.

COMPETITION. The freedom that business people have to choose the businesses they want to be in is matched by another equally important freedom. Individual consumers are free to choose the business people that they want to deal with. This explains why the word "competition" is so important in our economy. **Competition** in marketing refers to the efforts made by two or more businesses to win the same group of people as customers. When individual consumers decide to buy from a certain business, they are, in effect, casting a vote for that business. This is very like the vote cast in a voting booth for any government official. The candidate who gets the most votes wins the election. In a similar way, the business that gets the most votes wins out over its competitors.

Which businesses will get the consumers' vote? Certainly not the ones who sell poor-quality goods at high prices. Competition forces business people to think about whether they are answering the needs of the consumers. They know that their success or failure depends directly on the consumers' approval.

The Role of the Government

The government's role in our economy is a subject that is too large to be covered here, but we can summarize it by saying that the government wants to make free enterprise work for the benefit of the largest

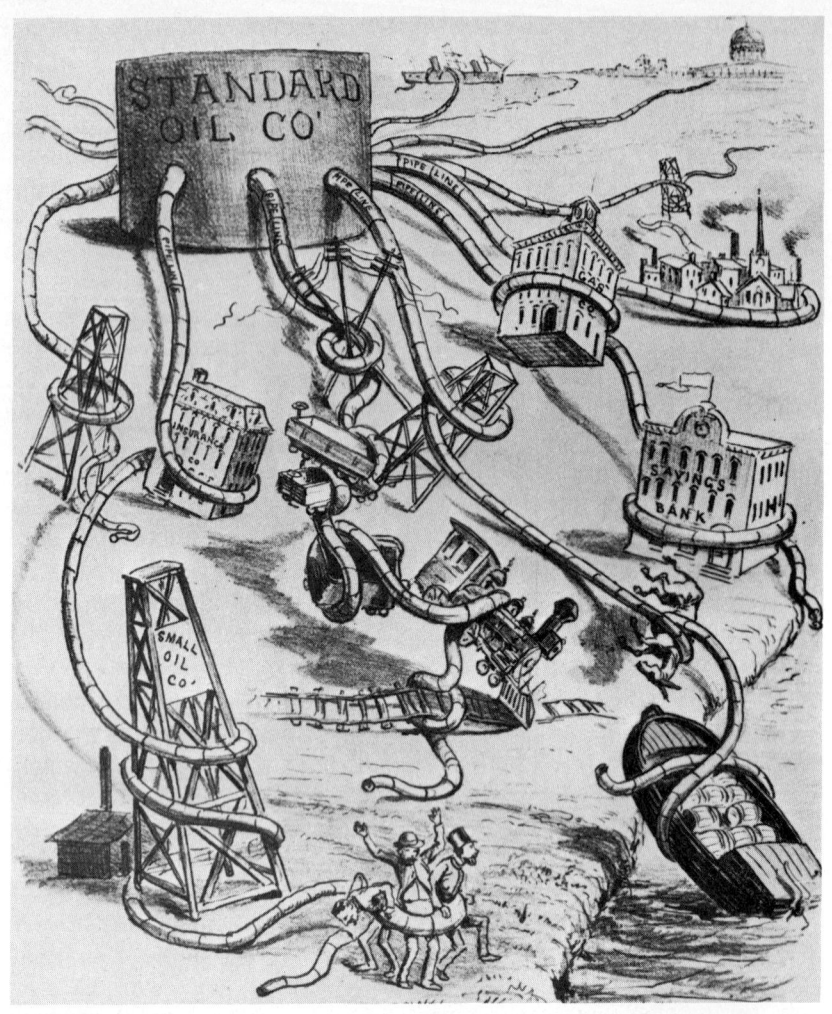

Before the Sherman Anti-Trust Act of 1890, there was no way for the government to prevent large companies from eliminating competition and establishing monopolies. This cartoon from 1884 reveals public feeling about the need to regulate monopolies. (*The Granger Collection*)

possible number of people. The government approaches this task from two different directions. On the one hand, it regulates certain business activities. On the other hand, it has many programs that provide assistance to business firms and workers.

In regulating business, one major concern of the government is to make sure that business firms are not so anxious to make a profit that they forget about the welfare of others. There are food and drug laws that keep harmful products off the market. And there are strict regulations on the sale of drugs and liquor. There are also minimum wage laws that establish the minimum amount of money employees must receive for their work. Employers may pay more if they want to, but they may not increase their profits by paying their employees less.

The government also tries to make sure that competition is working freely. When a company has no competitors, it is called a **monopoly**. In most instances, monopolies are illegal. When monopolies are necessary, as in the case of electric, gas, and water companies, their service and prices are regulated by the government.

One of the major ways in which the government helps business firms and workers, as well as the economy, is by gathering information and publishing reports on many subjects. Some of these reports give business people facts about the economy that help them to make wise decisions. Other reports give information about specific jobs—where they are, what the work is like, and what it takes to get hired. There are also employment services run by the government, which bring workers and jobs together. In addition, the government sometimes lends money to people who want to start their own small businesses.

These are just a few examples of the part that the government plays in our economy. You will be learning more about this very important subject as you move through this book.

HOW A FREE MARKETING SYSTEM SERVES THE PUBLIC

You would not be able to study about marketing without setting it against this background of modified free enterprise. The success of our marketing system is one of the best proofs you could find that individual economic freedom benefits the public at large. Our marketers, hoping to make a profit for themselves, have consistently tried to outdo each other in competing for the consumers' dollars. As a direct result of this competition, the public enjoys a high standard of living. **Standard of living** is a term that refers to the way people live. It is measured by the quantity and quality of the goods and services that people either own or have the use of. Marketing competition also keeps prices down, makes buying easy, adds to the value of goods and services, and keeps up with new living habits, as we shall now see.

Maintaining a High Standard of Living

You may have heard the saying, "If you build a better mousetrap, the world will beat a path to your door." Over the years, producers have believed that if someone makes a product that is better than anything

Please be patient. We're making our shoes as fast as we can.

Who ever heard of standing in line for a pair of shoes?

We're amazed. Really amazed. At first people called our EARTH* brand negative heel shoes strange and ugly. And now they're standing in line to get them.

And while the ends of the lines are waiting to get into our stores, the beginnings of the lines are buying up all of our shoes.

Of course we always knew Earth* shoes were a great invention. And we knew people would love them. But we had no idea the word would spread so fast.

It all started with Anne Kalsø.

It started in Denmark 17 years ago, when Anne Kalsø had the idea for the negative heel shoe. A shoe with the heel lower than the toe.

The concept was that these shoes would allow you to walk naturally. Like when you walk barefoot in sand and your heel sinks down lower than your toes. Anne was convinced that this is the natural way the body is designed to walk. And that this shoe would work in harmony with your entire body.

So she worked for 10 years refining every delicate adjustment. Until finally they were perfected.

The shoe that works with your body.

And the result was the Earth shoe. The shoe that's not just for your feet.

Not only is the heel lower than the toe, but the entire sole is molded in a very special way. This allows you to walk in a gentle rolling motion. And to walk easily and comfortably on the hard, jarring cement of our cities.

Even the arch of the Earth shoe is different, and the toes are wide to keep your toes from being cramped or squashed.

Now everybody wants them.

So you started buying them. You told your friends about them. And they told their friends.

Until finally it's happened. Now you want them faster than we can make them.

It takes time to make a good shoe.

Earth negative heel shoes take time to make. Of course we could knock them out fast, by

To get an idea of how the EARTH shoe works, stand barefoot with your toes up on a book. Feel what begins to happen.

leaving out a lot of important features. Or by not paying attention to quality. But then it wouldn't be the Earth brand shoe.

Lowering the heel isn't enough.

We knew we had a good idea. And we knew others would try to imitate us by making negative heel shoes too.

But just because a shoe looks like ours doesn't mean it works like ours.

The 10 years that went into perfecting the Earth shoe are very important. We have many, many features built into our shoes to make them work. And that is why they are patented.

So to be sure you're getting the Earth negative heel shoe, look on the sole for our Earth trademark, and U.S. patent number 3305947.

They're worth waiting for.

Please be patient. We're sending out more and more shoes to our stores

The EARTH shoe comes in styles for men and women, from open sandals to high boots. From $23.50 to $42.50. Prices slightly higher in the west.*

every month. And if they've run out of your size or style, they'll have it soon.

And when you do try them, you'll see, perhaps for the first time in your life, what it's like to walk more gracefully, naturally and comfortably.

And, believe us, that's worth waiting for.

earth shoe

EARTH is the registered trademark of Kalsø Systemet, Inc. for its negative heel shoes and other products.

Anne Kalsø.
Inventor of the EARTH negative heel shoe.*

Our shoes are sold at stores that sell only the EARTH shoe.

©1974 Kalsø Systemet, Inc.

You may have heard the old saying "build a better mousetrap and the world will beat a path to your door." Even today, with so many kinds of goods available, when manufacturers make a product that offers unique advantages, consumers will respond. (Courtesy Kalsø Systemet, Inc.)

36 • UNIT 1 • MARKETING: WHAT IT'S ALL ABOUT

else on the market, people will be very anxious to buy it. This explains the ongoing effort by producers to come up with new kinds of goods and services and to improve existing ones. The hand-cranked phonograph, invented when your grandmother was young, was replaced first by an electric model and then, in turn, by high-fidelity, stereophonic, and quadraphonic systems. Whenever one producer has gotten a new idea, it has been topped by another producer who sees a way to make something even better. The motive for each of these producers is profit. The result of their desire to make money is a national standard of living that is higher than ever before in history.

Keeping Prices Down

Marketers have also tried to outdo each other in keeping prices down. It is obvious that marketing has a cost. All the people involved in the marketing process have to be paid for what they do. However, marketers are constantly trying to figure out ways of keeping down their costs of doing business. They can then pass these savings along to their customers, as a way of beating their competitors.

A very important way for marketers to keep their prices down is by handling large quantities of goods at one time. This is because it costs less per item to sell a quantity of goods at the same time. For example, if you go into a store and buy one pair of socks, the salesworker has to do just as much work as if you bought two pairs. If the store's cost can be divided over two pairs, there is a saving that can be passed along to you. The next time you go into any kind of store, make a point of noticing how many times you are offered a chance to save money by buying more than one item at a time. Marketers try to take advantage of this principle all along the line, by finding ways of buying, transporting, and advertising quantities of goods at one time.

Making Buying Easy

Another way in which marketers compete with each other is in making it easier for the consumer to buy. Good examples of this are the many marketing businesses that have drive-in facilities, so that the customer doesn't even have to get out of the car. There are drive-in food stores, film developing services, banks, and eating places, all of them conveniently located. Other examples are the many stores that will accept orders over the telephone and then deliver the goods to the customer.

Marketing has always made buying easy for the public, making it possible for people to buy just the quantity of goods that they want when, where, and how they want them. But because of the constant pressure of competition, buying gets easier every day.

Adding to the Value of Goods and Services

By making buying so easy, marketing actually adds to the value of products. The producer has built a certain amount of basic worth into the product. But the product is worth more to the consumer when it is in the right place at the right time. As an example of this, think about a manufacturer in New Hampshire who buys leather and turns it into baseball mitts. These mitts have a value that is greater than the original value of the leather. But now think about the mitts from the point of view of a high school baseball team in Oklahoma City. The fact that there are mitts in New Hampshire doesn't do the team any good, nor would it help if the mitts could not be shipped from the factory until after the baseball season was over. These mitts can only be used and enjoyed by the players if the mitts are in the right place at the right time. This is where marketing comes in. The warehouse that stores the mitts, the trucking company that delivers them, and the sporting-goods store that sells them work together to add a time and place value to the basic value of the mitts.

Marketers also vie with each other in trying to think up ways of making products more usable for the people who will buy them. This is another way of adding to the product's value. For example, when you buy a pair of pants, the store alters them so that they fit properly and the legs are the right length. When a car needs new tires, the service station does not just sell the tires to the customer but also puts them on the car. When someone wants to paint a room, the paint store not only sells the person the paint but mixes it so that it is just the right color. In each of these cases, the motive of the marketers is profit. But, in the end, it is the customer who benefits.

Keeping Up with New Living Habits

Nobody has to be told that we live in a changing world, especially today, when the changes are coming at a faster pace than ever before. The marketers who want to be successful must think up ways to keep up with these changes. Any marketer who is using yesterday's methods cannot compete with the marketers who are finding new ways of answering the needs of today's consumers.

As an example of how marketing has to shift its thinking, let's consider the downtown central shopping areas of big cities. These areas were very popular before World War II because they could be reached easily by streetcar, bus, or subway. But after the war, our way of life changed drastically. One of the major reasons for this change was that more people owned automobiles. In addition, many people moved out of the cities and into the suburbs. The people who lived in the suburbs no longer wanted to go downtown to shop. There were marketers who recognized this fact and built large shopping centers on the outskirts of the cities. These shopping centers became very popular because they could be reached easily by car and offered ample parking. They also saved a lot of time for a population that liked to be on the go every minute.

Today the creation of shopping malls has given new importance to the central downtown shopping areas of many large cities. Two examples of this from the Nicollet Mall in Minneapolis are shown here. (*Courtesy Greater Minneapolis Chamber of Commerce*)

In recent years, there has been another major shift in people's living habits. Today many people are interested in returning to a slower pace of life. There is also widespread concern about the problems that so many automobiles have caused, such as crowded roads and air pollution. And the energy crisis has made it necessary for people to drive less. The result of this is that the downtown shopping areas are again becoming important, but in a new way. Many cities now have huge shopping malls, where many stores, and perhaps a restaurant or two, are connected by covered passageways. Many people have found that being able to stroll through these malls makes shopping a lot more fun. Some people even think these malls offer families the kind of shopping experience that the early farmers in our country had when they drove into town for market day.

As we have seen, success in marketing means recognizing and keeping pace with the new ways people want to live. The marketers who can give people what they want are the marketers who will win out over their competitors.

- **BUILDING YOUR MARKETING VOCABULARY**

Define each of the following terms and then use each one in a sentence.

competition
controlled economy
economy
free enterprise
law of demand
law of supply
modified free enterprise
monopoly
profit
standard of living

- **UNDERSTANDING WHAT YOU HAVE READ**

1. How does our economic system of modified free enterprise affect you as an individual?
2. List three checks and balances that are built into a modified free-enterprise system.
3. What is the effect of the laws of supply and demand on producers? What is their effect on the job hunter?
4. Explain the purpose of the following governmental activities: (a) reports about the job market, (b) minimum wage laws, (c) food and drug laws, (d) laws prohibiting monopolies, (e) employment services.
5. List five examples of how marketers can add to the value of goods and services.

• APPLYING WHAT YOU HAVE LEARNED

1. Write a paragraph discussing whether or not you think it is fair for the people who own businesses to make a profit.
2. A marketer decides to do five things to beat the competition. On a separate sheet of paper, write at least one way in which each of the following decisions benefits the public: (a) to advertise more widely, (b) to hold a special sale, (c) to provide a gift-wrapping service, (d) to sponsor a fashion show at a community center, (e) to give sewing classes.
3. "Success in marketing means recognizing and keeping pace with the new ways people want to live." What kinds of goods and services do you think will be in demand in the year 2000? Be prepared to defend your answers in a panel discussion. Some of the points you might consider are (a) the kinds of housing there will be, (b) the kinds of clothing people will wear, (c) the kinds of foods people will eat, (d) the kinds of jobs that will be available, (e) how much money people will be earning, (f) what transportation will be like, (g) how people will spend their free time, (h) other possible changes that might affect marketing.

    Use your imagination for this exercise, thinking about television programs and movies you have seen and books and magazines you have read. Of course, there are no right or wrong answers to this question.

part 5
What You Can Do for Marketing

After reading Part 5, you will be able—
- To distinguish between those marketing practices that are fair and those that are unfair to the consumer.
- To recognize an unfair marketing practice in your community and state (a) one way by which the marketer involved could correct the problem and (b) one kind of action that you personally could take against the marketer.

Some people don't want to hear any criticisms of our economic system. They say that anyone who doesn't like it should try living in a controlled economy for a while. But a modified free-enterprise system does have some problems, and these problems cannot possibly be solved unless they are brought out into the open. In a controlled economy, people have to accept whatever they get. But one of our most precious freedoms is the right to question things that are not working as well as they should. The point of such questions is not to destroy our economic system, but to try to make it work better.

If you think that you might be interested in a marketing career, you will have to think about the questions that people are asking. Marketing is not something that stands off by itself. It is tightly woven into the fabric of life in this country. The country's problems are marketing's problems, and marketing's problems are the country's problems. Thus, when you work to improve marketing, you are working to improve the quality of life for everyone. Within that framework, let's look first at some of the problem areas in marketing and then at what you can do to improve them.

DEMANDING HONESTY IN MARKETING
It is true that the goal of everything that happens in marketing is getting the consumer to buy. However, this does not mean that marketers are free to use any possible means to make a sale. Most marketers know

that honesty is a far better policy than trying to see how much they can get away with. They realize that maintaining a good name over the years is worth far more than a single sale. But unfortunately some marketers think that the marketplace is a jungle. They believe that people have a right to grab whatever they can in the same way that lions go after their prey.

It is because of such self-serving marketers that consumerism has become an important part of today's vocabulary. **Consumerism** is the effort to protect the interests of consumers. Because of the strength of the consumerism movement, there has been a great increase in the number of laws that enforce honest marketing practices. There are government offices on federal, state, and local levels whose purpose is to enforce these existing laws, to advise consumers of their rights, and to see where new laws are needed.

For many companies consumerism is not a new idea at all. These companies have a long history of being concerned with fair treatment for the consumer. They do not see the present consumerism movement as a threat but as a means of finding out how they can serve their customers better. Many companies have their own consumer affairs specialists who listen to what the consumer action groups are asking for. Then they recommend company policies that will answer the consumers' needs. Many companies also employ environmental protection experts to advise them on whether their policies are good for society as a whole.

There is also a strong self-policing movement in many marketing areas, whereby the honest marketers try to set and enforce high standards of conduct. It is encouraging that so many people are trying so hard to make marketing work as it should—for the benefit of everyone. However, as long as there are consumers who do not know what their rights are, the less-than-honest marketer will find a way to stay in business.

Let's look now at six of the problem areas in marketing: (1) guarantees, (2) quality, (3) pricing, (4) credit terms, (5) advertising, and (6) personal selling.

Satisfactory Guarantees

In the early days of marketing, the generally accepted attitude was "Let the buyer beware." Buyers had to inspect whatever they were buying with great care because, once the sale was made, the seller had no responsibilities at all. But today it is generally believed that consumers have a right to expect marketers to stand behind their goods and services. This is why the word "guarantee" is so important today. A **guarantee** is a statement from the seller to the buyer regarding the quality of the goods and services, the length of time they can be expected to last, and the obligation of the seller if anything is wrong.

Written guarantees are often given with specific purchases, such as automobiles, large or small appliances, or watches. The problem with such guarantees is that the salesperson may give the consumer the impression that the product is *fully* guaranteed, whereas the fine print may tell another story. It may be only the parts that are guaranteed. This leaves the consumer to pay all the labor bills, which are usually the most expensive part of repair work. The consumer may also find that some parts are completely excluded from the guarantee.

Besides the guarantee that is given on a specific product, there is also the question of the general policy of the seller. (A **policy** is a set plan that guides actions.) For example, most companies that sell by mail have a "satisfaction guaranteed" policy. If the customer is dissatisfied with the goods in any way, the goods may be returned, and the customer's money will be "cheerfully refunded." Many stores have a similar policy, which is, of course, ideal for the consumer. But this should not be taken to mean that marketers with different policies are cheating.

Some retailers have an **as-is policy,** meaning that the customer has to accept the goods in the condition they are in, usually at a greatly reduced price. Other stores will allow goods to be brought back, but only for **exchange.** This means that the seller will not refund the money but will allow the customer to pick out other items of equal value.

Consumers have the right to know the marketer's policy regarding the return of merchandise. *(Jeremiah Bean)*

With any sale, customers are being cheated whenever they are not made aware of the true situation. Informing the customer can be done by posting a large sign, by giving a written guarantee, or by telling the customer directly. Customers have a right to know *exactly* what they can expect from marketers if their purchases should turn out to be less than satisfactory. This is as true of a five-cent purchase as it is of a $500 one.

Reliable Standards of Quality

The necessity for a satisfactory guarantee has become even more important in recent years because many products are not holding up as well as they should. "They just don't make things as well as they used to." This has become an everyday complaint for customers, as they cope with all kinds of products, from automobiles to toys, that have defects, are unsafe, or don't last as long as they should. This is also a problem with many services, where customers do not receive the quality they are paying for.

A major cause of the decline in quality is the number of people who no longer take any pride in doing their jobs well. This cuts across every level of our economy. It includes factory owners who are satisfied with turning out inferior merchandise and factory workers who miss some of the bolts they are supposed to tighten. It also includes packers in the wholesaler's warehouse who constantly mix up orders, bus drivers who are grouchy, store salesworkers who think that waiting on people is a nuisance, repairers who fix one thing and break another in the process, and many more. This lack of pride in a job well done has become a very serious problem for our country. If we cannot produce and deliver high-quality goods and services, we run the risk of becoming a second-class economic power. Jobs in American industry will become scarce because foreign competitors will have taken away all our business.

Fair Prices

Marketers cannot be blamed for high prices that are beyond their control. When costs go up all along the line, prices have to go up all along the line too. For example, when the cost of raw materials goes up, the producer has to charge the wholesaler more; then the wholesaler must charge the retailer more; and the retailer, in turn, must charge the consumer more. When prices are very high throughout the whole economy, marketers still have a right to a fair profit. But they also have an obligation to help consumers get the most for their money.

In order to get the most for their money, consumers must compare

How would you like to sign the work you do?

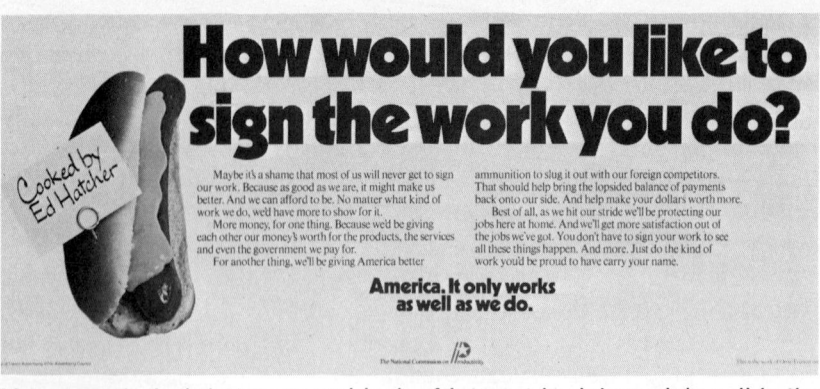

Maybe it's a shame that most of us will never get to sign our work. Because as good as we are, it might make us better. And we can afford to be. No matter what kind of work we do, we'll have more to show for it.

More money, for one thing. Because we'd be giving each other our money's worth for the products, the services and even the government we pay for.

For another thing, we'll be giving America better ammunition to slug it out with our foreign competitors. That should help bring the lopsided balance of payments back onto our side. And help make your dollars worth more.

Best of all, as we hit our stride we'll be protecting our jobs here at home. And we'll get more satisfaction out of the jobs we've got. You don't have to sign your work to see all these things happen. And more. Just do the kind of work you'd be proud to have carry your name.

America. It only works as well as we do.

Many people feel that a general lack of interest in doing a job well is the reason for the decline in the quality of American products. (*Courtesy The Advertising Council*)

prices. But comparison shopping is not always easy. This is especially true in food stores, where items are packed in cans and boxes of different sizes. The consumer who wants to compare prices has to do a lot of arithmetic. For example, does a 12-ounce box of crackers at 48 cents cost more or less than another company's 16-ounce box at 56 cents? To get the answer, the shopper has to do the following: 48 cents divided by 12 ounces equals 4 cents an ounce, and 56 cents divided by 16 ounces equals 3.5 cents an ounce. Therefore, the 16-ounce box is the better value.

Most people buy a lot of items in one shopping trip, and that adds up to a lot of work. This explains why there is a move toward requiring food retailers to state what their prices are, not for 12 ounces or 16 ounces but for one ounce. In other words, consumers are asking that the stores do the arithmetic for them. Pricing by the individual unit of weight or measure is called **unit pricing.** It is a very important step toward helping consumers exercise their right to choose what costs the least.

As another means of comparing prices, consumers have been asking for more accurate and complete labels. This helps shoppers to see which item is the better buy. For example, a customer might decide, on the basis of the labels, that a more expensive wash-and-wear raincoat is a better buy than one that has to be sent to a dry cleaner. Stores are also being asked not to give fancy names to cuts of meat, such as calling chuck steak "California Roast," so that customers can compare the meats offered by different stores.

The trends toward unit pricing and more descriptive labels are helping marketers give better service to consumers. However, there are still problem areas in pricing. The federal government watches closely to prevent situations where one big company gets a monopoly and can control the prices for certain products. It also forbids companies that should be competing with each other to join together to fix prices at high levels. There are also laws against charging the full price for a product that either weighs less than the consumer thinks or has been diluted in some way. But there are still some marketers who try to get away with such practices.

Straightforward Credit Terms

When consumers make large purchases—such as automobiles, appliances, and furniture—they may not have the money to pay the full price right away. In this case, they will ask for **credit.** This means that they can buy the merchandise now but pay for it at some future date. They are, in effect, borrowing the money to make the purchase. Whenever you borrow money, you have to pay something for the privilege. This is fair. But some marketers have explained the credit terms in such a way that the customers had no idea how much they were really paying. There are now laws that require that all credit costs be spelled out clearly and exactly. But it is still possible for marketers to take advantage of people who are inexperienced about borrowing money.

Truth in Advertising

An advertisement that doesn't make the product sound good is not an effective advertisement. But there is such a thing as making the product sound *too* good. An ad may make exaggerated statements about a

Without unit pricing, comparison shopping is a real test of a person's math skills.

product, promising things the product cannot do. If you are buying something relatively inexpensive, like toothpaste or shampoo, you will only be annoyed when the product isn't all that the ad said it was. But if the product is expensive, like an appliance, you are probably going to have to live with the results of being tricked by the ad for a long time.

To protect the consumer from this, the advertising business is policed by the Federal Trade Commission, which cracks down on all kinds of false advertising. This includes exercising strict controls over the advertising done by stores. Sometimes customers have gone to stores to purchase an item that was advertised as a bargain, only to find that the item was "out of stock." Once in the store, the customers would then be offered a higher-priced item.

It would be disastrous for our economy if consumers got to the point where they mistrusted all ads. The fact is that advertising contributes to the welfare of producers, marketers, and consumers. Its purpose is not just to persuade, but also to inform—to tell people what they have to know about new products. The many honest people in the advertising business are well aware of the importance of maintaining the public's confidence. They are working hard to establish and enforce standards that will eliminate all deceptive practices.

Honest Personal Selling

It is just as easy for the personal salesworker to make exaggerated claims for a product as it is for the advertiser. When you hear things like "once in a lifetime opportunity" and "special low rate just for you," you should be very suspicious. This is not the way that reliable salesworkers talk. Nor would reliable salesworkers ever try to force you to buy. They want to sell you products that will meet your needs. So they tell a straight story that depends on facts, not on overstatements.

Selling is a vitally important job. The people who do it honestly are helping in a very real way to keep our economy healthy. But this is not true of the fast-talking salesworker who sees everyone as a "sucker." There are laws that protect the consumer from such salesworkers in some instances. But as long as there are uninformed consumers, these salesworkers can find enough victims to keep them in business.

ACCEPTING INDIVIDUAL RESPONSIBILITY

There are people who think that they are doing all that is necessary by pointing out marketing's shortcomings. These people do not really understand what living in a democracy means. Life in a democracy is not

All too often a dishonest marketer is able to take advantage of a customer because, no matter how unlikely the marketer's claims about the product may seem, the customer wants to believe they are true.

"free" in the sense that you get all your rights for nothing. You must earn your rights by accepting the obligations that go along with them.

Rights and obligations go together in every facet of life in a democracy, including marketing. Thus, any discussion of what you think marketing owes you is only half the story. The other half has to be what you owe to marketing. What do you have to do to earn your right to live in a free marketing system and to enjoy its benefits? Can you just sit back and blame "them," meaning everyone but yourself, for what is wrong with marketing? Or do you have an obligation to replace negative criticism with constructive action? As a way of answering this question, let's look at what you might do as a consumer, a citizen, and a worker.

You as a Consumer

Let's suppose for a moment that every consumer in this country is a careful shopper who is well-informed about the marketing process and the obligations of marketers. What would happen then to the marketers who are less than honest? They need people whom they can "put something over on." But there wouldn't be any such people.

This may sound like an impossible dream. But there are a lot of people in this country who are working to make such an ideal situation a reality. Consumer protection agencies in the government, private consumer action groups, and marketers themselves are joining together to overcome consumer ignorance. Special things are being done for the people who are most likely to be victimized—the elderly, the people

Informing consumers is probably the most effective way to eliminate dishonest marketing practices, because informed consumers seldom allow themselves to be cheated. (*Courtesy Council of Better Business Bureaus, Inc.*)

who have just arrived in our country and don't know our language and customs, and the poor. It is hoped that these people, and all other consumers, can be provided with the most powerful of all weapons—knowledge! This includes telling people how to avoid being cheated and where to get help if they have been cheated. Government agencies and better business bureaus throughout the country want to help. But they cannot do anything unless problems are reported to them.

The people who are working to protect consumers and to preserve the environment need your support. Stay informed about what they are asking for and help them when you believe they are right. And most important of all, learn to be the kind of consumer that no one can take advantage of. You'll be helping yourself. What's more, you'll be benefiting the entire country, because you'll be closing one more door on dishonest marketers.

You as a Citizen

Another way in which you can improve marketing is by being a well-informed, concerned citizen. There are sharp differences of opinion in this country over how much economic control should be given to the government. Everyone agrees that some government control is necessary, but some people want to keep it to a minimum and others think that much more of it is needed. The problem is that every new government regulation means that some measure of freedom will be taken away from someone. The question that has to be asked in each situation is whether the freedom that will be taken away is more or less important than the benefits that the new regulation will provide.

This is why it is so important for you to know what the candidates for political office believe. Even before you are old enough to vote, you can work on behalf of the candidate that seems to represent your own ideas best. You can also influence your elected representatives by writing to let them know what you think. These are positive ways of working for those changes in our economic system and in marketing that mean the most to you.

You as a Worker

In many ways, the most encouraging signs about marketing's future are coming from within marketing, from the people who actually work in the field. Instead of trying to sweep the problems under the rug where they can be forgotten, many concerned marketers have been meeting them head-on. They not only have admitted that problems exist but also have accepted the most personal kind of responsibility for finding solutions. This concern can be seen on many levels, from the people who manage marketing businesses to the workers who have direct daily contact with consumers. For example, this concern may be seen through a decision to spend thousands of dollars for the benefit of consumers in general. Or it may be a matter of store salesworkers or service station attendants doing that something extra to help their customers, simply because that is what they believe is right. These people are all confident that the advantages of a free marketing system far outweigh its disadvantages, and they are trying to make it work as it should.

If you decide to work in marketing, you will have to decide what kind of worker you want to be. Will you be honest or dishonest in the amount and kind of work you do and in your dealings with your employer, fellow workers, and customers? Will you be concerned only with getting a paycheck or with giving a fair amount of service in return? The responsibility for making marketing work for everyone will not be "their" problem; it will be yours.

- **BUILDING YOUR MARKETING VOCABULARY**

Define each of the following terms and then use each one in a sentence.

as-is policy
consumerism
credit
exchange
guarantee
policy
unit pricing

- **UNDERSTANDING WHAT YOU HAVE READ**
    1. How is consumerism affecting marketing practices?
    2. How does the government help the consumer?
    3. Explain the meaning of "Let the buyer beware."
    4. Explain how accurate labeling can benefit the consumer.

- **APPLYING WHAT YOU HAVE LEARNED**
    1. State whether each of the following marketing practices is fair or unfair to the consumer: (a) three companies join together to fix prices; (b) as a customer is buying a sweater on sale, the salesworker reminds the person that the sweater cannot be returned for exchange or refund; (c) a supermarket displays unit-pricing signs with each item for sale; (d) a salesworker puts pressure on the customer to buy; (e) an advertisement claims that if you use a certain toothpaste, you will have more dates; (f) a toy packed in a sealed package is missing a part; (g) a store runs out of an advertised item but gives the customer a written promise to sell the item for the sale price when it is again in stock; (h) a food store sells goat meat, labeling it "chevron." In each case, give a reason for your answer.
    2. Prepare a report on an unfair marketing practice that you have observed or heard about. Your report should include answers to the following questions: (a) What was unfair? (b) What could the consumer have done to correct the problem? (c) What do you think will happen to the business if the problem is not corrected?

EXPERIMENTS IN MARKETING

1. Select 10 members of your class to play a game similar to that played on the television program "What's My Line?" You will need a moderator and four panel members. You will also need five contestants. The rest of the class will serve as judges. The moderator will introduce the first contestant with one of the statements listed in the left-hand column of the form below. The contestant will then make the corresponding statement listed in the center column. Each panel member is given one chance to identify the contestant's general line of work. After each panel member has given an answer, the judges decide which panel member is correct. The panel member who correctly identifies the greatest number of contestants wins the game. Five statements for the moderator and contestant are given below. You or your teacher may add more.

MODERATOR	CONTESTANT	LINE
Example: This person buys raw materials to make goods.	I buy sugar to make candy.	Industrial consumer
a. This person is a marketing expert.	I buy large quantities of goods from many producers, store them in my warehouse, and then divide them up for sale to many retailers.	
b. This person is a middleman.	I buy all the fish caught by a fleet of fishing boats and sell them to wholesalers.	
c. This person provides a service for producers.	I ask sample groups of people what kinds of products they want to buy.	
d. This person's work is a form of selling.	I try to get favorable stories about my company into the newspapers.	
e. This person produces and sells a product.	I grow apples and sell them at a roadside stand.	

2. Make a collage illustrating the variety of jobs that are part of marketing. You may use help-wanted ads from newspapers, pictures from magazines and newspapers, or your own drawings.

UNIT 2

After completing this unit, you will have increased your knowledge about yourself and about what a career is. You will understand that finding a career that is appropriate for you is a process that requires careful planning.

Unit 1 gave you a brief introduction to the field of marketing. Now it is time for you to think about what a career is and how important your choice of career will be to your life. In this unit, you will take a good look at yourself, in order to realize what makes you the unique person that you are. Understanding how and why you are an individual will help you to see why it is important for you to plan for a career that will let you be yourself.

You and a Marketing Career

part 6
Thinking About Careers

After reading Part 6, you will be able—
- To determine which of the three reasons for working would apply to a given job from your personal point of view.
- To state whether the person doing each job in a given list would be an unskilled, semiskilled, or skilled worker or a paraprofessional, middle manager, top manager, or professional.
- To define an entry-level job.
- To distinguish between the job changes that are part of a career ladder and those that are part of a career lattice in a given list of successive jobs held by an individual.

If you are going to be able to plan for a career that is right for you, you must know first of all what a career is. Is a career different from a job? If so, how? How does a career begin? How does it develop? These are all questions that will be answered in this part. But before you can even think about a career, you must answer another question: Why should you work? What are you going to get out of working that will make it worthwhile? Because this question is so important, we will start by trying to answer it.

WHY WORK?

There was a time in our country's history when questioning the value of working would have been considered very strange. Just about everyone accepted the "work ethic"—that is, the belief that work was the right and proper thing to do. But today there are young people who have chosen to drop out of the system. They have rejected the work ethic instead of accepting it. By doing this, they have called attention to the need for all of us to think through our own feelings about working. It is not enough anymore to commit yourself to a lifetime of working just because that's the way things have always been done or because that's what other people expect. Today's young people want answers that are more personal than that, answers that fit their own lives and times.

There was a time when the value of work was not questioned. People worked long hours and could take personal pride in the products they made. (*Courtesy Old Sturbridge Village*)

To help you find these answers for yourself, we will look at three reasons why work has been and still is a major part of human life: working for money, working to do your share, and working for self-fulfillment. Perhaps one of these three general reasons for working will give you the answer you need. Your personal answer may also be a combination of two of the reasons, or a mixture of all three.

Working for Money

When you are paid money for the work that you do, you then have a way of buying the things that you need in order to live. These include, first, the things that are absolute necessities, such as food, shelter, and clothing. They also include things that you don't really need but that you want in order to make your life more enjoyable—that is, things that could be considered luxuries.

Because people have very different ideas about how they want to live, they have different ideas about the importance of money. To some people, material things are not very important. These people do not need as much money as the people who want to live very comfortably with many luxuries. The amount of emphasis that you put on your own need for money is going to be a very personal matter, depending on the kind of life you want to lead. But unless you have some other means of support, you will have to earn at least some money in order to live.

For some people, like these communal farmers, working for money is not very important. What motivates them, then, to do the hard physical work necessary to maintain their simple life style? *(Mark Chester/Editorial Photocolor Archives)*

Working to Do Your Share

Why do retired schoolteachers, who offer their services free, spend many hours a week tutoring children who need extra help? Why do professional basketball players work without pay in community centers during their free time? And why do so many people who have inherited great wealth work in full-time jobs? There must be another reason for working besides having to earn money.

In Part 5, we discussed the idea that rights carry obligations with them. There are many people who believe that they are not entitled to a "free ride" through life, always taking and never giving anything in return. These people see work as a way of contributing their share to society. Some people talk a lot about how much they love humanity and how much they want to help other people. But the only ones who can prove that they mean what they say are the ones who actually work at it.

Working for Self-Fulfillment

Working for money and working to fulfill your obligations to society as you see them are both very important reasons for working. But there is a third reason that speaks even more directly to our times. Today people are very concerned with individual freedom. Instead of trying to make everyone conform, there is a new emphasis on allowing you as an individual to develop in your own way, to "do your own thing."

There are people who think that they cannot start "doing their own thing" until the workday is over. In other words, they see work only as something that they must do in order to support themselves. But actually your work and your life are not two separate things. For better or worse, your work is a part of your total life experience. That is why it is so important to learn how to go about finding the work that is right for you. The wrong work can stifle you. But the right work can bring a special kind of richness to your life, a richness that excludes boredom and sameness and includes people who interest you and situations that challenge you. Even the right work won't be 100 percent joy day in and day out. That is not the way life is. But the right work *can* help you grow in the directions that are right for you.

WHAT IS A JOB?

The word **job** refers to the work one does at any given time. For example, you may have a job pumping gas in a service station. When you leave that job, you may get another job as a mechanic for a bus company. Eventually you may have a job as the manager of a service station. And when you get older and want to slow down, you may take a job keeping service station records. You will have done each of these jobs at a certain time of your life.

Job Levels

There are four main levels of jobs. The first is for those people that are called **unskilled workers,** because they have not had any job training. On the second level, we find the **skilled workers,** who have spent the time and effort to learn how to do specialized jobs. The paraprofessionals are on the third level. *Para* is a prefix that means alongside of, and so a **paraprofessional** is a person who works with and is supervised by professionals in various fields. For example, a paramedic works in the field of medicine under the supervision of doctors.

There are two groups of people on the fourth level of jobs—professionals and top managers. A **professional** may be defined as a person engaged in a job requiring a long and intensive period of schooling to acquire highly specialized knowledge. Doctors and lawyers, for example, are professionals. **Top managers** are the people at the top of the line of responsibility in a company who are in charge of planning the course of action that the company will take and directing the efforts of the other workers.

In between these four main levels, there are some intermediate steps. When unskilled workers have learned how to do some tasks, they are referred to as **semiskilled workers.** Below the top managers, there is a step for the **middle managers,** who supervise the work of others but still have to report to top management. On this step too are the skilled workers who have gone into business for themselves.

There are four main levels of jobs. If, after a training period, you became an airline flight attendant, on which job level would you be working?

Unskilled Jobs: A Special Problem
Unskilled workers are not only on the lowest level of jobs but also the least secure in their jobs. There are more unskilled workers than there are jobs for them to fill. Unskilled workers generally do routine jobs that are done over and over in the same way. Therefore, unskilled workers are often replaced by machines. Even though the pay for unskilled workers is generally low, machines can do the same work for much less money. New machines are constantly being invented, so the outlook for unskilled workers is becoming worse every day. This means that education and training are becoming more and more important for anyone planning to enter the world of work.

WHAT IS A CAREER?
The words "job" and "career" do not mean the same thing and should not be used as if they did. Whereas a job is what a person does at a given point in time, a **career** is the whole series of jobs that a person will have in a lifetime. If a person stays in the same job throughout his or her working life, as many professional and skilled workers do, it is not necessary to distinguish between the person's job and career. For most workers, however, the distinction is quite important. Let's see why this is so by looking first at how a career begins and then at how it develops.

How a Career Begins
Your first job will be what is called an **entry-level job,** which gets its name because it represents a way of entering the world of work, a way of beginning. In hiring you for this job, your employer will take into account the amount of education and training you are bringing to the job. The more you know when you start, the better your entry-level job will be. For example, a person who has not finished high school and who has not learned any job skills would have to start in some kind of unskilled category—perhaps unloading trucks for a supermarket. But a person who has finished high school and also taken marketing courses might be hired by this same supermarket to be trained to become the head of a department.

In hiring you, the employer will also take into account many other factors, including your appearance and attitudes. If you look sloppy, you give the impression that you will do sloppy work. No matter what level of job employers are trying to fill, they want to hire the kind of person who will get along well with other people, care about the company's welfare, and be interested in learning how to do the job well. All this means that your career actually starts before you get your first job.

It starts while you are preparing yourself, or not preparing yourself, for the world of work.

The field of marketing offers the young person who is seeking that important first job some definite advantages. Marketing is one of the fastest growing parts of the business world, and growth means more jobs for more people. These jobs can be found wherever there are people—in rural areas, small towns, suburbs, and cities. Wherever there are people using goods and services, there are marketers working to see that these goods and services are right at hand, ready for the people who want to buy them. Furthermore, marketing offers many jobs for beginners, something that is not true of many parts of the business world.

Marketing is unique in that it offers many opportunities for part-time work. This is true because many marketing businesses have to stay open long hours. The workers who come to work early in the morning have to be relieved by another shift of workers for the later hours. Part-time workers are also needed because many marketing businesses have peak periods of activity. For example, food stores are busiest at the end of the week, so extra workers are needed then. Many young people get started on their marketing careers while they are still in school by taking advantage of marketing's need for part-time workers. Retail stores, service stations, hotels, and eating places are among the marketing businesses that offer young people excellent opportunities for part-time, after-school work.

How a Career Develops

Getting hired for your first job is an important step in your career. But it is even more important for you to learn how to stay hired. Your employer has to look at your performance on the job in terms of dollars and cents. If you are not worth what you are being paid, your employer will have to fire you. In that case, all you can hope for is to find another entry-level job so that you can start over. If you do well in your entry-level job, however, you will no longer be a beginner in the world of work. You will have some experience to offer an employer, experience that you can build on when you are faced with the necessity of learning new skills. By proving yourself in your first job, you will be in a good position to progress to other jobs.

CAREER LADDERS. One way in which your career can progress is by climbing a **career ladder,** moving up one step at a time in the same general kind of business. When you have shown that you can easily handle the job you are doing and are capable of more difficult tasks, you are promoted to the next level of responsibility. You are now worth more to your employer, and so you are paid more money. The jobs at the bottom of the career ladder are called entry-level jobs. Next come the career-level jobs, for those people who have learned their own jobs but do not supervise the work of others. Finally, at the top, there are the management-level jobs.

Marketing has been widely recognized as a field where it is especially easy to move up the ladder. In some fields, there are barriers between the levels of workers. For example, you cannot start out as a nurse and work your way up to become a doctor. A nurse would have to go back to school for many years to become a doctor. Even in fields that do not have such barriers, promotions may be given on the basis of who has been around longest.

A career in marketing offers you many opportunities to make both lattice- and ladder-type moves.

PART 6 • THINKING ABOUT CAREERS • 63

By contrast with these situations, there are few barriers in marketing, and promotions generally go to the people who deserve them. This means that in marketing it really is possible to start at the bottom and wind up at the top. There are many examples of people who have started out as junior salespeople for large companies and have moved up, step by step, to become the company president. Marketing also offers you the chance to own your own business and be your own boss. Furthermore, all this can happen while you are still young. Marketing is a field that is growing rather than standing still. Therefore, it welcomes and rewards young people with fresh, new ideas.

CAREER LATTICES. The second pattern that your career could follow is called a **career lattice.** Instead of moving up, you move sideways to another job in a related field that calls for many of the same skills. Being able to do this gives you a high degree of job security. For example, let's say that you have been working as the cashier in a movie theater. You suddenly have to move to another area of the country, where you find that there are no cashier jobs open. But you are able to get a job in a bank as a teller. This job requires you to accept the money that people want to deposit in the bank and give out the money that people want to withdraw. Your previous experience in handling money convinces the bank that you will have no trouble with the teller's job.

It is also possible to move sideways and up at the same time. For example, a person who has worked as an artist for a company that creates package designs might move into a large department store as the head of the display department.

The possibilities for lattice-type moves are very great in marketing. Because so many marketing skills are interrelated, it is easy for you to use what you have learned in one job on other jobs. For example, it is easy to make the switch from wholesaling to retailing or from personal selling to nonpersonal selling work. Also, having had experience selling supplies to producers, you might take a job doing the buying for one of the producers. The point is that marketing jobs, instead of being dead ends, have many turnabout opportunities, so you never have to feel hemmed in.

- **BUILDING YOUR CAREER VOCABULARY**

Define each of the following terms and then use each one in a sentence.

career	paraprofessional
career ladder	professional
career lattice	semiskilled worker
entry-level job	skilled worker
job	top manager
middle manager	unskilled worker

- ## UNDERSTANDING WHAT YOU HAVE READ
    1. Name the job level that each of the following workers would be on: (a) president of a company, (b) beginning worker with no skills, (c) teacher's aide, (d) manager of a department in a store, (e) beginning worker who can type, (f) doctor, (g) experienced salesworker.
    2. Why do unskilled workers have the least security in their jobs?
    3. If you live in a small town, would you be unwise to plan a career in marketing? Why or why not?
    4. List three advantages of jobs in marketing.
    5. Generally speaking, are marketing jobs dead-end jobs? Explain your answer.

- ## APPLYING WHAT YOU HAVE LEARNED
    1. Choose one of the following jobs: (a) bus driver, (b) restaurant owner, (c) salesworker in a hobby shop, (d) television repairer, (e) airline flight attendant. From what you've seen and heard of the job, try to imagine what it would involve. Then write a paragraph explaining how many of the three reasons for working discussed in the text would apply to this job from your point of view.
    2. Divide your class into teams and hold informal debates on the following issues: (a) the work ethic is dead, (b) working for money is selfish and wrong, (c) your work is one thing and your life is another.
    3. A list of the successive jobs held by Emily Hicks during her lifetime is given below. Make a diagram of Emily's career by representing each change as part of a career ladder or career lattice. The successive jobs are (a) part-time cashier in a movie theater, (b) store salesworker, (c) trainee in the store's display department, (d) store display artist, (e) store display director, (f) display director for a wholesaler.

part 7
Understanding Basic Human Needs

After reading Part 7, you will be able—
- To state which of the eight basic human needs each individual is trying to satisfy when you are given specific examples of human behavior.
- To state the order in which needs generally have to be satisfied.
- To define the word "frustration."
- To state one positive way and one negative way in which a given list of obstacles to the fulfillment of needs could be handled.
- To list five ways in which your work can satisfy your needs.

Now is a very good time for you to take the time to learn about what makes you the one-of-a-kind person that you are. Learning about yourself will help you in many ways. It will help you lead a fuller and happier life. It will also help you to make wise decisions about the kind of work you would eventually like to do and about the courses you should take to prepare yourself for that work. The more information you have about yourself, the easier it will be to narrow down your choices to the areas that would be best for you.

Another reason for taking the time to learn about yourself is that understanding yourself helps you to understand other people better. Knowing what it is that makes you an individual helps you to appreciate the individual qualities of the people around you. Actually, personal understanding is like a two-way street, because it is also true that the more you learn about other people, the more insights you gain into your own personality. You have probably heard the saying "Knowledge is power." The more you learn about yourself, the more power you have for understanding how to live with yourself and how to work with other people.

The best way to start this important study of your uniqueness is by learning about the needs that you share with all human beings. Knowing what these needs are and how important it is to satisfy them can teach you a lot about your own and other people's behavior.

DEFINING BASIC HUMAN NEEDS

You have a basic need when you are missing something that is important to your well-being. When you have this lack, what you want most is to satisfy it. So the need itself becomes a strong force, pushing you in the direction that will get rid of the need and take away the dissatisfaction you feel. Needs "motivate" us, which means that they cause us to act as we do. We may not be at all conscious of this motivation, but it is going on within us all the same. **Needs** are the things that we must have. They should not be confused with **wants,** which are the things we would like to have. Our wants also motivate us, but satisfying them is not absolutely essential to our well-being.

The list of basic human needs that follows is very similar to the list developed by Dr. Abraham H. Maslow. His studies about basic human needs have greatly influenced modern thinking on this subject. The needs that we will discuss are physical needs, the need for safety, the need for acceptance and love, the need for respect, the need to know, the need to understand, the need for beauty, and the need to become yourself.

When you are having a good time rapping with friends, you are satisfying the basic human need for acceptance. (*National Education Association*)

Physical Needs
When we talk about physical needs, we are talking about all the things that your body must have in order to stay alive and well. You must have fresh air to breathe and pure water to drink. Your body must get enough of the right kind of food so that it can grow and repair itself and provide you with plenty of energy. Being able to maintain an even temperature is also important to your body. Thus, you need protection from both the winter's frost and the summer's scorching sun. You also need enough space to live in and medical care if you get sick.

The Need for Safety
Have you ever been in a situation in which you were physically afraid? Perhaps someone bigger and stronger than you was threatening to beat you up. Or maybe you were walking along a deserted street late at night and were frightened by the shadows and strange noises. If you have ever had any such experience, you know how strong your need to feel safe is. As a human being, it is necessary for you to feel sure that you are not going to be injured or killed. Sometimes feeling afraid is good, because it helps you protect yourself. Being afraid can give you the energy to run away from a dangerous situation or the strength to fight, if necessary. But when human beings have to live in a constant state of fear, they cannot develop as they should.

The Need for Acceptance and Love
The good feeling that you have when you are with your friends comes from the need of all human beings to be accepted and loved. Occasionally you hear of someone who has spent her or his whole life living all alone, but that is very rare. Human beings are happiest living in groups because it is necessary for them to feel that they belong.

When you were an infant, it was your family that you counted on for acceptance and love. Then, as you grew and moved out into the community, you became part of other groups. You may have a special group of friends in your neighborhood and another at school. You may also belong to a church group, social club, or community center. All of these groups are important to you because they take away your feeling of loneliness. The warmth and security that you get from knowing that you are an accepted member of the group are vital to your well-being.

The Need for Respect
Besides being accepted and loved, you also have a need to be respected. You have to know that the other members of your group really appreciate what you are and what you can do. This need for recogni-

tion from the group motivates you to do the things that the group accepts as being worthy of respect and to avoid the behavior that the group disapproves of. Obviously, the ways of winning respect in a primitive tribe in New Guinea are not the same as the ways in Bloomington, Illinois. Wherever you live, however, you have this need to have the people around you approve of you.

When this need has been satisfied, you have something else that is vital to your welfare—self-esteem. Because you know that other people respect you, you can respect yourself.

The Need to Know

Suppose that one day, while your class was in session, a strange, very loud noise began coming from the hallway. What do you think the reaction of your teacher and class would be? Would you all just go on with your work? Isn't it more likely that you would stop until someone found out what was causing the noise? Your need to know would have to be satisfied. You can see this need in action with young children, whose curiosity is so lively that the questions come out faster than they can be handled.

Children are naturally curious about everything in the world around them. This curiosity comes from the basic human need to know. (*National Education Association*)

Human beings have a need for information about everything around them, from the laws of nature to the ways of people. Human curiosity extends to the past and to the future, as well as to the present. It is because of this need to know that we have schools, libraries, and newspapers.

The need to know serves many purposes. Sometimes people are afraid of other people who are different from themselves. But when people get to know each other, the fear disappears. Knowledge also helps people to live and work in a more efficient way. For example, knowing about people's needs and wants helps the salesworker to do a better job. Learning also makes people's lives more interesting. When you never learn anything new, your life is humdrum and boring. But when your need to know is continually satisfied, you feel stimulated and interested. Knowledge provides the variety that is indeed the "spice of life."

The Need to Understand

Human beings have a need to go a step beyond just knowing something to the point of really understanding it. You start out by knowing that water boils when it is heated long enough, but then you want to know why. What causes the water to change from a clear, still liquid to a fast-moving cloud of steam? The steam engine was invented because a man went on asking himself questions about that boiling water.

Sometimes human beings ask questions that science cannot answer. Some people get answers that satisfy them from their religions. Other people turn to philosophy, which is a subject that people study to help them make sense of their surroundings and experiences. This need to ask questions and to find out why things happen is a very important part of being human. It makes people very different from sheep, which just follow the leader blindly.

The Need for Beauty

The proof that human beings have a need to bring beauty into their lives is not hard to find. Nor is this proof to be found only in art museums and concert halls. You can see it all around you, in such everyday ways as the clothing and jewelry that people choose to wear and the concern that they have for making their homes look nice. You can see it in a gift-wrapped package, a table that has been nicely set for a meal, or a vase of flowers. This everyday need for beauty has been seen in the most primitive as well as the most advanced societies down through history. It is because this need is universal that it is included in the list of basic human needs.

The need for beauty is what motivates people to plant a flower and vegetable garden in the middle of a big city. (*New York* Daily News *Photo*)

The Need to Become Yourself
There are some young people who think that they invented the idea of doing your own thing. But actually human beings have always had, and always will have, the need to develop as independent individuals. Even though human beings have much in common, each person is distinctly different from everyone else. You are you, and you must grow in your own way, just as your friends have to grow in their own ways. Each of you needs to develop the best that is in you.

PUTTING NEEDS IN ORDER
You have just learned about eight basic needs. Dr. Maslow believes not only that these needs have to be satisfied, but also that they must be satisfied in the order in which they are listed above. An easy way to understand what this means is to imagine that these needs are on a staircase. The physical needs, which are the most urgent needs, are on the bottom step. And the need to become yourself is on the top step. You can't jump on the stairs somewhere in the middle. You have to climb one step at a time, satisfying each need as you go along.

Thus, people who have not eaten for days will take the chance of getting hurt in order to get food. And when they do get the food, they are certainly not going to stop to set the table before eating it. Until their need for food has been satisfied, people cannot satisfy their other needs. Likewise, babies will not explore their surroundings, even though their need to know is very strong, until they are quite sure that they will be safe.

Dr. Maslow ranked the basic human needs in the order in which they must be satisfied.

None of your needs can be satisfied once and for all. For example, your physical needs obviously have to be taken care of every day. But when you know that your physical needs have always been satisfied and that you have the means for satisfying them in the future, you are able to move up to the next step. When you have always had a great deal of respect, you can count on its continuing, and therefore you can go on climbing.

Being able to reach the top of the stairs is the best thing that can happen to a human being. This means that you have gotten from your environment everything that you need in order to be healthy in mind and body. Dr. Maslow calls this eighth level **self-actualization,** which means that the best that is in you has been able to get out into the open. It is no longer a question of what you could be but, rather, what you actually are.

WHEN NEEDS ARE NOT MET

Let's say that you have in a window box a plant that is supposed to flower. This plant needs water, sunshine, soil that is rich with plant food, and loving care. If it steadily gets all these things, it will grow strong and have many perfect flowers. But maybe the plant doesn't get everything that it needs all the time. Maybe the soil isn't quite rich enough, or maybe you occasionally forget to water it. Even though it won't be as perfect as it might have been, the plant can still grow and blossom. As long as most of its needs are met most of the time, the plant will not die.

For you as a human being, the situation is much the same. If all your needs are satisfied all the time, you will blossom to the fullest. And if your needs consistently go unanswered, you will either die or have a complete breakdown. These are the two extremes. But if you are like most people, you will live your life somewhere in the middle, where some of your needs get blocked some of the time.

Meeting obstacles is normal, in that it happens to most people. In fact, many very famous people have had serious obstacles to overcome. Franklin D. Roosevelt was a polio victim but still went on to become the president of the United States. And Stevie Wonder has become a famous entertainer even though he is blind.

The problem for each of us is how to handle the tenseness and disappointment—that is, the **frustration**—that we feel when our needs are not satisfied. If we keep frustrations all bottled up inside us, we may become angry and want to "get even" by hurting other people. We may also go in the other direction and stay completely away from people, so that they cannot cause us any more frustrations.

Many people have to overcome serious obstacles before they can satisfy their basic human needs and reach the level of self-actualization. For physically handicapped people, the most serious obstacle often is not their handicap but other people's attitudes. (*Courtesy The President's Committee on Employment of the Handicapped, The School of Visual Arts Public Advertising System*)

To avoid these two extremes, we each work out our own ways of coping with our anger and fears. Lots of people "blow off steam," just like a boiling tea kettle, by playing a very active sport or pouring out their troubles to a sympathetic friend. Other people make their frustrations seem less important by laughing at them. Still others daydream them away. There are also people who find something else for themselves in order to make up for the need that isn't satisfied. For example, a person who feels rejected may turn to drugs as a substitute.

People use such strategies because they must get relief somehow from the pressures of their frustrations. Knowing this helps you to understand your own actions, as well as those of other people.

SATISFYING NEEDS THROUGH YOUR WORK

When you have a job, you can earn money to buy the things that will answer your basic physical needs. This is vital. But if that is all your job is doing for you, it is not the right job for you. It is true that your work will not be your whole life. You will have a family and a social life away from work. But your work will be such a major part of your life that it should be a way of answering your other needs too, rather than an unending stream of frustrations.

Your need for safety must be met in your work, of course. When it is not because you have to do work that is dangerous, you should be paid extra money for taking these risks. Your need to belong should also be answered in your job. This is especially true in marketing jobs, where you work closely with other people. Many employers make a special effort to foster this sense of belonging by making the atmosphere of the business pleasant, printing newsletters about what the people in the company are doing, and sponsoring after-hours social activities, such as bowling leagues and various kinds of clubs. It is also common for employers to provide recognition for outstanding work so that the employees can enjoy the respect of their fellow workers for work well done. Your job also earns you the respect of the community at large, whose members appreciate you for what you can do.

Your job can also satisfy your need to know, for there is always more to be learned, no matter what your job is. Learning leads to understanding as you figure out causes and relationships. Your job can also be a way of answering your need for beauty. Many employers today recognize this as a real need and make every effort to provide their employees with attractive surroundings.

It is also to be hoped that your work will answer your need for self-actualization. This is much more likely to happen if you have given a lot of thought to what you want to do for a living. By finding out as much as you can about yourself and about possible careers before you start to work, you stand a much better chance of finding the right work for you. And that is work in which you can be successful and happy.

- ## BUILDING YOUR CAREER VOCABULARY

Define each of the following terms and then use each one in a sentence.

frustration   self-actualization
needs   wants

- ## UNDERSTANDING WHAT YOU HAVE READ

1. Explain two ways in which learning more about yourself can help you.
2. List six kinds of physical needs that all human beings have.

3. List the following needs on a separate sheet of paper, putting them in the order in which they have to be satisfied: need for beauty, physical needs, need to know, need to become yourself, need for acceptance and love, need for safety, need to understand, need for respect.
4. Why does your text say that it is normal to have obstacles in your life?
5. Give five examples of how your work can satisfy your needs.

• APPLYING WHAT YOU HAVE LEARNED

1. For each of the following examples of things people do, name the need that the individual is trying to satisfy: (a) swimming in the presence of a lifeguard, (b) hanging pictures in a home, (c) studying philosophy, (d) wearing warm clothes in cold weather, (e) winning a school letter for athletics, (f) wearing clothes that are considered "right" in your group, (g) developing your own interests, (h) asking questions about how things work.
2. A list of obstacles to the fulfillment of needs is given below. For each one, write one positive way and one negative way in which the individual could handle the obstacle. The obstacles are (a) being blind, (b) being the victim of discrimination, (c) not having books in your home to help you with your schoolwork, (d) having to be home at night before your friends do, (e) not having the money for a hobby that interests you.
3. Make a list of five things that happened in the past few weeks that made you angry. Think about why you were angry and whether what you did helped the situation or made it worse.
4. Have a class discussion about whether there should be any limits on the extent to which young people can expect to do their own thing.

part 8
Understanding Why You Are Unique

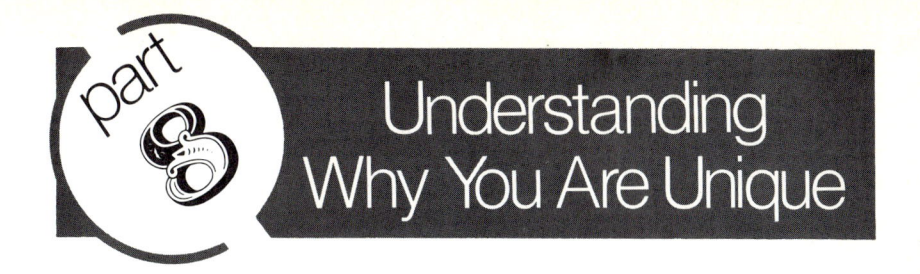

After reading Part 8, you will be able—
- To list three examples of customs observed by your family and comment on how each one has influenced your development.
- To list three ways in which your peer group has influenced your development.
- To explain the connection between a person's work and life style.
- To compare your present life style with the life style you hope to have in the future.

All you have to do to convince yourself that you really are unique is to look at the people around you. Look at your own brothers and sisters, if you have any, and at your classmates and friends. None of these people looks exactly like you. None of them talks, moves, thinks, acts, or reacts exactly as you do either. The process of conception and birth is the same for all human beings, so why are people so different from each other? Psychologists, scientists who study the mind and human behavior, explain the differences in people by talking about two factors: heredity and environment. In this part, you will learn what these words mean and see how they influence your development. You will also be able to think about the very important question of whether you have any control over your own development.

YOUR HEREDITY: THE BASIC PLAN

When we speak of your **heredity**, we are talking about all the characteristics that have been passed down to you not only from your mother and father but from generations back. Your heredity is responsible for such physical characteristics as your sex, the color of your hair, skin, and eyes, and your general size and shape. Heredity also provides the broad outlines for your emotional and mental makeup, setting out in a very general way what kind of person you will be.

All the special characteristics that you inherit from your ancestors are carried in "genes," which can be compared to tiny computers. To

Because heredity helps to determine how a person looks, very strong physical similarities often exist within families. (*Arthur Sirdofsky/Editorial Photocolor Archives*)

make a computer work, someone has to make a basic plan, or program, for it that tells it exactly how to proceed. When you were conceived, your genes were programmed in this same way, so that they would contain the basic plan for your development. A computer's program also tells it when to take each step. Likewise, your genes were given a timetable for your growth—a built-in schedule for when you would be strong enough to walk, when your first and second sets of teeth would grow in, when you would become an adult physically, and so on.

To understand why your program is different from everyone else's, you have to realize that there are many different kinds of genes and they can be combined in any number of ways. The particular combination of genes that you have is yours alone, and so no one else can have the particular combination of genetic qualities that you do.

THE EFFECTS OF YOUR ENVIRONMENT

When we talk about your **environment,** we are talking about everything around you—the place where you live, the things that happen there, the climate, the people, and the feelings and actions of those people. These are all things that affect your own growth and development, sometimes even in ways that go against the basic plan set by your heredity. For example, if you cannot get the right kind of food from your environment, you may not become as tall or as strong as your genes had you programmed for. And if your environment doesn't provide you with the opportunity to go to school, you may wind up with less brainpower than your heredity made you capable of.

The effect that your environment has on you is a lifelong process. Every day you have new experiences that are not exactly like anyone else's experiences. Each of these experiences has the same effect on you that a blow of the sculptor's chisel has on a piece of marble. Each blow of the chisel affects the final shape of the sculpture, just as each of your experiences shapes you. Another way to describe the effect your experiences have on you is to say that each experience teaches you a lesson about how to grow. To understand this point better, let's look at the seven main places where you get these lessons for growing.

Learning at Home

The learning process, which will go on as long as you live, starts at home. Your immediate family teaches you the basic skills and attitudes that act as a foundation for all the more advanced knowledge you will acquire later on. Some of this learning is direct, such as when someone in the family teaches you to tie your shoelaces or do household tasks. But much of what you learn comes to you in an indirect way through your family's **customs.** These are set ways of acting in certain situations, and they are not exactly the same in any two families. Examples of your family's customs are how, what, and when the family eats and how it celebrates holidays. Other examples are how the chores in the family are divided, who makes the decisions for the family, and how the family relates to outsiders.

Children learn many customs and traditions in the home. This Jewish family is celebrating Sukkoth, the autumn harvest festival. (*Charles Harbutt/Magnum*)

There are many factors that influence your family's customs, including your parents' backgrounds and education. The question of where you live also makes a difference. If you live in the country, your family will have different customs than if you live in a city or suburb. And if you live close to your grandparents, aunts, uncles, and cousins, your experiences will be different than if you have only your immediate family to teach you. The amount of money that your family has to spend also affects its customs, and so do the factors of how and by whom that money is earned. All of these things added together make an atmosphere, or climate, in your home that is different from the climate in any other home and that affects your development. You are part of this climate, because you are making an environment for the other people in your family just as they are making one for you.

The climate in your home is necessarily a changing one, for many things happen to families that force them to alter their customs. Babies are born, and people die. Parents may become separated or divorced. A job may be lost or a better one secured. The family may move. Children will leave home as they become self-supporting. This means that the things you learn at home may be quite different from the things an older or younger brother or sister learns.

One of the things that you learn at home is what it means to be male or female and—more important—what it means to be human. Some homes draw sharp lines between "woman's work" and "man's work." This is emphasized in many ways, including the relationships between the adults in the family. Also, different toys are given to boys and girls, and it is not expected that they could or should do the same things. But today more and more families are recognizing that most of the differences between the sexes are actually a matter of how and what they have been taught. These families are giving their boys and girls equal rights to choose their own directions and to do "human work."

What you have learned at home may satisfy you so completely that you will want to go on living in much the same way when you are on your own. There may, however, be many things that you will want to do differently. You may even want to go in a completely opposite direction. In any case, what you have learned at home will always be with you.

Learning in Your Neighborhood
You will have your first experiences outside your own home in your neighborhood. You may live in a neighborhood where the families are alike in many ways. In this case, the things that you learn at home will be "reinforced," which means they are given extra strength. But some

neighborhoods are made up of people who have very different backgrounds and customs. This can be very difficult if your experiences at home have taught you to dislike and fear certain groups of people or everyone who is different from yourself. When you make judgments about people based on the groups they belong to instead of on what they are as individuals, we say that you are "prejudiced."

Children can be taught to be unprejudiced as easily as they can be taught to be prejudiced. For this reason, many families today are deliberately choosing to live in neighborhoods made up of people from different races and national origins. These families hope to teach their children early that the differences in people do not have to be feared but can add a special interest and richness to life.

Growing up in a neighborhood made up of different races and ethnic backgrounds can help children develop unprejudiced attitudes toward all people. (Courtesy Police Athletic League, New York City)

Learning from the Groups You Belong To

Because of your need to belong, which is especially strong during the high school years, the groups that you belong to have a powerful influence on you. This is especially true of your own **peer group.** This is a term that you have probably heard before. It refers to the people who are roughly your own age, with whom you naturally have much in common.

Each generation has its own way of viewing the world. The older generation sometimes finds the views of younger people hard to understand, and so young people turn to each other for support. But the problem here is that people are not all alike, whether they would like to be or not. Sacrificing your own individuality may be too high a price to pay for being accepted as a member of the group. Also, young people do not all develop at the same rate of speed. When you are ready to move forward in your own development, you want to be sure that you have the freedom to move. It is possible for you to get so entangled in your friends' views of the world that your personal growth and development are forced to stop.

Learning at School

If someone asked you what you were learning in school this year, you would probably list the courses that you were taking. If you were asked about your teachers, you would name the people teaching those courses. But actually your courses, important as they are, represent only a fraction of what you learn in any school year, and the people who teach these courses are not your only teachers. You are also being taught by all the other people who work in the school, from the principal to the custodian. All these people are creating an atmosphere in the school that contributes to what you learn there. The other students are also part of this atmosphere, just as you are.

What are you learning from all these teachers? You are developing attitudes about yourself and about getting along with other people whose customs may be different from those of your family. You are also developing attitudes about learning itself and about what it means to be a thinking person. You are also developing attitudes about authority, individual responsibility, honesty, success, and many other subjects that will be important to you long after you have forgotten some of the facts that you are learning now.

Learning from the Media

The word **media** refers to channels of communication—that is, newspapers, magazines, radio, and television. The media have two distinct functions. The first is to keep us informed about current events. The media can now do that so successfully that we know what is going on halfway around the world, not weeks after the fact, but as it is happening. Getting the news is an obvious learning experience. When we know the facts, we are better able to think intelligently about what is happening in the world and to form valid opinions.

The media's second function is to entertain. Entertainment is also a significant learning experience. With so many people spending so many hours watching television every day, there is no doubt that television has great power to shape their development. Two popular programs, "Sesame Street" and "The Electric Company," represent an effort to use television's teaching power in a positive way for young children. When you are watching a television program, whether it is coverage of a sports event or a detective story, it can be an interesting experience to ask yourself what effect the program is having on you and other viewers.

You can broaden your experience of life by visiting new places. For example, you can tour museums in your own or a nearby community. (*Courtesy The Cooper Union*)

Learning from Traveling

A usual procedure in kindergarten is to take the class on a visit to the fire station. The children may have seen books about fire fighters and fire trucks, but the very best way of teaching them what a fire station is really like is to let them see it with their own eyes. You may not yet have had the opportunity to do much traveling. Perhaps you have not even traveled to other areas of your own city to see how other people live. But keep in mind that visiting different places, even if they are only other neighborhoods in your own city, provides you with very important learning experiences. When people from rural areas visit a large city, when Easterners go to the West, or when Americans travel in Europe, they are all learning that their ways of doing things are not the only ways there are. They are also learning that, despite their many different customs, people the world over have a great deal in common.

Learning at Work

When you begin working, you will find that you are doing two kinds of learning. The first of these has to do with the job itself. When your employer hires you, he or she will take into account all the skills and attitudes you have already learned. Once you are on the job, you will be expected to go on learning, piling more advanced skills and attitudes on top of those you already have, like so many building blocks. Along the way, you will have many teachers, including your employer, your co-workers, the customers, and yourself. What you will be learning from all these teachers are the more advanced skills and attitudes that will let you move on to better and better jobs over the years.

When you are working, you are also learning many things that will influence the way you live when you are not at work. An obvious example is that your eating habits may change because the people you work with may tell you about different foods or take you to new restaurants. Your clothing, your furniture, the way you spend your spare time and your money, and your attitudes about life in general will almost certainly begin to reflect the things that you are learning at work.

Your work is going to be a major influence on your total **life style,** which is the way a person lives. This is why you have to be so careful in choosing what you want to do. By working, you are not just learning how to do a job. You are also developing as a whole person. You have to be sure that the person your work will make of you is the person you want to be.

CONTROLLING YOUR OWN DEVELOPMENT

The subject of choosing your work brings up the question of whether you have any choices about what you are to become. Just how locked in are you by your heredity and environment? Do you have any control over your own development or not? It is true that you cannot change your heredity as such. But the older you get, the more possible it becomes for you to make changes in your environment, and sometimes these changes can alter personal characteristics that were determined by heredity.

An easy-to-understand example of this is your physical appearance. When you were a young child, everything was chosen for you, so that you had no control at all over how you looked. But now that you are older, the question of what other people see when they look at you depends on the choices that you make. The food that you choose to eat affects your weight. The kind and amount of exercise that you choose to get, or not to get, affects the shape of your body. Your choice of hairstyle, clothes, and accessories gives you the power to change your appearance.

You have this same freedom of choice in many other areas. Another way of saying that you have choices is to say that you have **options.** You have options about who your friends are and how you spend your free time. You have options about how much effort to put into your schoolwork.

You also have options about the basis on which you make your choices. For example, you can choose your food strictly according to what you like to eat. Or you can make the effort to learn about the kinds and amounts of food that your body needs to be healthy and choose foods on the basis of their nutritional value. You can choose a job because it is nearby and easy to get to. Or you can plan ahead and choose a job on the basis of its value to your growth as an individual. Learning how to make choices is a subject that you will have a chance to explore in more detail in Part 11. The point to be made now is that you do have choices about the kind of person that you are going to be. These choices give you a real responsibility for your own development.

- **BUILDING YOUR CAREER VOCABULARY**

  Define each of the following terms and then use each one in a sentence.

  custom
  environment
  heredity
  life style

  media
  option
  peer group

- **UNDERSTANDING WHAT YOU HAVE READ**

  1. Explain how heredity influences your development.
  2. List three examples of your family's customs and give an example of how each one has influenced your development.
  3. List three ways in which your peer group has influenced your development.
  4. Do you think it is true that television programs that are purely for entertainment are a "significant learning experience"? Support your written answer with references to a television show that you have seen recently.
  5. List five ways in which your work can influence your life style.

- **APPLYING WHAT YOU HAVE LEARNED**

  1. Think about your present life style by answering the following questions on a separate sheet of paper. You will not have to share your answers with your classmates.
     a. What is the size of your family?
     b. Do you live in a house or an apartment?
     c. Do you share a bedroom? With whom?
     d. What is the size and location of the community you live in?
     e. What kind of clothes do you like to wear?
     f. List your five favorite foods.

g. Does your family own a car? A television set?
   h. Who are your closest friends?
   i. List three things you most enjoy doing with your free time.
   j. What is the farthest point to which you have traveled?
   k. What is the thing about your life that you are most grateful for?
   l. What would you say is your main concern at the moment?
2. Imagine now that the time is ten years in the future and answer the following questions on a separate sheet of paper. Again, you will not have to share your answers with your classmates.
   a. In what city or area are you living?
   b. With whom are you living?
   c. Do you have a job? If so, what type of work are you doing? If not, where is the money that you need to live coming from?
   d. If you are married, does your spouse work?
   e. Do you have any children? If so, how many?
   f. Do you pay rent or do you own the apartment or house that you live in?
   g. Name five things you own that you could not give up.
   h. What did you do on your last vacation?
   i. List three things that you like to do in your free time.
   j. Would you describe your need for money as low, medium, or high?
   k. What changes would you like to make in your life?

part 9

Getting to Know the Real You

After reading Part 9, you will be able—
- To rate the degree to which you possess each one of a given list of physical characteristics on a scale of one to five, with one being the least and five the greatest.
- To determine which aptitudes in a given list you possess and the degree to which you possess them.
- To identify your interests and noninterests by thinking about how you spend your time and what you enjoy doing.
- To list five of your personality traits that you are proud of and five that you would like to improve.

Now that you have seen *why* you are different from everyone else, the next step is to see *how* you are different. Each individual is a complex combination of many qualities. In order to understand yourself fully, you must spend some time trying to define your particular qualities. This self-knowledge will help you on every level of your life, but especially when you are trying to make career choices.

When you are thinking about yourself, you should remember two things. The first is that it's just as important to know what qualities you don't have as to know what qualities you do have. For example, your noninterests can tell you as much about yourself as your interests. It is important that you know what you can't do as well as what you can. The second important thing to remember is that if you are not satisfied with the you that you see today, there is plenty of time and opportunity for change. Your physical growth will soon stop, if it hasn't already. But your mental and emotional growth are an entirely different matter. Because they never have to stop, you never have to feel discouraged about not being the person you would like to be.

YOUR PHYSICAL CHARACTERISTICS

What are some of the ways in which you differ physically from other people? First there are the differences that are immediately apparent—your facial features, coloring, height, weight, body type, and sex. Then there are other things that you may have to stop and think about. How does your energy level compare with that of your friends and classmates? Do you tire easily? How fast can you move? How strong are you? How easy is it for you to make various parts of your body do what you want them to do? In other words, how "well coordinated" are you? Another question is whether you are sick very much. Do you have any physical disabilities, which are called "physical handicaps"? Answering such questions can give you a picture of your physical characteristics that will help you to make realistic career choices.

Because this is such an important subject, it is emphasized in the *Dictionary of Occupational Titles* (DOT), prepared by the U.S. Employment Service. This book describes thousands of jobs in detail, giving specific information about what the work is like and what qualifications a person should have in order to do the work successfully. Among the work requirements listed are the **physical demands** of each job. These are defined in the book as "those physical activities required of a worker in a job."

Thus, the DOT indicates whether lifting, carrying, pushing, or pulling are necessary in a job. Jobs are classified as sedentary (meaning that the worker sits most of the day), light, medium, heavy, or very heavy work. The DOT also explains whether a given job requires climbing, balancing, stooping, kneeling, crouching, or crawling and whether the workers will have to reach, use their hands, or do skilled work with their fingers. Other areas of concern are how well you have to be able to see, hear, or speak in order to do a particular job.

The DOT also discusses **working conditions,** which it defines as "the physical surroundings of a worker in a specific job." Jobs may have to be done indoors, outdoors, or both. The worker may have to be in a place that is cold, hot, wet, damp, or noisy. The job may also involve some risk of bodily injury, or there may be dust or unpleasant odors.

This information about the physical demands for given jobs can be helpful to you only if you are willing to take an honest look at your own physical strengths and weaknesses. But, at the same time, you will be doing yourself a disservice if you are not honest about weaknesses that could be corrected if you were to make the effort. You will also be making things harder for yourself if you don't recognize the importance of good health habits in any job. Your employer must be able to count on your being strong and well enough to come to work every day and to stay alert and efficient throughout the day.

Your employer is also interested in your appearance, which is a physical characteristic that you can easily improve. The day when all business clothes had to be very somber has passed. Now a much wider

A service station attendant spends a lot of time working outside, in all kinds of weather. A person who works at this job must have good health.

range of clothing is considered suitable in the business world. But your employer will still expect you to have the highest possible standards of personal hygiene and to show good taste in your choice of clothing and hairstyle.

YOUR INTELLIGENCE

Your intelligence represents your general ability to learn and to make sense of the things that happen in your environment. The popular way of expressing this is to talk about how "smart" or "dumb" people are. In the school environment, young people rate each other on the basis of how well they do in their courses. Everyone thinks of the all-*A* student as a "brain" and the borderline student as the opposite.

It is true that your success in school is one indication of your intelligence. That's why employers want to know about your grades when you apply for a job. But when you are assessing your own mental abilities, you have to remember that you may not be using your mind to the best advantage. If you had poor grades, was it because you really couldn't understand the work? Or was it because you daydreamed in class and didn't do your homework? Actually, all human beings, even geniuses, use only a small fraction of their total brainpower. Possibly future generations will learn how to unlock all the additional power. But the question for you now is whether you are making the best possible use of your mental abilities.

A word also needs to be said about the tests that are used to measure intelligence. In recent years, people have realized that these tests are not as accurate as they were once thought to be. It is now obvious that the tests have been weighted in favor of those people who come from white middle-class backgrounds. Researchers are now trying to work out tests that take into consideration the backgrounds of other segments of the population, whose experiences have taught them different kinds of things.

It is important to get such new tests perfected, so that all young people will be able to get a fair measurement of their mental abilities. But, in the meantime, you may have to take such tests. If so, you may want to ask your guidance counselor about books and other materials that can help you become familiar with these tests and give you practice in taking them. Preparation and practice will increase your chances for a score that truly reflects your abilities.

YOUR APTITUDES

While your intelligence represents your general ability to learn, you also have certain areas where learning comes easily. For example, you may be able to learn quickly about anything that has to do with machines. In this case, you are said to have a mechanical **aptitude,** which means that you have a natural ability which helps you learn without trouble. You might have an aptitude for doing very fine work with your fingers or an aptitude for working with colors, shapes,

Getting to know the real you means finding out what aptitudes you don't have as well as those you do have. It doesn't make sense to take violin lessons if you have no musical aptitude. (*Courtesy Walker/Parkersburg, Division of Textron, Inc.*)

90 • UNIT 2 • YOU AND A MARKETING CAREER

numbers, words, or music. You might also have an aptitude for coordinating all your body's movements, as dancers and athletes do. Aptitudes are another subject that the DOT is interested in, because people have a much greater chance of being successful in their work if they have the right aptitudes for it.

Some of your aptitudes may be already apparent to you. This is especially true when you have an aptitude that is very strong, in which case it is called a "talent." But it is also true that you may have aptitudes that you are not yet aware of. This is like having money in the bank that you don't know about. Neither the money nor the aptitude is going to do you any good if you don't even know it is there. To remedy this situation, it may be possible for you to take one of the many aptitude tests that are now available, possibly through your school guidance counselor. These tests can give you a lot of information about the aptitudes you have and don't have, and they can also give you an idea of how strong or weak your aptitudes are. Having this information can help you to eliminate the careers that would not be good for your particular combination of aptitudes and to identify the careers that you should consider. Knowing what aptitudes you have will help you plan for your career in a realistic way.

YOUR INTERESTS

Your **interests** are the things that you enjoy doing or learning about. Often they go hand in hand with your aptitudes, because it is easier to like doing things that come easily to you. Of course, there are many exceptions to this rule, such as the people who have no athletic aptitude themselves but are very interested in following all sports events. You can tell a lot about what your present interests and noninterests are by thinking about what courses you particularly like in school, what extracurricular activities you have joined, and how you spend your free time.

Don't be fooled, however, into thinking that your present interests are the only ones you will ever have. You can't be interested in something you have never even heard of. As you have new experiences, you will find new areas to be interested in. Reading, traveling, and meeting new people are all ways to develop your interests.

You may find that you are interested in more things than you have time to pursue. In this case, you will go along with those interests that are the strongest. For example, you may be interested in student government but have never run for election because you have been more interested in the sports program. Thinking about the relative strengths of your interests can help you to see which ones are worth trying to tie in with a career and which ones would be better developed as hobbies.

Just as meeting new people can help you discover new interests, so pursuing your interests can bring you into contact with people you might otherwise not have met. (Kent Dannen)

To help you understand what your interests are and how strong they are, you could take one of the interest tests that are available today. These tests can be a help to you when you are trying to decide on a career. Studies have proven that the people who work in careers that are related to their interests are generally satisfied with their careers and happy in them. When careers and interests are well matched, the career becomes a vehicle for personal fulfillment rather than just a way to earn a living.

YOUR SKILLS

Your **skills** are the things that you are able to do–that is, the tasks that you have learned how to perform successfully. To give just a few examples, riding a bicycle is a skill, as are driving a car, taking correct telephone messages, and typing. Rather than being inborn, as aptitudes are, skills have to be acquired. Learning a skill always requires some degree of work, even if you have an aptitude in that direction. But there are definite advantages to putting in the effort to acquire skills.

Every skill that you learn is important because it serves as a foundation for more advanced skills. For example, the person who wants to do advanced work in mathematics has to learn to do simple arithmetic first. At this point in your life, you can be building for the future by acquiring good study skills. This means learning how to read, write, and listen in class. It also means knowing how to plan your time and to stick to an assignment without being distracted. These skills will be useful to you long after you are out of school, for they are the basis for success in almost any job.

As you move on through high school, you will be acquiring still more skills that will be valuable to an employer. And when you begin working, you will have more opportunities to go on learning. When you are thinking about what your skills are, the question is not how many skills you already have. It is more important to know whether you want to learn new skills or whether you are content to rely only on the skills you have already learned.

YOUR ATTITUDES

The easiest way to define an **attitude** is by saying that it is a way of looking at things. When we talk about your posture, we are talking about your physical bearing. Attitudes represent your mental bearing, the positions that you take on certain issues. Like your posture, your attitudes can be changed for the better. But this gets harder and harder the older you get, so that there is no time like the present for thinking about what your attitudes are and what they might be.

This subject is very important because your attitudes and your chances for success in living and working are very closely related. This is why employers are so interested in your attitudes. They want to know what your attitudes are about life in general. Are you so sure that disaster is always ready to strike that you don't even make any effort to avoid it? Or do you have a more positive way of looking at things? Being positive doesn't mean insisting that everything is wonderful when it obviously isn't. But being positive does mean believing that things can get better in the future and that it is worth the effort to try to solve problems.

Another attitude that interests employers is how you feel about yourself in relation to other people. Some people have such an inflated idea of their own importance that they think everything and everybody revolves around them. Other people see themselves as being absolutely worthless. Employers try to avoid both these extremes, which are equally difficult to handle. They look instead for people who can see themselves as important, worthwhile individuals, living among many other important, worthwhile individuals. This attitude allows you to recognize that each individual is different, but that each one, including yourself, has something valuable to contribute to the world we all live in. This attitude also allows you to see other people as adding greatly to the richness of your own life, so that you can really like them.

Employers are also interested in your attitudes about working. Do you think that the world owes you a living and that you therefore should not have to make any real effort on the job? If this is your attitude, you can go to work late, leave early, and do careless, incomplete work without ever feeling guilty. But perhaps you believe instead in earning your own way by doing the best job that you can. In this case, you will want to give your employer a full day's work for a full day's pay, being as reliable and dependable as you know how.

YOUR PERSONALITY TRAITS

Your **personality traits** are the ways in which you as an individual tend to behave. For example, you may work well or collapse under pressure. You may be patient about having to sit still or anxious to get up and get moving. You may laugh easily and often or tend more to the serious side. You may warm up to people quickly or take a while to make friends. You may lose your temper easily or it may be very difficult to make you angry. You may be easily discouraged or very determined.

You have to consider what your personality traits are when you are thinking about possible careers. For example, if you don't sit still easily, you wouldn't want to take a job where you sit at the same desk for the whole working day. You would be better off with a job where you could keep moving—perhaps in sales. On the other hand, if you don't react well to pressure, selling jobs might be the area for you to avoid.

When you are thinking about your personality traits, you have to recognize that some of them are going to be completely undesirable from any employer's point of view. This is true of everybody, for there are no perfect human beings. For example, suppose that you never stop to think before you speak but just blurt out the first thing that comes into your head. The result of your lack of self-control is that you hurt people's feelings more often than not. An employer wouldn't be able to trust you with the customers or even with the other employees. Once you understand why this is a problem, however, you can work on this bad habit until you have broken it. All you have to do is to care enough.

- **BUILDING YOUR CAREER VOCABULARY**

Define each of the following terms and then use each one in a sentence.

aptitude
attitude
interest
personality traits
physical demands
skill
working conditions

• UNDERSTANDING WHAT YOU HAVE READ

1. Why is it important for you to know what your own combination of qualities is?
2. Do you think that getting to know yourself is an easy job? Explain your answer.
3. Why do your interests often go hand in hand with your aptitudes?
4. Are your present interests the only ones you will ever have?
5. How do aptitudes and skills differ from each other?

• APPLYING WHAT YOU HAVE LEARNED

The four questions below will help you to evaluate yourself so that you can make realistic career choices. You will not have to share your answers with your classmates. Write your answers on a separate sheet.

1. Answer each part of the following questions about your physical characteristics by choosing a number from 1 to 5. Use 1 if you have the characteristic either not at all or to a very slight degree, 2 for below average, 3 for average, 4 for above average, and 5 for superior.
    a. Are you generally healthy?
    b. Do you eat well? Do you exercise regularly?
    c. What is your energy level?
    d. Can you move quickly?
    e. How able are you to lift a 100-pound weight?
    f. How easy is it for you to bend? to stoop? to reach? to climb?
    g. Are you generally coordinated?
    h. Can you work with your hands?
    i. Can you do work that requires a large degree of finger control?
    j. Can you sit for long periods of time without having to move around? Can you stand for long periods of time?
    k. How well do you see? Can you recognize differences in colors?
    l. How well do you hear? Can you recognize differences in musical notes?
2. The list of aptitudes below is to start your thinking about your own aptitudes. For each aptitude, write: X if you do not have the aptitude at all, V if you have it to some degree, H if you have it to a high degree, and U if you are not sure whether you have it or not.
    a. Working with machinery
    b. Working with things
    c. Working with people
    d. Working with data (facts and numbers)
    e. Mathematical
    f. Artistic

g. Athletic
   h. Scientific
   i. Verbal (speaking)
   j. Verbal (writing)
   k. Musical
3. To help you to find out what your interests and noninterests are, answer the following questions.
   a. Which school subjects do you like best? Which do you like least?
   b. What subjects that your school offers do you want to take? Which ones are you determined to avoid?
   c. If you were in charge, what subject(s) would you add to your school's course selection?
   d. What teams, clubs, and other extracurricular activities in your school have you enjoyed? Which ones would you take part in if you had more time? Which activity in your school appeals to you the least?
   e. What organizations do you belong to outside of school?
   f. Do you have any hobbies? If so, list them.
   g. What is your favorite kind of television program? Which kind do you never watch?
   h. Name your favorite free-time activity. Name one thing that you hate having to do.
   i. What do you do when "there's nothing to do"?
4. On a separate piece of paper, list five of your personality traits that you are proud of and five that you would like to improve. You will not have to share your answers with your classmates.

Part 10: Thinking About What's Important to You

After reading Part 10, you will be able—
- To weigh the relative importance to you of a given list of values.
- To list five goals—short-range, intermediate, or long-range—that you have for your own life.
- To name one resource you will need in order to reach each of the goals you have listed.
- To define standards and explain how your standards for yourself affect your goals.

There is another way in which people differ from each other besides the ways that we have already discussed. Each person has an individual idea about what is important in life. Have you ever thought about what is important to you? If you had been going to school 100 years ago, that question might not have been so difficult to answer. Life then was much more simple, and people had fewer choices to make.

But today life is anything but simple. The world is changing at such a rapid rate that events often seem to rush by us like a movie being shown on a speeded-up projector. When people don't know what they think is important, they are confused by all the changes taking place. They don't know what to be for or against, and therefore they don't know how to act. They are constantly frustrated because they don't know where they are going or why.

Fortunately there is another way to meet the challenge of change. Instead of being confused about what to think and do, you can learn to make definite, conscious choices on the basis of what you think really counts. Your ideas and feelings about what is important in life are called your **values**. When you know what your values are, you can steer a course to places that you want to go instead of having to drift wherever the tide of change sends you.

The way that you turn your values, which are only ideas, into action is by setting goals. Your **goals** are your aims in life. Your values give you your reasons for acting. Your goals give you a concrete way of directing your behavior so that your values can become a real part of your life style.

YOU AND YOUR VALUES

Your values, the things that you stand for, are yours alone. This is not to say that every one of your values is a completely unique idea. You share many values with the other members of your family, your friends and neighbors, and the larger society in which you live. But with values, as with everything else about you as an individual, what is unique is your particular combination. This combination is the result of *your* needs, *your* personal characteristics, and *your* experiences.

There have been many stories written in modern times about people who worked very hard to achieve certain things. But then they found that what they had achieved was not what they wanted at all. It might have been what someone else thought they should want, but it was not what they really wanted. This is why it is important to define your own personal combination of values, your own **value system**. When you do, you can lead the life that is right for you and no one else, in the way that is right for you and no one else. Being honest with yourself about what your values are has another advantage. It makes you better able to recognize that your values change as you learn and grow. When you are aware of the changes in your values, you can keep your life style in harmony with them.

Summarizing the Kinds of Values

There are many different kinds of values covering the whole range of human experience. They include our most ordinary, everyday concerns, such as the value of keeping dry when it rains and the value of being polite. Values also include the most lofty and significant questions facing humanity—questions about human dignity, equality, and justice. It is not possible for us to discuss every kind of value. What we can do, however, in order to start your thinking on this important subject, is to summarize the many kinds of values under three main headings: material values, intellectual values, and social values.

MATERIAL VALUES. When we talk about material values, we are talking about the values put on tangible things. Because of our basic physical needs, we all have to value the things like food, water, and shelter that keep us alive. We also place a value on the things that make it possible for us to get food, water, and shelter. On a tropical island, this might mean valuing a canoe that is used for fishing. In our society, it might mean valuing an automobile as a means of driving to work and thus earning enough money to live.

People value material things also as a way of answering their other needs. Door locks and automobile seat belts are two examples of things that are valued in our society as a way of keeping people safe. Material things can also be a way of gaining acceptance and respect from other

Material things such as the "right" clothes are often valued because they help us gain acceptance in our peer groups.

people. For example, most young people like to wear the same kinds of clothes their peers are wearing, so that they will be accepted. Other people try to get status through their homes or automobiles. It is even possible to get status by having the right friends, which shows that a material value can be placed on people too.

People who have a strong need to know and understand things value books and libraries and school buildings, which are all material things. Paintings and sculpture help to answer the need for beauty, along with musical instruments, records, museums, and concert halls. People also value the things that will help them to follow their own aptitudes and interests so that they can achieve self-actualization. This may mean placing a value on such diverse things as old machines that can be taken apart, flower gardens, or photographic equipment.

INTELLECTUAL VALUES. Because we have minds as well as bodies, we can value intangible ideas as well as tangible things. For example, we can value truth, goodness, mercy, justice, and beauty. Such intellectual values can help us determine what is right or wrong, good or bad, kind or unkind, fair or unfair, beautiful or ugly. We also make our judgments about the importance of rational thought, self-expression, originality, creativity, intellectual stimulation, and self-discipline on the basis of our intellectual values.

Our intellectual values do not have to be at war with our material values. Rather, they represent another way for human beings to answer their basic needs. For example, the person who values self-discipline will probably be much healthier than the person who does not. And valuing fairness has always been a way to win respect. In this sense,

The strongly held value of respect for life inspired *Guernica*, Picasso's powerful statement of protest against war. (*Courtesy Museum of Modern Art*)

our intellectual values can be just as "useful" to us in our daily living as our material values.

SOCIAL VALUES. Your social values have to do with your feelings about other people and about how people should live together. They range all the way from your values about friendship and family life to your values about the most desirable form of government. Your social values depend on what you think of other people. If you always think of them in a material sense, in terms of how useful they can be to you, you will have different social values than if you think of them as important in their own right.

Your social values also depend on who it is that you are talking about when you say "other people." For example, if you say you believe that everyone is entitled to life, liberty, and the pursuit of happiness, do you really mean *everyone*? When some people say that, they are only talking about people in certain special groups. You have to know what you think about these basic questions before you can sort out your other social values.

Weighing Your Values

You have to know not only what your values are but also which of them are genuinely important to you. To do this, you have to put your values on a scale, weighing one against the other. For example, you have to weigh the values of the past that you have been taught to accept against the values of the new generation to see which ones you want to keep. You might also have to weigh the value that you place on the rights of the individual against the question of what is good for society as a whole. Or you might have to weigh the value that you place on being accepted by the group against the value of loyalty to a particular friend.

If you believe in helping other people achieve a better standard of living, would you be willing to spend two years of your life teaching them the skills that will enable them to do it? (*Courtesy ACTION*)

You have to weigh your values not only against each other but also against the question of how much you would give up for the sake of each particular value. For example, if you believe in helping other people, what would you be willing to give up to make your value a reality? Would you give some of your own money? How much money would you give? Would you give some of your time and effort? Or would you go as far as to give all your time and effort for your whole life? As another example, suppose that you believe in saving the environment. Would you be willing to go around the school grounds and pick up the litter to be recycled? Or would you prefer saving the environment in some less unpleasant way?

When you are asking yourself such questions about your values, you should remember that there are no right or wrong answers. You are trying to find out not what you *should* value but what you *do* value. You may find that some of the things you thought were important to you really are not. You may also find that some of your values are so strongly held that they can be called ideals. If so, it will be interesting for you to think about where humanity would be now if there had never been any ideals in the history of the world. **Ideals** are the bigger-than-life dreams that have provided human beings with reasons for acting in bigger-than-life ways.

Dr. Martin Luther King, Jr., lived his life according to his ideal of a world free of racial prejudice. (*United Press International Photo*)

Living by Your Values

There is a name for the person who claims to have certain values but lives in a way that goes against those values. That name is "hypocrite." An example of a hypocrite would be the person who says that the world is too materialistic but then buys one luxury after another. The only way not to be a hypocrite is to keep your life style and your values in tune with each other. This is not a process that can be done once and then forgotten. You have to keep a constant eye on your values and your life style to make certain there are no contradictions.

Working by Your Values

Your career is going to be such a large part of your life that it has to be in tune with your values too. Perhaps what you value most is money and the good things that it will buy. You may also value security, prestige, or the opportunity to help other people. Perhaps you value interesting experiences, the opportunity to use your own special talents, or time off to be with your family. Or perhaps your value system calls for some special mixture of these things. In any case, there is a career that is right for you, a career that you can follow honestly, without feeling like a hypocrite. But to find that career, you have to know what your own value system is.

YOU AND YOUR GOALS

We have said that values are only ideas. You may value the idea of owning your own home, but you can't move into an idea. And you may value the idea of helping people who don't have enough to eat, but those people can't eat your idea. In order to move your values from the world of ideas into the world of reality, you have to set goals.

Goals are guidelines that tell you what course of action to follow or to avoid. In either case, they help you when you have to make large and small decisions about what to do. For example, let's say that you have set a goal to buy a ten-speed bicycle for exercise and fun. In order to achieve this goal, you make the major decision to get a part-time job after school. And when everyday questions such as whether or not to go bowling with your friends come up, your goal of saving your money will influence your decision.

In setting your goals, you have to be concerned with what is realistic. Is the goal one that you could actually achieve or is it just an impossible dream? There are three things for you to think about when you are trying to set realistic goals: what resources are available, how much time you need, and what standards you have to meet.

Making Use of Resources

Anything that you can use to help you reach a goal is called a **resource**. When you are setting your goals, you have to think about what resources are available to you and how you can make the best use of them. Sometimes people give up their goals as being unrealistic because they don't realize what their resources are. For example, sometimes young people want to go on with their education after high school. But they decide that this is not possible because they don't have enough money. Before giving up this idea, young people should investigate the many scholarships and student loans that are available.

The most important resource that can help you reach your goals is yourself. Your own intelligence, aptitudes, interests, skills, attitudes, personal characteristics, and values are all tools that you can use. There are also material resources that can help you. This might mean a piano in your home, if your goal is to become a concert pianist. Or it might mean a tennis court near your home, if your goal is to become a professional tennis player. Your relationships with other people can also help you to realize your goals. For example, the encouragement that your parents and teachers give you can be an important resource in obtaining a difficult goal. There are also many community resources that can help you, including such things as health clinics, hospitals, banks, libraries, schools, museums, and all kinds of social agencies that want to help young people.

Before you dismiss a goal as being unrealistic, you should be certain that you have checked all your resources. For example, suppose that you want to be an airline pilot. But you find that there is a problem with a very important resource, your eyesight. At first, it seems to you

By making use of resources available to her, Evonne Goolagong Cawley turned a natural aptitude into a professional skill. (*United Press International Photo*)

that you are going to have to give up your goal. But then you find out that, with your particular eye problem, you can go to an eye clinic and learn to do corrective exercises. In this case, you will need two other resources besides the eye clinic. You will need a great deal of self-determination and willpower. These are resources that can often make up for others that are missing.

Taking Time into Account

Besides thinking about what your resources are, you also have to think about the amount of time that you will need to achieve your goals. Some goals are what we call **long-range goals,** because they can only be achieved over a long period of time. The goals that can be reached relatively quickly are called **short-range goals.** In between the two are **intermediate goals.**

If your goals are in line with your values and your other personal characteristics, it is very likely that your long-range, short-range, and intermediate goals will reinforce each other. For example, suppose that you value independence, you have an aptitude for getting along with people, and you are interested in music. Your long-range goal is to own a record store of your own. Your short-range goal is to get an after-school job in a record store so that you can begin to learn the business. Your intermediate goals include finishing high school, getting more experience in record stores, and saving your money. In this case, you would be using time in a realistic way. But suppose that your goal is to lose 20 pounds and you decide to do that in a month. Is that realistic?

Or suppose that your goal is to pass a test in a subject in which you have not been doing well. Would it be realistic to leave yourself only a half-hour for studying? Time can help us to achieve our goals or keep us from achieving them, depending on how we use it.

Meeting Standards
Another way of deciding whether your goals are realistic is to think about whether you can meet the standards for whatever it is you want to do. **Standards** are models against which quantity, quality, and performance can be judged. For example, your teachers have standards of performance that they expect in their classrooms. Your grades are measures of how well you do compared with the teachers' standards. There are standards that you have to meet in order to play on a school sports team or in the school marching band. Employers have standards too. Whether your goal is to be the star in a school play right now or to become president of a bank someday, you have to ask whether you can meet the required standards.

So far we have been talking about the standards that you have to meet for other people. Your goals and your decisions about how to reach those goals can also be influenced by your own personal standards. The great athletes have always been the people whose personal standards were far higher than just the standards necessary for making the team. Whether you choose to work toward your goal in a way that is just good enough or far more than enough depends on what your personal standards are.

- **BUILDING YOUR CAREER VOCABULARY**

Define each of the following terms and then use each one in a sentence.

goal
ideal
intermediate goal
long-range goal
resource

short-range goal
standard
value
value system

- **UNDERSTANDING WHAT YOU HAVE READ**
    1. Why is it important that you know what your own value system is?
    2. Under what three headings can the many kinds of values be summarized?
    3. What does the word ''materialistic'' mean to you? Is everyone who places a value on material things materialistic? Explain your answer.
    4. How can you recognize a hypocrite?
    5. How do your standards for yourself affect your goals?

• APPLYING WHAT YOU HAVE LEARNED

1. Copy the following list of things that you might value. Put a line through the things that you do not value at all. Put a check mark next to the things that you value but do not feel strongly about. Put a star next to the things that are very important to you. Now make a new list of the things you have starred, putting them in the order of importance to you. If there are other things that you value highly, add them to the list.

   free time
   power
   pleasant surroundings
   honesty
   money
   helping other people
   justice for all
   an automobile of your own
   the opportunity to express yourself
   status
   fame

   good health
   intellectual stimulation
   a secure future for yourself
   a safe future for the next generation
   beautiful clothes
   friendship
   fun
   peace
   challenging situations
   a home of your own
   independence

2. List five goals that you have for your own life. They may be goals for tomorrow, next year, or many years from now.
3. Name one resource you will need in order to reach each of the goals you have listed.

part 11
Making Decisions

After reading Part 11, you will be able—
- To list five requirements for decision making.
- To list six steps for personal decision making.
- To give an example of a situation in which you personally had to make a decision and analyze how the decision turned out.
- To give an example of a group decision in which you recently were involved and state how the decision was arrived at.

If nothing in your life ever changed, you would not have any choices to make. You could just do the same things in the same way every day. You could even think the same thoughts. But life has the idea of change built into it. There are all kinds of changes going on all the time—changes in the environment, in yourself as you grow older, in other people, and in relationships. These changes require you constantly to be choosing new ways of thinking and acting. You can make your choices in a haphazard, spur-of-the-moment way, in which case change will control you. Or you can learn how to take control of your own life. You can learn how to make thoughtful, careful choices on the basis of your needs, values, goals, and standards. The deliberate process of making choices is called **decision making.** In this part, you will see how this process works.

THE REQUIREMENTS FOR DECISION MAKING

When you were a preschooler, your parents or other adults made most of the decisions about your life. As a small child, you were not mature enough to be able to decide things for yourself. The word "mature" is one that you have heard often. But you may not have known what it really means. It includes **physical maturity,** which is the result of the growth and development of your body. It also includes **psychological maturity.** This comes about when people have developed mentally and emotionally so that they can direct their own actions.

Let's take a look now at five of the most important characteristics of the psychologically mature person: (1) making a habit of thinking,

(2) keeping a sense of identity, (3) accepting reality, (4) being willing to wait, and (5) understanding what courage means. Each of the five is a requirement for decision making.

Making a Habit of Thinking

Being able to think means being able to handle ideas and put them together in various ways. For one thing, the thinking person can **generalize,** which means to look at individual items of information and see what they all have in common. The thinking person can also **analyze,** which means to see how a large block of information breaks down into parts and how those parts relate to each other. Generalizing lets you see the whole forest, and analyzing lets you take a good look at the trees.

The thinking person also understands the principle of **cause and effect.** This means that one circumstance (the cause) makes another circumstance (the effect) happen. For example, you drop a glass and it breaks. Your dropping the glass is the cause, and its breaking is the effect.

When you can generalize, analyze, and see cause and effect, you can organize your experiences in your mind. Instead of seeing each one as a separate thing, you can see how they all relate to each other. You can compare them and put them in order. First you learn to do this for things that have already happened. Then, as you mature, you are able to do it for things that haven't happened yet. In other words, you learn to predict the future on the basis of what you already know.

When you develop the habit of thinking about things that happen to you and in the world around you, you will achieve a better understanding of your own life and of the world. (*National Education Association*)

As an example, let's say that you are supposed to meet four friends and go with them to the movies. What you have generalized from your friends' past behavior tells you that if you are late (cause), they will leave without you (effect). You are then able to adjust your actions to get the effect you want. You will ensure being able to go with your friends by not being late. When you can foresee the results of your actions in this way, you can make realistic plans.

There is no doubt that thinking is work. Nor is there any doubt that it is possible to avoid thinking. There are people who go through life doing everything "off the top of their heads," involving their minds as little as possible. But making a habit of thinking is the only possible way to direct your own life. Fortunately, the more you think, the easier it gets. Unlike other kinds of energy that get used up, brainpower increases with use.

Keeping a Sense of Identity

Each of us has many different roles to play. For example, you play one role as a student, another with your friends, and still another at home. When you have a job, that will be still another role. You also have a role as a citizen. If you marry, you will have another role. And if you have children, you will have a role as a parent. Meanwhile, as long as your own parents are alive, you will still have a role as a son or daughter.

Each of these roles requires you to act in certain expected ways. For example, as a student, you are expected to work hard at learning and to be respectful to your teachers. As a friend, you are expected to be available to have fun. As a member of a family, you are expected to help with the chores and to be concerned with family problems. As a worker, you are expected to get your work done and to be interested in the welfare of the company.

The difficulty with trying to meet the expectations of all your roles is that it is sometimes hard to know who the real you is. This is one of the reasons why we have taken so much time in this unit to discuss what "you" means. The better you know yourself, the more sense of personal identity you have. It is this sense of identity that allows you to play your many roles and still be true to yourself.

Accepting Reality

When you are mature, you know that there is no such thing as complete freedom of choice. Your choices are limited by the framework in which you live. To see what this means, suppose that you want to travel by bus from your town or city to another town. In trying to decide when to go, you cannot just choose any time at all. Because the buses run only at certain scheduled times your choices are limited. You

Unless you have a sense of your own identity, the need to be different things to different people can cause you to feel confused and unsure about who you really are.

have to make your decision within the framework of the bus schedule. When you are ready to choose your courses for next year, you will have to do so within the framework of the programs your school offers. Likewise, when you are applying for a job, you are limited to what kinds of jobs are available.

You can't choose your family or the weather or to have time stand still. You can't choose to break the laws of the society in which you live, unless you are willing to pay the consequences. You can't pull resources out of the air. The fact is that there are many things that are beyond your control. When you recognize this, you are accepting reality. You are looking at the world as it actually is, instead of as you wish it were. By doing this, you are gaining something very important—the freedom to make choices that will work.

Being Willing to Wait

Infants only understand this moment—right now. When they are hungry, they want to be fed immediately. They don't want to wait; indeed, they don't know how to wait. As you mature, you learn what people mean when they say, "in a minute," "tomorrow," "next week," or "three years from now." You learn too that you can't always have everything you want as soon as you want it.

There are many times when the best way to get what you want is to wait. When you find people who must have everything immediately, you know that they are very immature. These people cannot set goals, because even short-range goals require that something be done over a period of time rather than instantly. When you are willing to wait, you may miss out on some immediate satisfactions. But you have a tool that will help you meet your long-range goals.

In terms of a career, being willing to wait is important. Many young people who are starting out in jobs complain because they are not given enough responsibility. Or they may feel that they are not being allowed to do the work they really want to do. For example, students who get part-time jobs in service stations may resent having to spend so much time pumping gas. They may feel that they should be made mechanics right away. But their bosses feel that they have a lot to learn before they can be given the responsibilities of a mechanic. The young person who is impatient may quit and get another job, where the same thing will happen. But the young person who is mature enough to wait will stand a good chance of becoming a mechanic.

Understanding What Courage Means

Making a decision means having the courage to take a stand. It means saying to the world "This is what I believe is the right thing." This is not as safe a position as just staying quietly in your shell. Like the turtle, you are more open to attack when you "stick your neck out." Taking a stand is very difficult when you are confused about who you are. You feel unsure of yourself—afraid of failing, afraid of being laughed at. But when you have a mature view of yourself, you know that you can survive being wrong. This knowledge gives you the courage to admit you have made a mistake, without looking for someone else to blame. It also gives you the courage to go on making decisions.

WHEN DECISIONS ARE NECESSARY

When there is only one possible way to think or act, you don't have to make a decision. But as soon as there are two or more ways, and you can only do one, you have to choose between them. Sometimes the decision is fairly simple. For example, there isn't too much to consider when you are trying to buy an ice cream cone in a store that is famous for its many flavors. This is just a matter of your personal likes and dislikes, and the pleasure of the moment.

But perhaps your decision to go into the store in the first place was more complicated. Perhaps you had to weigh your desire for ice cream against your goal of losing weight or of saving money for something very special. Or perhaps the money was change from your lunch money that you were supposed to take home. In this case, you have a conflict between your desire for ice cream and the value you place on being honest. Being expected to take the money home may also have conflicted with what your friends were expecting of you, which was to join them in buying ice cream. When two of your roles are calling for two different courses of action in this way, we say that you have a **role conflict.**

The story of the ice cream cone is a simple example of a large fact. Each of us has to face many conflicts between our needs, wants, values, goals, and standards, as well as our roles. Sometimes these conflicts involve only the individual. Sometimes they involve family, friends, and larger groups of people. These conflicts are seldom easy to resolve because the situations are not clear-cut. Making a decision is hard because there is much to be said for both sides. Furthermore, it is often necessary to make more than one decision to resolve a conflict. There might be a question first of whether a certain course of action would be desirable. Then you might have to decide if it could be done with the available resources in the available time. Finally you would have to decide how to get it done.

It is because resolving conflicts is not easy that decision making is so important. Learning how to make thoughtful, careful decisions is no guarantee that you will always be right or that you will be able to solve every problem that you face. But if you are not willing to try to make the best decisions that you can, all you have left is wishing. And wishing for something doesn't make it happen.

SIX STEPS FOR PERSONAL DECISION MAKING

How do you actually go about making a decision? This is a question that can't be answered in one simple way. There are too many different kinds of decisions for one method to cover them all. However, it is possible to generalize and to say that there are six steps that you can follow in many decision-making situations. These six steps are presented as general guidelines for you to adapt to your own special circumstances. You might go through them all in a matter of minutes or take a long time, depending on the decision. The six steps are (1) recognizing that you have a choice, (2) identifying the real alternatives, (3) getting the facts, (4) weighing the alternatives, (5) acting on the decision, and (6) analyzing the decision.

- RECOGNIZING THAT YOU HAVE A CHOICE
- IDENTIFYING THE REAL ALTERNATIVES
- GETTING THE FACTS
- WEIGHING THE ALTERNATIVES
- ACTING ON THE DECISION
- ANALYZING THE DECISION

Think about a decision that you made recently. Can you compare the thinking process that you went through to arrive at your decision with the six steps outlined here?

PART 11 • MAKING DECISIONS • 113

Recognizing That You Have a Choice

The first step in decision making is to recognize that you have a choice. This sounds almost too simple. But there has to be some way of putting brakes on your actions. For example, suppose that you are on your way to school and your friend suggests that you both cut school. You could just follow along automatically. Or you could stop and say to yourself "I have a choice. I can decide whether I should cut school or not." There are many times when we just go along with things, even when they don't suit us. Sometimes we actually don't have a choice in these matters. But more often we do have a choice but just haven't stopped to recognize that fact. This book is asking you to recognize that you do have a choice about your future as a first step toward choosing a career that is right for you.

Identifying the Real Alternatives

In order to make a decision, you have to know what the alternatives are. (An **alternative** is one of the two or more things that you are going to have to choose between.) Sometimes the alternatives are very easy to identify—to cut school or not to cut school. But suppose that you want to buy a new car. Would you consider each of the different makes and models on the market an alternative? Probably you would automatically eliminate some cars because of price, size, or some other feature. You would then be left with those cars that represent your real alternatives. Each of the cars would be one that you could actually choose.

If you have no aptitude for working with people, you cannot consider the possibility of a career in sales as a real alternative. If you have no artistic ability, a career as a display artist is not a real alternative for you. If your alternatives are only daydreams, the decision-making process is going to be a lot of work for nothing.

Getting the Facts

Once you have established what your alternatives are, your next step is to get the facts for each one. This will mean doing some investigating on your own. Sometimes this is easy, but sometimes you will have to be resourceful about finding out where to look for facts. You may also want to consult with "experts"—the people who are in a position to know about the particular decision you are making.

The facts that you are after are the advantages and disadvantages of each alternative. What will you gain from each one? And what will each one cost you? This is not just a question of money but also one of time, energy, and other resources. For example, suppose that you are trying to decide between two jobs. You have to know how much each one pays. You also have to consider what the chances for advancement are in each job and whether you will be doing work that you are really interested in. You also have to think about where the job is. If it is an hour from your home, it will cost you two hours a day in commuting time, plus the cost of your travel.

Sometimes the cost of an alternative is that you won't be able to reach a goal as soon as you had planned. For example, suppose that one of the two jobs you are trying to choose between pays less than the other one to start but has greater possibilities for advancement in a few years. You had hoped to buy a car as soon you started to work, but if you choose this job, you won't be able to realize that goal for a while.

Sometimes the cost of an alternative is that you will have to sacrifice a value. For example, let's say that you value time with your family. But one job requires that you work every weekend, which is when the rest of your family has free time. In this case, the rights of your family are also involved. Perhaps this alternative is going to cost them too much. On the other hand, perhaps they will benefit from having you earn more money. These are all questions that you must have answers for before you can try to make a decision.

Weighing the Alternatives

Now that you have the facts for each alternative, you are ready to weigh them against each other. One alternative may clearly be the best. But often the situation is not that simple. Then what you must do is to see which alternative has the advantages that suit you best and the disadvantages that bother you least. As you are figuring this out, you will want to take into consideration your own past experiences. Perhaps something you have learned can help you to predict which alternative has the best chance of working. You will also want to analyze the question of how much you are being influenced by other people. This influence is not necessarily bad, but you should know what its extent is. You want to be sure that the alternative you finally decide on is your own choice.

Acting on the Decision

You have not really made a decision until you have acted on it. Many people go painstakingly through the four steps to decision making we have just listed. They find the one alternative that suits them best, and then they stop right there. They are afraid that they might be wrong, and so they do nothing. It is true that there is no way to be absolutely sure that your decision will be right, no matter how hard you have worked. But it is also true that you have markedly cut down the risk of failure. Being able to act on decisions is really a question of motivation. If you are just along for the ride, you don't have to follow through. If you want to sit in the driver's seat, you must have the courage to act.

Analyzing the Decision

The last step in decision making is to analyze how the decision turned out. If it turned out well, ask yourself why. In making your decision, what factors were especially helpful? What did you do that you should do again? If the decision did not turn out well, see if you can figure out what went wrong. Perhaps you didn't get all the facts. Or perhaps the decision itself was all right, but the timing was bad. Or perhaps there were some results that you had no way of foreseeing. Analyzing what went wrong can often help you to see a new way that will work. The main thing is not to be discouraged and to remember that "live and learn" expresses a process by which we all grow and develop.

SOCIAL DECISION MAKING

Decisions become much more complicated when they have to be made with other people. If the decision is to be a good one, it must take into account the wants, needs, values, goals, and standards of each individ-

In our society, everyone has the right to his or her own viewpoint. Although this is necessary if we are to have a free society, it makes social decision making more difficult.

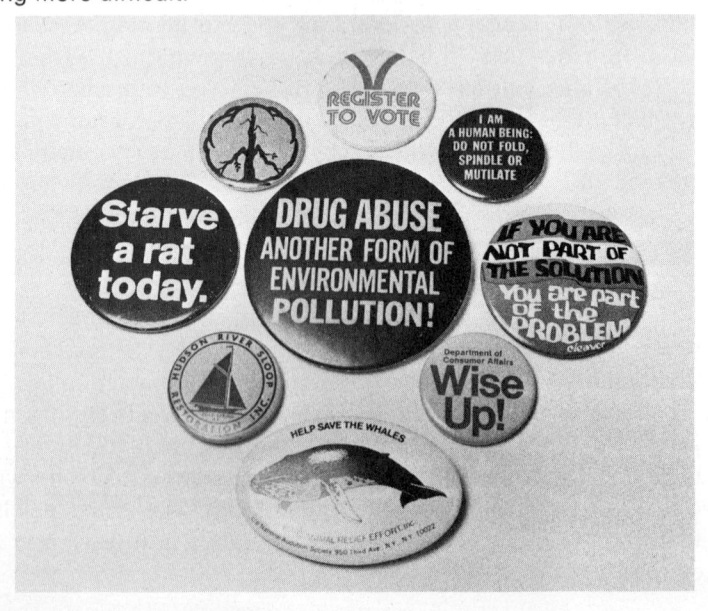

ual in the group. This has always been difficult, but in recent years it has become even more so. In our society, we have been moving toward being able to accept all the different viewpoints of all our different citizens, instead of expecting everyone to think alike. This makes social decision making both more difficult and more important.

Groups of people can arrive at decisions in three ways. One way is by **consensus,** which means that the majority of people decide for the group. This is the way our political system and most of our social clubs are run, on the basis of what the greatest number of people vote to do. Another way to make group decisions is by **compromise.** This means that each side is willing to give in on some things in order to keep other, more important things. The end result is a decision that gives everybody something, but nobody gets everything. Sometimes the difference of opinion is so great that neither consensus nor compromise will work. In this case, **compartmentalization** may be used. This is the process of separating the various parts of the problem. The group then agrees on as many parts as possible.

Whether the group you have to work with is your family, your co-workers, or the whole society, it is important to know how social decisions can be reached. The major requirement is that you be sensitive to other people's needs and viewpoints. It is hard work, but the future of the world depends on it.

• BUILDING YOUR CAREER VOCABULARY

Define each of the following terms and then use each one in a sentence.

alternative
analyze
cause and effect
compartmentalization
compromise
consensus
decision making
generalize
physical maturity
psychological maturity
role conflict

• UNDERSTANDING WHAT YOU HAVE READ

1. What are the five requirements for decision making?
2. What is the difference between brainpower and other kinds of energy?
3. Name four roles that you have to play at the present time.
4. Do you have complete freedom of choice? Explain your answer.
5. What word can be used to describe people who must have everything immediately?

6. When does it become necessary to make a decision?
7. What are six steps for personal decision making?

- **APPLYING WHAT YOU HAVE LEARNED**
1. List one person, place, and thing that could help you to get the necessary facts if you were faced with the following decisions: (a) buying a stereo set, (b) deciding how to get to a distant city, (c) choosing your courses for next year, (d) deciding between two part-time jobs, (e) deciding whether to continue studying after high school.
2. Think about a situation in which you recently had to make a personal decision. Write answers to the following questions:
   a. Why was it necessary for you to make a decision?
   b. What were the alternatives that you considered?
   c. Did you make any effort to get additional facts?
   d. Did you make up your own mind or follow someone else's advice?
   e. Has the decision turned out to be right? Why do you think it worked? If it turned out wrong, can you figure out what you should have done differently?
3. Think about a situation in which you recently were involved in a group decision. This could be a decision that was made at home, at school, in a club, or among your friends. Write answers to the following questions:
   a. What kind of decision had to be made?
   b. How many different viewpoints did the members of the group have?
   c. What method did they use for arriving at a decision?
   d. Did everyone participate fully in the decision or did certain people "take over"?
   e. What was decided?
   f. Was everyone satisfied with the decision?
   g. Should things have been handled differently? How?

Part 12: Putting It All Together

After reading Part 12, you will be able—
- To define what you personally want from a career by answering a series of career-related questions.
- To explain how the work of the Equal Employment Opportunity Commission affects you.

The process of deciding on a career begins, as does all decision making, when you recognize that you actually do have a choice. You don't have to just fall into your work, as so many people do. As a thinking person, you can make the decisions that will put you in control of your own future. It is important for you to accept this option to choose, because your career choice is a **central choice**. This means that it will influence most of the other choices you will have to make in setting your total life style.

Besides being so important, your career choice is also one of the most difficult choices you will ever have to make. It involves not just one quick and easy decision but a whole series of decisions that should be made carefully over a period of time. Some of these decisions will be negative, making it possible for you to weed out certain careers that would clearly not be right for you. Negative decisions can be an important way of narrowing your choices down to the real alternatives.

Some people make their negative decisions on the job. They start working and then decide that they are in the wrong field. This trial-and-error method is a costly way to reach a decision. It wastes time, money, and effort for both you and the employer. It is much more efficient to make as many decisions as you can, both positive and negative, *before* you start to work. This not only helps you to start out in the right field but also gives you time to learn the things that you have to know in order to be successful in your chosen field.

In trying to make a career decision, what you need most is information. You can get an idea of how important this is by asking some small children what they want to be when they grow up. They will name one of the very few occupations that they have had some direct contact with, such as teacher, fire fighter, doctor, television performer,

Very often little girls say that they want to be mothers when they grow up because motherhood is the only occupation for women that they have any contact with. *(Laima Turnley/Editorial Photocolor Archives)*

or whatever their parents and relatives do. These children can't tell you that they want to be package designers, wholesaling middlemen, or marketing researchers because they don't know that such occupations exist.

When you try to decide on a career on the basis of very limited information, you narrow down your alternatives drastically. What you are really doing is settling for a career rather than choosing one. True decision making calls for facts, facts, and more facts. It would be very difficult for you to get this mass of information by yourself. That's why your school is making courses such as this one available to you, to make you aware of all the career options open to you.

The field of marketing is a very important one for you to know about because of both the total number of jobs and the many different kinds of jobs that it offers. Exploring this field can only help you with your final career decision. Whether you accept or reject the idea of a career in marketing for yourself, you will have broadened your base of knowledge. And that will make your final decision more accurate.

In the coming units, you will be able to take a close look at what is involved in preparing for a marketing career. You will also be able to examine the individual parts of the marketing field, ranging from food stores to trucking companies. As a way of preparing for this specific information, we are going to summarize what you have learned so far about yourself, careers, and marketing. We can do this by thinking about how a marketing career lets you be yourself, what the disadvantages of marketing careers are, and whether we are including everybody when we use the word "you" in talking about marketing careers.

HOW A MARKETING CAREER LETS YOU BE YOURSELF

Your purpose in choosing a career is to find one that will be rewarding and satisfying because it is right for you. This means that it has to answer your needs and wants. You have to be able to handle the physical requirements for the work. And the career has to be in line with your intelligence, aptitudes, interests, skills, and personality traits. It also has to be in line with your values, goals, and standards as well as with the life style you hope to have. This is hardly a simple matter, but then marketing is not a simple field. The main advantage of marketing for the person seeking a tailor-made career is the wide variety of jobs that it offers. It also offers many variations of the same job.

As an example of this, let's think about the job of salesworker, which is only one of the many different kinds of jobs in marketing. There are some qualifications that all salesworkers should have. For example, they all have to be able to get along with other people. And

The ability to get along well with people is a quality that all salesworkers must have. (*Courtesy Jack Daniel Distillery*)

they all have to know the techniques of selling. But it would be a great mistake to think that all salesworkers should be alike in all ways. Just the fact that there are widely differing products calls for differences. The person who sells musical instruments needs different interests, abilities, and training than the automobile salesworker or the person who sells medical supplies to hospitals.

Sales jobs can also have very different working conditions. Some salesworkers work in stores, where the customers come to them. Others have to go to the customers' homes or places of business. Sometimes this requires a willingness to travel a great deal between cities or overseas. Salesworkers also differ in the amount of time they give to their jobs. There are many salesworkers who work only part time, while others work more than 40 hours a week.

This same kind of variation can be found in many other jobs in marketing. Clerks who reserve places for customers can work in such different surroundings as hotels, airports, and theaters. Waiters or waitresses can work in many different kinds of plain and fancy restaurants, in railroad dining cars, in the dining rooms of passenger ships, and at parties in private homes and clubs. Each of these situations calls for a different combination of qualities in the person filling the job.

It is obvious that marketing is a huge umbrella under which all kinds of very different people can fit. What is most important about this is that marketing doesn't just *put up with* the differences in people. Because marketing is such a varied field, it actually *needs* people from many different backgrounds, with many different personal qualities,

People with all sorts of different backgrounds, different interests, different qualities, different goals, and different life styles can find satisfying careers in marketing.

values, goals, and standards. Let's now examine this statement more closely, by looking at some of the ways in which marketing lets you be yourself.

Marketing Gives You Material Benefits

To understand the material benefits that you can get from marketing careers, you have to know how people are paid for the work that they do. Most people are paid both directly, in cash, and indirectly, by being given other things of value. Direct cash payments may be paid in the form of profits to the owners of businesses. Employees may be paid cash in the form of wages or salaries, both of which represent a certain amount of money for a certain period of time at work. When the amount of money is set by the hour or day, it is called a **wage.** When the amount represents a weekly, bimonthly, monthly, or yearly rate, it is called a **salary.**

When workers put in extra time on the job, beyond their usual hours, they may be paid **overtime,** which is pay for extra hours worked. This may be one and one-half times what they would normally earn. In some instances, they may even be paid double time. Overtime pay can be earned by both wage and salary earners. But when salaries are high, employees may be expected to get the job done regardless of the time involved—that is, without being paid overtime.

Cash payments can also be made in the form of tips. **Tips** are sums of money given directly to the worker by the customer as a way of saying thank you for good service. In fact, the word is a combination of the first letters of the words "*to insure prompt service.*" Tips are an important part of the income of such service workers as waitresses and waiters, porters, taxi drivers, and hairdressers. Another form of cash payment is the **commission.** This represents a percentage of the selling price that is paid to the salesworker for completing the sale. Often a worker is paid a base wage or salary and then is allowed to earn tips or commissions over and above that, depending on the job.

The indirect earnings of workers are called **fringe benefits.** These are all the extras that are paid by the employer on behalf of the employee. Some examples of fringe benefits are paid vacations, holidays, and sick leave; health, accident, and life insurance; and retirement funds. Sometimes these benefits are paid in full by the employer, and sometimes the employee has to pay some of the cost. For example, the employer and the employee usually make matching contributions to retirement funds. Also, they each have to pay half of the social security tax that is figured as a percentage of employee wages and salaries. This tax provides monthly cash benefits to people whose income has stopped because they are elderly or disabled and

Marketing jobs offer many fringe benefits, one of which might be the fun and relaxation of playing on a company baseball team. (*Courtesy Commonwealth of Puerto Rico*)

to the dependent children and widows of workers who have died. Social security is a fringe benefit that is required by federal law for almost all employees.

Fringe benefits can also include such things as clean uniforms, low-cost or free meals, the use of a company-owned automobile, and travel expenses. Many stores offer their employees discounts on purchases, which are usually figured as a percentage off the regular sale price. Also, many transportation companies offer their employees tickets at a discount. Some even offer completely free rides. In addition, an employer may offer such after-work activities as bowling leagues and clubs of all kinds.

What you want from a career in terms of cash and fringe benefits is a very personal matter. It depends on your needs and wants, as well as on your whole value system. If money is what you want most and you are willing to put in the time and effort to earn it, marketing gives you many choices. For example, there are hardworking salespeople who earn $100,000 a year and more from their commissions. Marketing executives, who have many responsibilities, can earn even more than that. But perhaps money is lower on your scale of values than free time to pursue your hobbies. In that case, you would care less about cash rewards and put more emphasis on short hours and long vacations. Likewise, someone who values traveling might prefer a job that offers discount plane tickets to a job that pays more in cash. These are just a few examples, but they point up one of marketing's main advantages. Because it is such a varied field, there is a good chance that marketing can offer you the combination of material benefits that suits you best.

Marketing Combines Security and Excitement

The field of marketing is famous for the job security that it offers. This means that marketing workers generally don't have to worry about being out of a job. There are three reasons for this. First, marketing is a growing field rather than one that is cutting back. In a growth situation, workers who have acquired marketing skills can be sure of being needed. Second, many marketing skills can be transferred from job to job in lattice-type moves. For example, what you learn in a food store can be transferred to other areas of retailing. This knowledge can also be transferred to food wholesaling or food advertising. Third, marketing is not a field that can be taken over by machines. There are machines, such as computers, that can do some of the routine jobs in marketing. But most marketing jobs are not routine or automatic. They involve people-to-people relationships, where things rarely happen twice in the same way. Because this is the major part of marketing, workers who develop skills in working with people don't have to worry about being replaced by a machine.

Sometimes we think of things that are secure as being rather dull. This is not the case in marketing, which is a constantly changing field. Customers change, products change, and market conditions change, so new ideas and new ways of doing things are constantly needed in every area of marketing.

Because marketing combines both security and excitement, you can get the blend of these two ingredients that suits you best. For example, you may choose the security of working for a well-established company, knowing that your job will be interesting. Or you may accept the challenge of going into business for yourself, knowing that you could transfer your skills to another marketing job if you had to. Whether you want a lot of security and some excitement or a lot of excitement and some security, marketing can give you what you want.

Marketing Lets You Work With People

Another of marketing's main advantages is that it allows you to work with people in the way that suits you best. You might like having authority and therefore enjoy supervising others. Or you might prefer to be supervised. You might like close teamwork with other people. Or you might like a career that gives you wide freedom of action and independence. What you want may be power or prestige. Perhaps you simply enjoy the stimulation of working with other people, finding that they give your life exciting new dimensions. You may feel this so strongly that you want a career where you can constantly be meeting new people. Also, your social values may be such that what you want most is to help other people.

Would it be possible for a person who is interested in painting and art to find a satisfying career in marketing? (*Bob Van Lindt/ Editorial Photocolor Archives*)

Any of these requirements, or any mixture of them, can be met in marketing. The only thing that marketing can't do is offer a career to someone who doesn't want to be around other people at all. Marketing is a people-to-people business in all its phases. Therefore, anyone who really does not like other people has very little chance of being successful in marketing.

Marketing Gives You Other Advantages

Marketing offers you a unique opportunity to work in a career that reflects your interests. Suppose, for example, that you like sports. You could work for a sporting-goods wholesaler or retailer or in the marketing department of a sporting-goods manufacturer. You could also work for one of the companies that arranges sports matches. It would also be possible for you to work in one of the health spas where people go to get physically fit.

The same kind of thing would be true if you were interested in art, music, machinery, photography, or anything else. In each case, you would find that your interest opened up a whole cluster of occupations to you. This is also true of your aptitudes and skills. You may work best with people, with machinery or other things, or with handling facts (data). Or you may work well with all these. In any case, marketing has much to offer.

Marketing also offers you ways of matching your other personal qualities. There are marketing careers for people who want a lot of schooling and people who don't, for people who are very ambitious and those who don't like to compete, for people who want a lot of activity and those who like peace and quiet. Because of the wide variety of occupations in marketing, it is a field where it is not unrealistic for you to plan to be yourself.

THE DISADVANTAGES OF MARKETING CAREERS

When you look only at the advantages of careers, you don't have enough information to make a decision. You also have to know what the drawbacks are, for no career is perfect. But talking in generalities about the disadvantages of marketing careers is difficult, because what is a disadvantage to one person is not a disadvantage to someone else. For example, many marketing jobs require that you travel. If you like seeing new places and faces all the time, this is an advantage. However, people who travel have less time to spend with their families, so traveling can be a disadvantage. Many marketing businesses are open in the evenings and on weekends, which can be a real disadvantage. But these long hours also make it possible for people to get part-time jobs in marketing or to work the shifts that fit in best with their lives. Also, marketing jobs often have an uneven flow of work. There may be periods that are slow and other periods that are very busy. Some people would be bothered by this, but others would not.

When you are thinking about disadvantages, you have to keep yourself in the center of the picture. The important thing is to know what bothers you, not what bothers other people.

DOES THE WORD "YOU" INCLUDE YOU?

When we say that *you* can choose the career that is right for *you*, we seem to be including everybody. But is this realistic? What about the two words "prejudice" and "discrimination"? These words describe an irrational way of holding individuals down because they belong to a group that some people consider inferior in some way. Our country's history includes discrimination against women and such minority groups as Afro-Americans, American Indians, Eskimos, Aleuts, and people with Hispanic or Oriental ancestry. Does this mean that the word "you" in the first sentence really excludes all these people?

The answer to this question is no. Since 1964 it has been a matter of federal law that qualified individuals cannot be refused employment or promotion on the basis of their race, color, national origin, religious belief, or sex. The federal Equal Employment Opportunity Commission (EEOC) has been able to enforce this law more rigidly with every passing year. A major turning point in the work of the EEOC came in 1972, when a major American company was required to pay millions of dollars in back pay to women and other minority workers that it had discriminated against. Similar charges of discrimination have been filed against other companies and some labor unions. These efforts make it clear that the federal government is committed to making prejudice in employment practices a thing of the past.

Many large companies are making a positive effort to seek out women and minority applicants for jobs. These companies, rather than

Today many women are working at jobs that used to be considered strictly men's jobs, and many men have jobs that used to be strictly women's jobs. (TOP *courtesy Volkswagen of America, Inc;* BOTTOM *courtesy AT&T*)

128 • UNIT 2 • YOU AND A MARKETING CAREER

discriminating against women and other minorities, are actually competing for the chance to hire them. Major efforts are also being made by business and government people to help women and other minority group members start their own businesses and to open up markets for the products of these businesses.

The result of this insistence on economic freedom for all is that everyone benefits. For example, in the past, men have been denied jobs traditionally held by women. But jobs can no longer be classified as "male" or "female." This means that the barriers have been eliminated for both men and women, except in those few cases, such as washroom attendant, where a person's sex is a necessary qualification for a specific job.

Because marketing is an activity that touches the lives of people everywhere, it has traditionally employed a broad cross section of the population. It has always had its doors open to women, although, in the past, few women advanced beyond the middle management level. But now there will be far more opportunities for women and minority-group members to find the marketing career that is right for them and to succeed in it. The problems are not solved by any means. But serious efforts are being made to eliminate prejudice in employment practices.

• BUILDING YOUR CAREER VOCABULARY

Define each of the following terms and then use each one in a sentence.

central choice	salary
commission	tips
fringe benefit	wage
overtime	

• UNDERSTANDING WHAT YOU HAVE READ

1. Why is it important to make as many career decisions as you can before you start to work?
2. What happens when you try to decide on a career on the basis of very limited information?
3. When you are trying to decide on a job, why is it important to know what fringe benefits are offered, as well as the rate of pay?
4. List three reasons why marketing jobs generally offer a high degree of job security.
5. Is there one type of person who stands the best chance of being successful in marketing? Explain your answer.

• APPLYING WHAT YOU HAVE LEARNED

1. To help you see what you want from a career, answer the following questions on a separate sheet of paper:
   a. Do you want a career that will let you live in the same area that you now live in? If not, would you prefer to work in a large city, middle-sized town, small town, suburban area, rural area, or foreign country?
   b. Once you were settled, would you accept a better job if it meant moving to another area?
   c. Would you like to travel for your job: not at all? occasionally? often? most of the time?
   d. Would you prefer to work indoors or outdoors?
   e. Do you prefer physical work or mental work?
   f. Is it important to you to work in a pleasant, attractive place?
   g. Would you mind some physical discomfort, such as working outside in cold or wet weather?
   h. Would you like to be paid a straight salary or wage so that you know exactly how much you will earn?
   i. Would you be willing to work strictly on commission, without any salary?
   j. Is a short workweek important to you?
   k. Would you be willing to work on the weekends and have your days off during the middle of the week?
   l. Would you work overtime for pay? without pay?
   m. Would you rather work steady hours or irregular hours?
   n. Which of the following things do you want from your career?

money	interesting experiences
prestige	self-satisfaction
independence	challenges
security	other things (list them)
opportunity to help others	

   o. Do you work well under pressure or would you prefer a job where you can work at a steady pace?
   p. Would you be willing to get more education to win a promotion?
   q. Which would you prefer: to have someone tell you how to do your job, to be fully responsible for your own work, or to plan and supervise the work of others?
2. Be prepared to participate actively in a class discussion on the work of the Equal Employment Opportunity Commission. Think about whether you agree with the principle that there should be no job discrimination based on "race, color, national origin, religious belief, or sex." What effect do you think this will have on your own career?

EXPERIMENTS IN MARKETING

1. In this unit we have discussed how important it is for you to find the job that is right for you. Write a paragraph discussing whether you think that it is important to the employer to get the right person in the right job, giving reasons for your answer. Be prepared to share your thoughts with the class.
2. Invite the person who does the hiring (who probably is called the personnel director) for a large marketing business in your area to come to your classroom. Ask this person to explain (a) what general qualities the company is looking for in its employees and (b) how decisions are made about filling specific jobs.

UNIT 3

After completing this unit, you will be able to relate the purposes, method, and content of your school's Distributive Education program to your own goals.

If you decide, at the end of this course, that you want to prepare for a career in marketing, you will then move into the Distributive Education program offered by your high school. To help you find out ahead of time if you will like this program, we are going to take a close look at what Distributive Education is and how it can prepare you for a marketing career. This will make it possible for you to see whether it seems like a good program for *you*.

Preparing for a Career in Marketing

part 13 Distributive Education: An Opportunity

After reading Part 13, you will be able—
- To define Distributive Education.
- To explain how the two methods that Distributive Education uses to make the student's education relevant reinforce each other.
- To identify and explain the purpose of the four sides to the DECA program.

In this part, you are going to begin your study of Distributive Education in order to see how it can help you to prepare for a marketing career. The first step is to define Distributive Education, so you will know what kind of a program it is. Then you will see how the program works on the high school level and what possibilities there are for getting additional training after you have finished high school. You are also going to be introduced to the Distributive Education Clubs of America, which is an exciting way of enriching your experience in Distributive Education.

WHAT IS DISTRIBUTIVE EDUCATION?

Distributive Education, which is often called simply DE, is an educational program whose purpose is to prepare people for careers in the broad field of marketing, including distribution. There are DE programs for high school students and for students who are continuing their formal education after high school. There are also evening courses for adults who want to upgrade their marketing skills.

Because DE's aim is to teach its students in the most meaningful way, it combines two methods. First, it teaches the principles, or "theory," of marketing. This means that it gives its students the whole body of facts and rules that they need in order to understand what marketing is all about. But theory alone only teaches what is supposed to happen, according to the facts and rules. To show the students what really does happen, DE's second method is to give the students direct experience with actual marketing practices.

By itself, theory can be an unexciting and difficult way to learn. The dry facts can be boring, and when things are boring, they are hard to understand and hard to remember. But when the facts are brought to life through direct, personal experiences, they are no longer dry. However, learning by experience alone is often called "the hard way." If you have to think through everything that happens to you on your own, you will learn much more slowly. By combining theory and experience, DE offers you a proven way of learning that is lively and stimulating. It never lets you forget that marketing is a real subject, about the real things that real people are doing.

THE DE PROGRAM ON THE HIGH SCHOOL LEVEL

The number of students enrolled in DE has been increasing at an extraordinary rate of speed in recent years. One circumstance that helps to explain this growth is that students are demanding that their education be relevant. They don't want school to be something that they have to "wait out" until they are ready for "real life." For these kinds of students, the DE program has much to offer. It makes it clear that school does not have to be something that is dull or irrelevant. Rather, it can be a lively beginning, a direct way of getting ready for a career and a life that are personally satisfying and rewarding. DE accomplishes this by bringing together "school," "work," and "life," both by what it teaches and by how it teaches.

What DE Teaches

As a DE student, you learn what the relationships are between marketing, production, consumption, and the economic health of our country. You also learn the facts about what marketing businesses are trying to do and how they are organized to get their work done. This includes learning what it means to be the boss and to have to run the business so that it makes a profit. It also includes learning what is expected of the workers in marketing businesses. This ranges all the way from learning the basic skills, attitudes, and personal qualities that are necessary in any job to developing special marketing skills.

DE also gives you details about a broad range of specific marketing jobs. You learn where the jobs are now, what their future is, what their advantages and disadvantages are, and what qualifications you need to get hired and build a career. This includes learning how much training is necessary for the job and where, how, and when that training can be gotten.

But DE does not just prepare you to work in marketing. It also gives you the background that you need to understand how democracy and modified free enterprise work, so that you can be a good citizen. DE also teaches you the importance of being true to yourself as an individual and of developing all your capabilities to the fullest. In short, DE's aim is to develop the whole person, as well as to prepare each individual for a career.

How DE Teaches

The DE program is not the same in all high schools. It varies according to the size and location of the school. It may be a one-, two-, or three-year program. But in any case, the basic DE idea of combining theory and experience is used. This is done first in the school setting. In many schools, it is also done by letting the student go to school part time and work part time in a marketing job, getting school credit for the work done. Let's see now how these two ways of teaching work out.

THEORY AND REALITY IN THE CLASSROOM. Some subjects can be taught successfully within the four walls of the classroom, with just a textbook and lectures by the teacher. But that is not the way that DE is taught. DE's method is to bring the realities of marketing into the classroom and to take the class out to where marketing is happening. This includes having people who work in marketing come to the classroom to discuss what they do at work. It also includes taking the whole class on field trips to let the students see with their own eyes how marketing businesses work. Homework assignments will also take students out into the field, by requiring all kinds of reports on marketing activities in the community.

Within the classroom, students will be assigned to projects that let them practice the principles they are learning. These projects might range all the way from creating displays to packing breakables so that they can be mailed safely. In many schools, DE students operate a school store, selling all kinds of school-related products to students and teachers. Such stores represent a service to the school, besides being a lively learning experience for DE students.

Another training method in DE is to set up situations that imitate real situations, just as a play imitates real life. For example, the classroom might be turned for a day into the office of an advertising agency. Some members of the class would play the roles of workers in the agency, and others would be representatives of a big company. Their job might be to analyze the company's current television campaign to see how effective it is.

COOPERATIVE EDUCATION. In many schools, DE students have a chance to become involved in marketing in the most direct way—by actually working in the field. They go to school part time, possibly in the mornings. Then they spend the rest of what would be their school

The DE students who operate this school store are acquiring valuable experience in many phases of marketing—including window display. (*Courtesy Distributive Education Clubs of America*)

time working in a job where they receive the going wage. This makes a two-way street of learning for the students. They get instruction in school that relates to their specific jobs. And their experiences at work, where they are closely supervised, show them how the principles they have learned in the classroom actually work out.

The person who helps the student to get the most out of this two-way process is the **teacher-coordinator.** This is the name that is given to a teacher who coordinates, or pulls together, a DE program. Teacher-coordinators are in charge of teaching the students in the classroom. Besides this, they contact business firms in their school areas to interest them in providing part-time jobs. Then they work with the employers and the students to get the right people into the right jobs. Teacher-coordinators also explain the program to the students' parents and get the parents' approval. And they constantly check back with the employers to see that the students are doing their jobs well.

DE is not the only area of study that offers cooperative work, but it is one of the best known. In Part 19, you will learn more about how this program works.

DE TRAINING AFTER HIGH SCHOOL

One of the main advantages of the DE program is that it allows students to get the amount of formal education that makes the most sense to them. Students who want to stop their formal education after high school are well prepared for the world of work. But it is also possible to go on with formal DE studies after high school. There are community colleges for just this purpose in many states. There are also post-high school DE programs in vocational-technical schools, junior colleges, and universities.

These post-high school DE programs allow students to concentrate on special areas of marketing. For example, students can choose to study in depth the marketing of fashions, home furnishings, or farm products. Students can also specialize in wholesaling or in the management of hotels, restaurants, transportation businesses, or recreation businesses. The quality of these specialized programs is so high that their graduates can enter the field of marketing as trainees at the middle-management level. This means that the extra time that is spent in school is a direct investment in the future for each student. This is something that you have to think about when you are trying to decide how much formal education you want for yourself.

DECA: TRAINING FOR LEADERSHIP

When you enroll in your school's DE program, you become eligible for membership in **DECA**. This stands for the Distributive Education Clubs of America, a program of DE-related activities for young people. The value of DECA to you is that it extends the DE program in all directions. It widens and deepens the learning experiences that DE offers. But teaching marketing skills is not DECA's only function. By offering recreation as well as instruction, DECA helps its members to develop more fully. Its activities are stimulating, interesting, and enjoyable. Let's see now how DECA goes about this.

How DECA Is Organized

When you join DECA, you will be joining three things all at once: your school chapter, your state association, and national DECA. You will be part of the High School Division, which is one of the five divisions of DECA. The other four are the Junior Collegiate and the Collegiate Division, for people who are continuing their DE education after high school; the Alumni Division, for DE graduates who want to continue their involvement in DECA; and the Professional Division, for such people as DE teacher-coordinators, employers, parents of DECA members, school administrators, and others who can contribute to the growth of DECA in a professional way.

The local chapter is run by the students themselves. They elect their own officers and plan their own activities, under the guidance of the DE teacher-coordinator, who serves as an adviser. In turn, the teacher-coordinator asks a group of local business people to help the chapter by serving as an Advisory Board. Parents are also asked to help to make the chapter run smoothly. The students elect their own officers on the state and national levels. There are 52 state associations, one for every state plus Puerto Rico and the District of Columbia.

How DECA Is Financed

DECA is financed partly by membership dues. Also, local chapters may conduct sales projects each year, where chapter members sell such frequently used things as school supplies, candy, and gift items. Sales projects represent both a way to make money for chapter activities and a direct experience in the realities of marketing. In addition, there are ways in which business people can make financial contributions to support DECA's programs. This includes a program for giving financial awards to members who want to continue their education.

The DECA Program

To carry out its aim of developing the whole person, DECA offers a varied and interesting program. There are four sides to this program: (1) vocational understanding, (2) civic consciousness, (3) social intelligence, and (4) leadership development. DECA believes that

A personal consumer survey is only one way in which DECA members learn about marketing and assist local retailers. (*Courtesy Distributive Education Clubs of America*)

PART 13 • DISTRIBUTIVE EDUCATION: AN OPPORTUNITY • 139

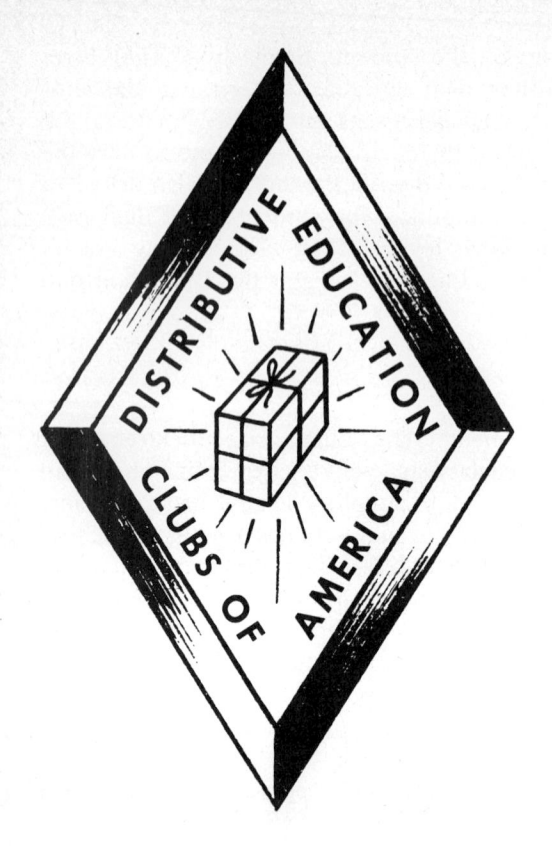

The emblem of the Distributive Education Clubs of America symbolizes the DECA program. The four sides of the diamond represent the four areas of development encouraged by the DECA program. (*Courtesy Distributive Education Clubs of America*)

each of these four areas must be developed if the student is going to get a well-rounded education. Let's see now what these four terms mean and how DECA brings them to life.

VOCATIONAL UNDERSTANDING. DE is classified as vocational education because it specifically prepares people for employment. The DECA program is planned to enrich its members' understanding of marketing, as a way of preparing them for marketing careers. This is done on the chapter level by planning programs for meetings that include guest speakers, panel discussions, and films. Members also work on various projects that are designed to make DE classroom work come alive. In some of these projects, the members of the chapter all work together, so that they learn the value of cooperative efforts. For example, the chapter may do a marketing research project for the town's retailers, studying such things as the need for more parking or the public's shopping habits. In other instances, individual members compete with each other on projects of their own. These projects include such diverse things as keeping a manual (notebook) about one phase of marketing, preparing a sales demonstration for a specific product, and developing a newspaper ad layout.

This competitive side of the DECA program is considered to be an important way of preparing students for positions of real responsibility in marketing. Our free-enterprise marketing system both needs and rewards people who have the initiative, energy, and skills to compete successfully. Students who do well in their chapters are eligible for prizes at the yearly state DECA conferences and at the national Career Development Conference. It is a tremendous honor to win one of these prizes. The competition for them each year is very keen. This makes the contests thrilling for the students who are taking part in them, as well as for those who are observing.

CIVIC CONSCIOUSNESS. When we talk about civic consciousness, we are talking about good citizenship. One of the most important ways that DECA develops this is by insisting that all its meetings be run according to strict **parliamentary procedure.** This term describes the rules of order that are used to conduct meetings in the most democratic way possible. Abiding by these rules ensures that everyone's viewpoint will be heard and judged with fairness.

DECA members also develop civic consciousness in other ways. They may sponsor or co-sponsor a charity drive, either for the whole town or for the school. They may work on a voter registration drive or a cleanup project, or they may adopt a needy family. They may also work on public relations projects in the belief that it is important for the community to know about DECA and what it does. Such projects might include building a DECA float for a parade or a DECA booth for a county fair or preparing newspaper releases and radio programs about DECA.

DECA members develop civic consciousness by sponsoring projects that benefit the community. A used clothing drive to help needy families is an example of such a project. (*Courtesy Distributive Education Clubs of America*)

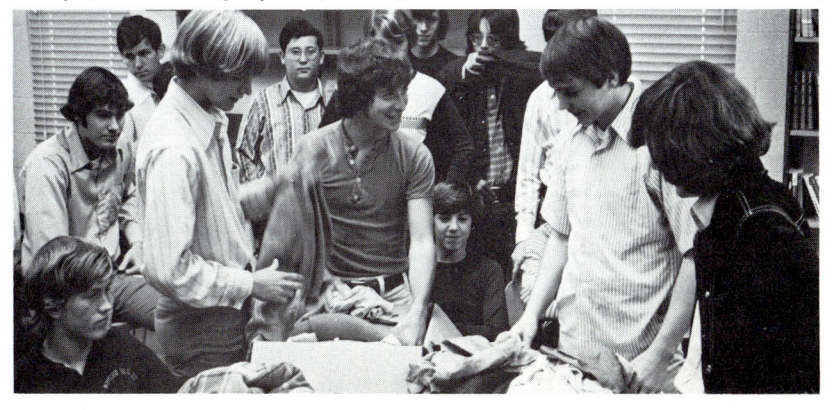

SOCIAL INTELLIGENCE. Because DECA is a social organization as well as a program for learning, it is a training ground for poise and good manners. DECA members have many opportunities to build comfortable social relationships, both with their peers and with adults. This is done at meetings, which are often accompanied by refreshments and some kind of entertainment. Such events as the Employer-Employee Banquet, Boss Breakfast, and Parents' Night give students a chance to practice their social skills. DECA members who attend state or national conferences have even more opportunity to develop their social intelligence. They meet people from many different localities whose customs may be different from their own. But their shared interest in DE and DECA makes it easy for them to become friends.

National DECA conferences give members the opportunity to make new friends and to develop social skills. (*Courtesy Distributive Education Clubs of America*)

LEADERSHIP DEVELOPMENT. A very important part of the DECA program is training young people to be the leaders of tomorrow. Because the future of our economy depends in so many ways on what happens in marketing, our country needs people who can make wise decisions for themselves and can point the way for others. Many DECA chapters elect officers as often as once a semester to let more members have leadership experience. Members also have a chance to serve as committee heads. But in real life, no one can be a leader all the time. So DECA also emphasizes the importance of knowing how to be a follower, when the situation calls for it. Thus, DECA members also learn to be effective committee members who can be counted on to do behind-the-scene jobs as cheerfully as they do the jobs in the spotlight.

• BUILDING YOUR MARKETING VOCABULARY

Define each of the following terms and then use each one in a sentence.

DECA
Distributive Education
parliamentary procedure
teacher-coordinator

• UNDERSTANDING WHAT YOU HAVE READ

1. What are the two teaching methods that DE uses to make the student's education relevant? How do these two methods reinforce each other?
2. Is DE taught only in high schools? Explain your answer.
3. What is the value of DECA to you?
4. What are the four sides to the DECA program? Explain the purpose of each one.
5. Why is DE classified as vocational education?
6. List ten activities that may be part of a DECA chapter's program.

• APPLYING WHAT YOU HAVE LEARNED

1. Participate actively in a class discussion about whether school should or should not be relevant to your life.
2. Invite a DE teacher or teacher-coordinator and two students who are presently studying DE in your school to come to your classroom to speak to you about your school's DE program and DECA chapter. If there is no DE program in your school, write to the State Director of Vocational Education at your State Department of Education, asking that arrangements be made to have a presentation about DE made in your school. Write a report summarizing what they said and your own reactions.

part 14 The Basic and Social Skills

After reading Part 14, you will be able—
- To name the four communication skills and explain how marketing workers use each one.
- To test your communication skills by reading a written guarantee and explaining its terms to the class.
- To list three reasons why mathematical accuracy is necessary in marketing businesses.
- To test your social skills by deciding what you would do in a given list of marketing situations.

There are some skills that you are going to need for anything that you want to do, whether it's further study, work, or just day-by-day living in our complex society. This includes, first of all, the basic skills. These are the skills that form the foundation for everything else that you will learn. The **basic skills** are the elementary skills in language and mathematics that you must have to be able to function as a thinking human being. Another set of skills that you must have in order to live and work comfortably with other people are the **social skills**. In this part, we will look at both the basic skills and the social skills to see why they are considered such an important part of the DE program.

MAKING LANGUAGE WORK FOR YOU

The purpose of language is to make it possible for people to **communicate**, which means to exchange information, ideas, and thoughts. But the only way that two people can really understand each other is if they are both speaking the same language. This means using words that mean the same thing to both of them. This is why there are dictionaries, so that everyone who is using the language can find out what the correct meanings of words are. But when you are talking to someone, you can't stop to look up words in the dictionary. So if you want to communicate quickly and easily, you have to make the effort to

144 • UNIT 3 • PREPARING FOR A CAREER IN MARKETING

The ability to use language effectively is necessary to communicate your thoughts and ideas to another person. (*National Education Association*)

build up your vocabulary. Fortunately, this is not hard. You can do it every day just by reading newspapers and magazines and watching television.

But you should remember that what you are trying to learn are words everyone will understand. Slang words are lots of fun, but slang is really a private language that is different in different parts of the country. When you are out of your own neighborhood, people may not be able to understand you if you rely too heavily on the slang that you and your friends use in talking to each other. This is not to say that slang is always wrong, only that there is a time and place for it.

Being able to communicate also depends on having everyone use the same grammar rules. Studying grammar may have always seemed to you like a waste of time. But grammar rules are the tools that you need to convey your thoughts to other people. You know that the proper tools make it easier to build a house or repair an engine. Likewise, grammar can help you form your thoughts into a message that other people can understand.

In your DE and DECA work, you will have many opportunities to practice the four basic communication skills as a way of preparing for working and living. You will be able to do this in the classroom and at DECA meetings, through such things as your textbook work, discussions, oral and written reports, role playing, and interviews. The four communication skills you will be practicing over and over are reading, listening, writing, and speaking.

PART 14 • THE BASIC AND SOCIAL SKILLS • 145

Reading Accurately

There is a big difference between just being able to read and reading accurately, so that you grasp what the writer is trying to communicate. For example, suppose that you are given an essay test. The directions tell you to answer three out of five questions. But because you don't read the directions accurately, you answer all five questions. When this happens, you are punishing yourself by not taking advantage of the choice that the teacher offered you. Being able to get the real meaning of written material is important in everything you want to do, from following the directions for taking care of a tape recorder to understanding the ballot in the voting booth.

Reading accurately is also very important in the business world. You have to be able to read accurately to fill out an application for employment. Often employees are given written statements of the company's policies and the obligations and rights of the employer and employee. Salesworkers have to be able to read in order to learn more about the products they are selling. In many cases too, employees have to be able to follow written directions. This is true for the repairer. This is also true for workers in toy stores, stereo equipment stores, bicycle shops, and other kinds of retail stores where products often must be assembled or adjusted before they are sold. To follow written directions, you must be able to read accurately and to act on what you have read.

Most important of all, employees have to read in order to learn the skills to advance to better jobs. In fact, reading is an effective way of broadening and deepening your knowledge on any subject that interests you. When you have learned to read comfortably and easily, you have a tool for self-education that will work for you for your whole life. Reading can help you be a better-informed citizen, a better-trained worker, and a more interesting person.

Learning How to Listen

Listening seems like a simple enough thing to do. But, in fact, many people don't know much about listening. They can't keep their minds on what other people are saying, either because they are daydreaming or because they are too busy thinking about what they want to say next. The process of communication is a two-way street. If you don't listen, you can talk *to* other people, but you can't talk *with* them.

When you are a good listener, you do more than just listen to the words people are saying. You also pay attention to the messages they are sending out through their facial expressions, gestures, and body positions. A smile, a frown, a brush of the hand, a tense posture, or a step backward can say a great deal. Putting this information together

Gestures and facial expressions can reveal a person's real feelings. (*Courtesy Allied Van Lines, Inc.*)

gives you a much more complete and accurate picture of what the person is thinking and feeling. If you can learn to be the kind of listener who meets people more than halfway in this manner, you will find that your relationships with people will be much more rewarding, both in social situations and at work. For example, knowing how to listen is vital for salesworkers. They cannot make sales unless they are able to listen effectively to their customers and determine the customers' needs.

Writing With Ease

The subject of writing has to do first of all with your handwriting. Good handwriting is largely a matter of caring enough to take the time to form your letters carefully and neatly, so that they can be easily read. You may have felt at times that your teachers were much too strict about your handwriting. But sloppy, illegible writing is a serious strike against you, both socially and in business. Poor spelling and punctuation are two more strikes against you, making you seem young and inexperienced.

There is also the question of whether you can present your ideas in a clear and convincing manner on paper. In order to do this, you must first be able to think through everything that you want to say. Next you have to organize your thoughts in logical order. Finally you must find the words that express your thoughts accurately.

There is no doubt that writing comes more easily to some people than to others. But you don't need a "writing talent" in order to write effective social and business letters. What you do need, though, is the willingness to spend the time and effort necessary to do a good job. You also have to remember that learning how to write is a matter of practice. The more writing you do, the easier it gets.

Speaking With Assurance

Speaking may not be something that comes easily to you either. But your DE and DECA experiences will give you many ways of practicing this skill and becoming comfortable with it. You will learn how to organize and deliver prepared speeches. And you will also develop the ability to speak on the spur of the moment.

Whether delivering a speech or speaking informally, you will have to think about how you speak. You will have to be able to pronounce each word clearly, so that people can understand you. If you run all your words together and swallow half of every word, you might just as well be speaking a foreign language, for all anyone will get out of what you are saying. It is also important that you try to develop a pleasant speaking voice that is neither too shrill nor too low, too feeble nor too loud, too fast nor too slow. You also have to learn to keep those annoying "ums" and "ahs" out of your speech. And you have to make sure you don't speak in a monotone that will put everyone to sleep.

Tape recording your speeches will help you pinpoint your problems so that you can concentrate on correcting them. (*Courtesy Today's Secretary*)

As with your written work, the success of your prepared speeches will vary in direct proportion to the amount of time and effort that you put into their preparation. Having to speak on the spur of the moment is in many ways more difficult. But you can prepare for this too by taking some time to think before you start to talk. When you do this, you will find that people can understand you more easily. You don't have to keep backtracking and saying "What I mean is . . .," because you are already saying what you mean.

DEVELOPING MATHEMATICAL SKILLS

You have been receiving training in the basic mathematical skills ever since the first grade. Math skills are part of everyone's basic education because they are needed for doing even the simplest everyday activities. Whenever you want to divide something equally with your friends or whenever you buy something, you use math skills. You need math to plan how to spend your money wisely. You even need math when you prepare a meal for yourself. You will also need a basic ability in math for almost any job in marketing. That's why DE puts a lot of emphasis on having students practice their math skills. To show you why this is such an important part of career training, let's consider the uses of mathematics in marketing businesses, the cost of errors, and the reasons for errors.

The Uses of Mathematics in Marketing Businesses

Let's say that you are a salesperson in a candy store. A person asks for half a pound of mints, three pounds of jelly beans, and a pound and a half of chocolates. In writing up the salescheck, you will have to deal with multiplication, fractions, and addition. If your state has a sales tax, you will also have to use percentages. Then, when the customer pays you, you will have to use subtraction to figure out how much change the customer should receive. Even if the candy store has a cash register that does some of that work automatically for you, you will still have to be able to make change and keep track of the money, in order to make sure that the money in the cash register equals the amount recorded on the cash register receipts. You will also have to be able to fill out records that summarize sales for the day, week, and month. And sometimes you will have to count the amount of candy and supplies on hand.

If you were the owner of the candy store, you would have still more uses for math. You would need it to decide how much candy to order, to check the charges for the candy, to figure out how much money to pay your employees, and to keep track of all the expenses.

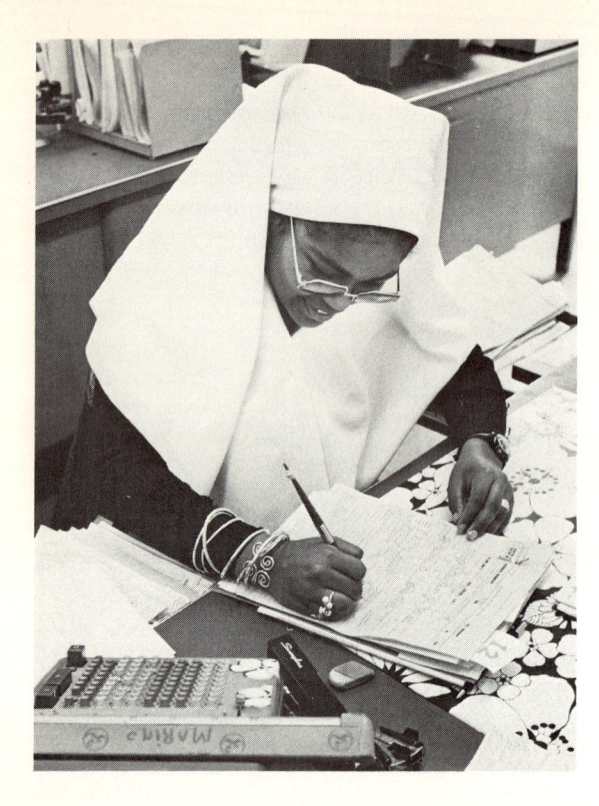

Being able to work accurately with numbers is important in all areas of marketing. *(Courtesy Metropolitan Life Insurance Co.)*

You would need math to make comparisons between your expenses and profits for various periods of time. And you would need it to help you predict future sales and profits.

The candy store is just one example of the importance of math in marketing. We might also have chosen a service station, restaurant, bank, skating rink, bus company, or insurance agency. In fact, we could have picked any marketing business. What this means is that if you want to work in marketing, you have to be able to work quickly, comfortably, and accurately with numbers. Sometimes students are weak in math because they've never been able to see that knowing it or not knowing it makes any difference at all. But through DE, you will be able to see that math is a subject that is a real part of your daily living and therefore worth learning.

The Cost of Errors

Mathematical errors are always expensive. Sometimes they cost the employer money in the most direct possible way. This is true when a salesclerk makes an error in addition and charges a customer too little. In other instances—for example, when errors are made in records—a lot of time and effort has to go into finding the errors. And time and effort cost money. Mathematical errors can also cost the employer the goodwill of the customers, who will feel that they have been cheated when they are overcharged for a purchase. And any error may make them lose confidence in the business. This all adds up to the fact that an employer cannot afford to have employees who can't handle numbers correctly.

The Reasons for Errors
Perhaps you make errors in math because you have never been sure of the mathematical rules. For example, you may get mixed up about where to place the decimal point when you are multiplying decimals or about how to express percentages as fractions. Because many students have such problems, your DE work will include a review of all the mathematical rules you have learned. You will also be given many opportunities to practice these rules and to become comfortable with them. Another major reason for errors is not being sure of number facts. Still another cause of errors is carelessness. Perhaps you write your numbers so poorly that you mistake one for another. For example, a hastily written 21 can look like a 4 and a sloppy 9 can be mistaken for a 7. Or perhaps you don't line up your numbers properly, so that you have no chance of adding or subtracting correctly. Perhaps you have turned the figures around, writing 89 when you mean 98. Another form of carelessness is to forget to check your answers. Remember that you can check addition with subtraction and multiplication with division, or the other way around. Fortunately carelessness is a bad habit that can be corrected with the kind of practice that your DE assignments will give you.

ACQUIRING SOCIAL SKILLS
Learning how to get along with other people is certainly one of the most important parts of your development as a human being. You will need this skill for everything you want to do, whether it's playing, working, or just daily living. If you want to work in marketing, getting along with others becomes even more important. Marketing is not a subject about things. It is about people, and that makes it a very broad subject indeed. Since no two people are alike in our crowded world, there is obviously a lot to be learned.

This explains why the study of **psychology,** the study of mind and behavior, is so important to marketers. In your DE classes, you will learn about how people's minds work and why people behave as they do. Another subject that you will learn about in your DE classes is

The root cause of bad manners is a basic lack of concern for other people.

human relations. This is the study of how people relate to each other individually and in groups. It is an important subject for both marketing employers and employees to understand.

While you are studying psychology and human relations, you will also learn about another subject that will help you get along with other people. This subject is **manners,** which are rules of conduct that tell people how to act in all kinds of situations. Manners are important because they take the friction out of people-to-people relationships.

Manners are the most helpful when they are based on a genuine concern for other people. When you care about people, you are naturally considerate of them. And consideration and good manners really are the same thing. For example, inconsiderate people can fail to show up for appointments, be late, take up more room than they are entitled to, make noises that disturb other people, and show their lack of manners in many other ways. If you care about other people, you wouldn't want to annoy or hurt them with such selfish behavior.

Through your experiences in DE and DECA, you will have many opportunities to develop the kind of genuinely good manners that make living and working with people both easier and more fun.

• BUILDING YOUR MARKETING VOCABULARY

Define each of the following terms and then use each one in a sentence.

basic skills   psychology
communicate   manners
human relations   social skills

- **UNDERSTANDING WHAT YOU HAVE READ**

  1. Is it always wrong to use slang? Explain your answer.
  2. Name the four communication skills and explain how marketing workers use each one.
  3. It is often said that listening is the most neglected of the communication skills. Explain what you think this means and tell whether or not you agree with this statement.
  4. Give three reasons why mathematical accuracy is necessary in marketing businesses.
  5. Why are social skills especially important in marketing jobs?

- **APPLYING WHAT YOU HAVE LEARNED**

  1. Think about a time when you have gotten into difficulty with a teacher, family member, friend, or other person because of a failure in communication. Write a paragraph describing what happened and how better communication would have kept the problem from arising.
  2. Find a written guarantee for a product or service in your home and bring it to class. Then test your communication skills by reading the guarantee and explaining its terms to the class.
  3. Test your social skills by writing on a separate piece of paper what you would do in each of the following situations:
     a. You are a retail salesworker waiting on a customer. Another customer comes over and says to you "Will you wait on me? I'm in a hurry."
     b. You are talking to another salesworker about your plans for the evening when a customer comes to your counter.
     c. You are a shoe salesworker. You have brought out a dozen pairs of shoes for a customer to try on, but the person leaves without buying anything.
     d. You are stocking shelves in a supermarket when a customer asks you where a certain item can be found.
     e. You are a bus driver. One passenger refuses to move to the rear of the bus to let other passengers on.

part 15: The Economic Facts of Life

After reading Part 15, you will be able—
- To explain why a marketer who buys a product for 50 cents and sells it for one dollar has not made a 50-cent profit.
- To list ten specific expenses that the owner of a given marketing business would have.
- To explain what shoplifting and unproductive work habits have in common.
- To define gross pay and take-home pay.

There are certain basic economic facts that everyone who works must know and that are especially important for marketing workers. These are the hard facts about money that make the difference between the success and failure of a business. These facts have to do with expenses, prices, and profits, and their relationship to each other. You cannot go into business for yourself without understanding these facts. And if you are going to work for someone else, this understanding will give you a much more realistic approach to your job. Because these facts are so important, they will be emphasized in your DE and DECA work in many ways. For example, if you take part in a sales project in your DECA chapter or if operating a store is part of your school's DE program, you will have a firsthand way of studying this subject.

UNDERSTANDING PROFITS

Suppose that a product costs 50 cents and a marketer sells it for one dollar. This dollar represents the **selling price** of the item, which is the amount of money a customer needs in order to buy goods or services. In this case, there is a 50-cent difference between the cost of the item and the selling price. Does this mean that the marketer's profit is 50 cents? You might think so, unless you remember that profit is the amount of money that is left over after *all* of the expenses of running the business have been paid. The cost of the product is only one expense. There are many other expenses that have to come out of that 50-cent difference. So the marketer's profit is going to be much less than 50 cents.

It's even possible that this 50 cents, which sounded like so much just a minute ago, isn't enough to cover all the expenses. When this happens, the business's outgo, which is another word for **expenses**, will be greater than its **income**, which is the amount of money that a business or individual receives or earns. When outgo is greater than income, the business is losing money, which it can't afford to do for very long. Success in marketing depends on knowing how both expenses and prices affect profits and on being able to keep expenses, prices, and profits in balance. To help you to understand what this means, we will look first at the kinds of expenses that marketers have and then at the ways in which profits can be increased.

The Kinds of Marketing Expenses

All marketers do not have the same expenses. An obvious reason for differences in expense is that there are many different kinds of marketing businesses. But expenses can also be different for businesses that are classified as being alike. Let's think about two stores that sell the same quality shoes, for example. One store has no "frills" at all. It is in a low-rent area and has only the bare essentials in the way of decoration. The customer must pay cash and may not return the shoes under any circumstances. By contrast, the second store is in the town's nicest shopping area, where rents are high. The store is elegantly decorated, and there is soft music. Customers may charge their purchases, have them delivered to their homes, and return anything they decide they don't like.

Even though the first store has much lower prices, both stores are very successful. This is because all people do not think alike about prices. Many people just want the lowest possible price. But others are willing to pay more *as long as* they feel that the extra money is balanced by the amount of convenience and service that they receive.

This means that marketers have to think carefully about what expenses are essential to their particular businesses. They have to think about what kinds of customers they are trying to attract and what those customers will expect. Keeping this background in mind, let's now look at the kinds of expenses that marketers have.

MAINTAINING A PLACE OF BUSINESS. The next time you go into a store, look carefully at all the things in the store that are not for sale. The display cases, lamps, rugs, and wall decorations all represent expenses for the storekeeper, as do the cash registers, and the typewriters, business machines, and file cabinets in the store's office area. In a restaurant, you will find the furniture in the dining area, a supply of dishes, silverware, and serving pieces, and a fully equipped kitchen. In other marketing businesses, you will find still other kinds of furniture and equipment, depending upon what goods and services are sold.

If you were a shrewd shopper, you might very well find a suit in the store above of the same quality as a suit sold in the store below, but for only two-thirds the price. What are the factors that cause the difference in price? (ABOVE *Michelle Stone/Editorial Photocolor Archives;* BELOW *courtesy John Bedessem/Carson Pirie Scott & Co.*)

156 • UNIT 3 • PREPARING FOR A CAREER IN MARKETING

Owners of marketing businesses have to plan for both the original cost of the furniture and equipment and the cost of replacing things that are worn out or outdated. Since these expenses are often large ones, owners may have to borrow the money for them. Then they have to pay off the loans, often in regular monthly payments. They also have to pay an extra amount of money called **interest.** This is a charge that has to be paid for the privilege of using money. Other regular payments that have to be paid to maintain a place of business are rent and charges from the electric, gas, water, and telephone companies.

BUYING GOODS, SUPPLIES, AND SERVICES. In buying goods for resale and the supplies that are needed to run the business, every effort has to be made to buy at the lowest possible price and still get the necessary quality. The marketer is also interested in the "terms of the sale," which are statements about how payment is to be made. If the seller will allow a reduction in the price, which is called a **discount,** in return for prompt cash payment, that will lower the price per item. Sometimes, however, it works out better if the marketer is allowed to wait to pay for the goods because this leaves the marketer's money free for other purposes.

Marketing businesses usually have to pay **shipping charges** on the goods that they buy. These charges represent payments to the transportation companies for their services in delivering the goods. Shipping charges may also include charges for packing the goods and getting them ready to be shipped. Marketers also buy insurance and many other business services. For example, there are companies that will clean the marketer's place of business. The marketer may also hire the services of an advertising agency or an accounting firm. Some marketers are able to perform these services for themselves. But others find that it is cheaper or more efficient to pay someone else to do them.

PAYING EMPLOYEES. The cost of labor is one of the largest expenses in any kind of business today. By worldwide standards, workers in our country are very well paid. Much of the credit for this has to be given to our country's **labor unions.** These are organizations of workers that make it possible for employees to bargain as a group with their employers for better pay and working conditions. Labor costs include more than just the amount of money on the workers' paychecks. All the fringe benefits also have to be paid for by the marketer.

PROVIDING SERVICES. Every service that marketers provide for their customers costs money, in terms of supplies, labor, or both. For example, when a store gift-wraps packages, it has to pay for the wrapping paper and ribbon. It also has to pay for the wages of the employee who does the wrapping. Allowing customers to return goods for exchange or refund is another example. This takes the time of the sale workers and stockroom clerks. Any credit services that marketers c cost money too. Whenever the customer can buy now and pay later, the marketer has extra bookkeeping expenses. And, there are always a certain number of people who don't pay their bills. This represents a complete loss to the marketer. Allowing credit also ties up some of the marketer's money, which may be needed for other purposes.

Another service that is expensive is waiting on customers. As a way of cutting down on this expense, many stores have turned to **self-service.** This is a system whereby the customer walks around the store selecting items and then takes them to a checkout counter where a clerk figures out how much the customer owes. Self-service works well for many kinds of items. But the more decisions the customer has to make about the material, color, style, possible uses, quality, and price of the item, the more help the customer needs from a salesworker.

There are other services that marketers may be expected to give. For example, salesworkers in camera shops are expected to take the time to give advice on how to take better pictures. Furniture stores hire professional decorators to give customers advice on styles and colors. Wholesalers serve their retailer customers by advising them about store layout and management, providing advertising and display materials, and running training programs for the retailers' employees.

ALLOWING FOR SPOILAGE AND SHOPLIFTING. There are some products, such as fresh fruits and vegetables, milk, and eggs, that can spoil on the way from producer to consumer. The marketers who handle

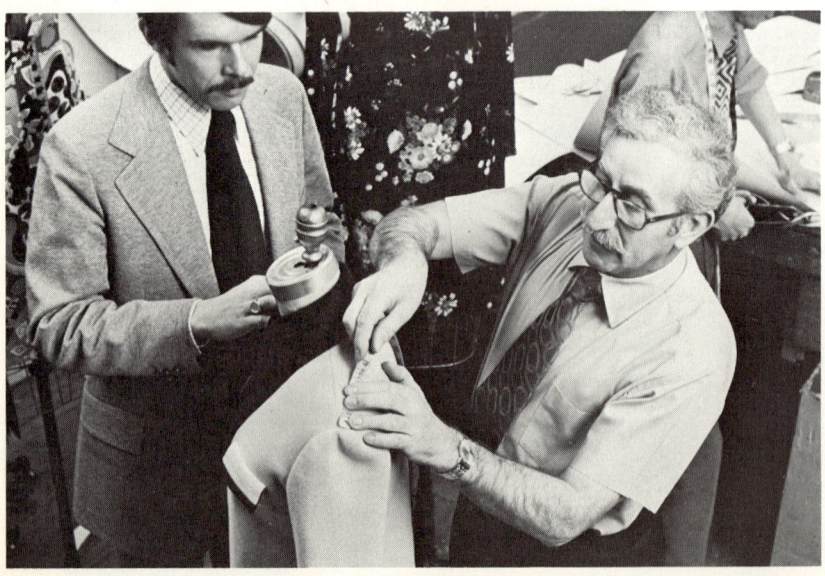

Many clothing stores are expected to offer alterations services. (*Courtesy Montgomery Ward*)

such products have to allow for spoilage when estimating expenses.

Another kind of loss that is becoming increasingly serious for retailers is **shoplifting**. This word, which means stealing goods from a store, has always been a part of the retailer's vocabulary. But, in recent years, what used to be a problem has become a crisis. Shoplifting is done by professional thieves, by people who steal because they are mentally ill, and sometimes by the store's own employees. It is also done by people who just want to see whether they can get away with it. For these people, "ripping off" the local storekeepers has become a game. In the end, this is a very expensive thrill. It results in much higher prices for the consumer because the retailers have to charge more in order to make up for their losses.

PROMOTING SALES. No matter how good a marketing business may be in every other way, it will grind to a halt if there aren't any customers. This is why advertising, display, and public relations belong on the list of necessary expenses for every marketing business, large or small. Marketers use sales promotion to get customers interested, to persuade them to buy, and to make them want to come back. Many marketers consider service to the community as sales promotion in the larger sense, in the belief that what is good for the community is good for business. This takes the form of contributions of time, materials, and money to support community projects.

PAYING TAXES. A **tax** is an amount of money that the government requires individuals to pay in exchange for governmental services. Tax money is used by local, state, and federal governments for such purposes as providing fire and police protection; maintaining roads, schools, and parks; and assisting people who are in need. When you pay taxes, you are "buying" your share of these and other services.

Taxes affect marketers in two ways. First, they have to pay taxes themselves. There are taxes on any land or buildings owned by the business. In many states, there is a tax on furniture and equipment. Some businesses must pay an income tax. Each business is also responsible for half of the social security tax paid on employees' wages and salaries.

Second, many owners of marketing businesses have to act as collection agencies for the government, besides paying taxes themselves. They have to collect the employee's half of the social security tax. They also have to help collect the federal tax on their employees' individual incomes. They do this by withholding a percentage of each employee's paycheck. The employer is responsible for sending this money to the government periodically. Marketers also collect the sales taxes that are required in many states and cities. There are some special taxes that apply to specific businesses. For example, there are excise taxes on gasoline, part of which goes to the state and part to the federal government. There are also excise taxes on cigarettes, alcoholic beverages, and telephone calls.

Keeping track of the money that is owed in taxes is a major job in every marketing business. It requires detailed recordkeeping, which takes time and is therefore expensive.

How Profits Can Be Increased

When you think about how many expenses marketers have, you can understand that making a profit is not an easy matter. And yet there must be profits if the business is to survive. Profits are even more necessary if the business is to grow. As an example, let's say that two partners open a store that sells small appliances at a discount. First they use their profits to increase the size of their store. Then they find that they have enough money to handle large appliances. In a few years, their profits enable them to open a second store, and then a third. This growth, which would have been impossible without profit, doesn't just benefit the partners. It means that more people can enjoy the low prices and convenience that the stores offer. The growth also means more jobs for more people, because all three stores must have workers.

Marketers don't have to be convinced of the importance of profits. But they do have to think about the three ways in which they can increase their profits: raising prices, increasing sales, and cutting expenses.

RAISING PRICES. Why should marketers ever have to lose money? When they see that their income is too low, why can't they just raise their prices? There are certainly many times when this happens. But there are also times when it is not possible to raise prices. One reason for this is competition for the consumer's dollars. This competition is not just from companies selling the same product but also from companies that sell other products that consumers might consider to be substitutes. For example, a motion picture theater and a skating rink in the same town would be competing to answer the consumer's recreational needs and would have to worry about each other's prices.

Marketers also sometimes have to face the problem of governmental controls on prices. For example, the prices that transportation companies can charge are controlled by the government. Also, in periods of inflation, the government sometimes orders a "price freeze," which means that prices are fixed at their current levels and cannot be raised. In some situations, the government may even order a "price rollback," which means that prices must be returned to an earlier lower level.

Still another factor that complicates pricing is consumer resistance to high prices. When consumers think that prices are too high, they can

In 1972, consumers demonstrated their resistance to high meat prices by staging a boycott. (*United Press International Photo*)

refuse to buy altogether. When a lot of consumers do this at the same time, there is less demand, and that pushes prices down.

These pressures on prices mean that marketers have to find other ways of increasing their profits.

INCREASING SALES. Another way of increasing income is to sell more goods or services. This will increase some expenses. For example, if you sell 200 sweaters instead of 100, you have to buy 200 instead of 100 from your supplier. But there are also many expenses that will stay the same. Costs for rent, electricity, interest on loans, and advertising, for example, will not change. This means that your total income will increase more than your total expenses.

When you can sell additional goods or services to the same customer, you can also save on labor costs. This may mean selling a larger quantity of the same item—three stereo tapes instead of one. Or it may mean reminding customers of other things that they might need. When a customer has selected a shirt, the salesworker suggests some ties. The furniture salesworker, having sold a desk, suggests a chair.

As a marketer, you can also increase sales by stocking items that have a "fast turnover," which means that they sell very quickly and thus make room for new items and more sales.

CUTTING EXPENSES. Another possible way of increasing profits is by decreasing expenses. When costs are rising throughout the whole economy, as they have been doing in our country in recent years, this can be very difficult. But it is important that the marketer try to reduce costs wherever possible. Probably the most important way of doing this is by reducing labor costs. This does not mean cutting wages. But it does mean not hiring two workers to do the work of one.

Take-home pay is gross pay after deductions are made for income tax, social security, and any fringe benefits.

It is a curious fact that many workers who would not steal as much as a postage stamp from their employers will steal time. Ten minutes late in the morning, five minutes late after lunch, and fifteen minutes spent watching the clock at the end of the day, five days a week—that adds up to two and a half hours a week. In a month's time, that amounts to more than a full day's pay—for nothing! If this same worker makes a habit of standing around during the day, the employer is being cheated even more. As costs climb, marketers will be less and less able to bear the expense of unproductive workers.

UNDERSTANDING YOUR PAYCHECK

Suppose that George Parnelli takes a part-time job in a retail store, doing odd jobs. He is told what his hourly rate of pay will be. He expects his first paycheck to be for an amount of money that equals his hourly rate multiplied by the number of hours that he worked. But when he gets his check, he finds that the amount is less than he expected. George's **gross pay,** which is the total amount of money that he earned, does equal the hourly rate times the number of hours. But George's **take-home pay** is different. This is gross pay minus all payroll deductions. George's share of the social security tax has been deducted from the paycheck. George's employer has also withheld money to pay George's federal income tax.

George's paycheck is a simple one. In some states, the employer also has to withhold money as insurance to pay workers if they become unemployed or disabled. Other deductions that may come out of paychecks are payments for health or life insurance and pension plans. In some companies, the employees may ask to have the company put a certain amount of money into a savings plan. Sometimes union dues may also be deducted.

Your take-home pay represents the amount of money that you can actually spend on things. But when you are thinking about what your "profit" is for the amount of work you have done, you have to consider all the fringe benefits of your job, as well as your actual pay.

- **BUILDING YOUR MARKETING VOCABULARY**

Define each of the following terms and then use each one in a sentence.

discount	interest	shipping charge
expenses	labor union	shoplifting
gross pay	self-service	take-home pay
income	selling price	tax

- **UNDERSTANDING WHAT YOU HAVE READ**

1. Explain why a marketer who buys a product for 50 cents and sells it for one dollar has not made a 50-cent profit.
2. Do people all think alike about prices? In other words, is everyone interested in paying the lowest price possible? Explain your answer.
3. Under what circumstances is it necessary for customers to be helped by salespeople?
4. Explain what shoplifting and unproductive work habits have in common.
5. Explain why marketers can't always raise their prices as a way of increasing profits.
6. Why is increasing sales an effective way of increasing profits?

- **APPLYING WHAT YOU HAVE LEARNED**

1. Mary and Ralph Engels have rented space and are planning to open a clothing store. They plan to hire one person to help them. Make a list of ten specific expenses that Mary and Ralph will have. List more if you can.
2. Write a paragraph explaining the following sentence: "When you work in marketing, it is the customer who pays your salary."

part 16 General Business Organization

After reading Part 16, you will be able—
- To define the various ways in which businesses can be owned.
- To define the various ways in which businesses can be affiliated.
- To assist in a class project to report on how the businesses in your area are owned and affiliated.

There are some terms that you have probably heard over and over without knowing what they really mean. For example, your family may buy food from a "chain store." You see newspaper articles about "corporations." Someone you know may be a "partner" in a business. And your town may have several automobile "dealers." These terms have to do with the various ways in which marketing businesses can be organized. This is a subject that you can't just "sort of" understand if you are going to work in marketing. The working conditions and opportunities can be quite different in different kinds of business organizations. So in order to make decisions about where you want to work, you must know about the ways businesses can be organized.

HOW BUSINESSES ARE OWNED

As you know, businesses in a modified free-enterprise system are privately owned, rather than being owned by the government. But this does not mean that they are all owned in exactly the same way. Some businesses are sole proprietorships. There are also partnerships, corporations, and cooperatives. How do people who want to start businesses decide among these four forms of ownership? To answer this question, let's see how each one works.

Sole Proprietorships

When a business is owned by one person, it is called a **sole proprietorship.** This is the oldest and simplest way to run a business. If you look around the area where your family shops, you will see many small stores that are examples of sole proprietorships. You will also see many small service businesses, such as beauty salons, barbershops, shoe repair shops, hand laundries, dry cleaners, eating places, and

When you are the owner of a sole proprietorship, you can take personal pride in the success of the business. (*Courtesy Manhattan Savings Bank*)

small motels. Sole proprietorships are the way the majority of businesses in this country are owned.

Of the four forms of ownership, sole proprietorships are the easiest to start. They are also the easiest to stop, since an owner may decide to sell or dissolve the business at any time. But probably their main advantage is that they allow people to work for themselves. If you are a sole proprietor, you are your own boss. You can make all the decisions and do everything your own way. And you can collect all the profits. However, in sole proprietorships, you also have all the responsibility. You have to raise all the money on your own. You have to know everything about running the business. Also, you are personally liable for the debts of the business. ("Liable," in this sense, means legally responsible.) If the business fails, you will have to pay all the debts. This may mean using not only any money that is left in the business, but also your own personal money and belongings.

Partnerships

A **partnership** is a business that is owned by two or more people. It works much like a sole proprietorship except that the responsibilities for the business can be shared. When they start the business, the

Two people may have skills that complement each other and by joining forces may begin a successful business partnership.

partners agree on how much money each person has to put into the business, how the profits will be divided, and what duties each person will have. Sometimes they do this with a "gentlemen's agreement," which means that they just shake hands on it. But it is wiser to have a written agreement so there can be no misunderstanding. You will find many examples of partnerships in your community.

This can be a very effective way to run a business. It is often easier for two or more people to raise money than it is for one person. Managing the business may also be easier, because the partners may have special abilities that complement each other. For example, one partner may know a lot about buying, selling, and sales promotion. The other may be very good at handling the finances and records.

But there are also some disadvantages to partnerships. All decisions should be made by mutual agreement, and that can be difficult. If one partner goes ahead and makes a decision without discussing it with the other partners beforehand, the other partners are just as responsible for it as they would be if they had helped make the decision. If one partner cheats or steals, the other partners are also responsible for that. If the business fails, the partners are all personally liable for the debts, just as the sole proprietor is. If one partner has no money, the other partners must pay that person's share of the debts as well as their own shares.

Corporations

Before you can understand the definition of a corporation, you have to know some facts about how corporations are set up. A corporation is more difficult to start than a sole proprietorship or partnership. This is because a corporation has to obtain permission to operate from the state in which it is located or, in the case of banks, from the federal government. We say that the government "charters" the corporation. Once the corporation is chartered, it begins to sell shares in the business, which are called shares of stock. The people who buy shares of stock in a corporation are called **stockholders** or shareholders. They are the owners of the corporation.

The corporation is managed by a board of directors. The members of this board are elected by the stockholders, on the basis of one vote for each share of stock they own. This means that the more shares of stock a person owns, the more control that person has over the management of the corporation. Profits are divided in the same way, according to the number of shares that are owned by each individual.

Often when people think of corporations, they think only of the very large, nationally known ones, such as the Exxon Corporation or the International Telephone & Telegraph Corporation (ITT). But corporations come in all sizes. There are many small businesses that are incorporated. These have only a few stockholders instead of tens of thousands of stockholders as the big corporations do. The stockholders in small corporations elect themselves to serve on the board of directors.

Small companies choose this form of business, even though it is more rigid than a sole proprietorship or a partnership, for one main reason. As the owners of the corporation, stockholders are not personally liable for the expenses of the business. Neither are the members of the board of directors. This is because the corporation itself is considered to be a legal person—that is, it is regarded, for legal purposes, as separate and apart from the people who own it. This means that the corporation itself is legally responsible for its own actions and affairs. The stockholders can lose the money they have invested in the corporation, but none of their personal money or belongings can be taken from them to pay the corporation's debts.

Another major advantage of the corporation is that the stockholders can sell their shares at any time. This makes people more willing to invest in stocks. The corporation gives average people the opportunity

At a stockholders' meeting, people who own shares of stock in the corporation assemble to hear reports on the corporation's activities and to ask questions of the board of directors. (*Courtesy Xerox Corporation*)

to share in the ownership of the country's largest and most important businesses. At the same time, the corporation benefits from this pooling of money from a wide group of people. The enormous sums of money that such businesses as airlines, electric companies, television networks, and large manufacturing companies need to do their job could not be gathered in any other way.

The corporation does have some disadvantages. It is much more closely supervised by the government than either a sole proprietorship or partnership. Also, its profits are taxed twice. Because the corporation is considered to be a person, it has to pay an income tax on its profits. Then when the stockholders get their share of the profits, they have to pay tax again on their personal income tax returns. However, these disadvantages clearly do not outweigh the advantages of this form of ownership for many businesses.

To summarize our discussion about corporations, we can say that a **corporation** is a business organization owned by its stockholders and chartered by government to act as a legal person.

Cooperatives

Another form of business ownership, the cooperative, is similar to the corporation in many ways. The cooperative also has to be chartered by the state in which it is located. It also raises money by selling shares of stock, and it has an elected board of directors. However, the people who buy shares of stock in a cooperative are called **members** instead of stockholders. Each member has only one vote, no matter how many shares of stock each individual owns. The cooperative's profits, instead of being related to the number of shares held, are divided according to the amount of business that each member does with the cooperative. For example, if you belong to a consumer cooperative that operates a food store, your profit will be paid on the basis of your total food purchases. Membership in such a cooperative is a way of lowering food costs, because the consumers who are members receive a share of the cooperative's profits.

There are also cooperatives that have been organized by industrial consumers. For example, a group of farmers may own a cooperative, so that they can buy seeds, fertilizer, and livestock feed. Other cooperatives act as assemblers, gathering together the products of the farmer members and then handling the marketing problems. A well-known example of this kind of cooperative is Sunkist Growers, Inc., which sells the oranges and lemons of many growers.

Thus, a **cooperative** can be defined as a business organization owned by the people who use its services and operated for their benefit. Today, only a small number of the total businesses in the country are organized as cooperatives, but their number is growing.

HOW MARKETING BUSINESSES ARE AFFILIATED

McDonald's famous hamburgers and french fries are sold in more than 3,300 fast-food restaurants in all 50 states, Puerto Rico, Guam, the Virgin Islands, Canada, Australia, Japan, West Germany, and the Netherlands. All the McDonald's restaurants are obviously related to each other, but how? How are the 1,700 J. C. Penney Company stores all across the country related?

We can answer these questions by looking at six of the ways in which marketing businesses can be set up: (1) as independents, (2) as corporate chains, (3) as cooperative chains, (4) as voluntary chains, (5) as franchised chains, and (6) as franchised dealerships.

Independents

When a marketing business is an **independent,** it has no connection with any other business. Independents can be any size. For example, there are large department stores, hotels, and wholesale establishments

Any business can be organized as a cooperative. This is a bicycle repair co-op, where members may bring their bikes for adjustment and repair. (Daniel S. Brody/Editorial Photocolor Archives)

that are independent businesses. But the greatest number of independents are small businesses that employ only a few people. Independent marketers usually own only one unit—one store, one motel, one restaurant. But there are some marketers who own several units (such as Harry who owned the food stores mentioned above). In this case, we speak of "multiunit independents."

Corporate Chains

When a marketing business has a number of units that are owned and operated from a central headquarters, it is called a **corporate chain.** The J. C. Penney Company is an example of a corporate chain. So are the Hilton Hotels Corporation and the F. W. Woolworth Company. There is no hard and fast rule about how many units make a chain. But the number that is often given is 11. There are "local chains," which are found in just one part of the country. Then there are "sectional chains," which cover a bigger part of the country. Finally there are the really large chains, the "national chains," which cover the whole country.

The main advantage of corporate chains has been their ability to keep their costs down. The buying for all the units is done from the central headquarters by highly trained specialists who know how to get the best buys. Because such large quantities of goods can be bought and shipped at one time, corporate chains save money and can pass these savings along to their customers. There are further savings because much of the advertising and sales promotion work is done centrally. Money is also saved by standardizing the way that the individual units are run.

Because of the quantity of goods that they buy, most of the large corporate chains deal directly with the producers. They then set up wholesaling warehouses where these large quantities of goods can be stored and broken down into smaller quantities to be shipped to the individual units as they are needed. Besides performing the wholesaling function in this way, some large corporate chains also have manufacturing divisions. For example, the Great Atlantic and Pacific Tea Company (A&P) owns and operates a bakery division that produces baked goods that are sold under the Jane Parker label.

Cooperative Chains

To get some of the buying advantages that the corporate chains enjoy, independent store owners sometimes form wholesaling cooperatives. The storekeeper members of the cooperative can lower their costs, and hence their prices, by buying through the cooperative. The members' stores are said to be a **cooperative chain.** This can be defined as an association of independent retailers who form a wholesaling cooperative for their own benefit. Sometimes the members of a cooperative chain use the same name and make their stores look alike so that people think they are chain stores. In other cases, they keep their separate identities.

The majority of cooperative chains have been formed by food stores. But they can also be found among drug, hardware, and stationery stores. An example of a cooperative chain is Certified Grocers.

Voluntary Chains

Another way of meeting chain store competition starts with the wholesaler, who offers to act as the supplier for independent retailers. The retailers are asked to sign an agreement to this effect. In exchange, they receive many of the advantages that chain store managers enjoy. For example, they get lower prices, advice on how to solve the problems of running the store, and help with sales promotion. This kind of setup is called a **voluntary chain.** It can be defined as an association of independent retailers who have agreed to buy from one wholesaler as a way of lowering their costs and increasing their efficiency. The retailers in a voluntary chain identify themselves with the group by using the chain's name and by making the stores look alike. Because of this, many people think that these stores are part of corporate chains. Examples of voluntary chains are Ben Franklin Stores, which are variety stores, and Independent Grocers of America (IGA).

Franchised Chains

A variation of the voluntary chain is franchising, which has been spreading at an extraordinary rate in recent years. Franchising is another way for people to enjoy the advantages of working for themselves while cutting down on the risks. In franchising, there is a parent company called the "franchisor," who is either a manufacturer or a wholesaling middleman. The franchisor grants an individual owner, called the "franchisee," the right to market whatever the parent company is selling. This may be a line of products or any one of a wide variety of personal or business services, including food service, motels, car and rental equipment, laundries, dry cleaners, and bookkeeping and employment services. Examples of such businesses are Baskin-Robbins, Inc., Travelodge International, Inc., Budget Rent A Car Corporation of America, and H & R Block, Inc.

The franchisor and the franchisee have an agreement that spells out exactly what their responsibilities are to each other. These agreements vary a great deal, according to what is being sold. The franchisee is usually expected to buy from the franchisor the products to be sold or the supplies used in producing the service. The franchisee is also expected to run the business according to the parent company's policies. This usually means attending a training course to learn these policies.

In return, the franchisee gets to use the company name and symbols (McDonald's golden arches, for example) and the right to market in a certain area. This right is usually "exclusive," meaning that no one else can market in the same area. The franchisee gets the benefit of the advertising and sales promotion carried out by the parent company. The franchisee may also get help with training employees, recordkeeping and management problems and sometimes can even borrow money from the franchisor to get started or to expand.

To sum up, we can say that a **franchised chain** is a group of independently owned businesses that have been given the right to market the products, services, or methods of a particular company in a given regional area.

Franchised Dealerships

There is one more variation of the voluntary chain and franchise ideas that you should know about. This is a system used by manufacturers as a way of making sure that their products will be marketed as they want them to be. The exclusive right to market the manufacturer's product

The owners of franchised businesses are expected to run their businesses according to guidelines established by the parent company. (*Courtesy Baskin-Robbins*)

in a certain area is given to marketers, called "dealers," who are in business for themselves. The correct marketing term for such a dealer is "franchised dealer." The manufacturer and the dealer have an agreement that states what is expected of each one.

Some products that are sold in this way are automobiles, trucks, and farm equipment. The manufacturer gives the dealer the kinds of help that all franchisors give, including the right to use the manufacturer's name and trademark, training courses, and management help. In return, the dealers have to run their businesses in line with the manufacturer's policies. This system is called a **franchised dealership.** It can be defined as an agreement in which a marketer is given exclusive rights to handle a specific manufacturer's product in a given area in exchange for following the marketer's policies. Examples of companies that offer franchised dealerships are General Motors, Mack Trucks, and International Harvester.

- **BUILDING YOUR MARKETING VOCABULARY**

Define each of the following terms and then use each one in a sentence.

cooperative	franchised chain	partnership
cooperative chain	franchised dealership	sole proprietorship
corporate chain	independent	stockholder
corporation	member	voluntary chain

- **UNDERSTANDING WHAT YOU HAVE READ**
    1. If you are a sole proprietor, who is your boss?
    2. If one person in a partnership makes a decision without consulting the other partners, are the other partners legally responsible for it?
    3. How can one person gain control over the management of a corporation?
    4. Why does a corporation have to pay an income tax on its profits?
    5. How many votes does a member of a cooperative have?
    6. What is a "multiunit independent"?
    7. Name five ways in which a franchisee may be helped by a franchisor.

- **APPLYING WHAT YOU HAVE LEARNED**
    1. Rule a form like the one below. In the first column, copy the following list of conditions: (a) personal liability, (b) profits divided according to number of shares, (c) profits taxed twice, (d) owned by stockholders, (e) owned by members, (f) decisions made by one person, (g) easiest to start and stop, (h) chartered by the state, (i) profits distributed by amount of business, and (j) elected board of directors. Place a check mark in the appropriate column to indicate the form of ownership to which the condition applies. You may check more than one if necessary.

CONDITION	SOLE PROPRIE-TORSHIP	PARTNER-SHIP	CORPOR-ATION	COOPER-ATIVE
Example: Personal liability	✔	✔		

    2. Assist in a class project to report on how the businesses in your area are owned and affiliated by taking the following steps:
        a. Agree with your class on what "your area" means. You may want to do just one major shopping district or center.
        b. Find out the names of the businesses in your agreed-upon area.
        c. Assign class members to work in pairs, visiting one or more businesses as needed, to ask each manager to explain how the business is owned and how it is affiliated with other businesses.
        d. Divide a bulletin board into ten sections corresponding to the ten ways in which businesses can be owned and affiliated. Put the name of each business on the bulletin board in two places, one to indicate how it is owned and one to indicate how it is affiliated.
        e. Summarize what the bulletin board shows in a class discussion.

Marketing Management

part 17

After reading Part 17, you will be able—
- To explain how making careful plans for the business in advance helps the marketing manager.
- To identify the five main areas into which marketers can group their individual tasks.
- To explain how a manager handles supervisory duties as a business expands and more workers are hired.
- To assist in a class project to draw a chart of the organizational plan of your school.

Let's suppose that you are a DECA member. You are asked to be in charge of refreshments for the coming year's meetings. In doing this job, you are going to have to make very careful plans about what refreshments to serve, where to get them, how to pay for them, when and how to serve them, and how to handle the cleaning up. You also have to decide whether you need help. If so, how many people do you need, what do you want them to do, and how can you be sure that you can count on them? If someone promises to bring cookies to a meeting and doesn't, you will be responsible. That goes along with being in charge.

By doing this job, or by holding any DECA office, you are getting direct, personal experience in a very important subject—management. You are learning how to look at a large job and see its parts so that you can make workable plans for getting everything done. You are also learning how to follow through on those plans so that the work actually gets done. Learning these management skills can help you in many ways in your personal life. Whether you are baby-sitting, going on a trip, or working on a long-term homework project, you can do a better job if you put yourself in charge instead of just letting things happen.

In the business world, the subject of management is even more important. As a way of defining **business management,** we can say that it is the process of planning, carrying out, and being responsible for the affairs of an individual business. The number of businesses that fail every year tells us that this is not always handled successfully. These

Creating an image for a business involves many things. These two stores sell the same general type of merchandise and appeal to the same age group. But how do their images differ? (ABOVE *photographed by Fern Urquhart-Logan at Bergdorf Goodman, On the Plaza in New York City;* BELOW *United Press International Photo*)

176 • UNIT 3 • PREPARING FOR A CAREER IN MARKETING

failures show that people should not go into business for themselves unless they understand what management is all about.

At the same time, a knowledge of the principles of marketing can help you even if you have no desire to work on the management level. When you understand the larger picture and know what the manager's problems are, you can be a much more effective employee. By making the manager's work easier, you make your own job much more secure.

When businesses are very competitive, it is especially important that management problems be handled skillfully. To be successful, marketers have to learn that the time to start solving the day-by-day problems of the business is before they come up. By making careful plans in advance, marketing managers can narrow down the many alternatives that they would otherwise be faced with. Because the planning that marketing managers have to do is so important, we are going to look at it from two different angles—planning an image for the business and planning how to do the work.

PLANNING AN IMAGE FOR THE BUSINESS

Let's say that you have decided what general kind of business you want to open—a bookstore, package delivery service, or whatever. You still have to define exactly what kind of business this is going to be and, equally important, what it isn't going to be. When you have a clear picture of what the business is trying to accomplish, you have guidelines for action. This means that each of the many problems that come up in a day's time does not have to be decided as though it were a completely separate problem.

When marketers are planning their businesses, they know that their success depends on pleasing the customers. But customers come in all ages and sizes, with different needs, wants, values, tastes, and amounts of money to spend. Because there are so many different kinds of people, very few marketers try to please them all. Instead they try to figure out what group of people they want to attract as customers. Then they set up their businesses according to what they think those customers will want. This is an important step, because no marketer has unlimited resources. Each business has limits of either space, money, time, or all three. So marketers have to try to make their resources count. They do this by concentrating their efforts in the areas that are most likely to win customer approval.

We are going to look now at four of the major areas that marketers have to think about in setting up their businesses: (1) planning what to sell, (2) planning what customer services to offer, (3) setting up a place of business, and (4) choosing employees who fit in. It is important to realize that no two marketers are going to make these plans in exactly the same way. There are so many different possibilities that no two businesses are ever exactly alike. Each one has a personality, or "image," all its own, just as people do.

Planning What to Sell

As soon as the type of business is decided on, the marketer has general guidelines about what to sell. For example, a small stationery store across the street from a school is going to sell school supplies and school-related items. But the stationery store can't sell every single stationery product that is available.

Obviously general guidelines aren't enough. To be able to narrow down the choices, each marketer needs definite plans about the specific kinds of merchandise to be sold, as well as the quality and price range of these items. To see why it is important for each marketer to think this through, ask yourself whether the stationery store near the school should try to sell $30 gold pens or plastic ones for under $1. Would you choose expensive leather notebooks for this store or cloth-covered notebooks? The gold pens and leather notebooks can be sold easily, but in another store, in a different place, and with different customers.

It is also important for service businesses to define exactly what they are going to sell. As an example of this, the policy of one beauty salon or barbershop might be to serve people who want to be ahead of the times and don't mind paying for it. Others might be aimed at people who are happy with the established styles and don't want to spend a lot of money, or people who want something in between. This same kind of thing is true of restaurants, movie theaters, and other service businesses. In each case, specific decisions must be made about what will be sold.

Planning What Customer Services to Offer

Marketers must make definite plans about the customer services that they are and are not going to offer. These plans should cover everything from how much sales help customers will be given to what kinds of guarantees will be offered.

The kinds of customer services that the marketer is expected to offer depend on the prices the business charges for goods. For example, there are retail stores that sell merchandise at reduced prices; these are called **discount stores**. These stores can afford to do this because they are willing to accept less profit on each item they sell. They believe that, in the end, they can make as much or more money by selling a lot of items at a low profit as they can by selling fewer

Tell me a story. Make me giggle. Make me laugh.

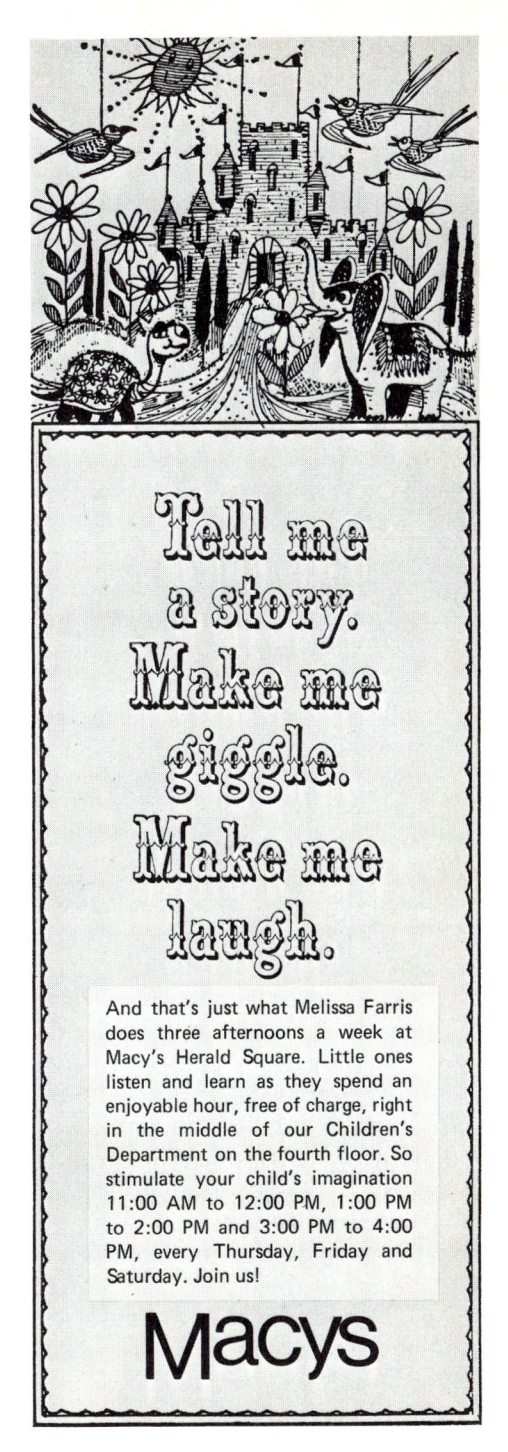

And that's just what Melissa Farris does three afternoons a week at Macy's Herald Square. Little ones listen and learn as they spend an enjoyable hour, free of charge, right in the middle of our Children's Department on the fourth floor. So stimulate your child's imagination 11:00 AM to 12:00 PM, 1:00 PM to 2:00 PM and 3:00 PM to 4:00 PM, every Thursday, Friday and Saturday. Join us!

Macys

What kind of image is this department store trying to create by offering a storytelling hour for children?
(Courtesy Macy's, New York)

items at a higher profit. To make this idea work, they also have to keep their expenses down. Price-conscious customers recognize this fact and are willing to accept fewer customer services in exchange for the lower prices.

However, marketing businesses don't eliminate services strictly on the basis of price. They also have to consider each service in terms of the amount of business it will bring in. Thus many discount stores allow their customers to charge their purchases and pay for them at the end of the month. Offering customer credit is very expensive for a business because charge accounts require a great deal of clerical work. But many discount stores have found that they sell more merchandise when they offer charge accounts. This increased business makes the expense worthwhile.

In choosing the customer services that they will offer, marketers are also guided by the image that they are trying to create in the customer's mind. For example, a small store that wants to be thought of as very friendly might serve coffee, giving the customers the feeling that they are welcome guests. A large store that wants to be thought of as a family shopping center might offer a playroom where children may be left while the parents shop. A hotel that wants to be thought of as offering every comfort might put a small ice-making machine in each room. In many cases, these special services cost very little in relation to the goodwill that they create.

Setting Up a Place of Business

The physical setup of the business—that is, the place where the business is carried out—is another factor in the personality of the business. The location of the business, its outside appearance, the arrangement of space inside, and the furnishings all require very careful planning. It is important to realize that these are not separate matters. They depend not only on each other but also on the kinds of merchandise the business will sell and the kinds of customer services it will offer. For example, suppose that you want to open a jewelry store in a small mining town. In this case, the location tells you that you should not plan to sell the most expensive jewelry you can find. Suppose, however, that your main goal is to sell very expensive jewelry. In this case, you have to choose a location that makes your goal possible, such as the fashionable shopping district of a large city.

The plans for the place of business should be consistent, so that they add to the image of the business rather than work against it. The expensive jewelry store needs a different kind of storefront and different furnishings than an appliance store that emphasizes low prices. The store that has a self-service policy needs a different layout than a

The most carefully thought-out store image can be destroyed if the employees who work there do not fit in.

store where customers are waited on. (**Layout** refers to the way the inside space of a place of business is arranged.) When careful plans are made to coordinate the design of the store with the kind of business to be carried on, there is a much greater chance for success.

Choosing Employees Who Fit In

By the time all the decisions we have discussed so far have been made, the marketer has come up with a blend of qualities that make the business unique. In order to sell this special blend to the customers, the marketer needs employees who can bring the image of the business to life.

To see why this is important, think about a "mod" clothing store. Wouldn't a salesworker who dresses conservatively destroy the image that the manager is trying to create? Managers know that the public is apt to think of the employees and the business as being one and the same. This is why it is so important to find employees who fit in.

PART 17 • MARKETING MANAGEMENT • 181

PLANNING HOW TO DO THE WORK

Think for a minute about a baseball game. One team is at bat, and the other team has nine players on the field. The players on the field want to prevent the other team from making any runs. But now the question is, what is the best way to go about this? Do you let the nine players figure it out on their own? Or do you give each one a specific area of responsibility? By assigning these players to the jobs of pitcher, catcher, and shortstop, as well as first, second, and third baseman and right, center, and left fielders, you can make sure that the whole field is covered in the most efficient way.

This same kind of thing is true in marketing businesses. If the business is to "win," the question of who is to be responsible for each job must be thought through very carefully. An organizational plan must be worked out that spells out the answer to this very important question. Otherwise some jobs will be repeated unnecessarily, and others won't be done at all. Working out this organizational plan means first listing all the tasks that have to be done and then deciding how to divide the responsibilities.

Listing the Tasks to Be Done

Because marketing businesses are so different, the specific tasks that have to be done will vary a great deal from business to business. However, marketers do find that it is possible to group their tasks into five main areas: (1) buying and selling goods (or producing and selling services), (2) maintaining the place of business, (3) handling personnel problems, (4) promoting sales, and (5) controlling the finances. Each of

Successful marketers must divide their attention among all five of the main marketing areas, without losing control of any one of them.

these five areas is equally important to the success of the business. This means that the marketing manager, like a juggler, has to keep all five areas going at once, without losing control of any of them. One way to do this is to list all the individual tasks that have to be done in each of the five areas of the business, as a first step in organizing the work.

BUYING AND SELLING GOODS (PRODUCING AND SELLING SERVICES). The word used to describe all the activities in a marketing business that have to do with buying and selling goods is **merchandising.** This includes figuring out what colors and styles people will want, which new items will be popular, and which basic stock items people will go on asking for. It also includes the big question of how much to buy, as well as where to buy and how to get the best possible price.

Merchandising also includes setting prices for the goods and actually selling the goods. The merchandise has to be carried to the selling area and arranged so that it will stay clean and be easy to find. The goods on hand, which are called the **inventory,** have to be counted, and records have to be kept of what has been sold and what customers are asking for.

Service businesses don't buy and sell goods, but they have comparable problems in producing and selling the service.

MAINTAINING THE PLACE OF BUSINESS. The activities in a marketing business that have to do with maintaining the place of business are called **operations.** These activities include buying and storing the supplies that are needed to run the business and keeping the furnishings, building, grounds, and parking areas in good condition. Also included in operations is the work of **receiving.** This is the process of receiving deliveries, unpacking the goods, and checking them against the order forms to be sure that the quantity and quality are right. The goods also have to be marked or tagged with the selling price and then either stored until they are needed or sent to the selling area. Other activities that are included in operations are running the delivery service, if there is one, guarding against theft and vandalism, and handling customer complaints.

HANDLING PERSONNEL PROBLEMS. It is easy to guess what the word **personnel** means, since it has the word "person" in it. It refers to the employees of a business. Thus, personnel problems have to do with choosing the employees for the business, deciding on their rate of pay, teaching them what they need to know, and promoting them to better jobs at the right time. Personnel problems also include handling all fringe benefits and providing for the safety of the employees.

PROMOTING SALES. Every business has the problem of attracting customers and persuading them to buy. As you know, this includes advertising, display, and public relations. The specific jobs that have to be done in all three of these sales promotional activities must be carefully listed, so that no important work will be left undone.

CONTROLLING THE FINANCES. The importance of handling the financial end of the business successfully cannot be overemphasized. This includes raising the money that is needed to start the business and keep it going. It also includes setting up a **budget** for the business, which is a plan for how money is to be spent or saved. The value of setting a budget is that it gives the marketer a chance to weigh each expense against its contribution to the success of the business. Budgets allow marketers to spend their money where it will do the most good. Budgets also keep marketers from spending more money than they should. Each business also needs someone to take the responsibility for collecting the money that is owed to the business, paying the bills, and keeping all financial records.

Dividing the Responsibilities

There are marketing businesses that are run by just one person. In this case, dividing the work is not a problem. It all has to be done by the only person available to do it. But let's say that the manager (who is probably also the owner) decides to hire a helper. Then it becomes important for the manager to know what tasks the helper can take over and to tell the helper exactly what the duties of the job are. This continues to be true as more workers are needed. To be sure that all five areas of the business are adequately covered, there must be a definite plan for who does what.

Each of the workers hired relieves the manager of certain specific tasks. But having employees gives the manager a whole new task—making sure that the employees do a good job. In other words, the manager has to oversee, or "supervise," the work that each employee is doing. The purpose of this supervision is to pull together the work of all the employees so they work together as a team and the business functions smoothly as a whole.

Each new employee gives the manager more supervisory work, so that eventually the manager cannot do it all alone. At this point, the supervisory work itself must be divided up. Instead of having each employee report directly to the top manager of the business, there have to be some middle managers who can each supervise certain employees and then report to the top manager. As the business grows, the supervisory work has to be divided even more, so that there are various levels of middle management.

HOW DEPARTMENT STORES ARE ORGANIZED. As an example of how important it is to have a definite plan for dividing and supervising the work, let's think about a large department store. These stores get their name because they are divided into departments, with each department selling a different category of goods. By strict definition, a **department store** is a store with 25 or more workers that sells some items in each of the following three categories: (1) clothing for men, women, and children; (2) furniture, home furnishings, and appliances; and (3) household linens and yard goods.

Many department stores are far bigger than the above definition suggests. They may have as many as 100 different departments, selling not only a broad range of merchandise but also such services as photography, hairdressing, and watch repair. One of these stores may have as many as ten floors, cover an entire city block, and have thousands of workers. If managing the five areas of marketing businesses that we have discussed is a problem for the small marketer, think how difficult it would be in a store this size!

To stay ahead of the problems that come from its great size, a large department store makes each of the five areas into a division of the store. Then most of the jobs in the store are set up under one of these five divisions, which are called (1) merchandising, (2) operations, (3) personnel, (4) sales promotion, and (5) control. Within each of these divisions, there is a clear plan for who is responsible for performing each single task and who is responsible for supervising each level of the work.

Besides setting up the lines of authority in this way, the large department store also employs people who are highly trained specialists. These employees are called "staff specialists." Their duties are to give advice and assistance, but they don't have supervisory duties. Examples of staff specialists are marketing research experts, who study consumer buying preferences, and fashion consultants, who advise the people who do the buying on fashion trends. Staff specialists report to the top managers of the store, who are also responsible for coordinating the work of the five divisions.

HOW OTHER MARKETING BUSINESSES ARE ORGANIZED. Other large marketing businesses have different forms of organization that suit their particular way of doing business. For example, a corporate chain must set up an organizational plan that shows how each individual unit is to be run. The plan also has to show how the individual units relate to the central headquarters, and to the various regional headquarters if the chain is a large one.

Corporate chains are like department stores in that they employ staff specialists whose job it is to increase the efficiency of the whole company. This kind of organizational setup, which is called "line and staff organization," is used by many large companies. To understand this term, you must first know what "line organization" is. When you draw a chart of a line organization, it looks like a pyramid. Each worker on the bottom level reports to a specific supervisor. Each of these supervisors then reports, in turn, to a supervisor on the next highest level, and so on. Finally you get to the one person at the top who has the final responsibility. With a line and staff organization, you have the same setup, but you also have staff specialists, whose advisory work is done outside the structure of the pyramid.

Whether a given company has a line organization or a line and staff organization, the important thing is that the plan be clearly stated. A definite plan takes the guesswork and confusion out of the day-by-day operation of the business. Workers on every level can be much more effective when they know what their specific jobs are and how their jobs fit into the total plan.

- **BUILDING YOUR MARKETING VOCABULARY**

Define each of the following terms and then use each one in a sentence.

budget	inventory	personnel
business management	layout	receiving
department store	merchandising	
discount store	operations	

- **UNDERSTANDING WHAT YOU HAVE READ**

1. Is studying management a waste of time if you don't want to work on the management level? Explain your answer.
2. How does making careful plans for the business in advance help the marketing manager?
3. Identify the five main areas into which marketers can group their individual tasks.
4. Explain how a manager's work changes as the business expands and more employees are hired.
5. Explain how a line organization works. How does a line and staff organization differ from this?

- **APPLYING WHAT YOU HAVE LEARNED**

1. Visit a store in your area and take notes on (a) its location; (b) its general appearance, including the front, windows, and inside decorations and furnishings; (c) the layout; (d) the kinds of goods it carries; (e) the kinds of customer services it offers; (f) its price range; (g) the kind of people who work in the store; and (h) the kind of customer the store seems to be aiming at. Be prepared to report what you have seen to the class and discuss whether you think the business is well planned.
2. Take an active part in a class project to draw a chart of the organizational plan of your school, showing who is responsible for the various jobs and how the work is supervised.

part 18 Marketing Skills

After reading Part 18, you will be able—
- To explain why marketers have to understand buying motives.
- To list the five steps leading to a sale.
- To list five questions that you might ask a salesworker when buying a product.
- To explain why marketing workers are encouraged to think in terms of accident prevention.

In your DE and DECA work, you will have an opportunity to practice many of the skills that are part of the field of marketing. You may not have to use all of these skills directly in your own marketing career. But it is still important for you to learn as much as you can about them all. You will find that they will increase your understanding of the work that you will do and help you see how your work relates to the whole marketing process. For example, think about a person who prepares advertisements or displays. Could this person do a good job without using some of the skills involved in personal selling? Then ask yourself whether the personal salesworker could benefit from knowing what the advertising and display workers are trying to do and why. This kind of interrelationship exists all the way through marketing. Therefore, the more you know about the whole field, the better you can do in a particular job.

UNDERSTANDING WHY PEOPLE BUY

An important part of preparing for a marketing career is studying about people—how they are alike, how they are different, and why they behave as they do. It is especially important for marketers to understand what makes people decide to buy goods and services. Unless this decision to buy is made and acted on, everything that happens in marketing is pointless. This means that everyone who works in marketing has to have some knowledge of why people buy.

Basically people buy to satisfy their needs and wants. But they are limited by the amount of money that they have to spend. To figure out

People spend their discretionary income for things that bring them satisfaction and enjoyment.

how much money a person is free to spend, one must first determine how much income a person has left after paying taxes. This amount is called **disposable income.** When planning how to spend their disposable income, people generally satisfy their basic needs first. The money they have left after paying for food, shelter, clothing, transportation, and medical care is called **discretionary income.** This can be defined as the amount of money that is left to spend after a person has paid for the basic costs of living.

Discretionary income can be spent in any way the person chooses, to satisfy whatever wants the person feels most strongly about. In our society, where discretionary income has been generally high, it has become more and more difficult for many people to distinguish between what they need and what they want. But whether an item like a television set is actually needed or just wanted, the drive to acquire a television set is still strong.

The drive to satisfy needs and wants provides people with reasons for buying, which are called **buying motives.** These are the personal advantages that people expect to get from buying goods or services. Because no two people see their needs and wants in the same way, there is a wide variation in buying motives, even for the same product. For example, some people see a high-priced car as a way of looking and feeling important. This would be an "emotional" buying motive, meaning that it is based on emotions or feelings. Other people might buy the same car because they think its size and weight make it safer to drive. This would be a "rational" buying motive, because it is based on reason and logic.

Most people like to think that they are making rational choices, and they want other people to think so too. Sometimes, therefore, when their real motives are emotional, they will think up reasons that disguise this fact. This process is called **rationalizing.** Thus the person who is buying the car for status may be able to give a long list of reasons why the car is the best buy, but these are not the real reasons behind the purchase.

For years, most car makers tried to produce cars faster and cheaper. We're trying to produce them slower and better.

At one time, the assembly line seemed like a great idea. Products could be made easier. And faster. And cheaper.

But the quality of products sometimes went down with the prices. Because working on an assembly line can be monotonous. And boring. And bored people usually don't do a very good job.

That's why we've gradually been replacing the assembly line with assembly teams: small groups of just three or four people who are responsible for a particular assembly process from start to finish.

We think assembly teams will mean less absenteeism and less turnover. So we will have more experienced people on the job. People who are more involved. People who care more. It's a slower, more costly system for us, but we know it builds better cars. And that's something that's very important to us at Saab.

That's why every Saab 99 is built with front-wheel drive, rack and pinion steering, power-assisted four wheel disc brakes, and roll-cage construction.

We want to give you the kind of car that every car should be.

Saab. It's what a car should be.

There are more than 300 Saab dealers nationwide. For the name and address of the one nearest you call 1-800-243-6000 toll free. In Connecticut, call 1-800-882-6500. All Saabs have a 12 month/unlimited mileage warranty.

To what buying motives does this advertisement appeal? (*Courtesy Saab-Scania of America and Cox & Co. Advertising Inc.*)

You can begin to develop the ability to understand buying motives by thinking about what your own motives are whenever you make a purchase and by observing your friends, relatives, and other customers in stores. "People watching" is one of the best learning experiences for someone interested in marketing.

LEARNING WHAT PRODUCT KNOWLEDGE MEANS

Suppose that you are a salesworker in a camera shop. The customers expect you to be able to give them exact details about the different kinds of cameras in the store. They want to know where they are made, what they can and cannot do, what guarantees they carry, how to get them repaired if they break, what extra equipment will be needed, how much they cost, and how they compare with other cameras in the store and with all other cameras on the market. If you were selling a carpet cleaning service, the same thing would be true. The customer would expect you to know the details of the service and to be able to answer any questions.

When marketers know all the facts about the goods or services they are selling, we say that they have **product knowledge.** This knowledge is obviously essential to all salesworkers. It is also important to many other workers in marketing. This includes the people who prepare labels and design packages, advertisements, and displays. It even includes packers and shippers, because many products have special features that require special handling techniques.

To emphasize the importance of product knowledge, DECA encourages students to compete for yearly prizes by preparing merchandise information manuals. Interested students prepare notebooks giving detailed information about a specific item of merchandise, such as men's shirts or television sets, for example. The students who prepare such notebooks get valuable experience in learning where to look for information, how to select the information that applies to the merchandise, and how to organize the information.

PRACTICING PERSONAL SELLING

A knowledge of the techniques of personal selling can help you not only in marketing jobs but also in your everyday life. There are many times when you have to sell your ideas to other people. When you understand what salesworkers do, you can also do your own personal buying more wisely.

To make a sale, salesworkers have to lead the prospective customer through five steps: (1) gaining attention, (2) arousing interest, (3) building desire, (4) winning conviction, and (5) getting action. The purpose of the first step is to win the favorable and immediate attention of

ATTENTION

INTEREST

DESIRE

CONVICTION

ACTION!

To be a successful salesworker you must understand these five steps in the selling process and be able to lead a customer from the Attention step through to the Action step.

prospective customers so that they are willing to listen to what the salesworker has to say. In the next step, the salesworker tries to interest the prospect in the possible advantages of the item or service. Then the salesworker has to increase the prospect's desire to buy by clearly demonstrating those advantages. In the fourth step, the salesworker must convince the customer that buying is the right course of action by answering any objections that the customer has. Finally the salesworker has to get the customer to act on the decision to buy.

When you think about these five steps, it is easy to understand how important product knowledge is to the salesworker. You cannot demonstrate the advantages of what you are selling or answer the customer's questions unless you know what you are talking about. You also cannot sell successfully unless you have a lot of knowledge

PART 18 • MARKETING SKILLS • 191

about what people are like. You have to be willing to make a real effort to find out as much as possible about the buying motives of each particular customer. This means that every salesworker has to know how to listen and has to be sympathetic to other people's needs and wants.

If you find in your DE and DECA work that you are especially interested in personal selling, you may want to compete in the Sales Demonstration event that DECA sponsors each year. This activity is another way in which DECA encourages students to develop specific marketing skills.

DEVELOPING GOOD BUSINESS HABITS

Have you ever thought about what people mean when they say that someone is "businesslike" or that something was done in an "unbusinesslike" way? These words tell us that the business world has certain standards of behavior for the people who are part of it. If just one employee in a firm has a casual or careless approach, the whole business suffers. When you get a marketing job, you will be part of this business world. To help you fit in, your DE classes will emphasize three areas where good habits are especially important: (1) filling out forms, (2) dealing with mail, and (3) using the telephone.

Filling Out Forms

Paper work is a very important part of every marketing business. Among the many special forms that are used in marketing are:

- Sales slips given to customers in retail stores
- Order forms
- Daily, weekly, and yearly summary records
- Forms for reporting taxes

In your DE classes, you will be given many opportunities to practice filling out forms. Since the purpose of the form is to communicate, it is very important that other people be able to read what you have written. If your handwriting is not clear, you should make a habit of printing as carefully as you can. Whenever you are faced with a new form, you should read it all the way through before you start writing. When you do this, you can see what the intent of the form is and thus have a better idea of what answers are expected. You can also avoid having to erase things that you've already written.

When the form is one that you are going to use often, such as a sales slip, you must always avoid being careless. Every space is there for a purpose, so you must be sure that you fill them all in every time.

Dealing With Mail

When we speak of mail, we are talking about written materials and packages that are sent through the U.S. Postal Service. For marketing businesses, mail is a vital means of communication. It allows people to request information, apply for jobs, keep customers informed about changes in business procedures, and advertise and promote goods and services. It also allows people to order and receive goods, send and pay bills, and make complaints and receive apologies. In fact, there are many business transactions that are carried out solely through the mails. The people involved do not meet each other in any other way. This is true not only of the mail order business but also in many other instances.

Because mail plays such an important part in marketing, you will be expected to learn how to deal with it. This means, first of all, learning how to handle incoming mail. To do this, you need some knowledge of how files are set up and maintained in business offices. Each company has certain special rules. But they all depend in one way or another on putting things in alphabetical order. If you know the alphabet backward and forward, you will find that filing is easy to learn.

Handling outgoing mail includes knowing how to write effective business letters. We have already talked about the importance of this. You also have to know how to wrap packages for mailing and be familiar with postal regulations concerning the size and weight of packages. You should also know about the various ways mail can be sent.

Using the Telephone

Because the telephone is another vital means of communication for marketing businesses, it is important that you learn how to use it to the best advantage. You will have many opportunities to practice this skill in your DE classes. In the meantime, there are certain basic rules that you can begin to think about. Whether you are making the call yourself or answering it, you have to remember to be well mannered and pleasant. You should sound friendly and anxious to help, rather than hurried or angry. You should also be sure that pencil and paper are at hand, ready for any messages.

When you are receiving a call, you should answer as promptly as possible, giving the name of the company or department and your own name. This is much more businesslike and much more helpful than simply saying hello. You should make sure that you have the correct spelling and pronunciation of the caller's name and that you don't make any mistakes in taking down any other details. If you are taking an order, you have to be sure you have *all* the required information.

If the caller is asking you for information that you must leave the telephone to locate, try to judge how long this will take. If it is going to take longer than a minute or two, suggest to the caller that you call back when you have the information. People do not enjoy having to wait. But neither do they like having to keep their line open for a call that never comes, so call back as soon as possible.

If you are making the call, always think about whether the time is appropriate. Remember too that time is money and that people will appreciate it if you will get to the point of the call quickly. When the telephone is used correctly, it is an efficient, effective way of transacting business. But when a business telephone call is handled poorly, it can be a very frustrating experience.

LEARNING TO USE MACHINES AND EQUIPMENT

While marketing is essentially a people-to-people business, there are some kinds of machines and special equipment that you will become familiar with through your DE work. To give a few examples, you will learn how to use the scales that are used to weigh many products, the yardage meters that are used to measure fabrics, the machines that are used in marking goods, and other special stockroom equipment. Perhaps the most important machine that you will learn about is the cash register. There are many types of cash registers, from the very simple ones that don't do much more than hold the money to the very complex ones that are hooked up to a computer.

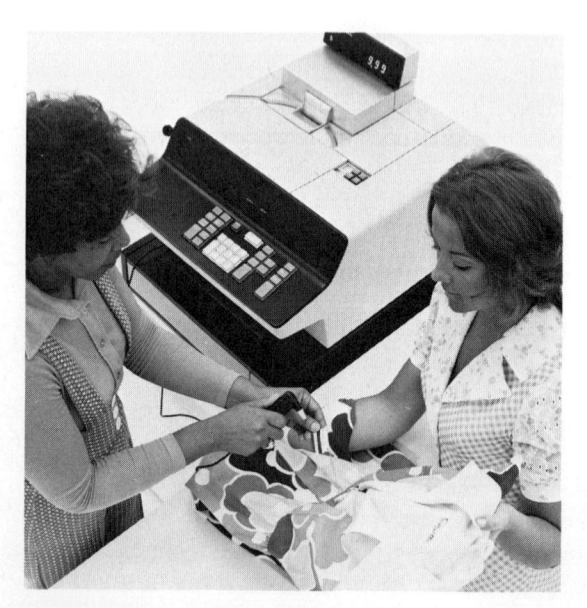

Cash registers that are hooked up to a computer that maintains sales and inventory records are being used in many retail stores today. (*Courtesy IBM*)

The special value of these new machines is that they save labor costs for the marketer, time for the consumer, and money for both of them. By relieving the marketer of tedious paper work, these machines make it possible for marketers to concentrate on those activities that involve people.

DEVELOPING A SAFETY SENSE

In a business that is as concerned with people as marketing is, it is important to have a sense of what is safe and what is not. This is necessary from your own viewpoint as a worker and also for the sake of the customers. To keep yourself safe from accidents, you should wear shoes that are comfortable and appropriate for your job. You should avoid loose clothing, especially loose sleeves, that can get caught on things.

You also have to make sure that aisles are free, so that no one can trip. If your job involves lifting, you should learn to do it so you don't strain your back. If you have to stack things up, you must make sure that they won't fall over. It is important to know where the fire exits are and how to call for help in case of fire or if anyone is hurt. It is also very helpful to know at least the basic principles of first aid.

Once an accident has occurred, it is too late to think of the ways in which it could have been prevented. In many situations, these ways are very obvious, but no one stopped to think about them. This is why your DE work will encourage you to think in terms of accident prevention in everything you do.

TRAINING IN SPECIALIZED MARKETING SKILLS

In Part 9, we noted that it is sometimes difficult for young people to know what their aptitudes are. This is why it is important for you to be able to sample some of the specialized marketing skills. Advertising, package design, display, public relations work, and marketing research are all areas of marketing that you might not think of in terms of yourself. You might not even dream that you could actually work in these areas, where so many talented people are needed.

In your DE and DECA work, you will have a chance to try your hand at actually doing some of these kinds of jobs. If you find that you have an aptitude for any one of them, you will be encouraged to concentrate your efforts in that area. DECA sponsors annual competitions in individual advertising, display, and marketing research projects. This highlights one of the main objectives of DE and DECA, to help each student become self-actualized—that is, to help students develop their own individual potentials to the fullest.

- **BUILDING YOUR MARKETING VOCABULARY**

Define each of the following terms and then use each one in a sentence.

buying motive
discretionary income
disposable income
product knowledge
rationalizing

- **UNDERSTANDING WHAT YOU HAVE READ**
  1. Explain why marketers should make an effort to understand buying motives.
  2. Suppose that two people decide to buy the same kind of car. Could their buying motives be different? Explain your answer.
  3. Explain why product knowledge is important to marketers.
  4. List the five steps leading to a sale.
  5. If you say that someone is "businesslike," what do you mean?
  6. Why is it a good idea to read a form all the way through before you start to fill it out?
  7. Explain why marketing workers are encouraged to think in terms of accident prevention.

- **APPLYING WHAT YOU HAVE LEARNED**
  1. Think of a product that you would like to buy. Make a list of at least five questions that you would ask about the product that the salesworker should be able to answer. List more than five if you can.
  2. Two students will be assigned to play the roles in each of the following situations:
     a. A customer is calling a salesworker to ask why an order promised a week ago has not yet been received.
     b. A customer is calling a store to ask if anyone found a package left on the counter.
     c. A worker in a store's delivery department is calling a customer to say when a piece of furniture will be delivered.
     d. A worker in a store that frames pictures is calling the customer to say that an order is ready to be picked up.

     After each situation, join in a class discussion of the telephone manners of the two participants.
  3. Students will be assigned to go to the school's lunchroom (or school store, if there is one) to practice using the cash register.

part 19 Cooperative Education

After reading Part 19, you will be able—
- To prepare properly for a mock interview with a marketing business of your choice.
- To participate in a mock interview.
- To list ten things that you can do to succeed in your job.

If your school's DE program includes cooperative education, you will find that this is one of the best possible ways of preparing for a career. The cooperative education program allows you to "try on" an area of marketing to see if it fits you before you have to commit yourself to it in a full-time job. Of course, it may not be possible for you to work in the exact area of marketing that you would like to be in eventually. This is especially true if your community is a small one. But your DE teacher-coordinator will make every effort to match you with the job that will interest you and give you experiences that you can easily transfer to your later work. What is most important is that you will be working under the supervision of both your DE teacher-coordinator and your employer. Together they will help you get the most out of what you are learning. They will also help you to relate your experiences in this single job to marketing as a whole.

To help you see what this experience will mean to you, we are going to discuss how you get a co-op job, what you have to bring to the job, and what your other schoolwork has to do with your DE experiences. If your school does not offer cooperative education, this information will still be useful to you. It can help you to get a job on your own and to understand what is expected of you when you work.

GETTING THE JOB
An important part of the DE teacher-coordinator's job is developing a close relationship with the marketers in the community. As you remember from Part 13, marketers are asked to give their help in many ways. This includes providing opportunities for co-op work if at all possible. The DE teacher-coordinator helps locate marketers who are

willing and able to provide jobs for cooperative education students. The teacher-coordinator then works very closely with students to match them with jobs that are appropriate to their career goals and interests.

But this is only the first part of the important process of getting a co-op job. If you are the student involved, you still have to be hired. You will have to have a face-to-face meeting with the employer, or with the personnel director if the company is a big one. The purpose of this meeting, which is called an "interview," is to give the marketer the chance to see whether or not you are suitable for the job. Even though marketers want to help the DE program, they can't afford just to throw their money away. They have to be sure that the people they hire will fit in and do a full share of the work.

In your DE program, you will be given many opportunities to practice your social skills. You will also take part in mock interviews where you practice answering the kinds of questions that employers ask. But it will still be up to you to make the real interview produce the result you want—a job. To do this successfully, you have to think about four things: (1) getting ready for the interview, (2) arriving for the interview, (3) making the interview work for you, and (4) analyzing turndowns. This will help you not only with this interview but also with all the other interviews that you will have in the course of your career. There will be many times when you will have to sell yourself to an interviewer. That's why it is so important for you to learn how to do this successfully.

Getting Ready for the Interview

Your DE teacher-coordinator may make the interview appointment for you. Or you may be asked to telephone the company and make the appointment yourself. If you have to do this, you will be grateful for the training in telephone manners that DE has given you. This phone call will give the marketer a first impression of you that may affect the interview itself.

Once the appointment is set, you should make an effort to find out as much as you can about the company. What does it sell? How is it organized? How many workers does it have? How long has it been in business? How long has it been connected with your school's DE program? Knowing the answers to questions such as these ahead of time will make you more comfortable in the interview. It will also help the interviewer know that you are interested in the company and in the job.

You should also do some thinking about yourself. Make sure that you understand why the DE teacher-coordinator selected you to apply for this particular job. How do your personal qualifications match the job? What do you think you can contribute to the company if you are hired? If you have thought this through, you will have an easier time with the interviewer's questions.

While you are thinking about yourself, you should also prepare a **personal data sheet** to give to the interviewer. This is a summary of the most important facts about a person who is applying for a job. [It is sometimes also called a resumé (reh-zoom-ay).] There is a sample personal data sheet on page 200 that will show you the kind of information that you should include. With this kind of summary in hand, the interviewer can get to the heart of the interview—that is, you—much more quickly. If the personal data sheet is going to work in your favor, it must be neatly typed with no misspellings or other mistakes.

It is important for you to decide well ahead of time what you are going to wear to the interview. This will give you time to make sure that your clothes are appropriate, clean, and in good shape. The interviewer will be spending what is really a very short time with you. Therefore, your appearance takes on an added importance. Knowing ahead of time what you are going to wear will also keep you from getting flustered by trying to make last-minute decisions.

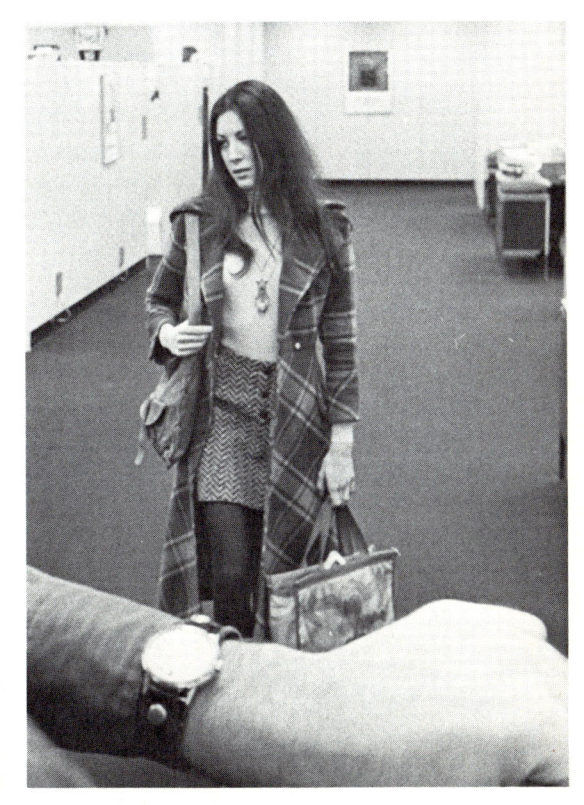

Would you be favorably impressed if this young woman were arriving for a job interview with you? (*Courtesy* Today's Secretary)

PART 19 • COOPERATIVE EDUCATION • 199

Andrew C. Masters
3476 Newcastle Road
Hamilton, Michigan 49419
(616) 555-2890

PERSONAL INFORMATION

Birth Date: August 8, 19--
Social Security Number: 385-99-7642
Health: Excellent

POSITION DESIRED

Retail salesperson

EDUCATION

Graduate of Alexander Hamilton High School, June, 19--
Business subjects studied: Marketing, salesmanship, retailing, business English, business mathematics, typewriting

WORK EXPERIENCE

The Record Hut. Salesperson-trainee during my senior year through the DE cooperative education program.

Shoppers Fare. Part-time check-out clerk during my junior year.

ACTIVITIES AND INTERESTS

Member of DECA
Member of Alexander Hamilton High School Concert Band
Hobbies: Rock music, photography
Sports: Tennis, gymnastics

REFERENCES

Mr. Jerome Klockman, Manager, The Record Hut, 1221 Main Street, Hamilton, Michigan 49499

Ms. Caroline Van Osterhoff, Manager, Shoppers Fare, Westgate Shopping Center, Hamilton, Michigan 49599

Ms. Mary Burdine, Distributive Education Teacher-Coordinator, Alexander Hamilton High School, Hamilton, Michigan 49499

One of the first steps you have to take when you are job hunting is to fill out a personal data sheet. By studying the sample printed here, you can see how this should be done.

You should also apply for a social security card if you do not already have one. Because many states have laws that govern where, how, and when young people can be employed, you may have to apply for a work permit too. Your DE teacher-coordinator will help you with both these forms.

Arriving for the Interview

You should allow yourself plenty of time to get to the interview and should arrive five to ten minutes early. No matter how much you'd like the support of a friend, you must go alone. Otherwise you give the impression that you are immature and unable to stand on your own two feet. You should give the interviewer's secretary your name and your reason for being there. The interviewer may very well ask the secretary later for an opinion of you. So while you are waiting, act as you would if the interviewer could see you.

You may be asked to fill in an application for employment before, or perhaps after, the interview. Your personal data sheet will help you do this. Besides being a way of getting information, the application is also a test to see whether you can follow directions. As with any form, you should read it all the way through before you begin writing. Then you should make every effort to be neat and to write clearly.

Making the Interview Work for You

There are two attitudes that will be especially helpful to you in an interview. The first is a positive attitude about yourself. This is much easier to come by when you know that you look your best and that you have done your homework for the interview. When you feel sure of yourself, you will have no trouble sitting still. People who are worried and nervous about what they have left undone can't do this. They have to wiggle and fidget as an outlet for their worries, which, in turn, makes the interviewer uncomfortable. The other attitude that you need is a respect for the value of the interviewer's time. Not wanting to waste time will give you a businesslike approach that will be greatly appreciated by the interviewer.

The interviewer will also appreciate being allowed to set the pace for the interview. This means that you shouldn't sit until you are invited to do so. You should answer all questions that are put to you honestly and fully. But you should also stick to the point of each question rather than rambling off in other directions. You should also be ready to respond positively when the interviewer indicates that the interview is over. You may be told immediately that the job is yours. Or you may be told that you will be given an answer within a few days. In either case, thank the interviewer for the kindness shown to you and leave! This is something that many people have trouble doing. But it is very annoying when people take forever to act on the word "goodbye" and go out inch by inch.

Analyzing Turndowns

It is hoped that you will get the job. But if you do not, it would be a mistake for you to feel discouraged. Instead, you should try to figure out how you can do better the next time. Your DE teacher-coordinator will help you to think back over the application and the interview to see what you could improve. The important thing is to accept each interview as a learning experience. If you will make a serious effort to learn from your mistakes, you will be in a good position to get the job next time around.

DOING WELL ON THE JOB

One of the main advantages of cooperative education is the supervision that you receive on the job. Instead of being on your own, you will be working under a **training plan.** This is a written statement of what each student trainee is expected to learn and where the learning is to take place—through classroom work, in individual sessions with the DE teacher-coordinator, on the job, or by a combination of these.

You will also have a **training agreement.** This is a form prepared by the DE teacher-coordinator stating how long the training will last and what the hours and rate of pay will be. It gives any other information that will help to make the student trainee's position in the cooperative program clear. The training agreement is usually signed by the student, the student's parents, the DE teacher-coordinator, and the employer.

When you report to work, you will be given a **training sponsor.** This is the person who is responsible for training and supervising the student trainee on the job. The owner or manager may act as the training sponsor or may appoint someone else in the company. Your training sponsor and your DE teacher-coordinator are very anxious for you to do well on your new job and will do everything they can to help you. Now let's see what you have to do to help yourself.

You and Your Job

What you have to bring to your job is a willingness to learn that reveals itself in every phase of the job. It may start with learning the schedules of the public transportation system in your town so you can get to work on time. Then you have to learn the company's policies and rules—how this particular company wants things done. You have to learn about the company's system for storing things so you can find the

Training sponsors are eager to help co-op students do well in their jobs. (*Courtesy Ford Motor Company*)

things you need without constantly asking other people. You also have to learn how your job fits into the total company picture so that you can understand why your job is important. Most necessary of all, you have to know exactly what your duties are and then learn how to carry them out in the best possible way.

As a student trainee, you will not be expected to learn all this on your own. You will have your training sponsor as a teacher. Your DE teacher-coordinator will check regularly with the training sponsor to see how you are getting along and what has to be done to help you. But although they will be making every effort to teach you, it won't work unless you are making an equal effort to learn.

Besides being willing to learn, you also have to be willing to give your company its money's worth. This means being willing to step in and help when you see you are needed. It means being cheerful about doing whatever you are asked to do, instead of acting as though you think you are being taken advantage of. It also means showing that you are the kind of person who can be counted on to finish whatever you start. The word that describes the person who sees each task through is "responsible." It is a trait that is a must in business.

You and Your Fellow Workers

You already know that it is important for you to be able to get along well with the people you work with. With so much else to be concerned about, your employer doesn't want to have employees arguing among themselves. But then what happens if you have to work with someone who is very difficult to get along with? In this case, one thing that helps is to look at the world through that person's eyes. There is probably something in the person's life now or something that happened in the past that is causing the unpleasantness. Sometimes finding out what this is helps you to be more understanding and sympathetic. If that isn't possible, you should remember that you don't really have to like this person. You just have to find ways of getting along on the job, which is an easier task.

You and the Customers

A subject that is always on your employer's mind is what the public thinks of the company. Customers will only deal with the company as long as they think it is well run, that its policies are fair, and that it is successful in its dealings with its customers. This is what public relations workers call a "positive image." It is important to all companies—large, small, and in between.

Your employer expects you to understand that you have an important role to play in building good public relations with the customers. This is true even if you never see a customer. For example, suppose that you work as a packer in the shipping room of a large store. If you pack the goods so carelessly that they are broken when the customer receives them, the customer is going to have a bad impression of the whole store. This is why it is important for you to do your own job, whatever it is, as well as you can.

If you do meet the customers in your job, you have to realize that the customers' impressions of the whole company are very much tied up with their impressions of you. By being polite and considerate, you can show the customers that you, and hence the whole company, really are concerned with pleasing them and satisfying their needs. It may take more time and effort to please some customers than others. But whatever extras you have to give, you should give them cheerfully and willingly.

REMEMBERING THE IMPORTANCE OF SCHOOL

You might become so interested in your co-op job that you lose all interest in your other schoolwork. But your other subjects are important for your future too. For example, you have to take English courses and American history courses in order to graduate. You may feel that they have nothing at all to do with your present or future life. But through your history studies and the books you have to read in English class, you can broaden your understanding of people. The more you know about what people are like and why they act the way they do, the

One of the major advantages of a co-op job is that what you learn in school and on the job reinforce each other.

better job you can do in marketing. Remember too that every time you answer a question aloud in any classroom or do a written assignment, you are practicing skills that are directly related to your success in marketing. This is also true of your gym classes, where you develop health habits that you need for working.

WORKING ON YOUR OWN

In schools that don't offer cooperative education, students can still sample the field of marketing by getting jobs on their own. Because of the long hours that marketing businesses are open, there is a real need for part-time workers in most communities. To get one of these jobs on your own is somewhat more difficult than it is in a cooperative education program. But you will find that your DE experiences will give you a distinct edge in getting hired. Because training workers is a time-consuming and expensive process, employers are generally glad to hire people who have already learned some marketing skills.

On the job, you will find that your DE experiences will help you to be successful. Even though your teacher-coordinator will not be supervising your work, you will be encouraged to relate your experiences on the job to your classroom work in many ways. The students in a DE class who have jobs are able to contribute a great deal to the class discussion and to benefit from it.

Whether or not your school has a cooperative education program, the DE program still fulfills its purpose—to give you the training and guidance that will prepare you directly for a career in marketing.

- ## BUILDING YOUR MARKETING VOCABULARY

  Define each of the following terms and then use each one in a sentence.

  personal data sheet training plan
  training agreement training sponsor

- ## UNDERSTANDING WHAT YOU HAVE READ

  1. What is the purpose of an interview?
  2. Why should you go alone to an interview?
  3. Who signs the training agreement?
  4. What is a "positive image"? Who is responsible for developing a positive image for the company?
  5. List ten things that you can do to succeed in your job.
  6. How can your classes in subjects like history, English, and gym help you with a marketing job?

- ## APPLYING WHAT YOU HAVE LEARNED

  1. Choose a marketing business in your area that you think you might like to work for. Pretend that an interview has been set up for you. Prepare for it in the following way:
     a. Find out all that you can about the company and make a list of this information.
     b. Prepare a personal data sheet, using the sample on page 200 to help you.
     c. Decide what you will wear to the interview and write a short description of your outfit.
     d. Write a brief plan for getting to the interview on time.
  2. Ask your teacher or a twelfth-grade DE student to play the role of the interviewer. Have that person interview individual members of the class. After each interview, participate in a class discussion to point out the good features of the interview and the ones that could be improved.
  3. If you do not already have a social security card, ask your teacher to obtain an application blank for you. Print the required information in ink and mail the form to the indicated place.

Unit 3: EXPERIMENTS IN MARKETING

Select one of the following projects:
1. Describe on 3 by 5-inch file cards five displays you have seen recently that you thought were particularly effective. Then prepare a display for the classroom, using such things as stamps, rocks, or anything that you collect.
2. As a way of evaluating what DE can mean to you, ask one or more of the following speakers to come to your classroom:
   a. An employer who has frequently hired DE-trained workers.
   b. A person who graduated from your school's DE program and now has a full-time job in marketing.
   c. A person who is studying in a post-high school DE program.
   Ask these people to speak about their personal views of DE. Write a report summarizing each talk and your reactions to it.
3. Choose a product that interests you and try to list all of its advantages. Use words that would be interesting to possible buyers, but be truthful.
4. Ask your local post office what the requirements are for mailing packages. First wrap a glass or china item as a gift and then wrap it for mailing.
5. Organize a committee to plan an end-of-term party for your class. Start by listing all the tasks that have to be done. Then decide how the work will be divided. Present your plan in writing to your teacher.

UNIT 2

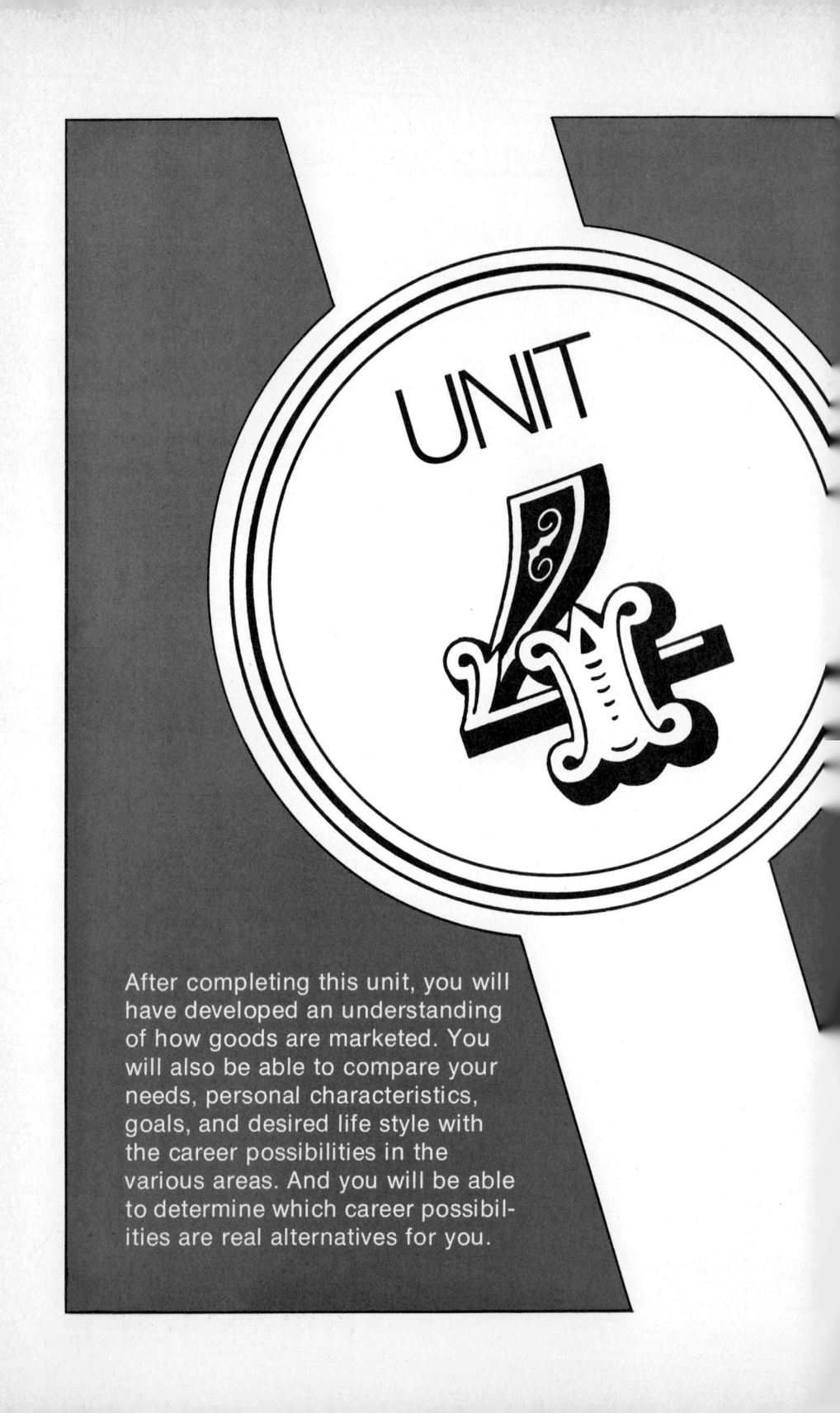

After completing this unit, you will have developed an understanding of how goods are marketed. You will also be able to compare your needs, personal characteristics, goals, and desired life style with the career possibilities in the various areas. And you will be able to determine which career possibilities are real alternatives for you.

You have learned how important it is to make positive decisions about your career. You have also learned that your chances for making the decisions that are right for you depend on the amount of information you have about your alternatives. To give you the background that you need, we are going to move now into a more detailed discussion of marketing. In this unit, you will have a chance to think about the businesses that market specific kinds of products, including food, apparel and accessories, home furnishings, health and beauty products, leisure-time goods, automotive products, farm and garden supplies, floristry products, and hardware and building supplies.

In studying these businesses, you will find that they are alike in many ways. These similarities emphasize that a general knowledge of marketing can be applied to many different businesses. At the same time, you will find many ways in which these businesses differ from each other. It is these differences that are important to you when you are trying to match the special person that we mean when we say "you" to a career.

The purpose of this unit is not to have you pick the one career that you want. Rather, it is to let you see the alternatives. Knowing the alternatives will help you discover the career possibilities that are in line with your understanding of yourself and your future.

Careers in Marketing Goods

part 20 Food Stores

After reading Part 20, you will be able—
- To explain why the food store business offers a high degree of job security.
- To define the four main kinds of food stores.
- To answer a series of questions designed to help you determine whether the food store business is or is not a real career alternative for you.

In this unit and the next one, we will be looking at the ways in which specific kinds of goods and services are marketed. We are going to start with an area that you already know something about—food stores. No matter where you live—in a rural, urban, or suburban area—there is a food store that serves your family. Altogether there are more than 200,000 food stores in this country. Because of the basic human need to eat, these food stores add up to more than a $100-billion-a-year business. You have been going in and out of food stores all your life, probably without giving them much thought. But now you are going to think of them in a new way, in terms of what they offer a person who is trying to get started on a career.

WHAT FOOD STORES ARE ALL ABOUT

The next time you go into a food store, take a careful look around you. You will see what many people in other parts of the world think of as an unbelievable variety of things to eat. You will see food that comes not only from different parts of our own country but also from many other parts of the world. There are spices and tea from the Orient, coffee and bananas from South America, and cheeses from Europe, to name only a few examples.

Not only is there a wide variety in the kinds of foods, but also a given kind of food comes in many forms. As an example of this, think about onions. You can buy fresh onions, either separately or already sorted and bagged. You can also buy either whole or minced onions that are peeled and frozen, all ready to be used in cooking. You can buy onions already cooked and packed in either cans or jars. You can also buy finely chopped onions that have been dried or made into a powder. You can buy frozen creamed onions or french fried onions that only have to be heated to be ready to eat. Furthermore, each of these different forms of onions is available in several different sizes, so that people who live alone and people who are shopping for large families can buy the amount that best suits their needs.

It is because of food stores that this wide range of food products can be bought and enjoyed by so many people. Food stores make it possible for us to buy a variety of foods in excellent condition, right near our homes. We can buy food when we want it, in the quantities that suit us best, and also enjoy very high standards of cleanliness.

A LOOK AT THE FUTURE OF FOOD STORES

At the present time, the food store business is the largest of the various retailing businesses in this country. To understand why this is true, you only have to remember that every one of the more than 220 million people who now live in this country must eat. Even though the birthrate in this country has decreased, the population is still increasing. This means that, in the future, there will be even more people who must buy food. In other words, the food retailing business is growing, and therefore even more workers will be needed in the future. These

The food store business offers a high degree of job security, because no matter what the economic situation, everyone must buy food. (*Courtesy Giant Food Stores*)

workers can look forward to *steady* employment. Some businesses have very busy periods, when they employ many workers, followed by very slow periods, when they have to lay off many workers. But food stores don't have such marked ups and downs. When incomes are low or prices are high, people watch their food purchases more carefully. They may buy less and cut out luxury items. But they can't stop buying food altogether.

This means that food stores offer a high degree of job security, so that when you work in this field, you don't have to be constantly worried about being out of a job. At the same time, the future of food stores holds out the promise of challenge and excitement. This is a highly competitive business. Therefore, anyone who works in a food store has to be quick to recognize new trends and adapt to new life styles, products, and marketing methods.

THE KINDS OF FOOD STORES

When stores sell only one line of goods or a group of goods that are closely related, as food stores do, they are called **limited-line stores.** There are four main kinds of food stores: (1) small food stores, (2) supermarkets, (3) superettes, and (4) convenience stores. Even though each of these kinds of stores serves a special purpose, their managers have to be constantly concerned with the new things that are being done in the other kinds of stores. To attract and hold customers, a constant effort has to be made to upgrade the goods and customer services that the store is offering, while keeping prices as low as possible. In the end, it is the consumer who benefits from this kind of competitive atmosphere.

Small Food Stores

A **small food store** is defined as any food store that does less than $150,000 worth of business a year. These stores are mostly **service stores,** meaning that a salesclerk waits on the customers. Although about 60 percent of all the food stores in this country are small stores, they account for only about 10 percent of the total food business. However, this should not be taken to mean that these stores aren't an important part of the total retailing picture, for 10 percent of $100 billion is still a lot of business.

There are two kinds of small stores. The first is the neighborhood store, which sells a general assortment of foods. This assortment has to be chosen very carefully by the store's manager because there are just so many items that a small store can hold. However, the manager of a neighborhood store usually knows the customers very well and can

Small food stores often specialize in the foods of a particular ethnic group or in unusual imported food products. (UPPER LEFT *Frank Lisciandro/Editorial Photocolor Archives;* UPPER RIGHT *courtesy New York Convention and Visitors Bureau;* BELOW *William Finch/Editorial Photocolor Archives*)

PART 20 • FOOD STORES • 213

tailor the store to the customers' needs. One store may go in the direction of providing especially high-quality goods—fresher eggs, bigger tomatoes, more tender meat, and so on. Another store might carry the kinds of food products that appeal to certain nationalities, such as Spanish, Chinese, or Italian foods. Because of their close relationship to their customers, neighborhood stores frequently offer such services as telephone ordering, delivery, and charge accounts.

The second kind of small store is the specialty food store, which sells one kind of food or a specialized group of foods. Examples of specialty food stores are fish stores, butcher shops, bakeries, delicatessens, cheese shops, and health food stores. These stores have the advantage of being able to offer a variety of goods in their special line.

Supermarkets

In direct contrast to the small food stores are the stores whose very name suggests "big." These are the supermarkets, which represent only 20 percent of all food stores and yet do more than 75 percent of the total food business. And *super*markets they are. Some of them are as big as an entire city block, with their own huge parking lots to hold the cars of the crowds of shoppers that fill the stores each day.

By definition, a **supermarket** is a food store that does at least $1 million worth of business a year and is organized into at least four departments: grocery, meats, dairy, and produce (fruits and vegetables). At least one of these departments must be self-service. In actual fact, most supermarkets have even more departments, and most of these departments are self-service. These departments may include frozen foods, fancy foods, bakery products, delicatessen foods, and such nonfood items as cosmetics and toiletries, magazines, nonprescription drugs, household supplies, and other general merchandise items.

In handling nonfood items, supermarkets are using a marketing method that is known as **scrambled merchandising.** This is the term that is used to describe a store's practice of stocking and selling merchandise outside of its regular line. In recent years, more and more emphasis has been placed on these nonfood items. They are seen as a way of increasing profits in a business where profits have always been low. As a result, supermarkets have been getting bigger and bigger. In fact, many stores have become so enormous that a new term is being used for them. They are called "superstores," and 20 percent or more of their very large selling area is devoted to nonfood items. Their aim is to allow the customers to make all their routine purchases under one roof.

Supermarkets have two special advantages. First, they can offer a really wide selection. It is common for supermarkets to carry as many

Specialized food stores, such as this candy and nut shop, offer interesting career opportunities. Do you have the will power it takes to work among such temptations? (*Anita Sabarese/Design Photographers International, Inc.*)

as 8,000 different items. Their second advantage is low prices. Because they buy and sell in quantity, they can keep their costs down. Their self-service policy saves labor costs. They generally also have a cash-and-carry policy, which again saves money. There are some supermarkets that put so much emphasis on keeping their prices down that they are called "discount food stores."

When supermarkets first started, the variety and low prices that they offered were enough to bring in customers. But now that there are so many supermarkets, each of them has to try to outdo the others in thinking up ways to attract and hold customers. Air-conditioning, electric-eye doors, modern lighting and decor, eye-catching signs, and piped-in music all have the same purpose—to make the customers enjoy their shopping so much that they will buy more than they had planned to.

Supermarkets also try to keep the customers happy by making it easy for them to find what they want. This is done by carefully planning where all items will be placed, so that they are easy to see and related items are together. Today many supermarkets are also competing with each other by trying to do everything they can to respond to the needs of consumers. These efforts to support consumerism range all the way from holding classes on how to plan inexpensive meals to making plans for better waste disposal methods.

Superettes

A **superette** is a food store that has some of the features of the small store and some of the features of the supermarket. Because it is larger than the small store, it can offer somewhat more variety. And yet, because it is smaller than a supermarket, it can still offer the personal services and attention that many people enjoy. Some superettes are set up so that the customers wait on themselves, as they do in supermarkets. But others are **semi–self-service stores.** This means that customers wait on themselves for some things and are waited on for others.

Convenience Stores

The trend toward bigger and bigger supermarkets has been matched by a trend toward **convenience stores.** These are small, carefully planned self-service stores that are open long hours and feature a limited line of popular, quick-selling items. The number of convenience stores is steadily growing. They fill the special need that consumers have to pick up often-used items quickly and easily.

Superettes feature self-service in some departments and salesperson assistance in others. (*Sally Rapelye/Editorial Photocolor Archives*)

HOW FOOD STORES ARE AFFILIATED

The largest number of food stores are owned independently. They have the advantage of being able to adapt quickly to the needs of the people they serve. Their main disadvantage is that they don't get the savings that result from buying and selling in quantity. This is why so many independent food stores have joined either cooperative chains, such as Associated Grocers, or voluntary chains, such as Red and White, Clover Farm, and Super-Valu.

About 20 percent of all food stores belong to corporate chains. Although each of the four kinds of food stores may be set up in this way, the majority of chain stores are supermarkets and convenience stores. Examples of supermarket chains that may be familiar to you are Safeway Stores, Winn Dixie Stores, and Food Fair Stores. Examples of chain-operated convenience stores are the 7-Eleven stores owned by the Southland Corporation.

In addition to its chain stores, the Southland Corporation has set up many 7-Eleven stores as franchises, which is a very popular way of operating convenience stores. Other examples of franchised convenience stores are Quik Stop Markets and Convenient Food Mart. Many speciality food stores are also operated as franchises. Examples are Cheese Shop International, Mother Nature's Nutrition Centers, and Swiss Colony Stores.

CAREERS IN FOOD STORES

Food stores offer some special advantages to anyone looking for a challenging and rewarding career. The food store field is a very easy one in which to get started. Food stores are open long hours. Some stores are even open all night. Even when the store itself is closed, the work of restocking the shelves may be done during the night. This means that food stores have a great need for part-time workers. Food stores also have a need for part-time workers during peak business times, such as on weekends, when many people do their shopping. These factors make it possible for you to get started in this field while you are still in school.

Another advantage of food store work is that you can earn as much money, if not more money, in this field as you can in many other retail businesses. The fringe benefits in this field compare well with those offered by other businesses. Still another advantage is that food stores are known for promoting their own workers to better jobs. Many of the managers of food stores started at the bottom and worked their way up as they gained experience and know-how.

Although these are important advantages, they are not the only things that you should think about when you are choosing a career. In order to provide you with more of the information you will need, let's look at the kind of work that is done in supermarkets and in other kinds of food stores. Then we will consider the requirements for food store jobs.

The Kind of Work Done in Supermarkets

Even though customers in supermarkets serve themselves, it takes a great many workers to make this self-service possible. Because of the supermarket's size, these workers don't do a little bit of everything, as they would in a small store. The supermarket can only run smoothly when each worker is given specific duties and responsibilities. The many jobs that have to be done in supermarkets are on three levels: (1) entry level, (2) career level, and (3) management level. Because there are no barriers between these levels, there are many possibilities for ladder-type moves. There are also many possibilities for lattice-type moves. The experience that you gain can be transferred to other departments in the supermarket, other kinds of food stores, food wholesaling, and other kinds of marketing businesses.

ENTRY-LEVEL JOBS. In supermarkets, there are many jobs for beginners. You might start out bagging customers' purchases at the checkout counter. Sometimes this job is combined with that of carryout clerk. This means carrying the customers' orders to their cars, gathering up shopping carts that have been left in the parking lot, and regrouping the carts in the store.

All the departments have jobs for beginning workers as trainees for career-level jobs. For example, the meat department hires people to train as meat wrappers. They learn how to handle the meat after it has been cut—that is, weighing, wrapping, and marking it. They also learn how to keep the meat counter and shelves clean and filled. A trainee for the job of stock clerk in the grocery, frozen food, dairy, or fancy foods department would learn how to keep the assigned shelves and bins clean and filled. This means learning how to bring goods from the stockroom as they are needed, to mark the price on each item, and to arrange the goods on the shelves or in the bins. This also means learning how to count the goods in the stockroom so goods can be reordered as needed. Trainee stock clerks also have to help unload delivery trucks and help with receiving and checking.

Trainees are also hired in the fruit and vegetable department to learn to be produce clerks. They have to learn the special ways in which fruits and vegetables are kept clean, fresh, and attractive. Trainees in this department also have to learn how to weigh and wrap produce. Beginners are also hired as trainees for the job of cashier. (Baggers and carryout clerks can also become cashier trainees.) This

There are many opportunities for beginning workers in supermarkets. And because many supermarkets are open in the evening and on weekends you have the chance to get started in a food store career while you are still in school. (ABOVE *courtesy* Chain Store Age; BELOW *courtesy* Food Fair/Pantry Pride)

PART 20 • FOOD STORES • 219

job involves learning how to ring up the customers' purchases on a cash register and make change. The cashier trainee also has to learn how to give out trading stamps if the store offers them, handle food stamps and coupons, and spot counterfeit money. Beginners may also be hired to be trained as bookkeepers and office clerks.

CAREER-LEVEL JOBS. The difference between a trainee produce clerk and a produce clerk is a matter of skill, experience, and knowledge. This is also the difference between a trainee and a meat wrapper, stock clerk, cashier, or bookkeeper. That is why these jobs, when they have been learned, are considered to be career-level jobs. Many people find that these career-level jobs are completely satisfying. For other people, these jobs are thought of as stepping-stones to management-level jobs or to other jobs in marketing.

It should be noted that the total number of cashiers and stock clerks will be reduced in the future because of the new use of computerized cash registers in checking out customers, counting stock, and reordering. The duties of these workers will have to be adjusted in order to match the new methods that will result from the use of computerized cash registers.

MANAGEMENT-LEVEL JOBS. If you are interested in management-level jobs, you will find that supermarkets offer many possibilities. For example, if you do a good job as a cashier, you may be promoted to the job of head cashier. This is a very responsible position which requires you to supervise the work of the cashier-trainees and cashiers. This means that you will assist in hiring and training them. You will also arrange their work schedules, keep them supplied with change, and collect the money from their registers. You will have to make sure that the amount of money in the cash registers agrees with the totals on the cash register tapes.

You can advance from the position of stock clerk or produce clerk to become the assistant manager of the department you are working in, and then you can become the department manager. As the manager of a department, you have to train and supervise the department's workers. You also have to do the ordering and reordering for the department and make sure that it runs smoothly and profitably.

From the job of head cashier or department head, you can move up to the job of assistant manager of the store, and then you can advance to the job of manager. In an independent supermarket, the manager is fully responsible for everything that happens in the store. In corporate chains, it used to be the case that the store manager was responsible for everything except meat and produce. However, many chains are now giving their managers full control of the store's operations and are also giving them the title "resident supervisor" as a way of indicating their broader responsibilities.

It is important to realize that management jobs on the store level are not the end of the line. Department heads and store managers for corporate chains can move up to more responsible jobs in the regional or central headquarters or can become supervisors for a group of stores. This is also true for managers of independent stores. Experience as a store manager can also prepare you for owning your own store.

The Kind of Work Done in Other Kinds of Food Stores

Most small stores can be run by the owner or manager and just one or two helpers. Often there is a need for a part-time worker to deliver orders and do odd jobs. The good thing about working in a small store is that you get to do all kinds of things, instead of just one special job. If you like to learn, you can develop a broad sense of what the food store business is all about. Although advancement possibilities are limited within the store, many workers eventually open their own stores. Or they use their experience to move into supermarket jobs or food wholesaling.

In superettes and convenience stores, there are fewer jobs than in supermarkets, but the jobs are similar to the ones found in supermarkets. Promotions can come even more quickly in convenience stores than in supermarkets. Because of the large growth in the number of convenience stores in recent years, the advancement from stock clerk to store manager is often very rapid.

Job Requirements

We have been talking about what food stores have to offer you, and this is an important thing for you to consider. But, at the same time, there is also the question of what a food store career would require from you. The people who work in food stores are not, by any means, all alike. In fact, their interests and life styles can be very different. But there are some basic requirements that you should be able to meet if you want to build a successful career in this field. These can be summarized as (1) personal characteristics, (2) physical requirements, and (3) educational requirements.

PERSONAL CHARACTERISTICS. The most essential requirements for food store work, no matter what job you are in, is that you like people and are genuinely interested in helping them. Food stores are not so different from each other that customers will put up with rudeness or indifference just to shop at a particular store. Suppose that the assistant manager makes fun of a customer who is making a complaint. When such things happen, customers change stores in a hurry! In a business as competitive as this one, no store can afford to let that

If a supermarket is to be successful and have loyal customers, everyone who works in the supermarket must be polite and willing to help.

happen. Every worker is expected to know that the success of the store is dependent on giving the customers complete satisfaction.

In hiring new workers, food store managers look for people who understand that satisfying the customer is a team responsibility. It requires the cooperation of all the workers in the store. It also requires that all the workers be thorough in their work. A meat counter that has been only half-cleaned is half dirty, and it is the dirty half that customers will see and remember. Food store workers also have to be clean and neat, because the customers tend to judge the store's standards by the employees' appearances. Still another requirement is the ability to work well under pressure. When the store is crowded and busy, workers have to be able to pace themselves accordingly. They must remain pleasant to their fellow workers, as well as to the customers, no matter how hectic things get.

Food store workers also have to cooperate with the manager by being willing to work when they are needed. Fortunately the people who work in food stores do not all want the same work schedule. For example, people with school children to care for will probably want to work during the daytime, whereas people who are going to school will want to work in the evenings and on Saturdays. It is one of the advantages of food stores that such special needs can be taken care of. But if you want a food store career, you have to remember that this is not a Monday through Friday, nine to five business. Thus you have to be willing to work when many of your friends are free.

If you want to work on the management level, you have to be

willing to accept the responsibility for other people's work as well as your own. You must have the ability to get other people to do their best, which includes setting a good example, being fair about what you expect from them, and making people feel that what they do is appreciated. It is not unusual for store managers to work well beyond the usual 40-hour workweek.

PHYSICAL REQUIREMENTS. A general requirement for food store workers is good physical health. There are some office jobs in the food store field, but most of the jobs require a lot of standing, walking, lifting, and bending. Even managers have to be on their feet all day. Therefore, this is not work that can be done by people who tire easily. Workers in the meat department have to go in and out of walk-in refrigerators all day. Most food store jobs also require good eye-and-hand coordination.

EDUCATIONAL REQUIREMENTS. As you know, you can be hired for food store work before you have finished high school. But it is necessary for you to have learned both basic skills and social skills. If you make your on-the-job training count, you can learn the marketing skills that you need in order to advance in your career as you go along. However, it is much easier to get hired in the first place and to move up to management-level jobs if you have had the kind of specific marketing training that DE high school programs offer.

If you want to start at the mid-management level, you should plan to go to a community or four-year college to acquire the necessary understanding and skills. The many scholarships being offered today make this a real alternative for a broad group of young people. There are even scholarships specifically set up for people who have been or are now employed in food stores.

Because of the flexible hours in food store jobs, you can easily go to school and work at the same time. There are also home study courses in food store management offered by Cornell University in cooperation with the National Association of Food Chains. If you are willing to put in this kind of extra effort, you will find that there are few areas in the business world where promotions come as quickly as they do in food stores.

- **BUILDING YOUR MARKETING VOCABULARY**

Define each of the following terms and then use each one in a sentence.

convenience store	service store
limited-line store	small food store
scrambled merchandising	superette
semi–self-service store	supermarket

- **UNDERSTANDING WHAT YOU HAVE READ**

    1. Explain why the food store business provides a high degree of job security.
    2. Even though supermarkets have many advantages, why do some people prefer to shop in small neighborhood stores?
    3. Why do many food stores carry nonfood items?
    4. What advantages do supermarkets have that make them so popular?
    5. What special need do convenience stores answer?
    6. Why do food stores need so many part-time workers?
    7. Does everyone who works in a food store hope to be a manager someday? Explain your answer.

- **APPLYING WHAT YOU HAVE LEARNED**

    1. Visit a supermarket in your area and take notes on how the layout is planned to make it easy for the customers to select their food purchases. Report back to your class on what you have seen. Then work with your class to prepare a summary report of what food stores should do to make the idea of self-service work.
    2. Answer the following questions using 0 for *no,* 1 for *maybe,* and 2 for *yes.* When you are finished, add up your score. A score of 18–24 is an indication that the food store field may be a real career alternative for you.
        a. In Part 6, you learned about the reasons why people work. Could a food store career answer your own reasons for working?
        b. Would food stores offer you the opportunity to work with people in the way that means the most to you?
        c. Do food stores in general seem like pleasant places to work?
        d. Do you meet the physical requirements for food store work?
        e. Would you be willing to see your appearance through the customer's eyes and make any necessary changes?
        f. Would working sometimes on weekends or in the evening and being off during the week or in the morning suit your life style?
        g. Do food stores offer you the opportunity to work on the job level that suits you best?
        h. Would you be willing to move faster during rush hours?
        i. Could you leave one task and take on another at a moment's notice without complaining?
        j. Does the job security that food stores offer seem important to you?
        k. Are you willing to make the effort to improve your basic skills while you are still in school?
        l. Would you like to learn more about how food stores work?

part 21
Food Wholesaling

After reading Part 21, you will be able—
- To list three ways in which food wholesalers cut costs for producers and three ways in which they cut costs for retailers.
- To make a comparative statement about food wholesaling when given a list of facts about food retailing.
- To list the advantages and disadvantages of a career in food wholesaling from your personal point of view.

The food products that are so easily available to you in your local food store come from many different sources. These include farms, meat-packing houses, fisheries, dairies, sugar refineries, flour mills, cereal-processing plants, frozen food plants, bakeries, canneries, and soft drink bottlers, to name only the most obvious. It would be impossible for food store managers to deal with each one of these producers individually. Trying to do this would involve too much time, energy, and money. Food store managers must find a way of cutting down on the number of suppliers that they deal with. This is why they rely heavily on the services of food wholesalers.

As far as the public is concerned, the middleman role of food wholesalers is a behind-the-scenes one. The customers in food stores tend to take the well-stocked shelves for granted. They are so used to being able to buy exactly what they want, when and where they want it, that they don't give it a second thought. Yet it is the food wholesaler who keeps the flow of goods even and steady, day in and day out. In this part, you will learn about how the food wholesaler goes about the important work of supplying food stores with goods for resale. The information that you will be gaining about food wholesaling will also help you to understand the wholesaling of other kinds of products.

THE FOOD WHOLESALER AND FOOD COSTS

Food wholesalers are like food retailers in that they buy goods and then resell these goods to their customers. This means that they need a place to put the goods after they have bought them and before they

Most consumers don't realize the importance of the food wholesaler's role in making food products available to them when and where they are needed. (*Bruce Anspach/Editorial Photocolor Archives*)

have sold them. The retailer uses a store for this purpose, whereas the wholesaler operates from a warehouse. Food retailers and wholesalers earn their money in the same way, by selling the goods for an amount of money that leaves a profit after all expenses have been paid. They also lose money on any goods that they are not able to sell.

Many people believe that the wholesaler's profits are the cause of higher consumer prices. People who don't know much about marketing are apt to talk about how much better it would be if we could "eliminate the middleman." But because they are highly skilled specialists in the field of marketing, wholesalers save money for consumers in many ways. For example, one of the wholesaler's main functions is **bulk breaking.** This is the process of buying large quantities of goods and then dividing them into smaller quantities for resale.

The people who can sell in large quantities to wholesalers obviously have much lower selling costs than they would have if they had to deal with the individual stores. Also, they don't have to worry about storing the goods until the stores need them. Because of these savings, they can afford to charge the wholesalers less for the goods. Shipping charges are also much lower when a large quantity of goods is shipped at one time. The savings can be passed along to retailers and consumers.

Because of the wholesalers' work, retailers also have much lower buying expenses. They have to spend much less time (which means money too) deciding what to buy and where to buy it. Because they don't have to deal with as many suppliers, they don't have to spend as much time doing paper work. They are also relieved of the cost of storing large quantities of goods because they can count on the wholesalers' well-stocked warehouses to keep them supplied on short notice.

The importance of the wholesalers' behind-the-scenes work in getting food from producers to consumers should not be underestimated. Everyone recognizes the overall efficiency of our farmers. The equipment and methods that they use have been constantly improved, so that the average amount of food that our farmers are producing per acre is at an all-time high. Our food processors, who turn basic food products into more usable forms, are equally well-known for their skill and efficiency. But farm products on the farm or in the food-processing plant are of no use to the consumers. The food has to be distributed as efficiently as it is produced, so that it is available when and where the consumers need it. The role that food wholesalers play in adding this time and place value to the food is far too vital to be eliminated.

THE DEVELOPMENT OF FULL-SERVICE WHOLESALING

Food stores don't buy everything that they sell from one wholesaler. But because of the number of products that they carry, they find that they do need one wholesaler to act as a principal supplier. To fill this need, there are wholesalers who carry a broad range of the products that food retailers want to buy. These wholesalers find that it is very much to their own advantage when their retailer customers are successful. The more the retailers sell, the more they buy from the wholesalers. To help retailer customers sell more, many wholesalers go beyond just supplying goods. These wholesalers, called **service wholesalers,** offer many services that will improve their customers' total business.

In recent years, many of these service wholesalers have broadened both the number of products and the kinds of services they offer their customers. As a result, they are spoken of in the food business as "full-service wholesalers." This term indicates the extent to which these wholesalers are capable of serving their retailer customers. To see how this change came about, let's look at the impact that the corporate chains have had on food wholesaling and at the reaction of the independent wholesalers to the competition from corporate chains. Then we will see how the reaction of the independent wholesalers has, in turn, affected the wholesaling methods of corporate chains.

The Impact of the Corporate Chains
The ways in which food wholesalers work have been greatly influenced by the fact that many of the large corporate food chains do their own service wholesaling. When corporate chains first began combining the wholesaling and retailing functions, they were able to offer exceptionally low prices. They saved money by buying in large quantities and by streamlining their management methods. They also employed highly trained management experts to help the individual store managers solve their problems in the most efficient way. There were people who predicted that the corporate chains would eventually drive the independent wholesalers and retailers out of business.

The Reaction of the Independent Wholesalers
When faced with this threat from the corporate chains, the independent wholesalers fought back, in the true spirit of free enterprise. They have been so successful that today they have many corporate chains as their customers. In many cases, corporate chains have found that it is easier

Corporate and voluntary chains hire experts to advise individual store managers on such subjects as store layout. *(Courtesy Pic N Pay Shoes, Inc.)*

to buy through independent wholesalers than to operate their own wholesaling facilities.

One thing that independent wholesalers have done to improve their position is to sell many more kinds of products in order to make themselves more useful to their customers. Besides a general line of grocery items, they now carry frozen foods, produce, meat, and dairy products. Since scrambled merchandising has become an accepted policy in many food stores, many wholesalers also carry health and beauty products and some general merchandise items. To see what else independent food wholesalers have done to compete with the corporate chains that do their own wholesaling, let's look at the growth of cooperative and voluntary chains. We will also think about the position of wholesalers who are "unaffiliated," which means that they don't have definite agreements that tie them to the retailers they serve.

THE GROWTH OF COOPERATIVE AND VOLUNTARY CHAINS. A very important way in which the independent wholesalers and retailers tried to meet the threat from corporate chains was by forming cooperative and voluntary chains. As you will remember from Part 16, the main advantage of cooperative chains, which are retailer owned, is their buying power. They allow independent retailers to maintain their independence, yet still enjoy the savings that come from quantity buying and shipping. Cooperative chains have become so important that 30 percent of all independent food wholesaling (that is, the food wholesaling not done by corporate chains) is now done by cooperative chains.

An even larger percentage—50 percent—of independent food wholesaling is done by the voluntary chains formed by wholesalers. Their aim is to give the retailers many of the advantages of corporate chains and still allow them to keep their independence. To do this, they have concentrated on matching the advantages that the corporate chains have in management and in buying.

Like the corporate chains, they hire experts to offer the individual store managers help with store layout, advertising, and display. They set up systems for counting the store's inventory. They also offer advice about what kinds of merchandise and how many items a particular store should order. Because wholesalers deal with many stores, they can keep more complete records and are able to make more accurate predictions about future sales than an individual store manager can. Voluntary chain wholesalers give expert advice about where to locate new stores and will even lend money to retailers to build new stores or remodel existing ones. They also provide training courses for the store's employees.

Some of the management aids offered by the voluntary chains are now being offered by the cooperative chains too, so that today both kinds of wholesalers are in a good competitive position.

NEW STRENGTH FOR UNAFFILIATED WHOLESALERS. There is yet another result of the competition in food wholesaling. The independent wholesalers who are not part of voluntary or cooperative chains have also worked hard to improve their position in the field. They now offer their retailer customers many of the same kinds of expert management services as the voluntary chains do. They have made a serious effort to introduce many more efficient methods in their own operating procedures in order to save money wherever possible. They have also concentrated on helping the individual store managers to do a better, more competitive job. Although they handle only 20 percent of independent food wholesaling, it is a strong 20 percent.

New Methods for the Corporate Chains

With their buying and management methods being copied by independent wholesalers, the large corporate chains that function as their own wholesalers had to take another look at their own operating methods. They realized that the independents had one special advantage—flexibility. The independents could put a new idea into effect before this same idea could get up through the levels of authority in the corporate chains.

To make themselves more competitive with the independents, many of the corporate chains have decentralized some of their operations. Recognizing that different communities have different needs, they are allowing more decisions to be made in their regional distribution centers, as well as by individual store managers. Decentralization makes it possible for them to respond to the needs and wants of their customers much more directly and quickly than they could before. Thus all the competition between the corporate chains and the independent wholesalers has had the effect of benefiting the public.

OTHER KINDS OF FOOD WHOLESALERS

There are three other kinds of wholesalers from whom food retailers buy. These wholesalers, who each have their own special ways of operating, are (1) specialty wholesalers, (2) rack jobbers, and (3) truck jobbers. In terms of the total volume of business that they do, these wholesalers are not as important as full-service wholesalers. However, the role that they play in helping retailers to round out their inventory benefits retailers and consumers alike and provides interesting jobs.

Specialty Wholesalers

The name that is given to a wholesaler who carries a wide selection in just one part of a line is **specialty wholesaler**. Examples of specialty wholesalers in the food business are those who sell eggs, meat, poultry, fish, produce, frozen foods, or health foods. Specialty wholesalers are the main suppliers for specialty stores, with whom they may have franchising agreements. Other food stores count on specialty wholesalers to supply those products that their full-service wholesalers don't carry. Or they may buy certain products from specialty wholesalers if they think the products are better in some way.

Rack Jobbers

Another kind of wholesaler is the **rack jobber,** who supplies the retailer with racks and keeps the racks full of merchandise in selected lines. Many corporate chains, as well as independent food stores, depend on rack jobbers to be responsible for supplying all the nonfood products sold in the stores. Rack jobbers take complete charge of selecting the kind and amount of merchandise to be sold. In doing this, they are careful to choose items for each particular store that will provide a fast turnover and a quick profit. They also mark the prices on each item, set up displays, and give the retailer full credit for items that don't sell. Because food store managers have so many things to think about and so many problems to deal with, they consider rack jobbing to be a very important service.

Truck Jobbers

A **truck jobber** can be defined as a wholesaler who combines the jobs of selling and delivering specific products. Truck jobbers usually handle products that will go stale or spoil and therefore cannot be stored for any length of time. Examples of such products are baked

It is the responsibility of this truck jobber to supply the supermarket with fresh eggs and take back any eggs that can no longer be sold. Therefore he must use good judgment in deciding exactly how many eggs will be needed so that the store has enough but not too many. (*Courtesy* Chain Store Age)

goods, potato chips, tobacco products, and candy. Truck jobbers also handle soft drinks. Their method of operation is to sign up food retailers as customers and then visit each one on a regular, frequent basis. The needs of each retailer can be filled on the spot, from the well-stocked trucks that give the truck jobbers their name. Truck jobbers take full charge of the products that they sell. They decide how many products are needed, take them into the selling area, arrange them on the shelves, and take back unsold items. For the store manager, this kind of dependable service is very important.

CAREERS IN FOOD WHOLESALING

Because it is so closely tied to food retailing, which is a growing business, food wholesaling offers the same kind of job security. Both areas will continue to be an essential part of our economy as long as people have to eat. However, there is very little room in food wholesaling for unskilled workers. In the well-equipped warehouses that many wholesalers now use, many of the jobs that used to be done by human musclepower are being done mechanically. A code, called the Uniform Product Code, has been worked out to identify many products instantly. This code is making it possible for computers to take over more and more of the work connected with receiving, sorting, shipping, billing, and inventory control. Because of these new machines, the unskilled jobs in food wholesaling are disappearing.

There is, however, a greater demand than ever for workers who have a broad base of knowledge about marketing and who can handle responsibility. For such workers, food wholesaling offers many challenging jobs. Food wholesaling could be called the heart of the food distribution process. From its position in the center of things, it pumps vitality back to the farmers and the food processors and forward to the food retailers. This two-way movement helps to keep our economy healthy and our standard of living high.

As a way of helping you to decide whether you might like to be part of this important work, let's think about getting started in food wholesaling, working at the career level, and moving into management.

Getting Started

It is not as easy to get started in food wholesaling as it is in food retailing. Obviously there are fewer wholesaling companies than there are food stores. Although food stores can be found in every village and city, there may not be a food wholesaler in your area. Another problem for people who want to get started in this field is that food wholesalers have very few jobs for part-time workers. Because most of the jobs in wholesaling require marketing skills, wholesalers prefer to hire and train full-time workers. Still another problem has to do with how the work is scheduled. Much of the order filling is done at night. The trucks are then loaded very early in the morning so they can reach the stores early in the day.

Despite these problems, there are DE teacher-coordinators who have worked out arrangements that allow their students to be assigned to wholesaling jobs. If this is not possible in your community, you will find that working in a food store is an excellent way of preparing for this kind of work.

Food wholesalers generally consider a high school diploma to be a requirement when they are hiring full-time employees. They also look for people who have a genuine interest in marketing and who can get along well with other people. Even workers who don't have direct contact with the customers have to be able to work smoothly with each other. Food wholesalers hire beginners to be trained as office workers or for warehouse jobs. Beginners in the warehouse start out doing the simpler jobs in the areas they are assigned to. They work under the guidance of career-level workers until they are ready to accept the full responsibilities of their particular jobs.

If you would like to start at a higher level, as a sales or management trainee, you may want to investigate the post-high school DE courses that allow you to specialize in wholesaling.

Working at the Career Level

The career-level jobs in food wholesaling offer many satisfactions. The pay is well above the national average, the fringe benefits are in line with those of other marketing businesses, and the work is never dull. Perhaps most important of all, career-level jobs in food wholesaling do not lock you in. You can make lattice-type moves, from a warehousing job to a position in sales or buying, for example. You can also move up, because food wholesalers, like food retailers, are known for promoting their own workers to better jobs. You can transfer the skills that you learn in food wholesaling to many areas of retailing, or you can move to the marketing department of a company that sells to food wholesalers. This mobility gives you a great deal of freedom, as well as job security.

There are career-level jobs in buying, selling, and warehousing. There are also career-level office jobs and jobs for staff specialists.

BUYING JOBS. The buying decisions in wholesaling are vital to the success of the business. The people who make these all-important decisions are called **buyers**. (This is the name that is given to those marketing workers who have the responsibility for buying goods for

Buyers must have a great deal of knowledge and experience in order to make wise buying decisions. (*Courtesy* IGA Grocergram)

resale.) Buying for the corporate, voluntary, and cooperative chains is done by a highly trained group of people. Each buyer needs an overall understanding of food marketing and an in-depth knowledge of a particular product or group of products. Buyers generally work from the central headquarters of the chain, but they have to do some traveling to the sources of supply. In some cases, they live in the areas where the central markets are located. Buyers need a high aptitude for data and the ability to make judgments about what, where, and how much to buy in order to get the best possible quality at the lowest possible prices.

Although the small independent wholesalers cannot afford the same degree of specialization, their buyers must be marketing experts, too. They must understand the problems of the food producers and processors, as well as the needs and wants of the consumers. They also have to stay aware of new trends and life styles so they can make accurate predictions about what consumers are going to want.

Many wholesale buyers were formerly department heads in food stores. Their buying experience on the retail level made it possible for them to take over the same kinds of duties in wholesaling.

SELLING JOBS. For any middleman, buying is only one side of the coin. The other side is selling. These are the two merchandising functions that are the basis of the wholesaler's business. However, the term "selling" does not mean the same thing in modern wholesaling as it once did. Today's wholesalers do not need salesworkers to sell particular products. Rather, they want people who can help to increase the retailer's total order. The only way to do this is to help the retailer in every possible way to do a better job and to sell more goods.

The voluntary chains, with their built-in customers, employ field representatives. The duties of these people are very similar to the duties of the independent wholesalers' salesworkers. Ordering has become so simplified that it can be done by phone, or by mail, or by a computer. Therefore, the job of the salesworker or field representative is largely a matter of giving the kind of service that will make the store more successful.

To do this, these workers have to be trained in all phases of wholesaling. They must know the details of the policies and products of the companies they work for. They also have to know a great deal about managing food stores so they can give the store managers realistic advice. This kind of work requires a high degree of self-discipline in order to plan the visits to the individual stores and to make the most of the time available. It also requires an aptitude for data, as well as a high aptitude for people.

A different kind of selling job in food wholesaling is the combination selling and driving job that is part of truck jobbing. The people who do this work are called "route workers" because they make scheduled deliveries along a definite route. Their selling duties consist mostly of being reliable and likable and knowing their merchandise thoroughly.

WAREHOUSING JOBS. Because so much of the work involved in running the warehouse is now being done mechanically, the number of jobs in this area has been cut down. Most of the jobs that are left are for workers who can make the kinds of decisions that machines can't make. Warehouse workers don't meet the customers directly. But they share the responsibility for making the retailer's business succeed. By doing their own jobs well, they make it possible for the retailers to get exactly what they have ordered, on time, and in good condition.

There are career-level warehouse jobs for order assemblers (sometimes called "order pickers") and packers, as well as for receiving, shipping, and stock clerks. All of these people need an aptitude for data and a concern for accuracy. The happy-go-lucky person, who doesn't like to pay attention to details, would not do well in this work.

The widespread use of laborsaving devices in food warehouses means that warehouse workers must be able to work with machines. This requires not only a degree of mechanical ability but also good coordination, a sense of responsibility, and a concern for physical safety conditions in the warehouse. Despite so many laborsaving devices, some warehouse work still requires good health and the ability to lift heavy boxes and cartons.

Today, much of the work done in warehouses requires skill in working with machines, such as this forklift truck. *(Courtesy Clark Equipment Co.)*

Physical strength is also necessary for the truck drivers who make deliveries to the stores. They must have safe driving records and the ability to keep to the schedule that is set for them.

OFFICE JOBS. The use of computers has drastically changed the way in which the office area of wholesaling businesses is run. Not all wholesalers use computers yet. But those that do use them are finding that they are revolutionizing the kinds of records that the wholesalers can keep. Wholesalers can now make very detailed and elaborate reports available to retailers that both summarize the past and predict the future. Computers and other advanced business machines are also used for processing orders, billing, and analyzing prices and profits. The people who work with these machines must have a high mechanical aptitude and an aptitude for data, as well as specialized technical training. Wholesalers also need people to work as secretaries, file clerks, telephone operators, and bookkeepers. These jobs are classified as sedentary.

Office jobs are not considered to be marketing jobs as such. But they have one important advantage for people who are interested in marketing careers. They represent a way of getting that all-important "foot in the door." You can use these jobs as a way of getting hired, gaining experience, and learning about what the company does and how it operates. This can help you to move into the jobs for which you need marketing skills.

STAFF SPECIALIST JOBS. To back up their merchandising activities, independent wholesalers, as well as corporate chains, may employ various kinds of highly trained specialists in staff positions. For example, they may hire marketing researchers, who can analyze buying trends, and people who can prepare advertisements to be used by the stores. They may hire display experts, who prepare display materials and give advice on display problems. Real estate experts and engineers help in planning new stores. Management and labor relations experts and lawyers are also needed.

Still another kind of special knowledge that is important in food wholesaling is "materials handling." This involves knowing how to move products safely in and out of the warehouse and how to store them properly. Because of the perishable nature of many food products, this work is especially necessary. Another kind of staff specialist, that is important in food wholesaling is the consumer affairs specialist, who may be trained in home economics and who advises the company on all problems related to consumers. In most cases, the people who are hired as staff specialists have had highly specialized training.

Moving Into Management

Because food wholesaling is such a competitive business, it has a great need for people with management ability. There are two ways to reach the management level. One is by working your way up within the wholesaling company. There are many presidents of wholesaling companies today who started out in the warehouse and moved up step by step.

The kinds of middle management jobs that you could move up to are head order assembler, head packer, or head receiving, shipping, or stock clerk. You could also become a dispatcher, who supervises the routing of the delivery trucks. Other management jobs are warehouse manager, merchandising manager, personnel director, advertising director, or controller.

The other approach to the management level in wholesaling is through retailing. For example, it is very common for the manager of a chain store to move to the job of store supervisor. This job is in many ways like the job of field representative for a voluntary chain, and it requires a great deal of knowledge about how food stores are run. People also move from management-level jobs in food store stock work to similar jobs in wholesale warehouses. In either case, it is possible to keep moving up. In a large corporate chain, you could eventually become the general merchandising manager or the general manager of the office and warehouse, working directly under the president.

Promotions in food wholesaling do not come automatically however. They come to those people who are willing to put in the time and effort needed to learn this complex business. This means learning on the job, taking the training courses that the company offers, and taking extra courses whenever possible.

- **BUILDING YOUR MARKETING VOCABULARY**

  Define each of the following terms and then use each one in a sentence.

  bulk breaking service wholesaler
  buyer specialty wholesaler
  rack jobber truck jobber

- **UNDERSTANDING WHAT YOU HAVE READ**

  1. List three ways in which food wholesalers cut costs for producers and three ways in which they cut costs for retailers.
  2. Explain how independent food wholesalers have reacted to the competition from the corporate chains.
  3. What effect have independent wholesalers had on the operating methods of the corporate chains?
  4. What is the significance of the Uniform Product Code?
  5. Name two different ways of getting into management-level jobs in food wholesaling.

- **APPLYING WHAT YOU HAVE LEARNED**

  1. Below is a list of facts about food retailing. Give a statement about food wholesaling that is comparable to each one.
     a. Job opportunities can be found in every village and city.
     b. Business operates from a store.
     c. Many part-time jobs are available for beginners.
     d. Ability to transfer to other marketing businesses exists.
     e. Marketer buys goods for resale to ultimate consumers.
     f. Field offers high degree of job security.
     g. Promotions from within the store are common.
  2. Invite one or more of the following people to come to your classroom to discuss the requirements and satisfactions of their kind of work: (a) a store supervisor for a corporate chain, (b) a field representative for a voluntary chain, (c) a salesworker for an unaffiliated full-service wholesaler, (d) a driver/salesworker for a rack jobber, (e) a driver/salesworker for a truck jobber, or (f) a truck driver for a corporate chain or full-service wholesaler. You can get their names from your local food store managers.
  3. List as many advantages and disadvantages of careers in food wholesaling as you can think of. Then write a paragraph stating whether your list shows that food wholesaling is or is not a real career alternative for you.

Apparel and Accessories

After reading Part 22, you will be able—
- To explain why there is a strong risk factor in the marketing of apparel and accessories.
- To list seven kinds of retailers that handle apparel and accessories.
- To explain why buying is an especially important function for apparel and accessories retailers.
- To answer a series of questions designed to help you determine whether marketing apparel and accessories is or is not a real career alternative for you.

The marketing of apparel and accessories is a multibillion-dollar-a-year business. It is concerned with selling clothing and the many other things that people wear with their basic items of clothing. The marketing of apparel and accessories is subject to rapid changes. In fact, there are few areas of marketing where the effects of political, social, and economic change are felt more immediately. People's clothing choices directly reflect their responses to what is going on in the world.

The marketer of apparel and accessories has to be able to predict accurately not only what people are going to want to wear but also when they are going to want it. When the right style is marketed at the right time, the marketer is a success. But when a style is put on the market before people are ready for it or after they are tired of it, it can be a marketing disaster. This means that there is a strong risk factor in marketing apparel and accessories. Also, the pace is very fast in this field, for the merchandise must be moved in and out of the stores before it is "stale." This has always been true. But today, when change is so rapid and so commonplace, anticipating people's wants means a faster pace and greater risks than ever before.

For people who enjoy the stimulation and excitement of constant change, the marketing of apparel and accessories can be very rewarding. People who have a special interest in style are also drawn to this field. This means being sensitive to how color, line, design, fabrics, and other materials can work together to improve a person's appearance. But it is important to see beyond the glamour of apparel and accessories. In this highly competitive business, the most effective way to balance the risks is to have managers and employees with a solid background of marketing knowledge and experience.

Now let's look at the apparel and accessories field more closely.

UNDERSTANDING THE INFLUENCE OF FASHION

What products are considered to be part of the apparel and accessories industry? The list includes the following categories:

Women's, misses', and juniors' outerwear and accessories: blouses, dresses, coats, suits, skirts, slacks, pants suits, hats, lingerie, scarves, hosiery, and costume and fine jewelry.

Men's and boys' outerwear and furnishings (*accessories*): coats, suits, trousers, sport jackets, shirts, work clothing, nightwear, underwear, ties, handkerchiefs, socks, jewelry, and other accessories.

Girls', children's, and infants' outerwear and accessories: coats, dresses, blouses, suits, shirts, slacks, playclothes, underwear, sleepwear, and jewelry items.

Leather goods: shoes, boots, slippers, gloves, belts, wallets, purses, and purse accessories.

Career apparel: uniforms and clothing that identifies the employees of such businesses as hotels and airlines.

It is important to realize that fashion is a major influence in all of these categories. A **fashion** is a style that is accepted by a group of people at a particular time. Fashion has always been a major factor in marketing women's apparel and accessories. But, in recent years, fashion has also become very important for men and children. Men's clothing today no longer looks as though it was all copied from the same drab model. Men now have their choice of a wide variety of styles, in every color of the rainbow. The same thing is true for children, and even in infants' wear, where things have moved far away from the old-fashioned standard of pink for girls and blue for boys.

The emphasis in fashion merchandising today is not to make everybody follow the leader. There isn't just one look that is acceptable, but a whole variety of looks that are based on individual tastes. People have always used clothing as a way of answering their needs—not only the physical need to be protected from the weather but also the need to be accepted and respected. Clothing has also always provided an important way of answering the basic human need for beauty. Today clothing is also widely accepted as a way to answer the need for self-actualization. It is now fashionable for people to express their own personalities through the clothing they wear.

SELLING APPAREL AND ACCESSORIES TO THE PUBLIC

The retailing of apparel and accessories is necessarily a very varied business. This is because no one retailer could possibly please all the various kinds of people that want to buy apparel and accessories. Think about how many different sizes and shapes people can be. They also have different tastes about styles and colors, different amounts of money to spend, and different ideas about what customer services are important. Instead of trying to take care of all kinds of people, each retail apparel and accessories business must know exactly what kind of customer it hopes to reach and make its plans accordingly.

This explains why retail apparel and accessories businesses are so different from each other. Some stores are dignified and elegant; others are "mod." Some are formal; some are friendly. Some are fancy; some are plain. These differences are important to you when you go shopping. They are also important if you want to find a job in this field that will let you be yourself.

Let us look now at the seven ways in which apparel and accessories are retailed: (1) limited line stores; (2) departmentalized specialty stores; (3) department stores; (4) other general merchandise stores; (5) factory outlet stores; (6) catalog retailing; and (7) direct selling.

In response to the current trend toward more casual clothing, there are many limited-line stores today that specialize in jeans and matching shirts and jackets. (*Courtesy Levi Strauss & Co.*)

Limited Line Stores

Any store that sells only apparel and accessories is a limited line store, just as a food store is. Some apparel and accessories stores sell clothing and shoes for the whole family. But most limit themselves even more, so that they carry either one or a few categories of apparel and accessories, in a particular size, style, or price range. For example, a store may just carry moderate-priced dresses in misses sizes or jeans and shirts for teenagers.

There are also limited line stores that carry a selection of related goods. For example, a store may sell toys, furniture, and clothing for babies. And still another kind of limited line store is the "boutique," which caters to the special tastes of a particular group of people by selling merchandise that is unique in some way. Apparel and accessories boutiques often sell merchandise that has been designed and made by one of the boutique's owners. Or they may sell merchandise that is representative of certain ethnic or national groups.

Most limited line stores are independent businesses, employing fewer than 20 workers. But they can also be part of such corporate chains as Lerner Stores Corporation and Three Sisters. Some chains, such as the Kinney Shoe Corporation, are owned by the manufacturer. And a few apparel and accessories stores, such as the Modern Bridal Shops, are franchised.

Departmentalized Specialty Stores

Some apparel and accessories stores are so large that they give the impression of being department stores. Because these stores are organized like department stores but carry a more limited range of merchandise, they are called **departmentalized specialty stores.** Sometimes these stores carry only apparel and accessories. For example, Barney's Clothes in New York City carries a very wide selection of clothing for men. There are other departmentalized specialty stores that carry primarily apparel and accessories but also have departments for household linens, gifts, and other kinds of merchandise. I. Magnin in San Francisco and the Neiman-Marcus Company in Dallas are examples of this kind of store.

The departmentalized specialty store usually has departments for different kinds of apparel and accessories, in different sizes and price ranges. There may even be departments that are set up as boutiques, to appeal to special interest groups. The total effect is that of a number of limited-line stores, all under one roof. Departmentalized specialty stores tend to be located in cities. To make it easier for their customers to reach them, many departmentalized specialty stores have opened additional stores in smaller communities. These stores are called

branch stores, because they are set up and run as offshoots of the parent store, offering the same general assortment of merchandise. They are often located in shopping centers, where there are a group of other stores and ample parking to attract customers.

Department Stores

Although department stores sell a very broad range of merchandise and even some services, the sale of apparel and accessories is usually the most important part of their business. In many department stores, the various apparel and accessories departments account for about 50 percent of the total sales. Examples of department stores are Rich's in Atlanta and Marshall Field & Company in Chicago.

Like departmentalized specialty stores, department stores may set up branch stores. They may also operate twigs, which sell just one line of goods rather than the full range of merchandise. (A **twig** may be defined as a limited-line store that is owned and operated by a department store.) Many twigs sell apparel and accessories.

Other General Merchandise Stores

When a store sells a variety of different kinds of merchandise, it is called a **general merchandise store.** Department stores are classified as general merchandise stores, and so are some departmentalized specialty stores. The general merchandise category can include all of the goods discussed in Unit 4 and some of the services discussed in Unit 5.

With this definition, it is easy to see that there are also some other general merchandise stores that are lively competitors in the retailing of apparel and accessories. Included in this group are the national chain department stores run by such companies as the J.C. Penney Company, Montgomery Ward and Company, and Sears, Roebuck and Company. These chains have developed an aggressive approach to fashion merchandising, so that they are often able to set trends rather than just follow them.

Another kind of chain store that sells apparel and accessories for the whole family is the **variety store,** which is a store that stocks a wide assortment of goods in a relatively low price range. Variety stores started as "five-and-ten-cent stores." But they have been gradually expanding the quantity and quality of goods that they sell, so that many of them are now called "junior department stores." Because these stores have been placing much more emphasis on fashion, they are doing a larger volume of business in apparel and accessories each year. Examples of such stores are the F.W. Woolworth Company, the S.S. Kresge Company, and the G.C. Murphy Company.

General merchandise discount stores have also been moving into apparel and accessories more forcefully. Like variety stores, discount stores have been trying to get away from the idea that they only carry standard items.

Factory Outlet Stores

There are apparel manufacturers who run outlet stores at their factories. These "factory outlet stores" provide a way of selling goods that are "seconds," meaning that they have a flaw of some kind. Samples, returned goods, and discontinued styles and colors are also sold. These are cash-and-carry stores and are usually plain in every way, offering almost no customer services. But because of their bargain prices, they are popular with price-conscious consumers.

There are other stores that are also called factory outlet stores but are not actually connected with a factory. These stores act as middlemen in buying the kinds of goods from the manufacturers that would be offered in regular factory outlet stores and offering them to the public. These are cash-and-carry stores too, offering no frills. In addition, they are often located in out-of-the-way places, where the rent is low. But many people believe that the low prices make up for the extra effort that is required to shop in such stores.

Catalog Retailing

There is another way for the public to buy apparel and accessories that has become increasingly important in recent years. This is **catalog retailing,** which is a form of retailing that allows the customer to order either by telephone or by mail from a catalog that gives a description and usually also a picture of the merchandise. The three giants in this field—Montgomery Ward, Sears Roebuck, and J.C. Penney—combine catalog retailing with their chain store businesses. Besides these giants, there are a great many other catalog-retailing companies. Some of them are general merchandise retailers, whereas others specialize in apparel and accessories. Sometimes these companies also run retail stores, but, in many cases, their whole business is catalog retailing. There are also some producers of apparel and accessories who market directly to the consumer in this way.

Direct-Selling Companies

Another form of nonstore retailing that is used for some apparel and accessories items is **direct selling.** This is a method of retailing where the salesworker contacts the ultimate consumer directly, usually in the consumer's home but sometimes in other places. For example, the line of clothing made by Doncaster, Inc., is sold by direct salesworkers from their own homes. They invite potential customers to come to see samples and pictures of the latest styles and then take orders for merchandise to be delivered at a future date. Another example of a direct-selling company in apparel and accessories is Sarah Coventry. In this case, the salesworkers go directly to the customers' homes to sell jewelry.

Catalog retailing is an important method of selling clothing and accessories. (*Courtesy L. L. Bean, Inc.*)

"Rugger" Shirt

Fine, light weight cotton knit shirts by Gant. Similar to Rugby shirts with white collar and wide 1½" stripes. Attractive, comfortable and washable.
Full proportioned with 3-Button placket and long square tails. Short, open sleeves. Weight about 6 oz.
Three patterns: Navy and Red Stripes. Navy and Green Stripes. Navy and White Stripes. Men's sizes: Small, Medium, Large and Extra Large.
1748 "Rugger" Shirt, $14.00 postpaid.

Bean's Walking Shorts

Designed for comfort and durability. British style with pleated front and wide, full legs. Inseam about 8½" to just above the knees. Self-belt waistband with adjustable tabs on sides. Deep, strong front and rear pockets.
Fabric is a sturdy Chino twill of breathable polyester/cotton. Washable. Color, Tan. Weight about 14 oz.
Men's even waist sizes 30 to 46.
1885 Walking Shorts, $17.50 postpaid.

Men's Velour Pullover

Fine cotton velour fabric. Double knit with a thick, soft and uniquely comfortable finish. The fabric is colorfast and gets even softer with age. Wash separately and drip dry; or dry clean.
Attractively styled with longer point collar and 3-button placket. Full length sleeves with knit wrists. Tailored for comfortable fit. Pleasingly warm for after swimming or tennis, or cool summer weather.
Weight 13 oz. Three colors: Forest Green. Beige. Swiss Blue.
Men's sizes: Small (38), Medium (40), Large (42) and Extra Large (44).
1774 Men's Velour Pullover, $22.50 postpaid.

Cotton T-Shirts

For hiking, cycling and other active sports. 100% combed cotton for absorbent comfort. Colorfast, pre-shrunk and machine washable.
Three colors: Navy. Green. Yellow. Weight 4 oz. each.
Men's sizes: Small (36), Medium (38-40), Large (42-44) and Extra Large (46).
1746 Cotton T-Shirts, $2.85 each. Three for $7.25 postpaid.

Men's Denim Shorts

Sturdy 10 oz. cotton denim with double-needle stitching throughout. Reinforced at stress points and will withstand a lot of abuse. Washable.
Four front pockets, two with inverted pleats and snap flaps for securely carrying small items. Two hip pockets with snap flaps. Wide 1¾" belt loops and brass zipper.
Color, Navy Blue Denim. Men's even waist sizes 30 to 42. Weight 16 oz.
1833 Men's Denim Shorts, $14.00 postpaid.

L. L. Bean, Inc. Freeport, Me. 04032

GETTING APPAREL AND ACCESSORIES TO RETAILERS

The job of buying the merchandise to be sold is always a very important one for any retailer. But in apparel and accessories it is even more vital. There are two reasons for this. The first is that relatively few apparel and accessories items are sold through wholesalers. Such staples as underwear, hosiery, and men's work clothing are sometimes wholesaled, and some clothing that comes from other countries is collected by wholesalers called "importers." But, in most cases, it is important to get apparel and accessories items into the stores as fast as possible before they go out of style. This means that in apparel and accessories the burden of buying is on the retailers, and the burden of selling is on the manufacturers.

The second reason that buying is especially important is that apparel manufacturers, especially in women's wear, tend to be small and highly specialized. They may manufacture just one size range, such as "junior," in just one narrow area, such as coats, dresses, or sportswear. Most independent retailers have to buy from many different suppliers in order to offer a good selection.

There is a definite trend toward large manufacturing companies. This is partly because the chain stores are asking for the reliability that the large companies can offer. It is also partly because today's high costs have forced some small companies out of business and caused others to "merge" (join together). The large companies have brought modern distribution methods such as computer ordering and mechanized order filling to the apparel and accessories industry. But there are still far more small companies than large ones, so that buying continues to be a major problem for most apparel and accessories retailers.

On the other hand, selling is a major problem for the manufacturers. They need salesworkers who have both training and experience in marketing. To get the required degree of skill, manufacturers may rely on their own salaried salesworkers. Or they may use salesworkers called **manufacturer's representatives** who are in business for themselves. These independent salesworkers are paid on a commission basis to sell a manufacturer's products.

Let's see now how the buyers for the retailers and the salesworkers for the manufacturers get together.

Selling and Buying Trips

Some manufacturers have traveling salesworkers who visit the retailers in their stores. In other cases, the buyers have to go directly to the showrooms of the manufacturers. Many buyers are attracted to New York City, where the largest number of women's wear manufacturers is located. Many stores also send their buyers to different parts of the

Buyers for apparel and accessories stores must travel to major cities to see and select new merchandise. These buyers are examining a jewelry manufacturer's new line at a trade show held in a New York City hotel. (*The New York Times/ Barton Silverman*)

world such as Paris, Rome, and the Orient, to satisfy their customers' tastes for the new or unusual.

The traveling that is involved in sending the manufacturers' salesworkers directly to the stores or the buyers directly to the manufacturers has a high cost in both time and money. To simplify the amount of traveling that has to be done, many manufacturers' salesworkers and representatives maintain permanent showrooms in certain major cities. These showrooms are grouped together to make it easier for the buyers and sellers to meet. In addition to grouping their showrooms, manufacturers' salesworkers and representatives work together to sponsor "market weeks" at those times of the year when the manufacturers want to introduce their new "lines."

Buying Offices and Store Groups

To simplify their buying problems, many stores use the services of "buying offices." These offices are located in the cities where showrooms are maintained. Buying offices sell advice. They study the apparel and accessories market carefully. They know what the latest trends are and which manufacturers are following those trends. They send special reports to the retailers not only about styles and prices but also about what other retailers are doing.

Another way to simplify buying is to join a "store group." This is an informal association of retailers who share information about where to buy. There may be a dozen or so members of the group. Their stores have to be quite similar. But they also have to be far enough apart geographically so that they don't compete with each other.

LOOKING AT THE KINDS OF JOBS IN APPAREL AND ACCESSORIES

It is not possible to do justice to the many interesting jobs in apparel and accessories in a book this size. But what we can do is to give you some idea of the kinds of jobs that have to be done. We are going to discuss buying, selling, and other merchandising jobs, as well as jobs in sales promotion, operations, personnel, and control. These are the same major areas that any marketer has to cover. We will also discuss jobs for staff specialists and top managers. As you are reading through this discussion, remember that, in the small store, the kind of specialization we are talking about is not necessary or possible.

Buying Jobs

We have already discussed the importance of buying to the success of the apparel and accessories business. In chain stores, the buying is done by a group of highly specialized buyers working from a central headquarters. Some department stores and departmentalized specialty stores are now doing their buying in a similar way. But many of them still use a system where the buying is handled separately in each department.

In this system, the buyer is also the manager of the department and is responsible for all the other workers in the department. This includes the sales and stock workers, as well as the people who manage the same departments in the branch stores. To handle this very responsible job, a high degree of skill in marketing is required. Most large stores have buyer training programs to which people who have had post-high school training in marketing are admitted. These people are given a chance to see how the store as a whole functions before they can become assistant buyers and eventually buyers.

Buyers can be promoted by being moved to more challenging departments. They may also move up to become merchandising managers, who are in charge of eight or ten buyers, and then general merchandising managers, who are in charge of the whole merchandising division.

Most apparel and accessories buyers must be willing to do some traveling. Because they have to figure out not only what items to buy but also how many in each size and color, they need a strong aptitude for data. They must be very up-to-date in their thinking so they can

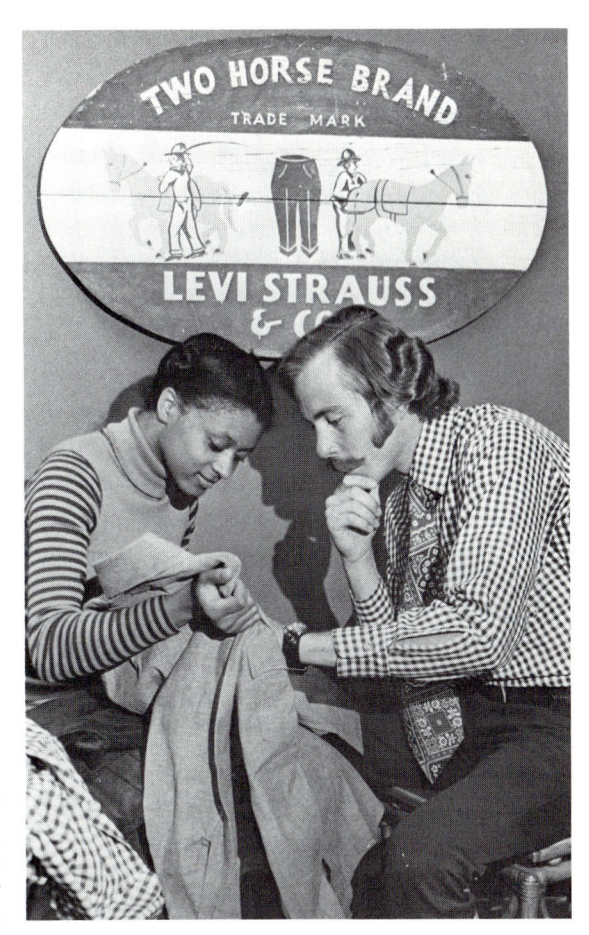

When buying apparel, retail buyers must inspect the merchandise carefully to determine its quality and wearability. *(Courtesy Levi Strauss & Co.)*

anticipate what people are going to want to wear. They must also have good taste and an understanding of what fashion is all about.

Selling Jobs

Because of all the needs people are trying to answer through their clothing choices, the salesworker in apparel and accessories has to know a lot about people. There is a big difference between selling people what *you* like and think they need and selling them what *they* like and really need. This is a job that can be as satisfying as it is difficult. In fact, many apparel and accessories salesworkers turn down promotions to management-level jobs in order to go on working directly with the customers. Because they often earn commissions on what they sell, skillful salesworkers can earn very good money.

Salesworkers in stores generally must be high school graduates

PART 22 • APPAREL AND ACCESSORIES • 249

with a good grasp of both basic skills and social skills. While they are learning the necessary marketing skills, they may be assigned to departments where no real sales ability is required. The people who give minimal sales assistance are called "salesclerks" rather than salesworkers. As they learn on the job, they are promoted to departments where the selling is more and more difficult. Thus the people who work in the better clothing departments are apt to be very seasoned workers. Often these people develop a following of their own, so that customers will refuse to be waited on by anyone else.

The salesworkers for apparel and accessories are usually expected to pay special attention to their own personal appearances. Customers are more willing to accept advice from someone who obviously has a sense of fashion. Salesworkers in this field should also know about the wearing qualities and care of various kinds of materials, the colors and styles that are "new," and what "goes" with what.

There are no specific educational requirements for direct salesworkers. But they must take the training courses given by the companies that they represent. Because they don't punch a time clock, they have to be "self-starters" who can make the most of their time. Salesworkers for manufacturers and wholesalers generally need more marketing skills to start with. Usually they are graduates of community college or four-year college marketing programs.

Other Merchandising Jobs

In chain stores, the head of each department is the department manager. Department managers have the same managerial duties as do buyers in department stores, but they don't do any buying. The department manager's job is part of the chain's management training program. People who have a potential for management may be hired for such training programs from post-high school DE programs. Some variety stores will hire people from high school DE programs who are outstanding and have had good part-time work experience. Department managers in chain stores can move up to the jobs of assistant store manager, store manager, and district manager, and then on to executive work in the regional or central office.

Depending on the store's organization, either the department manager or the buyer is in charge of the department's stockroom. Merchandise is sent from the store's main stockroom to the department's stockroom, where it is stored until it is needed on the selling floor. Stock clerks have an especially important job in apparel and accessories because of the necessity to keep the merchandise fresh and clean. Sometimes they have to wrap the customers' packages, and often they have duties related to inventory control. Thus stock clerks need some aptitude for data. They can be promoted to the job of head

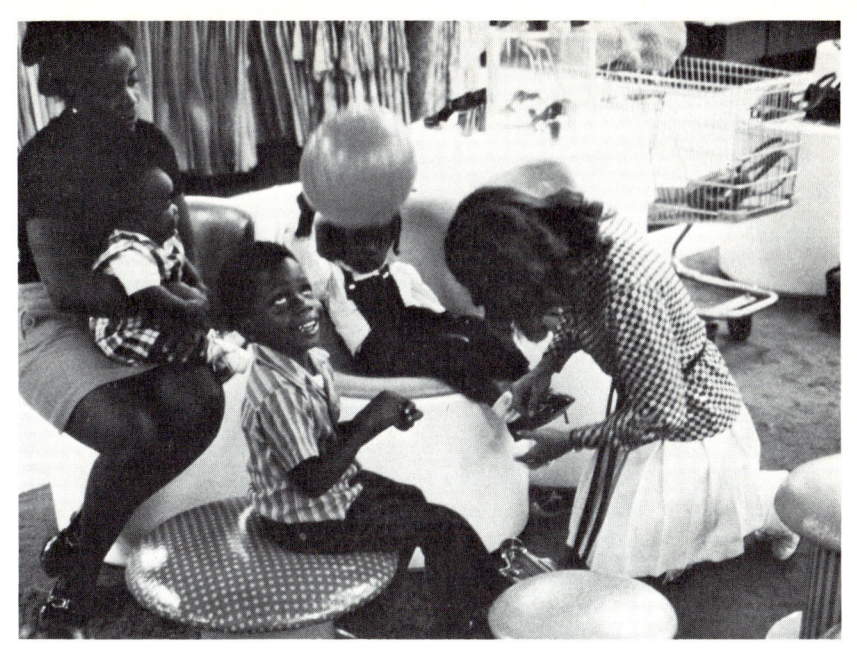

For salesworkers in the apparel and accessories business, there are as many different challenges as there are different products. For example, the person who sells children's shoes must cope with the problem of determining whether a shoe provides a proper fit for the foot of a squirming child. (*Courtesy Montgomery Ward*)

stock clerk or make a lattice-type move into the job of salesworker.

The merchandising division also has jobs for comparison shoppers, who go from store to store comparing prices and quality. Their reports help the buyers meet the competition from the other stores. High school graduates who enjoy shopping can be hired and trained for this work.

Sales Promotion Jobs

Because apparel and accessories must be sold before the season is over, the extra sales push that comes from advertising, display, and public relations is especially necessary. People who are skilled in these fields are much in demand to work for apparel and accessories manufacturers, chain stores, and department stores and to prepare the catalogs for catalog-retailing companies. There are sales promotion jobs for models, who may pose for photographs, model in fashion shows, or model informally in stores or manufacturers' showrooms. Models are chosen on the basis of how well they can show off clothes. Besides being attractive looking they must have a distinct flair for fashion.

Photographers, copywriters, artists, display experts, and public relations workers are all sales promotion workers. There are beginning jobs in sales promotion for people who want to learn these skills. The job of assistant display artist is an example of this. But to get these beginning jobs, young people have to show that they have talent along these lines.

Operations, Personnel, and Control Jobs

You are already familiar with many of the jobs that have to be done in operations, personnel, and control. If you are interested in working more directly with apparel and accessories, you may want to use the beginning jobs in these areas as a way of learning the business. You can also learn the business by working in one of the operations jobs that is peculiar to the apparel and accessories field. This includes jobs for people with sewing and tailoring skills to alter clothes and jobs for pressers to iron clothes that were wrinkled in transit.

You can use these jobs as stepping stones to jobs in merchandising and sales promotion. Or you may find them interesting in their own right.

Staff Specialist and Top Management Jobs

A very influential job in the area of apparel and accessories is that of fashion coordinator. This is a staff job in that the fashion coordinator

Models are often employed by retail stores for such sales promotion activities as fashion shows for the store's customers. *(Courtesy Community Services Administration)*

Bridal consultants help brides select gowns for themselves and their attendants and advise them in their wedding plans. (*Courtesy* Modern Bride)

works in an advisory capacity. The work usually includes advising the buyers on fashion trends and consumer preferences. It also includes setting a fashion image for the business. This image acts as a guideline to the buyers when they are making their decisions. People who are fashion coordinators often have moved up from the job of buyer or merchandise manager and have proven that they are capable of doing management-level work. Another staff specialist job is that of bridal consultant. This person advises brides on wedding customs and helps to coordinate the bridal merchandise that the store buys.

Every apparel and accessories business also needs a top manager, probably called a president, who can coordinate the work that is done in the business. These jobs are vital, especially now, when costs are high and making a profit is difficult.

COUNTING THE PLUSES OF AN APPAREL AND ACCESSORIES CAREER

One of the main advantages of apparel and accessories is that it is an easy field to get started in. Apparel and accessories stores are found all over the country. In many communities, they stay open in the evenings so families can shop together. Some stores are open seven days a week. These long hours mean that the stores need many part-time workers. Getting such a part-time job, either on your own or through your DE cooperative education program, is the best possible way to get started.

It is less easy to get started in a marketing job for a manufacturer. Apparel and accessories factories tend to be located only in certain parts of the country. They also have few opportunities for part-time work. But if you gain store experience, you can more easily move into these jobs at a later date.

Another major advantage of an apparel and accessories career is that it offers a high degree of job security to the people who have developed marketing skills. Even though the rate of failure for individual businesses is high, the industry as a whole is a strong one. Because it answers basic human needs, it has been growing steadily for many years.

A career in apparel and accessories offers you the opportunity to work with attractive things in what are usually very pleasant surroundings. The pay and fringe benefits are at least average and, in many cases, well above average. The discounts that most stores offer their employees on purchases can be considered as extra pay. But perhaps most important of all is the challenge of working in a field that is as alive and up-to-date as the news itself.

- **BUILDING YOUR MARKETING VOCABULARY**

Define each of the following terms and then use each one in a sentence.

branch store
catalog retailing
departmentalized specialty store
direct selling
fashion
general merchandise store
manufacturer's representative
twig
variety store

- **UNDERSTANDING WHAT YOU HAVE READ**

1. Explain why there is a strong risk factor in the marketing of apparel and accessories.
2. What basic human needs do people try to satisfy through their clothing choices?
3. List seven kinds of retailers that handle apparel and accessories.
4. Why is buying an especially important function for apparel and accessories retailers?
5. Explain what each of the following people does: (a) importer, (b) comparison shopper, (c) model, (d) fashion coordinator, and (e) bridal consultant.

- **APPLYING WHAT YOU HAVE LEARNED**

1. Write a report on a store in your area, explaining why you either buy or would like to buy your clothes there. Give the name and

address of the store and state what kind of store it is, according to what you have learned in this part. Discuss the store's fashion image and its quality, price, and customer service policies.
2. Answer the following questions on a separate sheet of paper, using 0 for *no,* 1 for *maybe,* and 2 for *yes.* When you are finished, add up your score. A score of 18–24 is an indication that the apparel and accessories field may be a real career alternative for you.
   a. Are you sensitive to how color, line, and design can work together to improve your own and other people's appearances?
   b. Do you like to keep up-to-date with fashions?
   c. Do you like helping your friends to decide what goes with what?
   d. Do you realize that marketing apparel and accessories is not all glamour?
   e. Do you enjoy working with all kinds of people?
   f. Do you recognize that a person's taste can be very different from your own and still be "good taste"?
   g. Are you patient and tactful?
   h. Could a career in apparel and accessories answer your own personal reasons for working?
   i. Would you be willing to work sometimes in the evening and on weekends?
   j. Would you be willing to learn the marketing skills that would give you job security in this field?
   k. Would you consider a discount on what you buy a desirable fringe benefit?
   l. Would you like to learn more about the apparel and accessories field?

part 23 Home Furnishings

After reading Part 23, you will be able—
- To explain how the concept of fashion affects the marketing of home furnishings.
- To explain why a knowledge of each of the following is important for home furnishings marketers: materials and construction methods, shipping methods, credit, and buying motives.
- To answer a series of questions designed to help you determine whether marketing home furnishings is or is not a real career alternative for you.

There is another area of marketing besides apparel and accessories that is particularly appealing to people who are interested in style, color, and design. This is the marketing of home furnishings, which is more than a $38-billion-a-year business. Part of the reason for the size of the home furnishings business is that people have a basic need to make a home for themselves—a home where they can eat, sleep, work, play, and live safely and comfortably. But this is not the only basic need that home furnishings answers.

From the earliest times, people have also considered their homes to be a way of answering their basic need for beauty. For some people, homes also serve as status symbols, a way of winning the respect of other people. But more and more today, people are seeing their homes as a way to attain self-actualization. They want their homes to reflect the kind of people they are and the life style they have chosen.

Because it helps people to answer their basic human needs, the home furnishings business is an important part of our economy. It is a field that is very diverse, for the people it serves have a wide range of tastes and interests, as well as different amounts of money to spend. It is also a field that is exceptionally challenging, because people tend to shop very carefully for home furnishings. For the most part, these are major purchases, and people want to be sure of their decisions. To meet this challenge, the people who work in this field have to have a broad base of knowledge about marketing in general and home furnishings in particular.

256 • UNIT 4 • CAREERS IN MARKETING GOODS

Included in the home furnishings field are the many products that people use to equip and decorate their homes, such as the following:

- Beds and bedding
- China, glassware, and silverware
- Draperies, curtains, and window shades
- Floor coverings
- Furniture
- Household appliances
- Household linens and fabrics
- Housewares
- Lamps and shades
- Mirrors and pictures
- Radios, stereo equipment, and television sets

In this part, you will learn what marketing these products is all about. You will learn why the home furnishings field is growing, how retailers sell home furnishings, how retailers buy home furnishings, and how you can build a satisfying career in home furnishings.

WHY THE HOME FURNISHINGS FIELD IS GROWING

Home furnishings used to be a rather staid business. Most people didn't move very often. They bought furniture just once, when they were married, and they expected it to last a lifetime. But today the picture is quite different. We have what is called a "mobile population," meaning that people move around a lot. People's jobs may take them to another part of the country. Or they may move from a small house or apartment to a larger one as the family grows and then back to a small house or apartment when the children grow up and become independent. With every one of these moves, the home furnishings business benefits to some extent. Things like curtains, draperies, rugs, and some pieces of furniture may not fit in the new home, and so they have to be replaced.

There are many new households being set up because of the "baby boom" of the late 1940s and early 1950s. These babies are now young adults, moving out of their parents' homes to be married or to start life on their own. Still another factor is that many people today own second homes. The second home may be a cabin in the mountains or a cottage at the seashore, or it may be a boat or a mobile home. Whatever it is, it has to be equipped with the kinds of products that the home furnishings business sells.

But even the people who aren't moving and who have only one home are buying more home furnishings. Today people are much more

People select home furnishings that fit their life style. What do these two rooms tell you about the people who live in them? (ABOVE *courtesy Scalamandré Silks, Inc.;* BELOW *courtesy J. Josephson Inc.*)

knowledgeable. They get around more. Magazines, newspapers, and television show them how other people live. To satisfy this more sophisticated taste, the home furnishings business has introduced the concept of fashion in a big way.

For example, there are several lines of household linens that have been designed by some of the most important dress designers. There are bright colors and designs to excite the eye in everything from ashtrays to bunk beds. There is also a lot more emphasis on bringing in unusual things from foreign countries. This emphasis on fashion, which came about because people were demanding it, creates in turn its own demands. When people see these exciting new products, they want them. People today are much less apt to feel that they have to hang on to a sofa or cabinet forever if something more interesting comes along.

The rising expectations that people have for their homes are also reflected in the sale of worksaving appliances. Things that are introduced as luxury items gradually become things that people are convinced they need. An example of this is the television set, which has become so commonplace that many households have more than one set. Today the microwave oven and the videotape recorder are luxury items. But, in a few years, these things may be an accepted part of the general standard of living.

HOW RETAILERS SELL HOME FURNISHINGS

The products that are classified as home furnishings are sold by many different kinds of retailers. Because the concept of scrambled merchandising has become popular in recent years, you can find home furnishings items in such places as supermarkets. However, the largest proportion of home furnishings are sold by seven kinds of retailers: (1) limited-line stores, (2) general merchandise stores, (3) warehouse showrooms, (4) catalog discount showrooms, (5) interior decorating businesses, (6) antique and secondhand stores, and (7) direct-selling companies. As you are thinking about these seven kinds of retailers, remember that there is a wide variation within each category. Home furnishings retailers are like all other retailers in that they each have their own plans for the kinds of customers they want to reach.

Limited-Line Stores

The limited-line stores that specialize in home furnishings are of four types. The first is the kind that sells a general selection of many different kinds of home furnishings. Often these stores are so large that they are organized into different departments and could therefore be called departmentalized specialty stores. The second kind of limited-line store is the one that limits its merchandise more specifically. This

A home furnishings boutique may specialize in patchwork quilts and other handcrafted accessories for the home. (*Courtesy Boston Flea Market, Inc.*)

kind of store may sell one style of furnishings, such as Early American, traditional, Scandinavian, or contemporary. Or it may handle only certain categories of merchandise, selling just lamps, linens, floor coverings, housewares, or appliances, for example. The third type of store may sell goods that are related by a common theme, such as all kinds of furniture and decorative accessories for the patio, or a wide sampling of things made of brass or wicker. The fourth kind of limited-line store may be set up as a boutique, offering an assortment of things that are very unusual.

The limited-line stores that sell such bulky merchandise as furniture and major appliances usually need warehouses as well as stores. The goods that the customers see in the store are floor samples, but the orders are filled from the stock in the warehouse. However, even the warehouse cannot hold a full assortment of merchandise. For example, a dining room table may be available in three different sizes, with each size available in teak, walnut, or rosewood. Likewise, a particular style of sofa may be available in different lengths and also in many different fabrics and colors. The store cannot keep all these choices in stock and therefore orders the goods from the manufacturer after the customer has placed an order. This means that the customer has to wait to get the merchandise, perhaps as long as three months.

General Merchandise Stores

The departmentalized specialty stores that are classified as general merchandise stores have various departments that sell household linens, housewares, and gifts for the home. Department stores have similar departments, and they also have departments that sell various categories of furniture and major appliances. Department stores carry the same range of products in their branch stores, and often they have twigs, where home furnishings are sold.

The national chain department stores sell the same broad cross section of home furnishings as do department stores. They do this not only in their retail stores but also through their catalog-retailing operations. Although the help that salesworkers can give is extremely important in many home furnishings sales, there are also many purchases that can conveniently be made by mail or phone.

General merchandise discount stores, junior department stores, and variety stores also compete in the home furnishings field, offering a wide assortment of popularly priced items that can be counted on for a fast turnover.

Warehouse Showrooms

The **warehouse showroom** is an attempt to answer the problem of having to wait for furniture. This can be defined as a low-overhead furniture or carpet outlet that offers a wide selection of popular merchandise that can be delivered immediately. Warehouse showrooms are usually located away from the high-rent center-city areas. They are often found on major highways, where they can be reached easily.

All the merchandise that is on display in the showroom is in stock in the warehouse, which is part of the same huge building. Warehouse showrooms are efficient rather than fancy. They keep their expenses down by eliminating customer services. This makes it possible for them to lower their prices on many items. Delivery charges are extra, so the customers can save still more money by making "do-it-yourself" delivery arrangements.

The inventory that warehouse showrooms have on hand can be worth as much as $1 million. Since this kind of investment is necessary, it is not possible for the small retailer to open this kind of business. An example of a company that operates a chain of warehouse showrooms is the Levitz Furniture Corporation.

Catalog Discount Showrooms

A relative newcomer in retailing is the **catalog discount showroom**. This is a low-overhead retailing establishment that offers low prices and quick delivery by combining catalog retailing with showroom retailing.

The catalog discount showroom prints a full-color, descriptive catalog that is used to inform potential customers of its merchandise offerings. If the customers want to see the goods, they can go to the showroom where samples are on display.

The customer can order at the showroom or place an order by phone or mail, using the catalog number for the item. The goods are either in stock and can be picked up immediately or they are available within a week. Catalog discount showrooms carry an assortment of general merchandise products, including such home furnishings items as china, silverware, housewares, small appliances, radios, phonographs, and television sets. An example of this kind of outlet is the chain of catalog showrooms run by the Best Products Company.

Interior Decorating Businesses

A job that is very important in the marketing of home furnishings is that of **interior decorator.** This is a person who is trained in the art of decorating and furnishing interiors. Interior decorators have to combine a natural flair for design with specialized training. They have to take courses on such subjects as the history of the various styles of furniture and the sources for unusual home furnishings today. Some interior decorators are employed by stores, while others work through independent retailing businesses. These businesses vary in size from a one-person business that is carried on from the interior decorator's own home to a large firm that has a whole staff of interior decorators, plus an office staff, and operates out of a studio.

Interior decorators sell advice along with merchandise. They show their customers, who are called "clients," pictures or samples of merchandise. Or they may accompany their clients to manufacturers' or wholesalers' showrooms. Often they plan every detail of the client's home and oversee any carpentry, painting, or papering work that has to be done. They may charge extra for this service. But if they have sold the client a great deal of merchandise, the service is apt to be free. Interior decorators specialize in things that are unusual rather than things that are mass-produced for the popular market. Sometimes they run regular retail stores in connection with their decorating businesses.

Antique and Secondhand Stores

By strict definition, an **antique** is an object that is at least 100 years old. But the word is loosely used to mean anything that belongs to the past. People who are interested in antiques in the broader sense of the word search through secondhand stores and antique shops with equal enthusiasm. Because tastes are so different, the things that one person

Secondhand stores and antique shops are a good source of home furnishings and accessories for people who are seeking unusual things for their homes. (*Courtesy Backroads Touring Co., Inc.*)

can't wait to get rid of are exactly the things that another person wants most.

Sales in antique shops and secondhand stores have been booming in recent years, partly because old things represent a nostalgic return to the "good old days." Also, there have been revivals of the fashions of the various decades of the 1900s—the '20s, '30s, '40s and '50s. Just as one example of how this affects the sale of home furnishings, during the 1930s, glass dishes and kitchen bowls made in molds were sold in "five-and-ten-cent stores" as an inexpensive alternative to china. Today this "Depression glass," which many families threw away as junk when times got better, is very much sought after.

The sale of old things is such a big business that there are more than 25,000 antique and secondhand outlets in this country. Antique stores range from very elegant, expensive places that seem like art galleries to country barns, where the cobwebs are part of the image. Mostly they are small stores, with only a few employees, which is also true of secondhand stores. There are also antique departments in many department stores.

Direct-Selling Companies

There are some home furnishings products, such as vacuum cleaners, cookware, china, tableware, and linens, that are sold directly to consumers rather than through stores. Examples of companies that use the

Manufacturers of home furnishings maintain showrooms where retail buyers come to select merchandise. (*Courtesy Kroehler Mfg. Co.*)

direct-selling method to get their home furnishings products to consumers are the Electrolux Corporation, which sells vacuum cleaners, and the Tupperware Home Parties Corporation, which sells plastic kitchenware. Tupperware products are sold by the "party plan," which means that the direct salesworker persuades homemakers to give parties for their friends. The direct salesworker then shows the Tupperware products to the group and demonstrates their usefulness.

HOW RETAILERS BUY HOME FURNISHINGS
Many home furnishings items are sold directly to the retailer by the manufacturer. This may be done through showrooms located at the factories or through showrooms that are maintained in some cities. Like the showrooms for apparel and accessories manufacturers, these showrooms tend to be clustered together. In many cases, they are in marts, such as the famous Merchandise Mart in Chicago, where there is also a Furniture Mart. The manufacturers' representatives or salaried salesworkers service the accounts for each area from these centrally located showrooms.

Home furnishings manufacturers introduce their new lines once or twice a year. They may do this by holding market weeks in the cities where they have showrooms. There are also home furnishings trade shows, where the manufacturers display their products in assigned areas in a large exhibition hall. For furniture, trade shows are held once a year in Chicago and twice a year in High Point, North Carolina. These trade shows make it easy for buyers to see many products at the same time. But many buyers who attend these shows also visit the factories. For example, furniture buyers who attend the trade shows at High Point usually visit at least some of the approximately 50 factories located within a 100-mile radius of High Point. Buyers from this country also visit the trade shows that are held abroad because of the heavy demand for home furnishings made in other countries.

Many home furnishings products are sold through independent wholesalers. These wholesalers may work for just one manufacturer, who finds it easier to turn over the selling problems to the wholesaler. For example, the products of the General Electric Company and the Westinghouse Electric Corporation are distributed in this way. The wholesaler may also specialize in one area of home furnishings, such as giftwares, housewares, or household linens. This kind of wholesaler gathers together the products of many manufacturers for the convenience of the retailers. Those wholesalers who are importers make it easy for the buyers in this country to get hold of items from other countries. Many wholesalers maintain permanent showrooms, just as manufacturers do, and participate in trade shows.

To compete with larger stores and chains, small stores sometimes join in store groups. This cooperative effort makes it possible for them to enjoy the savings that come with large-scale purchasing.

HOW YOU CAN BUILD A CAREER IN HOME FURNISHINGS

Anyone who wants to build a career in home furnishings has to be willing to acquire product knowledge. Information about materials and construction methods is vital not only to buyers and salesworkers but also to warehouse and delivery workers, repairers, and sales promotion workers. Likewise, the special problems connected with shipping home furnishings have to be generally understood—by buyers so they can make realistic plans, by salesworkers so they can explain the situation accurately to the customers, and by warehouse workers who must physically handle the merchandise.

Another major area of concern in home furnishings is credit. Because of the cost of many home furnishings items, many customers could not buy unless they were allowed to pay for the merchandise over a period of time. Home furnishings workers have to understand the various ways in which this may be done.

Home furnishings workers must be willing to learn as much as they can about people and their buying motives. They also have to like people. They must enjoy the differences in people, rather than being disturbed by them, for this is a field where differences are a matter of routine. One customer loves blue, and the next one hates it, and that's the way the day goes. To cope with these differences, home furnishings workers need a special degree of tolerance—a tolerance that must extend to new ideas as well as to people.

For example, it was once thought that pink, red, and orange could not be used together. But today that combination of colors is widely accepted. It was also once thought that every piece of furniture in a room should be the same style. But today people mix and match as they choose, so you might see antique carved wood chairs around a modern chrome and glass table. These are the kinds of turnabout situations that the home furnishings worker must be able to deal with. This is a business that is constantly changing and that needs workers with enough imagination and verve to be able to change with it.

With these general requirements in mind, let's now see how you get started in this field, what working at the career level means, and what management-level jobs there are in the field.

Getting Started

There is a shortage of skilled workers in the home furnishings field. Because of this, beginners who show promise have a good chance of being hired. This is especially true of beginners who have had DE training and who therefore have a good sense of what marketing home furnishings involves. Your best chance of getting started is in retailing. Manufacturing and wholesaling businesses are localized in areas that may not be close to where you live. But there is almost certainly some kind of home furnishings store within commuting distance of your home.

Because home furnishings stores are open long hours, they need part-time workers. Thus you can begin learning this business while you are still in school. If you cannot find part-time work in a home furnishings store but want to work in this area eventually, you will find that any kind of retailing experience will be helpful. This is especially true of jobs in apparel and accessories stores, where you learn to work with fashion and the individual tastes and needs of many different kinds of people.

Beginners may be hired to work in the store's stockroom, warehouse, or office. They may also be hired as salesclerks, to handle the kinds of sales where very little assistance is needed by the customer. Stores with a self-service policy may hire beginners to be trained as cashiers. Still another way to begin is to work as a helper to a display artist or interior decorator. In this case, you would run errands, gather the merchandise for display, and do other miscellaneous jobs. To be hired for this kind of job, you need artistic talent.

Working at the Career Level

Acquiring the skills that are necessary to work at the career level in home furnishings isn't difficult. Manufacturers' associations, as well as wholesalers, sponsor courses for home furnishings employees, who are often paid for the hours that they spend taking these courses. It is also possible to take courses at local business schools in the evenings, or during the day if you work the late shift. Making this effort to learn is very worthwhile.

Because skilled workers are in demand in this field, there is a high degree of job security for trained career-level workers. There is also security in that the skills you learn in this field are easily transferred to other areas of marketing. Just as one example, someone who has been a buyer for a home furnishings store could move over to a buying job with a hotel. This kind of flexibility is an important advantage.

People who sell home furnishings must have a good sense of color and design so that they can help people select things that complement one another. (*Courtesy Montgomery Ward*)

The career-level jobs in home furnishings fall into six groups: (1) buying jobs, (2) selling jobs, (3) interior decorating and display jobs, (4) warehousing jobs, (5) service jobs, and (6) other career-level jobs.

SELLING JOBS. Salesworkers in home furnishings have the satisfaction of being able to work directly with people. Because many of them get commissions on what they sell, their earnings can be high. Also, selling often gives salesworkers the opportunity to follow their own interests. For example, a person who enjoys fine cooking can work in a shop that sells the utensils needed for special recipes. Selling home furnishings can be so rewarding that many people make it their lifetime career.

The people who sell such "big-ticket" merchandise as furniture and carpets have usually worked their way up through more and more difficult departments. Many of them have learned so much along the way that the stores where they work call them "home furnishings counselors." Their customers rely heavily on them for advice and expect them to be patient and understanding. Salesworkers who have these advanced skills may be assigned to "in-the-home selling." In this case, the salesworker takes samples and photographs to the customer's home and gives on-the-spot advice. The people who do in-the-home selling for stores, like the salesworkers who work for the direct-selling companies, must have the ability to make people feel at ease and must also have a good deal of tact.

Selling for manufacturers and wholesalers is a highly skilled job. People who have had community college or four-year college training can be hired for sales training programs on this level. Retail salesworkers can move over to these training programs too. Salesworkers for manufacturers and wholesalers have so much product knowledge that they are able to teach courses for retail salesworkers, to help them improve their selling abilities.

BUYING JOBS. There are training programs for community college or four-year college graduates who want buying jobs in home furnishings. People who work in other areas of home furnishings often go to school part time to qualify for these buying jobs. Buyers may work in stores, in the central headquarters of chain stores, and for wholesalers. They have to be very sensitive to changes in life styles so they can buy the things the consumers will want. They need an aptitude for data so they can order the right quantities at the right prices, and they must be willing and able to travel.

INTERIOR DECORATING AND DISPLAY JOBS. In home furnishings stores, it is especially important to spark the customer's imagination through vivid displays. By putting things together in new ways, the stores can give customers ideas for their own homes—ideas that translate into sales. To do this work, stores need display artists and interior decorators to work with customers in an advisory or selling capacity.

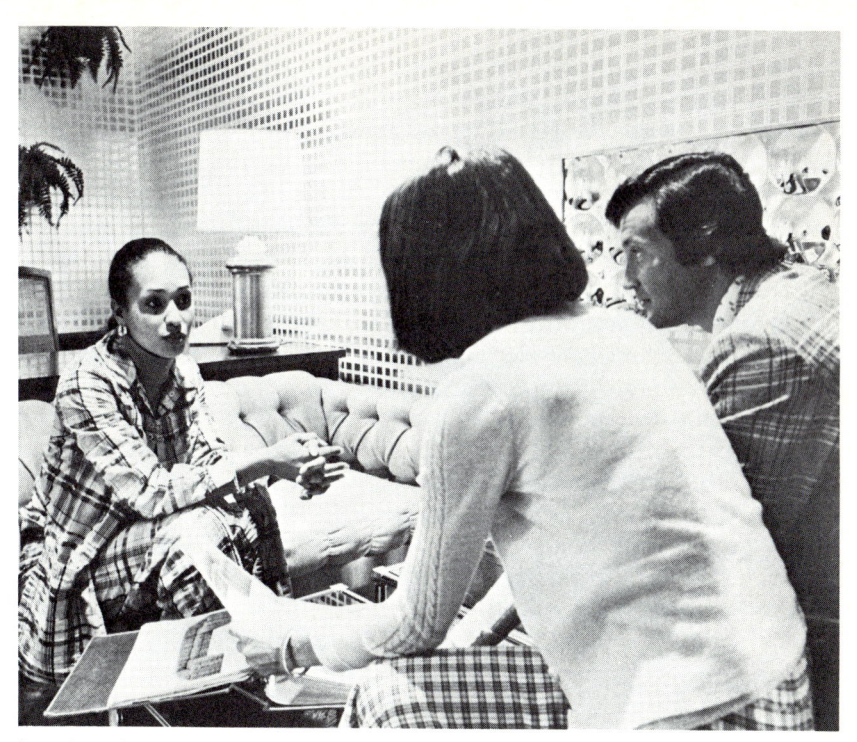

Interior decorators must be good listeners. In order to design a room decor that the customers will be happy with, they must first know the customers' tastes and style of living. (*Courtesy Sears, Roebuck and Co.*)

Interior decorators may also give decorating clinics for civic groups or young people who are starting their own homes.

Display artists and interior decorators also work as staff specialists in chain stores and for wholesalers and manufacturers. People with artistic talent who start out as helpers can work their way up to becoming full display artists or interior decorators if they make the effort to get the additional schooling.

Interior decorators who work directly with customers must know how to draw people out and find out what kinds of things they like and how they want to live. Besides being good listeners, interior decorators also have to be able to speak clearly and simply so the customers can understand the plans that are being presented.

WAREHOUSING JOBS. There are warehousing jobs in home furnishings with manufacturers, wholesalers, and retailers. Because there is so much automation in modern warehouses, warehouse workers have to be able to work with machines in a responsible way. Receiving clerks sometimes assemble merchandise that has been shipped knocked down, so they must have an aptitude for working with their

PART 23 • HOME FURNISHINGS • 269

hands. Stock clerks have to know how various materials should be handled so the merchandise will be undamaged. Truck drivers and delivery workers also have to know how to handle merchandise. Claims clerks must know how to investigate and handle customer complaints. They have to be very tactful and able to handle customers who may be angry.

SERVICE JOBS. The customers for many home furnishings products expect special services. For example, people who buy major appliances expect to have them installed and serviced. This service may be supplied by the store, or the store may arrange for it to be done by the manufacturer's or wholesaler's staff of service workers and repairers. In any case, it is usually the manufacturer who trains these people. A strong mechanical aptitude is needed for this kind of work.

There are also career-level jobs for floor covering installers and drapery installers, as well as for people who can make draperies and slipcovers to order. These jobs also require an aptitude for working with your hands. You could start out as a helper in these jobs, doing the easy parts of the work under close supervision, and then advance to the harder jobs as you learn.

OTHER CAREER-LEVEL JOBS. The maintenance jobs in home furnishings are very important, because a model room or display area covered with dirt would not promote many sales. There are also important jobs for bookkeepers, accountants, and other office workers. Career-level jobs exist for artists, photographers, copywriters, and layout artists to prepare advertisements, brochures, and catalogs. This kind of work often has a high pressure element to it because new ideas must constantly be thought up and deadlines have to be met.

Working in Management

There are management-level positions in all six of the job areas we have just discussed. The wholesaler's salesworker can become a sales manager, and the salesworker for the manufacturer can become a regional, and then national, sales manager. In many stores, the buyer for the department is also the boss of all the department's workers and is responsible for the successful operation of the department.

In the warehouse, there are supervisors of the various kinds of clerks. There is also the traffic manager, who is in charge of all shipping problems. This involves knowing the schedules and rates of various shipping companies. Because freight costs are so high in home furnishings, this is an extremely important job, as is the job of warehouse manager. This person has to have very specialized knowledge about how modern warehouses are run. People who want to advance to the jobs of traffic or warehouse manager must plan to get additional schooling.

Other management-level jobs are head interior decorator, display director, advertising director, service manager, personnel director, and controller. There is also the job of store manager, which can lead to executive jobs in the chain stores that sell general merchandise or home furnishings exclusively. Examples of home furnishings chain stores are Friendly Frost Stores and W. & J. Sloan.

It would also be possible for you to open your own home furnishings store. There are some franchise possibilities, such as the Bed & Bath Fashion Shops. And some manufacturers will give store owners various kinds of assistance in setting up and running their stores. However, you should not try to open your own store until you have gained a lot of direct experience in this field. The marketing of home furnishings is not for amateurs.

• BUILDING YOUR MARKET VOCABULARY

Define each of the following terms and then use each one in a sentence.

antique
catalog discount showroom
interior decorator
warehouse showroom

• UNDERSTANDING WHAT YOU HAVE READ

1. What basic human needs does the home furnishings business answer?
2. Explain how the concept of fashion affects the marketing of home furnishings.
3. Are all home furnishings products marketed directly from the manufacturer to the retailer? Explain your answer.
4. Explain why a knowledge of each of the following is important for home furnishings marketers: materials and construction methods, shipping methods, credit, and buying motives.
5. How can experience in apparel and accessories help you in marketing home furnishings?

• APPLYING WHAT YOU HAVE LEARNED

1. Divide your class into committees to visit the home furnishings stores in your area. Each committee will be expected to present an oral report to the class on how successfully the store used display to make people want to buy.
2. Answer the following questions using 0 for *no,* 1 for *maybe,* and 2 for *yes.* When you are finished, add up your score. A score of 18–24 is an indication that the home furnishings field may be a real career alternative for you.

a. When you go to someone's house, do you notice the way it is decorated?
b. Do you ever think about how you want your own home to look, when you have one of your own?
c. Do you like to look at pictures in magazines of attractive rooms or do you "window shop" home furnishings stores?
d. Do you enjoy being around things that are colorful and well designed?
e. Could a career in home furnishings answer your own personal reasons for working?
f. Would a home furnishings career offer you the chance to work with people in the way that means the most to you?
g. Do you enjoy the differences in people's tastes and life styles?
h. Can you be patient when people are slow to make decisions?
i. Are you willing to work in a field where the working hours are not regularly 9 to 5, Monday through Friday?
j. Would you be willing to acquire the product knowledge that you need in order to work in this field?
k. Did the material in this part interest you?
l. Would you like to learn more about how home furnishings are marketed?

part 24
Products for Health and Beauty

After reading Part 24, you will be able—
- To define each of the three kinds of drugstores.
- To explain why wholesaling is important in the marketing of health and beauty products.
- To assist in putting together a class report on the marketing of health and beauty products in your community.
- To write a summary of why you think the marketing of health and beauty products is or is not a real career alternative for you.

Another business that answers basic human needs is the marketing of health and beauty products. To understand the importance of this business, you have to be aware that the term "physical fitness" is no longer something that applies just to athletes. The number of years that people in this country can expect to live has been steadily increasing. In 1900, men could expect to live 46.3 years, and women 48.3 years. But the most recent estimate of the life expectancy is 67.4 years for men and 74.9 years for women.

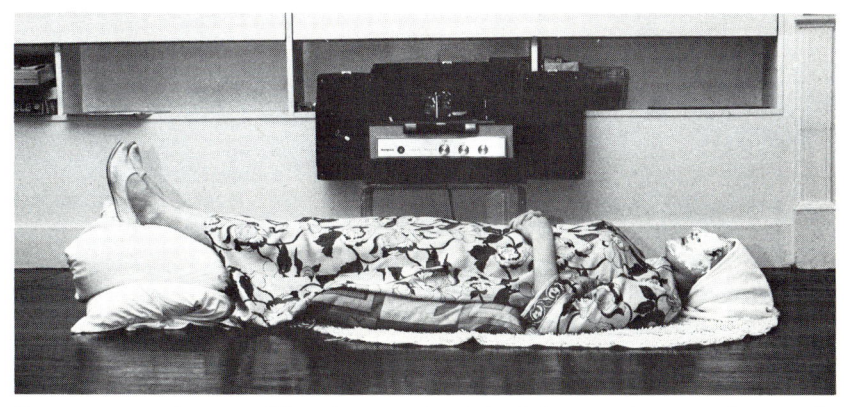

Because people are willing to spend a lot of time and money to remain healthy and attractive looking, the marketing of health and beauty products has become a vital business. (*Bonnie D. Unsworth*)

One reason for this increase is that much more is known today about how to take care of the human body. Medical science has made astounding advances in the treatment and cure of many diseases. Also, people are generally much more aware of how important it is to safeguard their health. Today it is a commonly accepted fact that taking care of yourself not only helps you live longer but also helps you feel the effects of old age less. Because people now feel young so much longer, they are interested in looking as young as they feel.

There is a wide range of products that help people fulfill their need to keep their bodies healthy and attractive and also their need to win the respect of other people. The marketing of these products is a very important part of our economy, providing career opportunities for many different kinds of people—perhaps for you.

RETAILING HEALTH AND BEAUTY PRODUCTS

There are many health and beauty products that are sold to ultimate consumers by retailers. The kinds of retailers that handle these products include drugstores, stores that specialize in selling beauty products, supermarkets, variety stores, general merchandise discount stores, department stores, and departmentalized specialty stores. Beauty products are sold in two other important ways: by direct selling in the customer's home and by service businesses. Now let's take a look at the ways in which these various kinds of retailers handle the sale of health and beauty products.

Three Kinds of Drugstores

The key part of every drugstore is the **prescription department,** where the medicines that doctors have prescribed for their patients are prepared. This work must be done by **registered pharmacists.** These are people who have been trained in the science of "pharmaceuticals" (drugs) and are licensed by the state in which they work. Pharmacists have to meet such rigid educational requirements that they are considered professional people.

About 10 percent of all drugstores are **professional drugstores.** These drugstores handle only prescriptions and some health products and first aid supplies that can be sold "over the counter."

The majority of drugstores, about 76 percent, are **general drugstores,** which carry a range of products besides drugs and health products. General drugstores do a large business in beauty products. These products used to be restricted to women, but they are now becoming more important for men too. General drugstores also carry such items as candy, stationery, paperback books, greeting cards, hosiery, and film. They often have lunch counters too.

Doctors' prescriptions for medicines are filled by pharmacists, who are trained professionals licensed by the state in which they work. (*Courtesy Unity Drug*)

A third type of drugstore is the **variety drugstore,** which is a combination drugstore and variety store. In these stores, the idea of carrying nondrug items has been expanded to include many different kinds of general merchandise items. Besides the things that the general drugstore carries, the variety drugstore may stock toys, small appliances, housewares, jewelry, clothing items, and sporting goods. Variety drugstores work on the low-profit, fast-turnover concept. Except for their prescription departments, they are self-service stores. Because their drug prices are generally lower than those of other drugstores, they are thought of as discount drugstores. Variety drugstores may be part of corporate chains, or they may be franchised. Also, some companies have some company-owned and some franchised units. An example of this kind of company is the Walgreen Company.

Other Stores That Sell Health and Beauty Products

There are some stores that specialize in the sale of beauty products. For example, there are stores that sell just wigs. These stores are expected to give the customers expert advice about the kind of wig to buy, as well as to have a styling service. There are also stores that specialize in the sale of the cosmetics made by one manufacturer. A good example of such stores are the Merle Norman Cosmetic Studios. There are more than 2,300 of these franchised stores in all 50 states, Canada, and abroad. Expert advice and cosmetic treatments are an important part of the business in such stores, as you would expect.

Over-the-counter health products and beauty products are carried in supermarkets and in variety stores. Large general merchandise stores, such as general merchandise discount stores and department stores, often employ registered pharmacists to run prescription drug departments. These stores also sell a wide variety of other health and beauty products. Departmentalized specialty stores are less likely to handle health products, but they emphasize the sale of cosmetics.

Direct Sales of Beauty Products

Direct selling is a very important way of selling beauty products, accounting for 25 percent of all beauty product sales. Examples of companies that do this kind of selling are Avon Products, Vanda Beauty Counselors International, and the Fuller Brush Company. Direct selling works especially well for cosmetics because of the personal attention that each customer receives. Customers want cosmetics that "fit," that answer their own needs exactly, and so they like having the individual attention of the salesworker.

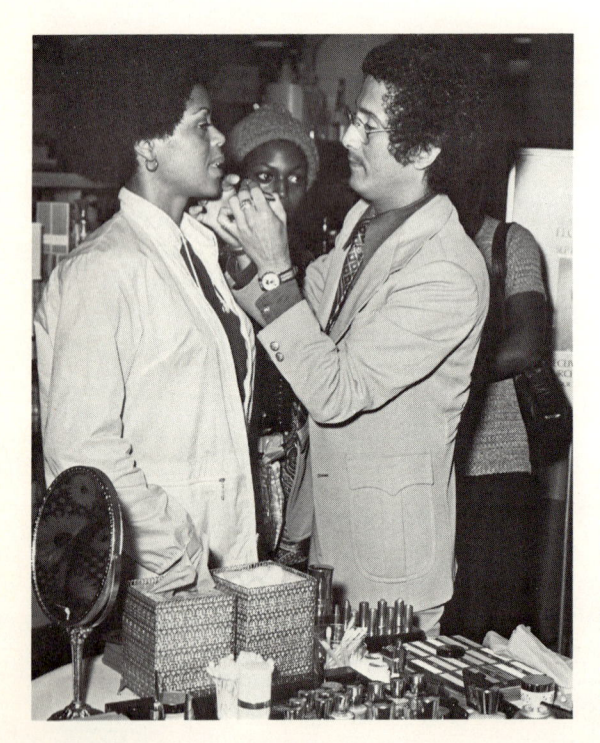

Often manufacturers of beauty products employ beauty experts. They visit stores where the products are sold to advise customers about using makeup and cosmetics and to promote sales. (*Courtesy Flori Roberts, Inc.*)

Sales of Beauty Products by Service Businesses

Many beauty salons and barbershops, which are primarily in the business of selling services, also sell beauty products. They do this as a way of making extra profits for themselves, and also as a service to their customers. People find it convenient to be able to pick up cosmetics while they are already thinking about their appearance.

Sometimes beauty salons and barbershops sell products that are also available in stores. But often they sell a line of products that are not marketed through stores. For example, Redken Laboratories sells its consumer products only through beauty salons and barbershops. The shops that handle Redken consumer products also use many Redken industrial products in producing their services. Thus customers think of the consumer products as an extension of the services they have received.

GETTING HEALTH AND BEAUTY PRODUCTS TO THE RETAILERS

When we talk about health and beauty products, we are talking about an enormous number of products, ranging from cough drops and bandages to hairbrushes and bath oil. To get some idea of how many products are involved, go into a drugstore and see how many different kinds of products and how many different brands of each kind of product there are. With this kind of variety, it would be much too difficult for the druggist to deal with each individual producer. The same thing is true for the other retailers who handle health and beauty products. This is the kind of situation where wholesalers are definitely needed.

Drugstores that have a very large prescription business can buy some of their pharmaceutical supplies directly from the manufacturers. This can only be done when the store is going to buy a quantity of goods that makes direct ordering worthwhile. The major cosmetic lines are also bought directly from the manufacturers. For most health and beauty products sold by retailers, however, the wholesaling process cannot be skipped. Many of the chain stores do their own wholesaling. But the average retailer depends heavily on the many wholesaling companies working in this field.

Some retailers, such as supermarkets, depend on rack jobbers to keep them supplied. Beauty salons deal with industrial distributors called "beauty dealers," who handle the products that the salon uses and the ones it sells. Beauty dealers are service wholesalers who give the kind of assistance that makes running the business much easier.

Druggists rely most heavily on those wholesalers who stock a full line of health and beauty products. This includes small, local wholesalers, as well as chain wholesalers. Two of the best known of the wholesaling chains are McKesson & Robbins and Bergen-Brunswig, whose operations cover the whole country. There are also cooperative drug wholesalers, which are owned by their retailer members. An example of this kind of drug wholesaler is Drug Trading, which has wholesale houses across Canada and thousands of store members.

SUPPLYING THE HEALTH CARE INDUSTRY

Hospitals, clinics, rehabilitation centers, nursing homes, research laboratories, blood banks, doctors, dentists, and medical and dental schools all need many, many different kinds of products to produce their services. The kinds of products that the health care industry uses range from disposable plastic gloves to the finest precision instruments for surgery and from tongue depressors to huge X-ray machines. Some of these products can be bought directly from the manufacturers. But because there are so many different products on the market, most of them have to be handled by wholesalers.

An example of the kind of company that works in this field is the American Hospital Supply Corporation. This company offers over 70,000 different items. Some of these items are manufactured by the company, but most of them are purchased from some 6,000 different suppliers. These figures make it clear how important the work of companies such as this one are to the health care industry. With its buying problems simplified, the health care industry can concentrate on its most important job, providing health care services.

BUILDING A CAREER IN HEALTH AND BEAUTY PRODUCTS

Because health and beauty products answer basic human needs, people go right on buying them even when the economic outlook is not good. There is even some evidence that people buy still more health products when they are worried about other things. They may cut out items that are obviously luxuries, but they still have the need to feel and look their best. This means that if you work in this field, you enjoy a high measure of job security. You also have a special opportunity to help other people, as well as to foster your own interests and talents. If you have always had an interest in medicine, for example, but don't want to work in any of the health care jobs, this could be a good field for you. Or if you have a flair for using cosmetics yourself and like to help your friends, you could turn this flair into a career.

To see what working in this field is all about, let's look at what the various selling jobs are like, what other kinds of career-level jobs there are, and what kind of future you can look forward to in this field.

Working in Sales

In health and beauty products, there is a wide range of selling jobs, from the salesclerk to the person who sells very complicated medical equipment. Each kind of selling job has some special requirements. But they all require a willingness to keep up-to-date. In the field of health and beauty products, new products are constantly coming on the market as new scientific discoveries are made. Thus the salesclerk who thinks that learning the store's stock is a onetime process will very quickly be behind the times. So will the skilled personal salesworker who doesn't keep up with new products and recognize how people's needs change.

SELLING IN STORES. There are many times when it is possible for stores to sell health and beauty products on a self-service basis. Customers may have been presold by advertisements. Or they may be able to make their choices on the basis of information given on the package. Or they may be buying products that they use regularly. To take advantage of this fact, stores display many health and beauty products so customers can easily wait on themselves.

At the other end of the scale are the health products that can only be sold by a registered pharmacist filling a doctor's prescription. Besides knowing how to prepare the prescriptions, pharmacists must have a friendly, reassuring manner that makes the customers feel that someone cares about their problems. In many stores where pharmacists work, they are also expected to be able to answer the customers' questions about nonprescription health products. People want to get a "straight story" from someone as knowledgeable as the pharmacist about what these products will and will not do.

Cosmetics salesworkers must be helpful and understanding about their customers' needs.
(*Courtesy John Bedessem/Carson Pirie Scott & Co.*)

In between the salesclerk and the pharmacist are the jobs that have to be done by people who do not have the professional education that the pharmacist has but who must be very skilled in personal selling. This is true of many of the people who sell cosmetics in stores. They are expected to have the facts about the products they are selling and about competing products as well. They also must be trained in the art of applying cosmetics so they can demonstrate to the customer how the cosmetics should be used for the best effect. This important training is handled in many instances by the cosmetics manufacturers. Cosmetics salesworkers have to be skilled with their hands, as well as tactful and understanding about how sensitive people can be about their appearance. They have to be good listeners so they can find out what each customer wants. And they must use cosmetics to the best effect on themselves so they set a good example.

SELLING DIRECTLY. The salesworkers who sell beauty products directly have many of the advantages of being in business for themselves and few of the risks. They are trained by the companies they work for and are assigned to a certain geographical area under a supervisor who helps them with their problems. But they don't have definite working hours, and they don't get a salary. They work on very generous commissions, in the neighborhood of 25–40 percent of the selling price of each item. Thus their earnings are tied to their own initiative, drive, and energy, just as a small storekeeper's earnings are. But direct salesworkers don't have to put up large sums of money to get started, as a storekeeper does. They usually pay for their sales kit and for the catalogs and small presents that they give to the customers. They also have to pay their own car expenses. But with just those expenses, they are ready for business.

Because direct salesworkers call on people in their homes, they must be very well groomed and have attractive personalities. They have to be sure of themselves so they are not overly disappointed by the turndowns that they are bound to encounter. They also have to know their products, because the customer has plenty of opportunity to ask questions in this kind of situation. There is no special amount of education required for this work, which is frequently done on a part-time basis. Very successful and busy direct salesworkers sometimes need part-time helpers to deliver orders for them. This can be a good way to find out what working in this area is all about.

HANDLING SALES IN SERVICE BUSINESSES. In many service businesses, the actual selling of beauty products is done by the hairdresser or barber. Then the customer just pays the cashier, who may also be the receptionist. Many products are also sold from racks. But there are service businesses that sell so many beauty products that they assign full-time salesworkers to this end of the business. These jobs are very similar to jobs selling cosmetics and other beauty products in stores.

The job of the detail salesworker is very challenging because detail salesworkers must present the manufacturer's products to highly educated health care professionals. *(Courtesy Parke, Davis & Co.)*

SELLING FOR A MANUFACTURER OR WHOLESALER. Routeworkers employed by rack jobbers must be able to judge how many items will be sold within a period of time. They also have to know how to display the goods so that they look attractive and are easy to find. And they must be able to keep accurate records. These are skills that can easily be learned by high school graduates. However, it is much easier to be hired for selling jobs with manufacturers and wholesalers if you have college-level training. These salesworkers have to know a lot about their own products and about their customers' businesses. This makes it possible for them to give their customers the kind of advice and assistance that adds up to more orders.

Sometimes the salesworkers for the manufacturers or wholesalers of health products were premed students in college but then changed their minds about going to medical school. This kind of background is especially helpful, but not necessary, for a **detail salesworker.** This is a salesworker whose job is promoting sales rather than actually selling merchandise. Detail salesworkers are employed by the manufacturers of pharmaceuticals to visit doctors, dentists, pharmacists, and other health care professionals to introduce the company's new products. The point of the detail salesworker's job is not to sell the product but just to point out its advantages over competing products so it will be prescribed and used.

Any salesworkers who deal with health care professionals have to be highly skilled in order to work with such well-educated customers. These salesworkers receive extensive training by their companies.

Looking at Other Career-Level Jobs
Career-level jobs in the marketing of health and beauty products are to be found in other areas besides selling. There are the buying jobs for wholesalers and retail chains. Many of these jobs are highly specialized, so the buyer works in one limited area and becomes expert in it. To be hired for these highly skilled jobs, you generally need post-high school education or experience in related areas of marketing.

There are also jobs in operations. This includes stock work for retailers. It also includes the various jobs that have to be done in the warehouses of chain stores, wholesalers, and manufacturers. There are also many office jobs to be done in marketing health and beauty products, as well as jobs for cashiers in self-service stores. Another important area is sales promotion. Health and beauty products are advertised especially widely. Packaging is also extremely important in this field.

Planning Your Future
You might want to test out the field by taking a part-time job in health and beauty products while you are still in school. Your best bet for getting such a job is to apply to a retail store as a salesclerk, stock worker, cashier, or office worker. Because retail stores stay open such long hours, many of them need part-time workers.

Taking one of these jobs can help you not only to see what this field is really like but also to decide how you could fit in. For example, a beginning job in a store might make you realize that a career in cosmetics is what you really want. By learning all that you can about the products and their uses, you put yourself in a good position to be hired as a salesworker trainee. Then you can move into a buyer training program or go to work in the wholesaling division of a cosmetics manufacturer, possibly giving training courses for retail salesworkers. Owning your own store is another possibility, especially with the franchising opportunities available.

For the people who prefer working on the career level, many lattice-type moves are possible. Those people who want management responsibilities will find that the marketing of health and beauty products can be very rewarding. The chain drugstores have management training programs leading to jobs in store management and to top jobs in the chain. These training programs are open to graduates of community college marketing programs. But it is also possible for employees who have proven their worth to get into these programs. There are other roads into management too. Salesworkers can become sales managers, buyers can become head buyers, and warehouse workers can become warehouse managers. These are also jobs that can lead further up in the health and beauty products field or over into other areas of marketing. Thus a starting job in health and beauty products can be an open door to the kind of future that is right for you.

• BUILDING YOUR MARKETING VOCABULARY

Define each of the following terms and then use each one in a sentence.

detail salesworker
general drugstore
prescription department
professional drugstore
registered pharmacist
variety drugstore

• UNDERSTANDING WHAT YOU HAVE READ

1. How does the general interest in physical fitness affect the marketing of health and beauty products?
2. Why is direct selling an effective way of marketing cosmetics?
3. Explain why wholesaling is important in the marketing of health and beauty products.
4. Can health and beauty products ever be sold on a self-service basis? Explain your answer.
5. List six requirements for cosmetics salesworkers.

• APPLYING WHAT YOU HAVE LEARNED

1. Divide your class into teams to visit the various stores and service businesses in your area that sell health and beauty products. Have each team answer the following questions:
    a. What is the name and address of the business?
    b. How would you classify the business on the basis of what you learned in this part?
    c. What kinds of health and beauty products does the business carry?
    d. What are the pricing policies of the business?
    e. To what extent does the business use the idea of self-service?
    f. What customer services does the business offer?
    g. What hours is the business open?
   Put the reports of all the teams together to make a directory of the businesses in your area that sell health and beauty products.
2. Invite a direct salesworker and a detail salesworker or a salesworker who sells supplies to your local hospital to come to your classroom on different days. Ask them to discuss the requirements and satisfactions of this kind of work.
3. Write a summary of why you think the marketing of health and beauty products is or is not a real career alternative for you.

part 25 Leisure-Time Goods

After reading Part 25, you will be able—
- To list five reasons why the field of leisure-time goods has become an important area of marketing.
- To list the names of the retailers in your community that sell a particular leisure-time product and state what kind of a retailer each one is.
- To choose one of your own leisure-time interests and show how you could develop this interest into a career in marketing leisure-time goods.
- To list five reasons why you either would or would not consider a career in marketing leisure-time goods.

One hundred years ago, only wealthy people had to worry about what to do with their free time. The average worker had a 70-hour workweek, and vacations were almost unheard of. But today the picture is very different. Because of modern machinery and methods, a worker can produce much more work in far less time. So the average workweek is now 40 hours, and in many businesses it is only 35 hours. Vacations of two weeks are standard today and many companies offer three or even four weeks. Also, people do not work as many years as they used to. Because of retirement plans, there are many older people who have free time to enjoy themselves and to do things that they never had time to do before. There is more leisure time in the home too. Automatic washing machines, dishwashers, clothes dryers, and other household appliances have cut down on the number of hours that must be spent on household chores.

All these factors have contributed to the growth of the sale of leisure-time goods—products that people use in their free time to expand and enrich their lives. These products are not seen as frivolous luxuries but as necessities that help people to stay healthy both physically and mentally. People once believed that they should slow up as they get older. But today doctors tell their patients that it is important to stay active physically and to keep themselves busy and interested throughout their lives. Thus leisure-time goods are sold to every age

Leisure-time goods are marketed to every age group. (*Bob Main*)

group. This includes children, who need toys and games to help them grow, and senior citizens, who buy leisure-time goods so they can stay young.

The marketing of leisure-time goods has become an important part of our economy, creating many interesting career opportunities. In this part, you will be able to see whether any of these opportunities would be right for you.

HOW LEISURE-TIME GOODS ARE MARKETED

Included in the term "leisure-time goods" are a wide variety of products. There are toys (which include dolls and stuffed animals), games, and playground equipment for children. There are also games specifically designed for adults, as well as model and craft kits. There are also the supplies that people need in order to pursue their favorite hobbies, ranging all the way from musical instruments to equipment for keeping pigeons on apartment house roofs. Leisure-time goods also include all kinds of pleasure boats, the airplanes and gliders that people fly for fun, and such recreational vehicles as bicycles, snowmobiles, trailers and campers that can be towed by a car, truck-mount campers, and motor homes. Also included are all the supplies and equipment needed for a long list of many different kinds of active sports, from camping, fishing, and hunting to baseball, basketball, football, and volleyball.

To see how important the marketing of leisure-time goods is, take any of the categories listed above and see how many products you can name that go with it. For example, campers need such things as tents, sleeping bags, air mattresses, backpacks, insulated food and beverage containers, cooking utensils, flashlights, and portable stoves. Just this one example makes it clear that the list of products included in leisure-time goods is long and varied.

Furthermore, these products are bought by a variety of customers. For example, Ping-Pong tables can be sold to individual homeowners, schools, community centers, retirement homes, hospitals, military bases, and hotels, as well as to the table tennis parlors that charge a fee for the use of the equipment. Thinking about the variety of goods to be sold and the variety of customers for them makes it clear that the marketing of leisure-time goods is big business. Let's see now how this business is carried out by looking first at how leisure-time goods are retailed and then at how they are wholesaled.

Retailing Leisure-Time Goods

As you would expect from the variety of leisure-time goods, they are sold to the ultimate consumer in many different ways. Because of the popularity of scrambled merchandising, you can find some items for sale in supermarkets, apparel and accessories stores, home furnishings stores, drugstores, service stations, and hardware stores. But the six most important ways of retailing leisure-time goods are (1) limited-line stores, (2) retailing at recreational services, (3) toy supermarkets, (4) general merchandise stores, (5) franchised dealers, and (6) brokers.

LIMITED-LINE STORES. There are limited-line stores that carry a general assortment of leisure-time goods, including sporting goods, games and toys, and hobby and craft supplies. Sometimes these stores also carry the clothing that is needed for active sports. They are sometimes so large that they can be called departmentalized specialty stores. Other limited-line stores are more specialized, selling only sporting goods, only toys, or only pet or hobby supplies. There are other stores that limit themselves even further. For example, a store may handle just records, just musical instruments, or just tropical fish. Another store may concentrate on things for boating or for tennis, perhaps also carrying some of the clothing that goes with these sports.

In these stores, product knowledge is vital. The salesworkers in a store that sells a general line of sports equipment may not play every sport themselves, but they should know as much as possible about each one. They should also know how to help people to find the exact product that best suits their individual needs. This is true to an even greater extent for the salesworkers in highly specialized stores. It would not make much sense to go to a golf shop and be helped by a salesworker who did not know what the various clubs were used for.

RETAILING BY RECREATION SERVICES. Often sporting goods can be bought at the places where sports are played, such as golf courses, tennis courts, and bowling alleys. In some cases, the right to sell merchandise at such a facility is given to the person who teaches there, such as the golf, tennis, or skiing "pro." In other cases, the merchandise is sold by the recreation service company itself, as a way of making extra profits.

There may be a regular store or just a small area set aside for the retailing operation. Usually the fastest-moving items, such as golf balls or tennis balls, are kept on hand, so that they can be purchased when the customer needs them. But special equipment is usually sold from samples. The goods are ordered after the customers have decided what they want to buy, so that a large inventory doesn't have to be maintained. The customers who buy at recreation services expect the most expert kind of advice and a great deal of individual attention.

TOY SUPERMARKETS. A special kind of limited-line store is the toy supermarket. These stores are as big as food supermarkets and carry a

What kinds of leisure-time products are needed by these mountain hikers? *(Courtesy Irish Tourist Board)*

much larger selection of all kinds of toys, games, and hobby supplies than the average limited-line store. They are laid out as food supermarkets are, to make self-service easy for the customers. Because of their mass merchandising approach, they can keep their prices down.

GENERAL MERCHANDISE STORES. Many small department stores do not handle leisure-time goods at all, except perhaps for a limited assortment of toys and games. But large department stores that are aimed at the whole family sell a broad cross section of leisure-time goods in various departments. In many department stores, toys are sold either on a self-service basis or by salesclerks. But salesworkers in the sporting goods departments are expected to be able to give the customers expert advice. Chain department stores also sell a wide range of leisure-time goods, both in their retail stores and through their catalog-retailing operations.

Popularly priced, fast-moving leisure-time products can be found in general merchandise discount stores. Junior department stores and variety stores also sell leisure-time goods. But they are likely to concentrate more on games and toys, placing less emphasis on sports equipment than general merchandise discount stores do.

FRANCHISED DEALERS. There are many leisure-time products that are sold through the franchised dealers that you learned about in Part 16. As an example of this, the Schwinn Bicycle Company has authorized 1,600 dealers to sell its bicycles. There are also dealers for other kinds of recreational vehicles and for boats and airplanes. Some dealerships are small operations, where the dealer can do most of the work with a minimum of help. Other dealers have several sales centers, with a staff of salesworkers at each one, plus a staff of repairers who can service the products. These large dealerships also need an office staff, cleaning help, and a manager for each sales center.

BROKERS. Another way of handling the sale of large and expensive leisure-time products is through brokers. "Brokers" are middlemen who do not buy the goods for resale but simply make all the arrangements between the buyer and the seller so that the sale can take place. Brokers relieve the manufacturers of their selling problems and make it easy for the customers to satisfy their needs. For this very important service, they receive a percentage of the selling price as a commission on each sale. The large pleasure boats that are called "yachts" are sold by brokers, as are some airplanes.

Wholesaling Leisure-Time Goods

Retailers buy leisure-time goods for resale in two ways. They can go directly to the manufacturers' showrooms or sales offices, dealing either with the manufacturers' salaried salesworkers or with the manufacturer's representatives. Or they may deal with the wholesalers and importers who gather the products of many manufacturers together. An example of a wholesaler who serves retailers in this way is Greenman Brothers, in Farmingdale, New York. This wholesaler has 450 retailer customers and stocks approximately 5,000 varieties of toys, as well as sports equipment and hobby supplies. The many industrial consumers who buy leisure-time goods also deal with both manufacturers and wholesalers. Examples of such consumers are recreational services, professional teams and players, day care centers, schools, community centers, hospitals, retirement and convalescent homes, hotels, and military bases.

To make wholesale buying easier, there are trade shows each year in major cities open only "to the trade," rather than to the general public. Examples are the toy shows that are held each year so retailers can place their orders in ample time for the Christmas rush. There is a special problem in retailing toys. More than half of the entire year's sales are made during November and December. This means that the toy buyer must make very accurate judgments and needs as much help as possible from manufacturers, wholesalers, and importers.

HOW A CAREER IN LEISURE-TIME GOODS DEVELOPS

The marketing of leisure-time goods offers you a special opportunity to build a career on the basis of your own interests and preferences. For example, you may have a strong interest in a particular sport. If so, you can consider a job buying or selling the equipment for that sport. You may be interested in early childhood education, and therefore helping parents to choose the right toys for their children may sound good to you. Perhaps your interest in high-speed racing bicycles points to a job servicing and repairing them. Or perhaps you are simply interested in helping people to get more out of life. In this case, the marketing of leisure-time goods has many possibilities for you.

However, you have to realize that a special interest is only the foundation for a career in marketing leisure-time goods. In order to build a sound structure on top of the foundation, you need marketing skills. This is a highly competitive field, which means that the person with the know-how is the one who is going to get the business. Customers today are much more knowledgeable and have much higher expectations than they used to.

Things have not been standing still in the leisure-time goods field any more than they have been in the other areas of marketing you have read about. Color and good design have been introduced into such products as bowling balls, bags, and shoes; tennis balls; basketballs; golf clubs and bags; and skis. Some games have been designed to be decorative additions to the customer's living room. In short, there is a fashion element to the marketing of leisure-time goods that needs to be

What career possibilities in the field of leisure-time goods might there be for this cellist? (*National Education Association*)

understood. This puts pressure on marketers to buy, sell, and promote sales in the most skillful and effective way. The squeeze on profits caused by high prices also makes marketing skills essential in this field.

Because marketing skills are so important in leisure-time goods, employers look for the kind of people who are willing to develop these skills. With this as a background, let's see what job opportunities there are in leisure-time goods on the entry, career, and management levels.

Entry-Level Jobs

The easiest way to get started in the marketing of leisure-time goods is in retailing. Manufacturers and wholesalers are not located all across the country, as retailers are. Thus retailing offers you a better chance of finding a job within commuting distance of your home. The retailers of leisure-time goods are open long hours. They do much of their business in the evenings, on Saturdays, and even on Sundays in many communities. They also have a special need for extra help at Christmas time. This means that there are many opportunities for part-time work in retailing.

290 • UNIT 4 • CAREERS IN MARKETING GOODS

On the retail level, you can be hired to be trained as a salesclerk or as a cashier in a self-service store or department. You can also be hired for office or stockroom work. These beginning jobs are very similar to the beginning jobs in other kinds of marketing businesses. Their advantage is that they put you in a position where you can learn. By keeping your eyes and ears open in these jobs, you can acquire a great deal of specific knowledge about products, suppliers, and customer likes and dislikes.

If you have a mechanical aptitude, you can be hired to be trained as an assembler. As a way of saving on shipping costs, many leisure-time products are shipped knocked down and have to be put together in the store. Also, some leisure-time products have to be installed. For example, a customer may buy a basketball net and backboard on the condition that they be mounted at the customer's house. Beginners who are good at working with their hands are often assigned as helpers on such jobs as a way of learning the skills involved.

When you are ready for a full-time job, any of these kinds of beginning experiences in retailing will be very helpful to you. You can start out in the warehouse or in the office of a manufacturer or wholesaler right from high school. But if you want to start as a management or buyer trainee for a department or chain store your best bet is to plan to go on with your education after high school.

Career-Level Jobs

Among the career-level jobs in leisure-time goods are retail selling jobs. A great deal of patience is required for these jobs, along with product knowledge and selling ability. This is a field where people ask a great many questions and like to think over the answers. They don't want to be hurried through their buying decisions. The more expensive the purchase is, the more a customer dislikes being rushed. Thus brokers and the salesworkers for dealers are usually highly skilled people who have had previous experience in selling. Their jobs are seldom limited to a regular 9-to-5 schedule. But because they work on a commission basis, their rate of pay is tied directly to the amount of effort they put into their jobs.

The salesworkers for manufacturers and wholesalers also have to be very skilled in selling. Their training usually includes learning all the other parts of the business, so that they can answer all their customers' questions. Because these people often have to give training courses to retail salesworkers, they must have exceptionally good communication skills.

There are also career-level jobs in buying for wholesalers and chain stores. These people must be closely tuned to changing life styles

The customer's desire for a leisure-time product provides the strongest motivation for buying, but the salesworker must be able to give complete and experienced answers to any questions the customer may have. (*Courtesy Yamaha International Corporation*)

so they know what people are going to be asking for. For example, the present strong interest in camping is a reflection of the desire of many people to get back to the simpler life. Buyers have to recognize such trends and be ready for them.

Warehouses and stockrooms offer such career-level jobs as order assemblers, packers, and receiving, shipping, and stock clerks. There are also jobs for assemblers, repairers, mechanics, and truck drivers. Cashier jobs, office jobs, and jobs in advertising, display, and public relations are also available.

A career-level job in leisure-time goods is not a dead-end job that leads nowhere. The skills that you learn in one of these jobs can be easily transferred to other jobs, either in this field or in other areas of marketing. For example, if you are a salesworker for sporting goods, you could move to a job selling sportswear. Or if you have worked as a mechanic for an airplane dealer, you might go to work for an airline.

Management-Level Jobs

If you want the responsibility and challenge of supervising the work of others, you will find that there are many possibilities for management-level jobs in leisure-time goods. A salesworker for a manufacturer can move up to the job of district, and then national, sales manager. A wholesale salesworker can also become a sales manager. A buyer for a wholesaler or chain store can become a head buyer and then move up to a top management job, and department store buyers have equally good chances for advancement. Warehouse workers can become warehouse managers, and from there they can move up to top management positions. There are also such management-level jobs as personnel director, advertising director, display director, and public relations director.

In leisure-time goods, it is also possible for you to open your own store, if you have the necessary marketing skills. Good marketing skills are the key to success in owning your own business. They are also the element that provides job security for workers on any level in this field. When you are willing to think of learning marketing skills as an ongoing process, you don't have to worry about being out of a job.

• UNDERSTANDING WHAT YOU HAVE READ

1. List five reasons why the field of leisure-time goods has become an important area of marketing.
2. What is the special problem in retailing toys?
3. Does the word "fashion" have anything to do with leisure-time goods? Explain your answer.
4. Why is retailing the easiest way to get started on a career in leisure-time goods?
5. What can workers in this field do to make their jobs more secure?

• APPLYING WHAT YOU HAVE LEARNED

1. Divide your class into teams of about four students each. Assign each team a specific leisure-time product, such as a bowling ball, guitar, basketball, etc. Have each team do some shopping research and prepare a list of all the retailers in your area that sell the product. State what kind of retailer each one is, using the material in your text to help you.
2. Choose one of your own leisure-time interests and show how you could develop this interest into a career in marketing leisure-time goods by choosing an entry-level job and then diagraming the ladder- or lattice-type moves that you could make as you developed marketing skills.
3. List five reasons why you either would or would not consider a career in marketing leisure-time goods.

part 26 Automotive Products

After reading Part 26, you will be able—
- To list five products and five services that are sold in service stations and five services that may be provided free of charge.
- To explain why service station experience can help you get a job with other automotive products marketers.
- To answer a series of questions designed to help you determine whether marketing automotive products is or is not a real career alternative for you.

Rather than being considered luxuries, automobiles are thought of today as a very basic part of a family's standard of living. As a result, four out of five families in this country own cars today, and about one-fourth of the families that own cars own two or more. If you live in a suburb or rural area, you don't have to be told how necessary the automobile is. Many of these areas are not well served by such public transportation facilities as buses and commuter trains, and driving is the only way to get around. Many of the people who live in cities need cars for their everyday work too. People also depend heavily on their cars for recreation and vacation travel.

With the energy crisis, there has been a lot of emphasis on getting people to use their cars less. Many people are joining car pools for driving to work, and some are riding bicycles. But since the end of World War II, this country has encouraged a dependence on cars by putting more emphasis on building highways than on developing public transportation facilities. The way of life that has resulted from this cannot easily be changed. Thus, for some years to come, we can expect the automobile to continue to be an essential part of our lives. This is also true of trucks, which are the only means of transporting goods to the many areas that cannot be reached by planes, ships, and trains.

There are well over 100 million cars and trucks on the highways of this country. Keeping these vehicles running is a vast undertaking that provides jobs for many people. In this part, we are going to look at some of the marketing businesses that do this work. We are going to

Since the energy crisis, more and more people are using bicycles for short-distance transportation. But, despite this trend, the automobile is still essential to our way of life. (*Daniel S. Brody/Editorial Photocolor Archives*)

give the greatest amount of attention to service stations for two reasons. First, this is where most of the part-time jobs are for people just getting started. Second, people who have had service station experience find it easy to move into the other businesses that sell automotive products. After we have looked at service stations, we will see the career opportunities that are connected with oil product wholesalers, automobile and truck dealers, and parts and accessories retailers and wholesalers.

SERVICE STATIONS

The freedom to go wherever they want that the drivers of cars and trucks have would not be possible without the many service stations that are scattered all across the country. These stations are located on rural roads and city streets. Motorists can be many miles from their homes and still be able to purchase everything they need to keep their cars running properly. To see what it would be like to work in one of these service stations, let's look at this business more closely.

The Service Station: A Retail Store

The service station is really a kind of store. In fact, some of the big oil companies that own service stations are referring to them as "retail stores" or "retail outlets" instead of calling them service stations.

Like many other stores—for instance, a jewelry store that sells and repairs watches or a camera shop that sells and develops film—the service station sells both goods and services. Like all stores everywhere, it also has certain services that it gives to its customers. Just as a store doesn't try to be all things to all people, so the service station directs itself toward certain customers by offering the particular combination of products and services that those customers want. These various factors work together to give each service station a definite personality, as we shall now see.

THE SERVICE STATION CHOOSES ITS CUSTOMERS. The first thing the service station owner has to do is to decide what kind of station to open. A **neighborhood station,** which is a service station near a large group of homes, primarily takes care of the passenger cars of the people who live in the area. A **heavy traffic station** is a service station in a busy downtown area. This kind of station services the cars and trucks of the people who do business in the area. The customers for a **highway station,** which is a service station located on a highway, are the travelers who pass by in cars and trucks, as well as the people who live nearby.

For people in a hurry, there are **multipump stations.** These are service stations that have many gas pumps. These stations are usually located in heavily traveled areas. More and more of them are becoming self-service stations, where the customers pump their own gas. This means that these stations need a minimum of help and can therefore afford to charge less for the gas. Often there is an area, separated from the pumps, where any mechanical problems with the car can be taken care of.

Two other kinds of service stations are the truck station and the rural station. A **truck station** is a service station that specializes in the fuels and services that trucks need. This kind of station tends to be quite large and is usually located on a main highway. The **rural station** is a small service station in a country area. These stations may have only one pump because of the limited amount of business that they do. Besides those service stations strictly for cars and trucks, there are also marine stations that sell gasoline for boats and airport stations near the airports for private planes.

THE SERVICE STATION SELLS GOODS. Service stations sell gasoline, motor oil, various motor lubricants, and antifreeze. If they service trucks, they also sell butane and diesel fuel. Most stations also sell "TBA," meaning tires, batteries, and such accessories as windshield wipers, radiator caps, flashlights, chains, polishes, and waxes. Service stations also sell such routine replacement parts as spark plugs, oil and air filters, fuses, fan belts, and light bulbs. Most stations don't keep any large or very special replacement parts on hand. But sometimes they will special order them from the car manufacturers or their local representatives.

In addition to automotive products, many service stations, especially highway stations, carry items that people like to pick up while they are getting gas, so that they don't have to make two stops—things such as soft drinks, candy, cigarettes, ice, postcards, and small toys.

THE SERVICE STATION SELLS SERVICES. The idea of going to a service station for expert service is very much a part of modern living. In fact, most motorists think that the service station employee is a kind of doctor who can give a car regular checkups, decide what's ailing it, and then cure it. It is not unusual to see the term "diagnostic center" used for the area of the station that does this work.

The services that motorists can buy in service stations include such things as lubricating the engine, fixing flats, rotating the tires, putting on chains, tightening the brakes and clutch, adjusting the steering, tuning up the motor, washing and waxing the body of the car, and supplying road service or towing service to cars stalled by the roadside. All stations do not necessarily do all of these things. But whatever services they sell must be done expertly.

THE SERVICE STATION GIVES SOME SERVICES AWAY. Customers don't expect to pay for all the services they receive in a service station. Such free services as checking the battery and the oil and water levels are done automatically in many stations, along with washing the windshield and rear window. In other stations, these are done at the request of the customer. If the customer asks, the service station employee will also check the air in the tires or look at the engine for some problem such as overheating.

Very often this free service leads to extra sales. For example, motorists buy oil when they see that they need it. But washing the windows doesn't sell anything, so there must be another reason for this free service. That reason can be summed up in one word: *goodwill.* Like all stores, the service station has the problem of keeping its customers happy and making them think so well of the station that they will come back again.

Goodwill explains the other things that service stations do for their customers, too. They provide clean rest rooms, and some even have waste disposal facilities for campers. They keep their stations open for long hours for the customers' convenience. They make it possible for their customers to charge their purchases, either through the station itself or more often with a credit card. They may even drive customers home or to work when they leave their cars for servicing. Not all of these services are available in all stations. But whatever services the station does give away should be given cheerfully. Otherwise the services will not fulfill their purpose of bringing in more business.

Checking the oil and cleaning the windshield are two examples of free services provided by service stations. (*Courtesy Exxon Corporation*)

The Service Station and Its Suppliers

A service station generally sells the gasoline and oil products of just one supplier. The supplier may be one of the big oil-producing companies, such as the Phillips Petroleum Company, Texaco, the Exxon Corporation, the Amoco International Oil Company, and the Shell Oil Company. Or the supplier may be an oil **jobber,** which is another way of saying wholesaler.

The relationship between the service station manager and the supplier is always a close one. In some stations, the supplier is actually the station manager's boss—that is, the supplier owns the station as part of a chain, and the manager is hired to run it. In other cases, the supplier buys the land, builds the station, and then leases (rents) it to the manager on a franchising basis. The owner of the station is thus self-employed, and yet the supplier is assured of customers. Still another arrangement is for the service station to be owned outright by its manager. In this case, the manager makes an agreement with the supplier to furnish the necessary gasoline and oil products.

With any of these arrangements, the success of the service station and the success of the supplier are tied so closely together that the service station manager can expect all kinds of help from the supplier. This help will include advertising the oil products on television and in magazines and newspapers, as well as providing sales posters and racks to display the merchandise to the service station's customers. The supplier may also offer such things as training courses for the service station's employees, bookkeeping aids, and credit cards for the station's customers. The service station manager also buys merchandise from wholesalers of tires, automotive parts and supplies, and various other products.

Careers in Service Stations

Since the service station is really a kind of store, the service station manager has to worry about the same five problems that any storekeeper does: merchandising, operations, personnel, sales promotion, and control. This means that the manager has to buy and sell. It is also vital to keep the station itself and all the equipment clean and in good working order. The manager also has to find, hire, train, and supervise the employees and worry about attracting and holding customers. Although the suppliers do a lot of national advertising, the manager still has to handle local advertising and sales promotion and set up displays. Finally, the manager has to keep very accurate records and make careful financial plans to be sure of making a profit.

In a small station, all these jobs can be handled by the manager. But the bigger the station, the more maintenance and repair work it does, and the more hours it is open, the more help the manager needs. Let's see now how the work is divided in service stations, what the requirements are, and what the future holds for anyone starting out in this field.

DIVIDING THE WORK IN SERVICE STATIONS. Some service station employees are specialists. For instance, the manager may hire someone, perhaps on a part-time basis, to do the bookkeeping. In stations that do a lot of repair work, there are employees who are such expert mechanics that they spend all their time on repair work. There are also some employees who are salesclerks. They pump gas and perform routine services, but they do nothing that requires any advanced skill. These workers, who are often hired part time, fill in during the day and cover the station in the evening hours. They also work in multipump stations. But most service station employees are neither specialists nor clerks. They are expected to understand what the whole business is about. They should be prepared to help the manager wherever and however they are needed.

Many service station managers are now calling their employees service salesworkers instead of service station attendants, because this seems to explain what is expected of the employees more accurately. They should know what products the station carries, what they are used for, and how they should be installed. They also should know what services the station will and won't provide for its customers, and they should know how to do most of those services. They have to know if the station has done any special advertising and must be prepared to make good on what the advertising promised. They have to think ahead to what the customers will be needing in the future and suggest those things to the customers. They also have to be prepared to explain *the reason why* to customers who can't decide whether or not to spend the money for a recommended service or replacement part.

When the attendants are not busy with customers, they work on the cars that have been left in the station for servicing or repairing. They also share the work of maintaining the station. They may have to receive a shipment of goods, unpack it, and put it in the right place. Or they may have to count the stock or arrange a display. They also have to do their share of recordkeeping, by filling out the charge slips and using the cash register properly.

Service station managers also need people with management abilities. If the station does a lot of repair work, there may be a head mechanic. There must be someone who can take care of the station when the manager is not present. This person, who may be called the assistant manager, has to be able to supervise the other workers and keep things running smoothly.

CHECKING THE REQUIREMENTS FOR SERVICE STATIONS. Perhaps the best thing about the service station business for the young person who is interested in a career is that it has many openings for part-time beginners. Young people who are still in school can either work in a station as co-op students or get jobs on their own after school and on weekends.

However, this is not the right business for just any beginner. There are some special qualities that you need in order to be successful in this work. You must have an aptitude for working with your hands and with engines, so that you will be able to master the necessary skills. You must also be willing to keep learning, because this is a business where there is always something new. For example, there are new car models every year, and the equipment for diagnosing car problems is always being updated.

As a service station worker, you have to like people and be able to get along with your boss, your co-workers, and the customers. You also need exceptionally good health. Much of this work has to be done outdoors in all kinds of weather, and there is a lot of lifting, bending, and carrying. You also need the basic skills. You must be able to read directions and explain things to customers to whom engines may be a

Service station attendants do many things besides just pumping gas.

PART 26 • AUTOMOTIVE PRODUCTS • 301

mystery. You also have to be accurate with figures and know how to fill out forms. If you want to be given management responsibilities, you must have an extra measure of common sense, along with the ability to plan ahead and make decisions.

LOOKING AT THE FUTURE. Many people find career-level jobs in service stations very rewarding. Wages tend to be good. In many cases, commissions can be earned on the merchandise that is sold. The work is never dull, for each day brings new and different problems to be solved. Also, if you learn the skills necessary to do this work, you will find that your job is very secure. This is especially true if you want to make the effort to become a well-trained mechanic. You can do this relatively slowly, on the job. Or you can plan to attend a vocational-technical school or trade school.

Jobs in service stations give you many opportunities to move out or up. When you have enough experience, you can become the manager of a company-owned station or open one of your own. Because of the many franchising opportunities, this is fairly easy to do. Being the manager of a service station generally means working very long hours, so you have to decide whether you are willing to put that much time into your job. Service station experience can also be used in any of the other businesses that sell automotive products, which we will be discussing next. You might also go to work for one of the companies that sells transportation services.

OIL PRODUCTS WHOLESALERS

There are three kinds of customers for wholesale oil products: (1) service stations, (2) retailers who sell home heating oil, and (3) the many industrial consumers who use oil products in running their businesses. These customers may buy their oil products either from the large oil-producing companies, who do their own wholesaling, or from independent jobbers. Oil products are wholesaled from **petroleum bulk stations** instead of regular warehouses. These are large storage tanks where oil products can be stored until needed. With this information in mind, let's see what kinds of jobs there are in wholesaling oil products.

Selling Wholesale Oil Products

Oil producers and jobbers need a variety of salesworkers to act as links between the company and its customers. They employ route workers, who drive the large storage trucks and make routine deliveries. Because the products that they carry could catch fire easily, these route workers must be especially good drivers. They don't have to be skilled in selling, but they must be pleasant and courteous.

There are also jobs for sales representatives, who can work with the independent retailers to help them run their businesses more effectively. This is the same kind of help that any service wholesaler gives. Its purpose is to make the retailers more successful so they will buy more of the wholesaler's products. The sales representatives who deal with service stations have to know a great deal about the service station business. This, then, is a job for people who have had service station experience, college-level training in marketing management, or both.

When there are company-owned stations, the sales representatives are the supervisors of the managers in their territory. This is a job to which service station managers are often promoted. The sales representatives who deal with retailers of home heating oil have to understand the problems of that business. Often they are people who started out in retailing.

Salesworkers are also needed to deal with such industrial consumers as bus and truck companies, airlines, railroads, steamship lines, and factories. Some of these salesworkers have to be **sales engineers.** These are salesworkers who have had technical training related to the products they sell. Usually they are graduate engineers who have also learned selling skills. They are called upon to solve technical problems for their customers that are related to the use of petroleum products.

Salesworkers can advance to the job of district sales manager, regional sales manager, and then general sales manager. Route workers can become truck dispatchers. Or, if they want to do some extra studying, they can become sales representatives.

Sales representatives are expected to be thoroughly familiar with the areas in which they work. Thus they are in a position to help decide where new stations are needed. (*Courtesy Gulf Oil Corporation*)

Other Wholesaling Jobs

Oil producers and jobbers employ warehouse workers to run the petroleum bulk stations. Since these storage facilities are highly mechanized, the jobs in this area are for people who can make the decisions that machines cannot make. Many of these jobs can be learned on the job by high school graduates. Experience in these jobs, combined with additional schooling, can lead to the job of petroleum bulk station manager or to other jobs in wholesaling or retailing oil products.

Jobbers need buyers to handle the purchases from producers. They also need a large staff of office workers, as do the producers. Because of the scope of the business of the large oil producers, they need many kinds of staff specialists. They need advertising and display experts and management experts to give training courses to the retailers. They need real estate experts to find new locations for service stations, as well as lawyers, financial experts, consumer affairs specialists, and environmental specialists to advise them on problems related to preserving the environment. The oil companies do so much of their business overseas that they offer special opportunities to anyone who is interested in living or working abroad.

AUTOMOBILE AND TRUCK DEALERS

Automobile manufacturers reach the consumers through franchised dealers who are spread out all across the country. These dealers may represent American or foreign manufacturers. They run showrooms, where the public can see the latest models on display. When customers buy new cars, they usually trade in their old cars. This means that the dealer buys the old car and takes the purchase price off the bill for the new car. The dealer must then sell these used cars. Sometimes the dealer runs a used car lot, in order to sell directly to the public. In other cases, the dealer sells the cars to a wholesaler who specializes in buying used cars. Truck dealers also take trade-ins on used trucks when they are selling new ones.

Besides the new car and truck dealers, there are used car dealers who buy and sell used cars and trucks. To see what it would be like to work for an automobile or truck dealer, let's look at selling jobs and service jobs.

Selling Jobs

Car and truck dealers have a staff of salesworkers who must be very skilled in selling. This includes having very complete product knowledge, an understanding of people, and excellent communication skills. There are no specific educational requirements for this job. But it

A successful automobile salesworker must have excellent communication skills and the ability to inspire confidence in the customers. (*Courtesy Burroughs Corporation*)

would be very hard to be hired without at least a high school diploma and some previous experience in selling. Many automobile and truck salesworkers have also worked in service stations. The pay, which is in the form of commissions, can be very high. Salesworkers often open up dealerships of their own when they have gained enough experience.

Service Jobs

New car and truck dealers are expected to provide service for the cars that they sell. Some used car dealers also have service departments. They need people who can wash and wax cars and handle such routine jobs as oil changes. These are jobs for which beginners can be hired and trained, sometimes even on a part-time basis. It is possible for such beginners to become the kind of highly trained mechanics that dealers need. People with strong aptitudes for this work and some previous experience are often sent to the factory for extensive training in order to make them thoroughly familiar with the particular make of car.

The dealer also needs a counter worker to run the parts department, where the supplies are handed out. This job includes receiving, checking, and storing the merchandise, as well as keeping track of what to reorder. The important thing in this job is product knowledge,

Car and truck dealers employ highly trained mechanics to provide service for the cars and trucks that are sold. (*Courtesy Ford Motor Company*)

so some previous experience in working with cars is needed. Thus this is another job that the beginner can work up to.

Even more experience is necessary to become a service adviser, who writes out the directions for the mechanics and explains policies and costs to the customers. Service advisers are the salesworkers for the service department. They must have pleasant personalities, as well as a great deal of product knowledge. At the head of the service department is the service manager. This job, which requires experience and the ability to schedule and supervise work, is also one that an ambitious beginner could work up to.

PARTS AND ACCESSORIES RETAILERS AND WHOLESALERS

Although most people turn the care of their cars over to experts, there is a growing number of do-it-yourselfers who take care of their own cars. These people buy the products that they need from parts and accessories retailers. These retailers also sell many things that people can use to personalize their cars. The amount of business that these stores are doing is increasing all the time, undoubtedly because of the high cost of labor involved in minor maintenance tasks.

The retailers that sell parts and accessories include the chain department stores, which also run service stations, as well as family department stores and general merchandise discount stores. There are also many limited-line stores in this business. These include stores that carry a wide, general assortment of parts and accessories and those that specialize in certain types of parts and accessories. There are stores that carry parts for foreign cars and others that carry parts for sports cars. There are also the "speed shops" that sell equipment to make cars go faster. There are stores that specialize in the sale of tires, car sound systems, mufflers, and seat covers. Some of these stores are strictly for the do-it-yourselfer. But others will install the products. Thus they are like highly specialized service stations, as are the many companies that specialize in such things as repairing brakes and transmissions, replacing broken glass, and repainting the bodies of cars and trucks.

What you have learned about how stores and service stations are run can help you to understand what jobs are like in these businesses. Both the service workers and salesworkers have to be very well informed about what the business sells. The people who use these businesses ask a lot of questions, and they expect complete and accurate answers. This is why service station experience is so valuable. Many of these stores are run under franchising agreements with such companies as the Firestone Tire & Rubber Company and Midas, Inc. This could make it possible for you to own your own store, if this prospect interests you.

Many of the companies that retail parts and accessories also have wholesaling divisions of their businesses. They sell, at a discount, to service stations, car rental agencies, and taxi, bus, and truck companies. There are also many companies that are strictly wholesalers of parts and accessories.

For the wholesaling business, there have to be "inside salesworkers," who may also be called counter workers. They handle the sales to walk-in customers. There are also "outside salesworkers," who pay calls on customers in their own places of business. Both kinds of salesworkers must know a great deal about the products that they handle, because they frequently have to give advice about what products would be best. These salesworkers may have gotten their start as stock workers, or they may have had service station experience.

The employees of parts and accessories retailers and wholesalers can look forward to moving up in the company. They can also easily transfer their skills to the other businesses that sell automotive products or to other areas of marketing.

- **BUILDING YOUR MARKETING VOCABULARY**

    Define each of the following terms and then use each one in a sentence.

    heavy traffic station
    highway station
    jobber
    multipump station
    neighborhood station
    petroleum bulk station
    rural station
    sales engineer
    truck station

- **UNDERSTANDING WHAT YOU HAVE READ**

    1. List five products and five services that may be sold in service stations and five services that are provided free of charge.
    2. Why is goodwill important to a service station?
    3. List three relationships that can exist between the service station manager and the supplier.
    4. Explain why service station experience can help you to get a job with other automotive products marketers.

- **APPLYING WHAT YOU HAVE LEARNED**

    1. Use the Yellow Pages to compile a list of the businesses in your area that sell automotive products.
    2. Answer the following questions using 0 for *no,* 1 for *maybe,* and 2 for *yes.* When you are finished, add up your score. A score of 18–24 is an indication that the automotive products field may be a real career alternative for you.
        a. Do you like to look at cars, and are you able to recognize many of the models?
        b. Are you looking forward to having a car of your own?
        c. Do you have a mechanical aptitude?
        d. Do you have a mechanical interest?
        e. Do you have the physical requirements for service station work?
        f. Do you think you can learn to fill out forms, reports, and sales slips accurately?
        g. Are you willing to learn the basic skills?
        h. Could a career in automotive products answer your own personal reasons for working?
        i. Would a career in automotive products offer you the opportunity to work with people in the way that is most meaningful to you?
        j. Are you willing to work in the evenings and on weekends, if necessary?
        k. Could you handle the pressures of rush hours?
        l. Would you like to learn more about how automotive products are marketed?

part 27 Farm & Garden Supplies and Floristry

After reading Part 27, you will be able—
- To explain the importance of product knowledge in relation to (a) supplying the needs of farmers, (b) supplying the needs of home gardeners, and (c) floristry.
- To name one ladder-type and one lattice-type move that would be possible from each of a given list of jobs in marketing farm and garden supplies and in floristry.
- To assist in preparing a class report on the opportunities in marketing farm and garden supplies and in floristry in your area.
- To list five reasons why you would or would not consider a job in this field.

In this part, we are going to discuss the marketing businesses that sell supplies and equipment to farmers and those that sell to home gardeners. We are also going to discuss **floristry,** which is the business of growing and selling flowers and ornamental plants. These businesses are very much in the news today. The combination of a rapidly expanding world population and critical food shortages in many areas is putting large demands on American and Canadian farmers. They are being asked to increase their production, which is already at a higher level than that of other countries, as a way of feeding the many hungry people in the world. Because farmers are under this pressure, they expect more from the businesses that sell them the supplies and equipment that they need in order to do their work.

At the same time, people in this country are becoming increasingly interested in home gardening. They are again planting the kinds of vegetable gardens that were called "Victory Gardens" during World War II. This is a reflection of rising food costs and also of the growing interest in ecology. Many people look upon the idea of growing part of their own food as a way of making the most of the earth's resources. But they can't do this alone. They too are dependent on the people who sell the supplies and equipment that make home gardening possible. The interest in ecology also helps to explain why the floristry business has been growing so rapidly. People want flowers and green plants in their

The increasing number of rooftop and terrace gardens in large cities reflects the growing interest in ecology and a desire to return to nature. (*Courtesy The City Gardener, Inc.*)

homes to give them a release from the concrete and steel that is so much a part of modern life.

This all adds up to the fact that the marketing of farm and garden supplies, flowers, and green plants is as vital as today's headlines. Rather than being an old-fashioned kind of business for old-fashioned people, it is for people who understand the directions in which the world is moving and who are willing to move too. If you are this kind of person and if you are also interested in nature and growing things, this could be the right field for you.

SUPPLYING THE NEEDS OF FARMERS

In 1840, one farm worker in the United States could grow enough to feed 4.6 people. In 1972, one farm worker could grow enough to feed 52.4 people. And today the yield is even higher. This increased efficiency can be explained by the supplies and equipment that are available to today's farmer. Scientific research and modern technology have made extraordinary improvements possible in seeds, plants, fertilizer, pesticides, and livestock feed. Also, the machinery that farmers use is being constantly improved, and new machines are steadily being invented to take the drudgery out of farming. The milking stool and pail that were once the symbol of the dairy farmer have been replaced by automatic milking machines. The wheat farmer now uses a huge "combine," which cuts the wheat and threshes and cleans the grain in one operation.

Every improvement that has been made in farm supplies and equipment has made the marketing process both more important and more difficult. The marketers of farm supplies and equipment today have to be trained in two directions. They must know a great deal about farming and the needs of farmers in order to determine which products can best answer the farmers' needs. And they must also be well trained in modern marketing techniques. Today's farmers are not "hayseeds." They are experts in their own field, and they want to deal with marketers who are understanding, knowledgeable, and efficient.

The Kinds of Businesses That Sell to Farmers

If you live in a city, you may never have had the opportunity to see just how far the marketing of farm supplies and equipment has progressed from the old general stores that you see on TV "Westerns." A few of these stores, which sell a little bit of many things, still exist. But they can't begin to carry the range of products that today's farmer needs.

Furthermore, farmers today expect a range of services that are far beyond the scope of the general store. The places where farmers buy their supplies and equipment may make deliveries and offer various credit plans. They may have a repair service and perhaps a rental service for things that the farmer uses only occasionally. They may also make recommendations, based on the farmer's specific situation, about what fertilizers and pesticides to use or when and how to plant. Let's see now where farmers go to obtain the goods and services they need.

FARM EQUIPMENT DEALERS. The large machines that farmers use are sold by franchised dealers, who function in much the same way as do automobile dealers. An example of a company that sells its products in this way is Deere and Company. This manufacturer of major pieces of farm equipment—such as tractors, combines, planters, and fertilizer and pesticide applicators—has 3,500 dealers in North America and 1,500 abroad. The company works with these dealers through sales branches, which are set up in various geographic areas. These sales branches are actually handling the wholesaling function for the manufacturer.

FARM SUPPLY STORES. The small pieces of equipment and the supplies that farmers need are sold in farm supply stores. In these stores, farmers can buy such small equipment as wheelbarrows, various hand and power tools, and an assortment of basic hardware. Farmers can

Manufacturers of agricultural products often set up exhibits at state and county fairs to give farmers an opportunity to learn about new products and equipment available to them. (*Daniel S. Brody/Editorial Photocolor Archives*)

also buy fencing materials, equipment for taking care of animals and poultry, seeds, fertilizer, pesticides, and the petroleum products that are needed to run farm equipment.

In many farm supply stores, the sale of services has also become an important part of the business. For example, a store may have trained crews of service workers who can plant, cultivate, and harvest a particular crop for the farmer on the farmer's land. Or the person who owns the farm may want to have the entire operation of the farm taken over by the crew of the farm supply store. The sale of these services usually includes the sale of such products as seeds, fertilizers, and pesticides.

Farm supply stores may be businesses that are run by independent marketers. Or they may be cooperatives that are owned by a group of farmers as a way of keeping their costs down.

OTHER BUSINESSES THAT SELL TO FARMERS. Most farmers now buy at least part of the feed that they use in order to provide their livestock and poultry with a scientifically balanced diet. Consequently, there are feed mills that make a specialty of custom mixing feed for farmers, according to their individual needs. There are also rural grain elevators that buy the farmers' grain products and sell supplies too. The national chain stores also sell some of the supplies and small equipment that farmers use, both in their stores and through their catalogs.

Careers in Farm Supplies and Equipment

Many young people who live in rural areas do not realize how many career opportunities there are in marketing farm supplies and equipment. These opportunities all represent alternatives to the role of farmer, and yet they don't require that rural young people move to the city and change their way of life altogether. Young people who have been raised in the city but who want to live close to nature may also find that these jobs represent a way of achieving what they value.

There are some opportunities to do part-time work in this field while you are still in school. A beginner with an aptitude for people could start out as a salesclerk for a farm supply store, selling some of the routine items. There are also beginning jobs in stock work. These jobs generally require physical strength because many farm supply products are packed in 100-pound sacks. The crews that do service work for farm supply stores can also use beginners with physical strength and the willingness to follow directions. Beginners can also do maintenance work in a farm supply store or in a dealership.

To advance from these jobs, the beginner must obtain more knowledge both about marketing and about farming. Subjects related to agriculture are taught in many high schools in rural areas. Often this is done through a cooperative program that allows students to combine school and agricultural work experience, just as the DE cooperative program combines school and marketing experience. Either program would help the student to prepare for a career in marketing farm supplies and equipment. The student who studies agriculture in high school might study marketing in a community college or four-year college, or vice versa, to become expert in both areas. This kind of studying could be done in night school courses, and there are also many scholarships available.

The career-level jobs in this area can be very rewarding. There are inside and outside salesworkers, many of whom are specialists in one line of products, such as feed, seeds, fertilizers, or pesticides. The people who sell large farm equipment are also specialists. They have to understand the needs of the farmer, the mechanical principles of the machinery, and personal selling. There are also many career-level jobs for buyers, mechanics, warehouse and stockroom workers, and people who can handle advertising, display, and sales promotion work. These people must have the same aptitudes and skills as the people who have comparable jobs in other marketing businesses, along with product knowledge about farm products.

For all these people, there are excellent possibilities for advancement. Such job titles as warehouse manager, service manager, sales manager, branch manager, and director of marketing indicate that this is a field where there are many management opportunities.

Farm supply salesworkers visit their customers' farms to give expert advice about soil conditions and growing techniques. (*Andrew Sacks/Editorial Photocolor Archives*)

SUPPLYING THE NEEDS OF HOME GARDENERS

The marketing of supplies, equipment, and plants to home gardeners is another area where product knowledge is very important. Some people garden because they feel that they must keep up the appearance and value of their property. Others plant vegetable gardens in order to save money on food. And many people garden as a hobby. But no matter why people garden, they need expert advice and information when they are making buying decisions. So the people who market supplies to home gardeners have to be well informed about home gardening techniques. Anyone who runs a **nursery**—which is a place where plants, including trees and shrubs, are grown and sold—has to be an expert on the kinds of plants that the nursery handles.

Let's see now how nursery and garden supplies are retailed, how they are wholesaled, and what careers in this marketing area are like.

Retailing Nursery and Garden Supplies

In a recent year, home gardeners spent roughly $100 million for seeds alone. This figure gives you some idea of how important home gardening has become. The gardener who buys seeds also needs such products as fertilizers, soil conditioners, pesticides, weed killers, lawn sprinklers, hoses, nozzles, peat moss, hand and power tools, containers for plants, and gardening books. Where does the home gardener go to buy these products?

GARDEN EQUIPMENT DEALERS. There are franchised dealers for such large pieces of garden equipment as power mowers, garden tractors, chain saws, leaf blowers, and snow blowers. Sometimes garden equipment dealers are franchised by more than one manufacturer. Sometimes they also sell other kinds of garden supplies along with the large pieces of equipment. Garden equipment dealers are usually expected to service the products that they sell, so there are many jobs for mechanics in this area.

RETAIL NURSERIES AND GARDEN SUPPLY STORES. Maintenance plays a very important role in the nursery business, because the plants cannot be neglected even for a day. The selling jobs are also challenging, because the salesworker must know the characteristics of each plant and how it should be cared for.

Some retail nurseries sell only plants, but most of them sell at least some garden supplies. Many of them run very complete garden supply stores. There are also garden supply stores that have just a small nursery business. In any case, these businesses play a major role in supplying the needs of home gardeners. Often they sell such products for outdoor living as lawn furniture, grills, and above-the-ground swimming pools. They stay busy in the winter by selling pumpkins, cider, bird feeders and seed, Christmas trees and greens, Christmas decorations, and firewood.

Retail nurseries and garden supply stores often have a service department, so that it is possible for a customer not only to buy plants but also to have them delivered and planted. Some customers want to have fertilizer applied to their lawns. Others may even want to buy full lawn maintenance service.

CATALOG RETAILING. A favorite pastime of many home gardeners during the winter months is poring over the catalogs that offer seeds, bulbs, plants, and garden aids for sale by mail order. These catalogs, which are often in full color, give the home gardener the chance to make plans for the coming season well in advance. The W. Atlee Burpee Company is an example of a company that markets in this way.

GENERAL MERCHANDISE AND OTHER STORES. There are many general merchandise stores that do a large business in nursery and garden supplies. This includes variety stores, general merchandise discount stores, and department stores, especially in their suburban branches. Because of the popularity of scrambled merchandising, nursery and garden supplies can sometimes be purchased in supermarkets and service stations. Hardware stores also routinely carry a broad selection of garden supplies and equipment.

Wholesaling Nursery and Garden Supplies

The retail nursery may grow its own stock. Or it may buy from a producer who grows the plants for the wholesale market, selling them to retailers rather than to ultimate consumers. There are also jobbers who

The maintenance jobs in a nursery are very important because the plants can't be neglected for even a day. (*Courtesy Julius Roehrs Company*)

are in the business of buying nursery stock from producers and reselling it to retailers. These jobbers are often experts at finding rare plants. In addition, there are wholesalers who handle the small equipment and supplies that are sold in garden supply stores. The garden equipment manufacturers keep their dealers supplied through branch offices, where many of the wholesaling functions are carried out.

Building a Career in Nursery and Garden Supplies

Nursery and garden supply stores have to be open in the evenings and on weekends, when home gardeners are free to shop. This means that it is possible to get a part-time job to find out what part of the business interests you most. You may find that you have the ability to work successfully with plants, which is called having a "green thumb." You may find that working with machines suits your aptitudes and abilities best. Or you may find that you have the right qualifications for working directly with people, helping them to satisfy their needs through skilled sales work. If you have a talent for art, a part-time beginning job could also eventually lead you to a job in catalog retailing, maybe designing seed packets, catalogs, or promotional materials.

The various career-level jobs in the nursery and garden supply business can be very satisfying. They also offer a high level of job security to anyone who is willing to make the effort to acquire the product knowledge that is vital in this business.

There are also many opportunities for management positions in marketing garden supplies. These opportunities range from being in charge of the maintenance of a nursery to heading a department in a general merchandise store or being the vice-president in charge of marketing for a garden equipment manufacturer. It would also be possible for you to own your own business or to transfer what you have learned in the marketing of garden supplies to the marketing of farm supplies. You might find yourself interested in the floristry business. So an afterschool beginning job in this field can open many doors for you.

PLANNING A CAREER IN FLORISTRY

In 1917, the American Florists' Society first began using the slogan "Say it with flowers." In the years since then, the florist shop has been accepted as the place to go for presents for a wide variety of occasions and reasons. So the gift market is a very important part of the floristry business. But people also buy flowers for themselves—for their weddings and parties and just to make their homes more beautiful. So the floristry business is not just concerned with flowers. It is also concerned with people. To work successfully in this field, you have to care about both.

The floristry business is a marketing business, and all the marketing skills are required. Just as one example of how important this is, think about the buying for a florist shop. Florists have to buy the vases, ribbons, and other supplies that they use for flower arranging and that they may also sell to their customers. But most important, they have to buy fresh flowers. Because flowers are perishable, the buying has to be done daily. If the manager orders too many flowers, some will have to be thrown out, which represents a loss of money. But, if too few flowers are ordered, business may be lost. The manager must know how to order the right kinds of flowers in the right amounts, and this requires both training and experience.

The manager of the retail or wholesale floristry business also has to worry about selling the goods, operating the place of business, handling personnel problems, promoting sales, and controlling the profits, just as all other marketers do. Let's see now what this means to you if you want to work in a florist shop or a plant store or for a flower or plant wholesaler.

Working in a Florist Shop

Generally speaking, the easiest way to get started in the floristry business is by taking a part-time job in a florist shop. There are peak periods of activity in this business, when extra help is needed. This is

Buying flowers for one's home is a way of satisfying the basic human need for beauty. (*Courtesy New York Convention and Visitors Bureau*)

true of Christmas, Valentine's Day, Easter, and Mother's Day, which are all popular times for sending flowers as gifts. Florists can use beginners with physical strength to help with maintenance work, either in the shop itself or in the greenhouse that is part of some florist shops. Beginners who can work with people can become salesclerks, taking orders in person or over the telephone for the floral arrangements that will be made up by the floral designers. There are also office jobs that beginners with an aptitude for data can learn to do. Young people who have driver's licenses and a high level of responsibility can be hired to make deliveries.

These part-time jobs give you the opportunity to see whether working in this field interests you. These jobs also give you the opportunity to begin acquiring the product knowledge that is necessary for career-level work. You can acquire this product knowledge slowly, on the job. Or you can learn more quickly and thoroughly by taking specific courses related to floristry. If you are very artistic and good at working with your hands, you may want to attend one of the many floral design schools that are located throughout the country. The courses in these schools last from one to six weeks and teach the basic principles of flower arranging. In some states, short courses relating to other aspects of florist shop work are sponsored by the state florists' associations. There are also two- and four-year college programs in **floriculture,** the study of how plants and flowers are grown. Many of the schools that offer such programs include special courses in retailing.

It is also possible to prepare for a career in this field by majoring in marketing management and taking whatever courses in floriculture the school offers. In either case, the idea is to learn about flowers and plants and about marketing. When you are trained in these areas, you enjoy a high level of job security. You are also in a good position to open your own business if that appeals to you.

Working in a Plant Store
Although florist shops sell plants as well as flowers, they usually don't handle very rare or special plants. They leave that to the plant stores. The widespread interest in ecology has brought about a great increase in the number of these specialized stores. Some of them are small stores that call themselves "plant boutiques." It is possible for the managers of these small stores to run them single-handedly or with a helper. But there are also large businesses that offer many of the same kinds of career opportunities that florists do.

Working on the Wholesale Level
Eighty-five percent of the indoor ornamental plants that are sold in this country are grown in Florida. They are shipped from there each week to wholesalers all across the country in huge tractor-trailer trucks. These wholesalers, who generally operate greenhouses, then distribute the plants to florist shops and plant stores.

Fresh flowers are also wholesaled, even though they are very perishable. This is a necessary step, because the producers have to be able to sell the flowers as fast as they are grown. The producers can't take the time to work with many retailers. They want to make as few individual sales as possible. On the other hand, the retailers want to be able to buy the relatively small quantities of flowers that they need. For this reason, the wholesaler's traditional role as a bulk breaker is very important in the floristry business.

The busiest part of the day for the flower wholesaler happens very early in the morning. This is when the truck drivers, who have driven during the night, bring the flowers in from the producers. It is also when the orders must be shipped out to the retailers. Because of the work schedule, this is not work that can be done while you are still in school. But when you are ready for a full-time job, there are many jobs for beginners in flower and plant wholesaling.

Plant stores offer exciting career opportunities for people who enjoy working with plants and are knowledgeable about plant care. (*Courtesy The City Gardener, Inc.*)

Besides office jobs, there are the jobs that have to be done in receiving and shipping the flowers. Because flowers are fragile, this work cannot be done by machines. It is physical work that requires lifting, bending, and stooping, and it may have to be done outdoors when the weather is cold or wet. You can move from these jobs to jobs in sales or in buying, and then on to top management jobs.

The wholesaling and retailing of flowers and plants are so closely related that people can easily move from one area to the other. Or they can transfer their skills to the marketing of farm or garden supplies and equipment.

• BUILDING YOUR MARKETING VOCABULARY

Define each of the following terms and then use each one in a sentence.

floriculture   floristry   nursery

• UNDERSTANDING WHAT YOU HAVE READ

1. Explain why the marketing of farm and garden supplies, flowers, and green plants is "as vital as today's headlines."
2. If you live in a rural area, do you have any alternatives other than becoming a farmer or moving to a city? Explain your answer.
3. How do garden supply stores stay busy during the winter months?
4. Why are flowers wholesaled?

5. Explain the importance of product knowledge in relation to (a) supplying the needs of farmers, (b) supplying the needs of home gardeners, and (c) floristry.

- **APPLYING WHAT YOU HAVE LEARNED**
   1. Name one ladder-type and one lattice-type move that would be possible from each of the following jobs: (a) salesworker for a farm equipment dealer, (b) stock worker in a garden supply store, (c) greenhouse worker for a florist, (d) receiving clerk for a flower wholesaler, and (e) helper in a plant boutique.
   2. Work with your class on a group project to analyze the job opportunities in marketing farm and garden supplies and in floristry in your area. Take the following steps:
      a. Use the Yellow Pages to find out how many such businesses are located in your area. Be careful to find *all* the businesses, including sales branches, wholesalers, and retailers. Remember too that manufacturers have marketing departments.
      b. Put the name of each business on a card and put the cards on a bulletin board that you have divided into the following sections: (1) supplying the needs of farmers, (2) supplying the needs of home gardeners, and (3) floristry.
      c. Write a summary report of what your bulletin board indicates about the opportunities in marketing farm and garden supplies and in floristry in your area. Explain your findings in terms of the characteristics of your community.
   3. List five reasons why you personally would or would not consider a job in marketing farm and garden supplies or in floristry.

part 28 Hardware and Building Supplies

After reading Part 28, you will be able—
- To explain why wholesaling is important in the hardware business.
- To list ten career-level jobs in marketing hardware and building supplies.
- To assist in a class comparative shopping project involving the retailers in your community that sell a given list of hardware and building supply products.
- To prepare a list of 12 questions that you could use to help a friend decide for or against a career in marketing hardware and building supplies.

If you have always enjoyed working with your hands—building and repairing things—you may want to consider a career in marketing hardware and building supplies. These are the products that are used to build, maintain, repair, and remodel homes, as well as commercial and industrial structures and public buildings. When there is a lot of new construction going on, this business is extremely profitable. But even when there is a slowdown in **housing starts** (a term that refers to the number of new houses being started), the marketers of hardware and building supplies still have work to do. When people want to move but can't, they spend money fixing up the homes they are already living in.

To show you what it would be like to work in this field, we are going to discuss the kinds of products, the kinds of customers, and the kinds of businesses involved in the marketing of hardware and building supplies. Then we will take a look at the opportunities for building a career in this field.

THE KINDS OF HARDWARE AND BUILDING SUPPLY PRODUCTS

When we talk about hardware and building supplies, we are talking about a wide range of products. We are going to list the major categories into which these products fall. We are also going to give some examples of the kinds of products that are included under each particular category. This will give you a good idea of the breadth of the

322 • UNIT 4 • CAREERS IN MARKETING GOODS

hardware and building supply business. The seven major categories are as follows:

Hardware: nails, screws, nuts, bolts, hinges, knobs, pulls, rods, screening, hand and power tools.
Masonry supplies: sand, gravel, cement, stones, bricks, marble, granite.
Electrical supplies: wiring, cables, fuses, circuit breakers, electrical fixtures.
Plumbing, heating, and cooling supplies: pipes, fittings, kitchen and bathroom fixtures, furnaces, air-conditioning equipment.
Lumber: boards and beams for construction work, plywood, wood trim, finished plywood paneling, flooring.
Paint and wallpaper: paint, paint remover, stains, varnish, shellac, solvents, brushes, rollers, wallpaper, paste, special tools.
Glass: glass for windows, doors, and greenhouses, putty, and special equipment.

THE CUSTOMERS FOR HARDWARE AND BUILDING SUPPLIES

A major group of customers for hardware and building supplies are homeowners, who need many of these products for the everyday upkeep of their homes. Besides using these products for maintenance,

Even unconventional do-it-yourselfers need hardware and building supplies to carry out their imaginative decorating ideas. (*Courtesy Pratt Institute*)

many homeowners today are dedicated do-it-yourselfers and want to be able to buy the supplies that they need for their remodeling projects in a convenient way. People who live in apartment houses also have many projects for which they need hardware and building supply products, from hanging pictures to refinishing furniture. In fact, every time a new household is set up, there is a new customer for the hardware and building supply business.

Another group of customers for hardware and building supply products are the people who work in the building trades—building contractors, masons, electricians, plumbers, carpenters, painters, and paperhangers. It is very important that these people be able not only to get the supplies that they need but also to get them on time. When supplies are missing, work on building projects has to be delayed. This loss of time can be expensive in terms of money and the customer's goodwill.

THE BUSINESSES THAT MARKET HARDWARE AND BUILDING SUPPLIES

The marketers of hardware and building supplies have the same basic job as all the other marketers of products that you have learned about so far. They have to keep the products that they sell moving along smoothly, for the benefit of both the people who have produced them and those who want to use them. The hardware and building supply business is also like the other businesses you have studied in that this work is done in a wide variety of ways. Let's see now who the marketers of hardware and building supplies are and how they work.

Hardware Stores

Hardware stores could be called the general stores of the hardware and building supply business. Besides carrying the broad assortment of hardware that gives them their name, these stores carry a selection of electrical, plumbing, heating, and cooling supplies, as well as paint, and wallpaper. They also carry tools, supplies, and equipment for lawn maintenance, gardening, and farming. Housewares is another group of products that is traditionally carried in hardware stores. They may also carry sporting goods and recreational supplies.

Although this is the general range of products to be found in hardware stores, the proportion of the whole business taken up by each of these categories varies a great deal from store to store. Some stores place a lot of emphasis on housewares, including small and even large appliances. Stores in rural areas may place more emphasis on sporting goods, especially hunting, fishing, and camping supplies. Other hard-

This self-service lumber and building supply area is part of a large departmentalized home improvement center. (*Courtesy* Home Center *Magazine*)

ware stores are aimed at the do-it-yourselfer, carrying such things as plywood paneling, wallpaper, floor and ceiling tiles, and perhaps even kitchen cabinets and bathroom fixtures. These stores often call themselves "home centers" or "hardware/home center retailers."

The salesworkers in hardware stores are now expected to be able to give expert advice on the use of the products they sell. It isn't just the do-it-yourselfers who need this advice. The professionals in the building trades buy from hardware stores too, and they depend on the store's salesworkers for information about products and how they should be used.

Specialized Retailers of Hardware and Building Supplies

There are some retail stores that are more specialized than the hardware store is, carrying just masonry or electrical supplies and equipment or supplies and equipment needed for plumbing, heating, and cooling. There are also specialized stores that sell paint and wallpaper or glass, along with the necessary equipment. There are lumberyards, which are really stores for selling wood that has been cut into various thicknesses and lengths. Some lumberyards concentrate on the woods that are the most generally used in building. Others specialize in rare woods from such places as Central and South America and the southern coast of Asia. Many lumberyards also have departments for hardware and masonry supplies so carpenters and masons can find everything they need in one place.

The specialized stores have the advantage of being able to carry a very wide selection of items in their particular category. The people who work in these stores are expected to have the kind of product knowledge that allows them to give expert advice.

General Merchandise Stores

General merchandise stores are also in the business of selling hardware and building supplies. The national chain stores do a sizable business in this field, both in their retail stores and through their catalog-retailing operations. General merchandise discount stores and variety stores also sell hardware and building supplies, as do department stores, especially through their suburban branches.

These stores sell an assortment of the things that well-stocked hardware stores sell. However, they tend to emphasize the popular items that have a fast turnover. Because of their mass merchandising approach, they can sometimes charge less than a neighborhood hardware store for the same item. To meet this competition, the hardware store emphasizes its ability to give the customer personal attention and good advice.

Hardware Wholesalers

A major problem for hardware stores is the exceptionally large number of items that must be included in the store's inventory. This makes it essential to buy most items through wholesalers instead of trying to buy everything directly from the manufacturers. Stores generally look for a principal supplier who can provide the majority of the products they need. In selecting a wholesaler to be its principal supplier, a store can choose from the same general types of wholesalers with which you are already familiar, except that in the hardware business some of these wholesalers have different names. There are four basic types of hardware wholesalers:

1. Stores that want to be completely independent can choose an independent service wholesaler as their principal supplier. These wholesalers supply their customers with a broad range of merchandise, as well as a number of services designed to help the retailers be more successful.
2. Another kind of hardware wholesaler is the **program wholesaler,** who operates in much the same way as voluntary wholesalers in other areas of marketing. An example of a program wholesaler is Sentry Wholesaler, which is an association of 14 different wholesalers who are spread out geographically so they don't compete with each other. These 14 wholesalers service a total of 4,000 retailers.
3. The hardware wholesalers who are organized as cooperative wholesalers are called **dealer-owned wholesalers.** A well-known example of a dealer-owned wholesaler is Cotter and Company, whose members use the name "True Value" for their stores.

4. The hardware business also has franchising wholesalers. The Stratton and Terstegge Company, which is based in Louisville, Kentucky, is an example of such a wholesaler. This company has a network of 600 "S & T" retailers.

Although hardware stores do their major buying from one of the above wholesalers, they also depend on specialty wholesalers for some of their needs. These wholesalers specialize in just one part of the inventory of the hardware store. But they carry that part in depth. Thus if a hardware store finds that one department is especially popular with the customers, it can expand the offerings in that department by buying from a specialty wholesaler.

Building Supply Wholesalers

There are wholesalers who are specialists in various parts of the building supply business. These wholesalers sell to the specialized retailers in this field, as well as to people who work in the building trades and various other industrial users. Included in this group of wholesalers are the wholesale lumberyards that gather together a stock of lumber from various sawmills. These large wholesale lumberyards then sell to the

This is the showroom of a manufacturer of electrical supplies. Builders can bring their clients here to select lighting fixtures for a new home or office. (*Courtesy Koch and Lowry Inc.*)

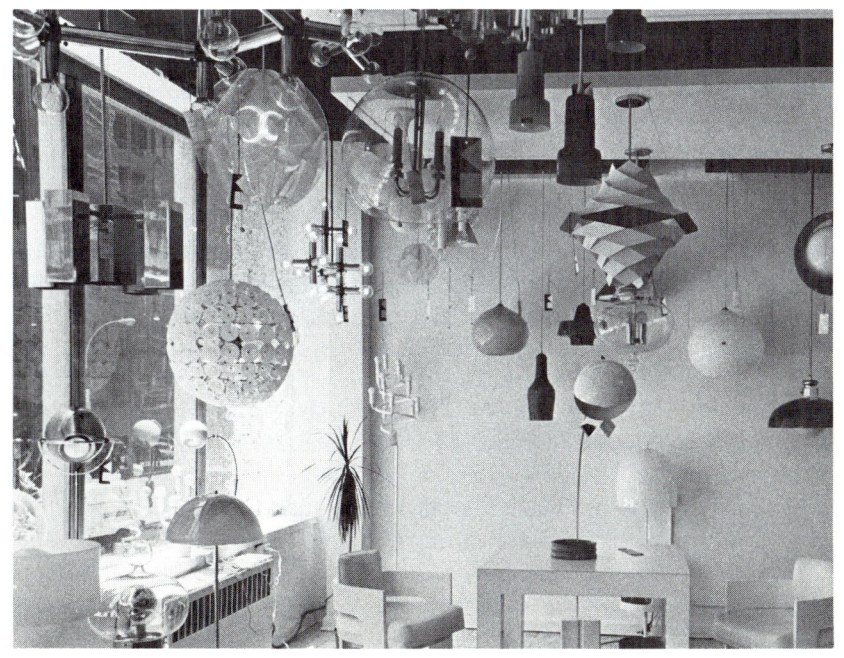

smaller retail lumberyards. They also sell to large construction companies, to factories that use wood as a raw material in the production process, and to utility companies.

There are also wholesalers who deal in either electrical or plumbing, heating, and cooling supplies. These wholesalers are service wholesalers, and they perform many services for the retailers and building trade workers who are their customers. For example, they often operate showrooms to which a builder can take clients to pick out all the electrical or plumbing fixtures for their houses.

Besides maintaining showrooms, these wholesalers maintain an outside sales staff to call on customers at their places of business. They help their customers estimate how much specific jobs are going to cost so the price can be set correctly for the ultimate consumer. They prepare catalogs and other sales promotion materials to give the customers up-to-date decorating ideas. They may even draw up a floor plan, showing how to use the products in the way that will be the most satisfactory for the people who are going to be living with them. They also sponsor trade shows so their customers can see what is new in the field, and they may print trade magazines or newspapers for this same purpose.

The Producers Who Market Directly

Although wholesalers are important in the hardware and building supply business, there are also many producers who market directly to retailers and to the construction industry. For example, most masonry supplies are marketed directly. There are also some manufacturers of consumer products who have extensive marketing departments and therefore prefer to deal directly with the retailers.

However, most manufacturers don't like to sell in small quantities, as wholesalers are willing to do. Although buying in quantity may be an advantage to the large retailer, it is a burden for the smaller stores. It means that a lot of money has to be tied up at one time in inventory. Providing storage space for these goods is also a problem. But buying in this way helps to round out the retailers' stock so they can offer their customers a larger selection.

CAREER POSSIBILITIES IN HARDWARE AND BUILDING SUPPLIES

A special problem in marketing hardware and building supplies is the large number of items that retailers and wholesalers must stock. Furthermore, many of these items do not have a very fast turnover. This means that a lot of money is tied up in inventory. This is another factor that makes marketing skills important in this field, because it is hard to make a profit unless the business is well run in every respect.

The need for marketing skills makes the DE program an excellent way of preparing for this kind of work. It would also be a good idea for you to take the industrial arts courses that your school offers, which are now open to girls as well as boys in most schools. Through these courses, you can begin to get some of the product knowledge that is so important in this field. You can also begin to learn the special words and terms that go along with the building trades so you will be able to talk to the customers in the language that they understand.

Let's now see what jobs are like in retailing and wholesaling hardware and building supplies and in working with direct-marketing producers. As you are reading about these jobs, remember that experience in one of these areas can easily be transferred to the other areas. Also, the experience that you gain in marketing hardware and building supplies can help you to get jobs in other marketing businesses.

Jobs in Retailing

The best way to get started in the hardware and building supply business is through retailing, where it is easy to get part-time jobs while you are still in school. Do-it-yourselfers tend to shop in the evenings and on Saturdays, when they are not working at their regular jobs. These are peak times when more help is needed.

The work that has to be done in retailing hardware and building supplies is in many ways similar to the jobs in other retailing businesses. Thus beginners in hardware and building supplies need the basic and social skills, plus a neat appearance and a willingness to work hard. Beginners can start out doing maintenance work. They can also do stock work—receiving and marking goods and placing them in the right place in the stockroom or on the selling floor. The beginner might also wrap orders. Exceptionally responsible young people with driver's licenses can be hired to make deliveries.

The value of one of these beginning jobs is that it offers you the opportunity to begin acquiring knowledge about the special products that are sold in this business. This is particularly true of stock work, where the beginner can learn such things as who and where the suppliers are, what kind of products sell the fastest, and how the various products are used. To help the ambitious young person move on to the selling jobs, there are home study courses, such as the Advanced Course in Hardware Retailing offered by the National Retail Hardware Association. This course gives the hardware store employees a chance to learn details about the different kinds of products that the stores sell so they can deal with the customers who need advice.

Although all the basic skills are important in retailing hardware and building supplies, skill in arithmetic is especially necessary. As an example of why this is so, a salesworker in a paint and wallpaper store may have to figure out how many gallons of paint or how many rolls of wallpaper will be needed for a certain size room. Likewise, salesworkers in lumberyards may have to determine how much wood would be needed for a specific job. Retail salesworkers in this field, as in the other areas of marketing you have learned about, have to enjoy working with people. They must also have the tact and patience that make this possible. They have to enjoy the challenge of helping customers to solve their problems. A mechanical aptitude is also usually necessary in this field.

Salesworkers who have made the effort to develop their marketing skills can become assistant managers of independent stores. In order to do this, however, they must have shown that they can assume responsibility for their own work and the work of others. They can also be taken into the training programs that lead to the jobs of department head or buyer in general merchandise stores. It is possible for them to become the managers of multiunit or chain hardware and building

Salesworkers for hardware and building supply businesses must be familiar with what they sell so that they can advise customers about what they will need to do a job. (*Courtesy Sears, Roebuck and Co.*)

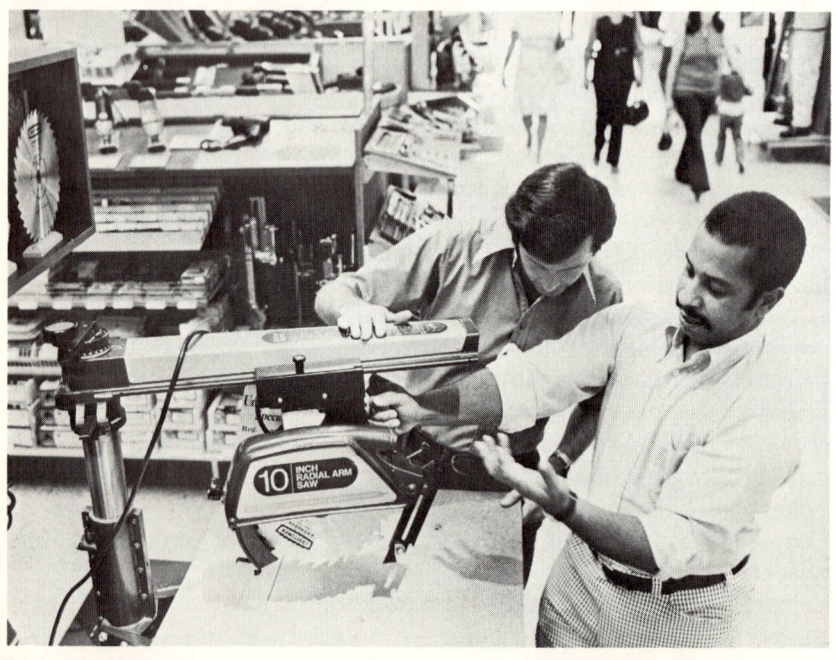

supply stores, although the chances for this are not as great as they are in some other marketing businesses.

In hardware and building supplies, the largest majority of the retailing businesses are independently owned, and there are no really large national chains in this field. Because this is a field that is not dominated by chains, your chances for owning a store of your own are good. The help that the wholesalers in this field are prepared to give, especially the program and franchising wholesalers, may be enough to put store ownership within your reach.

Jobs in Wholesaling

The widespread use of computers among hardware and building supply wholesalers has cut down on the number of unskilled jobs that have to be done. This explains why people who have developed retailing skills are especially welcome in wholesaling jobs. It is also possible to get beginning jobs in the warehouse directly after graduation from high school, without previous experience, but you must be the kind of person who is eager to learn. People who have had college-level training can be hired directly as buyers or sales trainees, but they too must want to learn as much as they can about the business. Let's now look more closely at the various kinds of jobs that have to be done with hardware and building supply wholesalers.

BUYING JOBS. The buyers for hardware and building supply wholesalers tend to be highly specialized, so that each buyer handles one particular type of product. For example, one buyer may buy electrical supplies, another one paint and paint supplies, and another one housewares. Because of this, buyers get to be experts in their particular lines. They make sure that they know all the manufacturers and all the products that they can buy so they are really able to make the best choice. They do this mainly by receiving calls from manufacturers' salesworkers. They may also visit factories and trade shows. Buyers need an aptitude for data because they have to judge how much, where, and when to order and how to get the best possible terms. This requires that they be able to analyze reports and estimate future needs.

SELLING JOBS. Hardware and building supply wholesalers employ inside salesworkers and outside salesworkers. The inside salesworkers may start by working at a counter, serving the walk-in customers. Then they may move to the job of taking orders over the telephone. Or they may be assigned to the wholesaler's showroom to work with industrial consumers and their clients. Inside salesworkers may be promoted to outside selling, which calls for the ability to set their own pace. In many ways, outside salesworkers are their own supervisors, planning their own time and taking full responsibility for their own actions.

An outside salesworker who serves retailers may take inventory for the retailers, decide how much merchandise is needed, and write out the orders. All the retailers have to do is approve the orders. The outside salesworkers who work with customers in the construction industry often are sales engineers, who are highly trained in both engineering and selling. These salesworkers have to be able to do the kind of creative thinking that solves problems. In other words, they have to be able to put the knowledge that they have to work in new ways.

All salesworkers for hardware and building supply wholesalers must understand how their own company works and what its policies are. They also have to know a great deal about the businesses that their customers are in so they can give the most helpful kind of advice. This is especially true of the sales representatives who work for program and franchising wholesalers. Although they don't have any selling duties as such, they have to serve as the link between the wholesaler and the store. Their aim is to help the retailer sell more goods and thus improve the business of the wholesaler. These are people-to-people jobs that require highly developed social skills.

WAREHOUSING JOBS. The warehouse of the hardware and building supply wholesaler is generally a pleasant place to work. Although some heavy outdoor work must be done in lumberyards and masonry supply outlets, most hardware and building supply warehouse workers have the benefit of many laborsaving devices. However, they still need good health and physical stamina to do the work. Some jobs require a high aptitude for data, and others require mechanical aptitude.

There are jobs for receiving clerks, order pickers, order checkers, packers, and shipping clerks. These workers generally have to be high school graduates, as do the truck drivers who are hired to make deliveries. Besides requiring a safe driving record, driving jobs require good vision, physical strength, and a stable personality.

Because the warehouse workers are in a position to learn so much about how the wholesaling company operates, it is very common for them to be promoted to better jobs. This may mean being given management duties in the warehouse or in other parts of the business.

SALES-SUPPORTING JOBS. Hardware and building supply wholesalers need people who can prepare advertising and display materials that the wholesalers' customers can use. People are also needed to prepare catalogs and sales brochures. These jobs are done by artists, designers, and writers who must not only be talented in their own field but also know how the wholesaling company works and what it is trying to do.

Another kind of job that supports the work of the sales force is designing rooms and laying out plans for industrial consumers in the building trades. The people who do this work may be trained as engineers. Or they may be trained as interior architects, which means that they have learned how to plan interior spaces. Still another sales-sup-

This person, who has been trained as an interior architect, is employed by a hardware and building supply wholesaler. She works in a sales-supporting capacity planning interiors for the wholesaler's customers. (*Courtesy The Cooper Union for the Advancement of Science and Art*)

porting job involves planning educational materials and running educational programs for the wholesalers' employees and customers. These jobs require experience in speaking, writing, and teaching. The people who work in these sales-supporting jobs are usually hired on the basis of their special talents and abilities.

OFFICE JOBS. Much of the paper work and recordkeeping that has to be done by hardware and building supply wholesalers is done with computers. This includes keeping inventory records, setting prices, and estimating costs for industrial consumers. It also includes keeping track of the income and expenses of the business in order to be sure of making a profit. Wholesalers need people with the skills to run these computers. They also need people who have acquired the specialized office skills needed to be secretaries, typists, and accountants.

TOP MANAGEMENT JOBS. Wholesaling companies need people at the top who can coordinate all the work that is being done in the various departments of the company. Although it is possible for beginners in the warehouse to work up to these top management jobs, such promotions are much more likely to come about if courses in marketing management are taken along the way. The top managers of wholesaling companies must have a broad range of both experience and education in order to do their jobs properly. If you know ahead of time that you want to work on the management level, you should plan to attend a community college or four-year college. This gives you the chance to start partway up the ladder rather than on the bottom rung.

Jobs With Direct-Marketing Producers

Marketing jobs that have to be done for the producers who market directly are very similar to the jobs in wholesaling. This is because these producers are, in effect, acting as their own wholesalers. The differences are that there are no jobs for buyers and there are more jobs at the top in selling. Many of the producers who do their own marketing are large companies whose customers are spread all over the country and perhaps in other countries. Thus they need regional sales managers, a national sales manager, and a vice-president in charge of marketing. It is important for you to know about the marketing jobs with producers because they give you still another way of building a career in the hardware and building supply business.

- **BUILDING YOUR MARKETING VOCABULARY**

  Define each of the following terms and then use each one in a sentence.

  dealer-owned wholesaler   housing starts   program wholesaler

- **UNDERSTANDING WHAT YOU HAVE READ**
  1. Why is product knowledge important in this field?
  2. Explain why wholesaling is important in the hardware business.
  3. Name four kinds of wholesalers that hardware stores may choose as their principal suppliers.
  4. List ten career-level jobs in this field.

- **APPLYING WHAT YOU HAVE LEARNED**
  1. Divide your class into three teams. Assign each team a specific hardware and building supply product, such as a hammer, sack of ready-mix cement, gallon of paint, etc. Each team must do the following things:
      a. List the names and addresses of each retailer in your area that sells the product.
      b. Assign individual team members to visit each retailer and report on the quality, prices, and customer services that each retailer offers.
      c. Summarize the results and prepare an oral report for the class.
  2. Using the list of questions that follow Parts 20, 22, 23, and 27 as a guide, prepare a list of 12 questions that you could use to help a friend decide about a career in hardware and building supplies.
  3. Think about how you would personally answer the questions you have prepared and write a paragraph explaining why you would or would not be interested in a career in this field.

EXPERIMENTS IN MARKETING

1. Together with other members of your class, make a list of the ways in which the businesses that market goods are alike. Here are three examples to start your thinking:
   a. They are all concerned with maintaining the goodwill of their customers.
   b. They all have to keep careful records.
   c. They all add a time and place value to the goods that they sell.
2. Does the fact that businesses that market goods have so much in common mean that you could be equally happy in any of them? Have a class discussion on this question.
3. Ask each person in your class to do the following:
   a. Choose a business that markets goods, such as a food store, hardware wholesaler, florist shop, direct-selling manufacturer of cosmetics, etc.
   b. Pretend to be the person who does the hiring for the business. Draw up a list of at least 12 characteristics that you are looking for in the people you hire. Here are two examples to start your thinking: (1) neat appearance and (2) honesty.
   c. Compare the individual lists in class and make a master list of the qualities that are needed for success in marketing goods.
4. Name five jobs that you could do in marketing goods if you are (a) artistic, (b) mechanical, (c) a good driver, (d) eager to travel, and (e) happiest in a job that offers wide freedom of action and independence.

UNIT 5

After completing this unit, you will have developed an understanding of how services are marketed. You will also be able to compare your needs, personal characteristics, goals, and desired life style with the career possibilities in the various areas. And you will be able to determine which career possibilities are real alternatives for you.

In the last three decades, the sale of services has been rapidly overtaking the sale of goods. With a larger and larger share of the consumer's dollar being spent for services, many economists are predicting that the sale of services will soon be the most important part of marketing. In any case, service businesses already represent a major source of jobs, offering many different ways to build satisfying careers.

In this unit, you will have a chance to learn what the major kinds of service businesses are like. You will see many similarities among them, just as you will see many similarities with the businesses that market goods. You will also learn about the special problems and satisfactions of marketing each particular kind of service. This will help you to decide whether any of these areas of marketing has something to offer you personally.

Careers in Marketing Services

part 29 Food Services

After reading Part 29, you will be able—
- To explain the importance of the food service business.
- To list seven requirements for a given food service job.
- To list three advantages and three disadvantages of a career in marketing food services from your personal point of view.

We are going to begin our study of the marketing of services by looking at a service business that you have surely had some contact with. If you have ever bought a hamburger, you have been a customer of the food service business. When you bought the hamburger, you were buying not only the food itself but also the preparation and serving of it. The food service business has so many customers that it accounts for about 9 percent of all retail sales. It serves more than 39 billion meals annually and employs nearly 3½ million people, more than any other marketing business. Let's see now how the food service business works and what kinds of careers it offers.

FOOD SERVICE: A VITAL BUSINESS

There are a number of reasons that explain why the food service business is so large. Most people today have jobs that are some distance from their homes. They can't go home to eat the meals that they need during the working day. In many families, both husbands and wives work, which means that there is less time and energy for cooking and more money for eating out. More and more people use the food service business to help them entertain their business associates and friends. Many business people like to make the most of their working day by holding meetings at lunchtime, sometimes for very large groups of people. Also, more people are traveling for business and pleasure, and more people are eating out just because they like to. Going out for meals has become a form of recreation as well as a necessity.

These reasons for eating out explain why there are food service businesses wherever there are people living, working, traveling, or having fun. This includes small towns, big cities, and the highways

338 • UNIT 5 • CAREERS IN MARKETING SERVICES

When people dine out, eating becomes a form of recreation as well as a necessity. (*Courtesy Fairmont Hotel and Tower*)

between towns. The main purpose of most food service businesses is food service. But there are also food service facilities that are part of other businesses, such as drug, department, and variety stores. There are also food service facilities on trains and passenger ships and in hospitals, schools, factories, and office buildings.

When you add all this together, you can see that the food service business is a vital part of our economy. It is a business that gives you the opportunity not only to serve other people but also to build a satisfying career for yourself.

THE KINDS OF FOOD SERVICE BUSINESSES

There are two basic kinds of food service businesses. The first is the **restaurant**, which can be defined as a public eating place. The second is the **catering service.** This is a food service business that has an agreement with a customer to provide either food preparation alone or food preparation and service. In some cases, the cooking is done in the kitchen of the catering service and delivered to the customer. In other cases, it is done in the kitchen of the customer.

There are many food service businesses that are quite clearly either restaurants or catering services. But there are also many food service companies where the two overlap. There are many restaurants that also offer catering services, and there are many catering service companies that have opened restaurants. This shows that food service businesses are like all other marketing businesses in that there aren't sharp distinctions between the kinds of businesses. The important thing is not how a business should be classified but how well it serves its customers. With this in mind, let's now take a closer look at how restaurants and catering businesses operate.

Defining Restaurants

Within the restaurant category, many different names are used, such as diner, lunchroom, luncheonette, cafeteria, cafe, tearoom, coffee shop, steak house, chop house, tavern, grill room, and so on. It is very difficult to define many of these terms in any conclusive way. For example, the dictionary definition of a luncheonette is "a place where light lunches are sold to be eaten on the premises." But many so-called luncheonettes are open long hours. They serve breakfast and substantial meals at the dinner hour, and they often package food for their customers to take out.

A much better way of differentiating between the many kinds of restaurants is to get at their individual qualities. For each restaurant, the owner/manager must make some basic decisions that define what the business will be like and what it will try to do. In making these decisions, the restaurant manager has to try to please the customers. But it isn't possible to please all the customers all the time. There are too many different kinds of people, and even the same people have different needs at different times. Thus each restaurant has to be planned so it fills special needs. In other words, the restaurant has to have a personality, or image, just as other marketing businesses do, so the customers know what to expect. The decisions that the manager must make are actually all tied in together. But they will be easier to understand if we look at them one by one.

STYLE OF COOKING. The style of cooking of a restaurant is called its **cuisine** (kwih-zeen). Many businesses have what is known as a "general cuisine." In such cases, their **menu,** which is the list of foods offered by a food service business, gives the customers their choice of a group of popularly accepted dishes. Other businesses feature elaborate menus, offering very special dishes that have to be prepared with painstaking care. There are restaurants that concentrate on the cooking of a particular nationality—French, Chinese, Japanese, Italian, German, Greek, Polish, or Mexican, for example. Other restaurants may feature soul food or kosher cooking. Still others serve the specialities of a particular region, such as the South, New England, or the Southwest.

Some restaurants offer a "limited menu," which means that they specialize in certain kinds of foods, such as steaks, seafood, snack foods, hamburgers, or pancakes. Often those restaurants that have a limited menu offer **short-order cooking**. This is a method of cooking where the food can be prepared very quickly. This kind of cooking lends itself to assembly-line techniques. In fact, many limited menu businesses have streamlined their operations to such an extent that they have brought the term **fast-food business** into the language. This is a food service business that uses the techniques of mass production to prepare and serve food very rapidly. McDonald's and Burger King are examples of fast-food businesses.

METHODS OF SERVICE. Another extremely important factor in the image of the restaurant is how the food is served. There are five ways in which this may be done. Some restaurants use only one way, whereas others use a combination of methods.

1. **Table service** is the method of food service where the customers are seated at tables or booths and are served everything they need by waitresses or waiters. This can be very informal or very elegant.
2. **Cafeteria service** is the method of food service where the customers help themselves or are served at a buffet-type counter and then take the food to a table to eat it. In a cafeteria, the customer takes a tray and walks the length of the counter, usually choosing the cold foods without assistance but getting help from counter workers with the hot dishes. At the end of the counter, the customer pays a cashier.

Can you identify the two types of service shown here? (LEFT *courtesy Harrison Conference Centers*)

Counter service and takeout service are two popular ways of serving food. (LEFT *courtesy Bryan Mah/Hyatt Corporation;* RIGHT *courtesy Marriott Corporation*)

3. People in a hurry appreciate **counter service.** This is the method of food service where the customer is served and eats at a counter. A counter worker serves the food, which is usually of the short-order type. Many restaurants have both counter service and table service.
4. Short-order cooking is also a feature of the restaurants that offer **drive-in service.** This is the method of food service where the customer parks outside the restaurant and the prepared food is carried out to the car. A carhop takes the order and brings the food on a tray, which hooks onto the car window. Thus the customer doesn't even have to get out of the car.
5. Another very popular method of food service is **take-out service**, where the customers take the prepared food out of the restaurant and eat it wherever they want. There are restaurants that will package an entire dinner to take out from their regular menu. Take-out service is generally featured by fast-food businesses.

SIZE OF THE RESTAURANT. Restaurants come in many sizes. Although about three-quarters of them are small businesses with fewer than ten employees, there are also restaurants with several dining rooms where hundreds of people can be served at one time. Restaurants can be independently owned. Or the owner may be a franchisee of such chains as Chicken Delight, International House of Pancakes, and Taco Time International. In such cases, much of the personality of the business has already been determined by the parent company. There are almost always very specific requirements about details ranging from the architecture of the building to the recipes for the food. Restaurants can also be owned by corporate chains, such as Stouffer's Restaurants.

ATMOSPHERE OF THE RESTAURANT. It isn't possible to talk about restaurants very long without getting around to the word "atmosphere." This has to do with how the restaurant makes the customers feel. There are many things that help to form the atmosphere, including the method of service, the style of cooking, and the size of the restaurant. The location of the building or room is also a factor, as are such things as the lighting, furniture, type of decoration, tablecloths, dishes, glassware, silverware, and uniforms of the employees. The employees themselves are also part of the atmosphere. If you want to work in a restaurant, you should think about the kind of atmosphere you prefer.

PRICE RANGES IN RESTAURANTS. Restaurants are like other marketing businesses in that they don't all have the same price policies. Some are planned for the people who want to pay as little as possible, whereas others are very expensive. But whatever the restaurant charges, it has to give its customers their money's worth. The customers have to feel that the quality of the food, the way in which it is prepared and served, and the atmosphere all add up to a total experience that balances the amount of money that is being charged. Otherwise they will go somewhere else.

HOURS THAT RESTAURANTS ARE OPEN. Many food service businesses don't open until noon because they serve only lunch and dinner. Others don't open until late afternoon because they serve only dinner. Some open very early in the morning to serve breakfast and then perhaps close early in the evening. Others are open 24 hours a day. Restaurants also tend to be open on weekends and holidays.

There are restaurant jobs that can be done during the regular working day. But there are also many jobs that require hours that can be a reason either for or against working in this field, depending on your point of view. Some people find that working in the evenings and being off during the day fits in very well with their life styles. There are even some people in this business who work a "split shift." This requires that they work for two separate periods of time with a break in the middle. For example, a waiter/waitress might work during the lunch period and then be off duty until dinner time. Although this may sound inconvenient, there are people who find that such a schedule suits their needs and preferences. The variety of food service businesses gives you a good chance of working out the schedule that fits in best with your life style.

Some catering services specialize in providing food and elegant settings for formal banquets. *(Courtesy Marriott Corporation)*

Defining Catering Services

Catering services can be as different from each other as restaurants are. Some have a general kind of menu. Others are highly specialized, offering only New England clambakes, for example, or only snack foods. There are catering services of all sizes. At one end of the scale is the business that can be run completely by one person out of a home kitchen. On the other end of the scale are such large national corporations as Canteen Corporation, Servomation, and ARA Services. These companies have large ultramodern food preparation centers in the various geographic areas that they serve.

Catering services may be sold to private individuals who are having parties, weddings, or other social events. Besides preparing the food, the caterer may supply everything else that is needed, including waiters and waitresses, linens, china, silverware, tables, and chairs.

Catering services are also sold to business customers. This may mean simply supplying and delivering the prepared food to such customers as airlines, who then serve it to their own customers. Or it may mean serving the food in the cafeterias or dining rooms of factories, office buildings, schools, hospitals, and recreation areas. In such cases, the catering company may prepare the food in its own kitchen or in the kitchen of the customer. Sometimes such previously prepared foods as soups, salads, sandwiches, hot and cold drinks, and desserts are placed in automatic vending machines. In other instances, prepared snack food is placed on trucks that have refrigeration facilities. These trucks make routine stops so people who are not near restaurants can buy food conveniently.

CAREERS IN FOOD SERVICE BUSINESSES

It has been estimated that 27 percent of the workers in the food service business are people in their teens. There are two conclusions that can be drawn from this. The first is that there are many entry-level jobs for which no previous training or experience is needed. The second is that this is a very easy field in which to get after-school or summer work.

These entry-level jobs can all lead to more advanced jobs. If you are willing to make the effort to learn the skills that are needed in this business, you will find that it is easy to move up. You can do this by starting at the bottom and moving up step by step as you gain experience. Or you can get a "running start" by going to one of the schools that specialize in preparing people for food service work. With the odd hours in this business, it is very easy to go to classes while you are working.

To see how a career in the food service business could develop, let's look first at the kinds of jobs that have to be done and then check the advantages of food service work.

The Kinds of Jobs That Have to Be Done

When you are looking at the kinds of jobs that have to be done in food service businesses, you will find many things that you are already familiar with. This is because the businesses that sell services have many things in common with the businesses that sell goods. Because of these similarities, it is easy to transfer food service experience to other areas of marketing, and vice versa. But while you are watching for similarities, you should remember how many differences there are between marketing businesses.

BUYING SUPPLIES. In the food service business, it is necessary to buy many supplies in order to produce the service on a continuing basis. This ranges from the food and paper supplies that are needed each day to replacements for broken dishes and worn-out equipment. The business also has to buy some services. For example, it may buy the services of a linen rental company that supplies clean tablecloths, napkins, and uniforms. In small businesses, the buying duties may all be divided between the cook and the manager, who may be the same person. In large businesses, however, there are purchasing agents who do this work. (A **purchasing agent** is a marketing worker who buys goods and services to be used by an industrial consumer.) The corporate and franchised chains may have large staffs of highly specialized purchasing agents working from the central headquarters. Purchasing agents in this field need skills that are similar in many ways to those needed by buyers for stores and wholesalers, with an emphasis on the special needs of the food service business.

PREPARING THE FOOD. There are some food service businesses where the job of preparing the food does not require special skills. For example, in many fast-food restaurants, beginners can easily be trained for this work. At the other end of the scale is the job of "chef," which is the name that is given to a highly skilled cook. Chefs are not considered to be marketing workers, but many of them do have a need for marketing skills. For example, some chefs are in charge of buying the food for the restaurant and so need buying skills. Also, chefs sometimes open their own restaurants, which means that they need a knowledge of marketing management.

Chefs must have intensive training in special cooking schools. In return, they enjoy a high degree of job security because there is a general shortage of trained cooks and chefs. If you think that you might be interested in this kind of work, you can get a beginning job as a kitchen helper. This will help you determine whether you have the interest in cooking and the ability to work with your hands that are required.

SERVING THE FOOD. The number and kinds of jobs that have to be done to serve the food depend on the size of the business and the method of service. In a large cafeteria, there aren't any waitresses or waiters because the customers wait on themselves. But workers called "waiter's assistants" (busboys and busgirls) are needed to clean up the tables and take the dirty dishes back to the kitchen. The situation is quite different in a restaurant that is the same size as the cafeteria but offers table service. In this case, a whole staff of waiters and waitresses is needed, plus a staff of waiter's assistants, who not only clear off the tables but also reset them for the next customers.

The job of waiter's assistant is an entry-level job from which you can work up to the job of waiter/waitress. It is possible to be hired directly as a waiter/waitress in some businesses and to be trained either on the job or with a few days' schooling. In other restaurants, the job of waiter/waitress is a highly skilled one, requiring both experience and special training. For example, in an elegant restaurant, the waiter/waitress must know how to do some cooking at the table, to carve meat, and to serve in the most gracious way.

Waiters or waitresses who rush customers through their dinner ignore their responsibility to see that customers are enjoying themselves.

Large restaurants employ a hostess or headwaiter to greet the guests and seat them. In some restaurants, these people have no other duties and therefore need no special training. In other cases, they supervise the waiters and waitresses, as well as the waiter's assistants. For this kind of supervisory work, experience or special training is necessary. Two other ways to get started in food service are by working as a carhop or as a counter worker. This is experience that can be transferred to other food service jobs.

Serving jobs require a high aptitude for handling things. The waiter's assistant who drops a trayfull of dishes breaks both the dishes and the mood. The waiter/waitress who spills coffee into the saucer or onto the customer loses friends for the business very quickly. Serving jobs also require a very high aptitude for people—that is, you must enjoy working with them and seeing to it that they enjoy themselves. Many serving jobs also require an aptitude for data. The waiter/waitress is often responsible for adding up the customer's check. The counter worker in a fast-food restaurant acts as both server and cashier.

Still another requirement for serving jobs is good health and plenty of energy, because these are not jobs where you can sit down. Also, you can't be the kind of person who falls apart when things don't go smoothly. There are rush hours in this business when it seems that everyone wants to eat at once. You have to be able to take these busy times in stride.

MEETING CLEANLINESS STANDARDS. It is essential that everything about the food service business be spotlessly clean. This is partly to please customers. But cleanliness is also a requirement of the state and local health departments that license food service businesses. There are constant inspections, and places that are not clean can be shut down. Every employee is expected to help with this problem. There may also be a staff of cleaning workers for the building and grounds. In addition, there are cleanup jobs in the kitchen, including loading and emptying the dishwashers that most businesses now use.

Cleaning jobs can be filled by people with no previous training, as long as they have an aptitude for things and enough physical strength and energy to do the work. For someone who is willing to learn, these jobs can be stepping-stones to other jobs in the business that require marketing skills.

CONTROLLING THE FINANCES. There are many jobs for cashiers in food service businesses. To be hired as a cashier, you may not need previous experience. But you do have to be good in arithmetic and careful in handling money. Each food service business also has the problems of setting prices, planning a budget, paying bills, and keeping financial records. In the small business, these are all problems for the manager. But large businesses employ bookeepers, accountants, and office workers.

PROMOTING SALES. The food service business has the same problem of attracting customers that any marketing business has. Although the manager has to handle these problems in the small business, large businesses employ specialists in advertising. Some companies also employ people to think up promotional "gimmicks" that will attract customers. For example, children may be given small toys or books when they visit the restaurant. The people who fill these jobs usually have had both training and experience in their particular fields.

MANAGING THE FOOD SERVICE BUSINESS. Because of the number of food service businesses, there are many opportunities for people to reach the top management jobs. There are also many opportunities for people to own their own businesses. The number of franchised chains makes this a very real possibility for you if this is where your interest lies. But before you try to go into business for yourself, you should get the kind of experience and training that would entitle you to be a manager. You might come to the manager's job from food preparation or

Food service businesses need people with a high aptitude for data to do office work. (*Jeremiah Bean*)

food service work. Or you might be trained in the financial side of the business, starting out as a cashier perhaps.

Along the way, however, you have to make the effort to learn how all the other parts of the business work, preferably by taking courses in food service management. You must be able to put all the parts together so the business functions smoothly as a whole. You must also be able to bring out the best in the people who work for you. When food service businesses fail, as many of them do, it is often because the people at the top did not have all the necessary management skills.

The Advantages of Food Service Work

The pay in food service businesses compares well with the pay in other marketing businesses. If the basic salary is low, as it may be with waitresses and waiters, the tips that are part of this business make the actual take-home pay very attractive. Most food service companies provide such fringe benefits as health and life insurance, paid vacations, and retirement plans.

But the most important advantage of food service work is that it gives you the opportunity to build the career that is right for you, while offering a very high degree of job security. This career might be either in the food service business or in another area of marketing, such as other kinds of service businesses or food retailing or wholesaling. Because food service experience is transferable, you are opening many doors for yourself when you take an entry-level job in this field.

• BUILDING YOUR MARKETING VOCABULARY

Define each of the following terms and then use each one in a sentence.

cafeteria service
catering service
counter service
cuisine
drive-in service
fast-food business

menu
purchasing agent
restaurant
short-order cooking
table service
take-out service

• UNDERSTANDING WHAT YOU HAVE READ

1. Explain the importance of the food service business.
2. Explain the meaning of the term "split shift."
3. What kinds of business customers buy catering services?
4. What conclusions can be drawn from the fact that such a large percentage of the workers in food service businesses are in their teens?
5. How can you get a "running start" on a career in food service?

• APPLYING WHAT YOU HAVE LEARNED

1. Describe a food service business that you have visited, writing one sentence dealing with each of the following points: (a) style of cooking, (b) method of service, (c) size, (d) atmosphere, (e) price range, and (f) hours.
2. Select one job from the list below. Try to imagine what the job would be like and then list seven requirements for it. Use your text as a guide but also do your own thinking.
   a. A counter worker in a fast-food restaurant
   b. A cashier in a large cafeteria
   c. A waiter's assistant in a small, expensive restaurant
   d. A hostess or head waiter who shows people to their tables in a family-style restaurant
   e. A manager of a catering service
3. List three advantages and three disadvantages of food service work from your personal point of view. Then write a paragraph summarizing how you feel about the possibility of pursuing a career in this area.

part 30 Hotels and Motels

After reading Part 30, you will be able—
- To explain why it is significant that the customers in hotels and motels are always spoken of as "guests."
- To choose one entry-level job in hotels and motels and diagram the ladder- or lattice-type moves that a person can make from it.
- To participate in a class discussion on the requirements for being successful in the hotel and motel field.

If you enjoy meeting new people, people who are interesting because they come from faraway places, the hotel and motel business may very well be for you. With jet planes, high-speed trains, high-powered automobiles, and superior roads, people are on the move for pleasure and business on a scale that has never been known before. Our citizens are traveling not only within this country but also abroad. This foreign travel is a two-way movement, with people from other countries coming here just as freely. When you read the guest list in any hotel or motel, you find people that come from all corners of the world.

The hotel and motel business provides not only a place to sleep but also many of the comforts of home for these travelers, who are always spoken of as "guests." This makes it clear that the main concern of this business is serving people, meeting their needs, and making sure that their stay is as pleasant and enjoyable as possible. This is a task that has no beginning or ending hours. It goes on all around the clock. In fact, it is such a large task that about 1 million people are now working at it.

These people work in a wide range of jobs calling for many different skills. Some of them work in the small hotels and motels that have fewer than 25 rooms. Some of them work in places that have 1,000 rooms or more. Some of them work in independently owned businesses. Others work for such chains as Americana Hotels. Still others work for themselves, either by owning their own hotels or motels outright or as franchisees with such companies as Holiday Inns and Quality Courts Motels. Because there are so many and such different career opportunities in the hotel and motel business, it deserves the attention of anyone who is making plans for the future.

Today, hotels and motels have become so much alike in terms of the services they offer that it no longer seems necessary to say which is which. Whether it is called a hotel or motel doesn't really matter. Its business is the same—to take the hassle out of traveling and to make its guests feel welcome and comfortable.

THE SERVICES OFFERED BY HOTELS AND MOTELS

Hotels and motels can be divided into three main categories: (1) commercial hotels and motels, where guests stay for fairly brief periods of time; (2) resort hotels and motels, which provide recreation facilities and entertainment for people on vacation; and (3) residential hotels, where people live on a permanent basis. Since one of the main purposes of each of these types of hotels and motels is to provide its guests with a private place to stay, much of the space in them is taken up by bedrooms. These rooms are either "singles" or "doubles," which means that they can be occupied by one person alone or by a couple or small family together. A room may have a private bathroom, or the guest may share the use of the bathroom with other guests.

The price that is charged for the room depends on how many people are sleeping in it, whether the bathroom is private, the size of the room, and its location in the hotel or motel. For instance, one side of the hotel may offer a "view," perhaps of a rolling countryside, perhaps of a city's skyline. The other side may look out onto a highway, or the view may be blocked by a wall. The room with the better view usually costs more because it is more attractive and perhaps quieter.

The price of the room also has to do with the general quality of the hotel or motel and what it offers its guests besides the basic room. A television set in every room, air-conditioning, a good restaurant, room service that carries food to the guests' rooms, and laundry and dry-cleaning services have all become common. Many hotels and motels also help their guests to get plane and train tickets or theater tickets and give them advice on what to see and do in the area. Many hotels and motels also have swimming pools. Often there is a gift shop in the building, and perhaps a beauty salon, barbershop, and flower shop.

The big hotels and motels may have not just one but several restaurants in different price ranges. They may also have ballrooms where very large parties can be held, as well as meeting rooms and exhibition halls for the use of business people. They may hire people to entertain the guests at dinner and employ orchestras that provide music for dancing. In resort areas, hotels and motels may have golf courses or putting greens and tennis courts, as well as playgrounds for the children.

For a while, the trend in the hotel and motel business was to provide more and more services. But now that costs are so high, there

How would the accommodations and services offered by this large urban hotel differ from those offered by this mountain lodge? (ABOVE *courtesy St. Francis Hotel:* BELOW *courtesy Indian Cave Lodge*)

PART 30 • HOTELS AND MOTELS • 353

is a trend in the other direction. There are a number of new "budget motel" chains, such as Motel 6 and Suisse Chalet. Because the companies that run such chains have kept costs foremost in their minds, they are able to offer consumers a new option—the chance to enjoy a night's lodging in a clean, modern, but more simple room, with fewer "extras," for less money. In many ways, these motels are a return to the original motel idea. Yet they answer a need that is very much a part of today's economic picture—the need to stretch the dollar as far as possible.

These budget motels have not put the more expensive hotels and motels out of business because people don't all think the same way about services and prices. If they did, the small country hotels that call themselves "inns" would have had to close their doors long ago. These inns cannot afford all of the modern luxuries that the big hotels and motels offer. To make up for this, they play up their quiet and charming atmosphere, in order to attract people who want to get away from the frantic pace and impersonal tone of the big city. Because the hotel and motel business serves people and because people are so different, there is room for a variety of approaches to the problem of how to please the guests.

CAREER OPPORTUNITIES IN HOTELS AND MOTELS

One of the main advantages of the hotel and motel business is that it allows you to work wherever you want. Because there are hotels and motels all across the country, you don't have to go very far from your own home to get a job. On the other hand, you can choose to go to any place that interests you. This might be in this country or abroad, because there are many hotels around the world that are owned by American companies. There are even some people who spend their winters in warm Florida and their summers in cool Maine by working in the resort hotels. Some resort hotels have peak seasons, when they need larger staffs. Others are open only certain parts of the year, although there is a trend toward keeping resort hotels open year-round.

One of the main requirements for this business is that you like people and enjoy helping them answer their needs. But you also have to be realistic about what people are like. You can't expect everyone you meet to be your favorite kind of person. In any business that serves the public, there are bound to be some people who try the patience of everyone who has to deal with them. Others may have emergency situations that will make your job harder for a while. But if you really like people in general, these things become part of the game—a game that is as stimulating as people themselves are.

Now let's be more specific about what the career opportunities are. To see if there is anything in this business for you, you must know how to get started, what kinds of jobs there are, and what kind of future you can look forward to.

Getting Started

It is not difficult to get into the hotel and motel business. This is a 24-hour-a-day business, with three shifts of jobs to be filled each day. There don't have to be as many people on the late shifts, but this still leaves a great deal of opportunity for people who want to get started either full or part time. Also, it is generally easy to get summer work. Many hotels and motels have more guests in the summer, so they need more workers then. They also need replacements for their regular workers who are going on vacation.

The important question to ask yourself when you are entering this business is how far you ultimately want to go. It is becoming more and more unusual for people who start in the less skilled jobs, such as bellhop, to advance to the job of manager. Like the food service business, this is a field for which specialists are being trained in special schools and colleges. This means that a high school education is a minimum if you hope to advance in this field. Even then you should plan to take special courses in hotel management. The odd hours in this business, the many scholarship possibilities, and the opportunities for studying through correspondence courses make it very easy to work and study at the same time.

The Kinds of Jobs in Hotels and Motels

When you think about all the things that hotels and motels do for their guests, you can see that this is a business that can make use of people with many different kinds of skills. There are "front-of-the-house" jobs for the employees who work directly with the guests. There are "back-of-the-house" jobs for the employees who keep things running so smoothly that the guests are not even aware of all the things that go on behind the scenes. There are jobs for people who like to work all day with other people, jobs for people who like to work with their hands or with machines, jobs for people who like working with data, jobs for people who like to think up new ideas, and jobs for people who like to organize things and make them run smoothly.

The hotel and motel business also offers a variety of working conditions. If you like constant action, you can find it in the large commercial hotels in the downtown areas of major cities. Even at 2 A.M., the lobbies of such hotels can be busy places. If you like a more peaceful kind of life, you can find it in the small motels and country inns. The resort hotels can offer you a way of living in an area where you can

The people who work at the reservation desk of a hotel or motel must have a high aptitude for data, because mistakes and mix-ups in reservations can have serious consequences.

enjoy active sports and an outdoor life. This means that there isn't just one life style that goes with the hotel and motel business. This is a field that has room for many different kinds of people, as long as they are interested in the basic idea of helping people to be comfortable and to enjoy their stay away from home.

With this in mind, let's look at the different parts of the hotel and motel business one by one.

FRONT OFFICE JOBS. The front office of the hotel or motel is an important area because it keeps track of the guests and knows which rooms are occupied. It is to this office that the letters, telegrams, and phone calls come, asking that rooms be saved for certain guests for certain days. A guest coming in without one of these "advance registrations" would have to apply at this office too.

Besides renting rooms and getting the incoming guests to sign in, or "register," this office has to give the guests the keys to their rooms, sort the guests' mail, take their messages, and check them out when they leave. If the hotel or motel is a very small one, there may be just one person to do all these jobs. In a large operation, however, there may be a staff of clerks, each one assigned to a special part of the front office work. There may be separate clerks in charge of reservations, the front desk, the keys, the rack that indicates which rooms are occupied, messages, and information.

If the hotel is very large, each of these clerks may have an assistant. There also has to be a staff of telephone operators to handle incoming and outgoing calls. Although a small number of clerks and telephone operators can double up on the jobs during the late shift, the front desk does have to be staffed around the clock. The work of this department is supervised by a front office manager and an assistant front office manager.

People in front office jobs must be able to work accurately with data. They must also be very skilled at getting along with people. Besides having good communication skills, they must always be in control of their own tempers and moods and able to treat every guest courteously, no matter how difficult the situation. Because of the number of guests visiting this country from overseas, people who can speak a language besides English are very much in demand for front office jobs. This is especially true of Spanish, which has become the second language in New York, Miami, and the Southwest. Many large hotel and motel companies use front office jobs as a training ground for management jobs.

CASHIER AND ACCOUNTING JOBS. When the guests check out of the hotel or motel, they have to pay what they owe for their rooms and for such extras as food service, laundry service, and telephone calls. In many cases, the clerks at the front desk handle the checkout procedure entirely, collecting the money in cash or by check or accepting payment by credit card. In large hotels, however, the cashier's job is a separate one. This is a job that requires the ability to handle money with accuracy. Large hotels and motels need bookkeepers and accountants to keep the financial records and make sure the business is earning a profit. The person who is in charge of this phase of the business is the controller.

SERVICE DEPARTMENT JOBS. Although everyone who works in a hotel or motel is in some way serving the guests, there are some jobs that are specifically called service jobs and are the responsibility of the service department. The size of this department depends on the size of the hotel or motel. The range goes all the way from the lone person at the front desk, who is both the desk clerk and the whole service department, to a very large staff of doormen, bellhops, elevator operators, baggage porters, checkroom attendants, parking lot attendants, and transportation clerks, who help guests buy tickets and ship their baggage.

The people doing service jobs may have to take turns on the late shifts. They need physical strength and a natural kind of courtesy that makes the guests feel welcome. These people can earn tips, which

Hotel doormen and other people in service jobs must be polite and courteous at all times. *(Courtesy Intercontinental Hotels)*

means that their earnings are tied to the amount of effort that they want to put in. People who are not high school graduates and who have had no special training can be hired for many of these jobs. However, such people generally have to work twice as long and twice as hard to win promotions. If they are willing to do this, they can advance to the job of bell captain or superintendent of service. They can also move to front desk jobs or to other jobs in the hotel or motel.

HOUSEKEEPING JOBS. The task of keeping the hotel or motel neat, clean, and ready at all times for its guests is an enormous one that requires careful organization. Each day the rooms have to be "made up." This includes cleaning them and putting fresh linens on the beds and clean towels in the bathrooms. The hallways, lobby areas, and elevators have to be cleaned too. Furniture, floors, and metal fixtures have to be polished, and furnishings repaired or replaced on a regular schedule. These jobs fall to the executive housekeeper and however large a staff of assistant housekeepers, cleaners, linen room attendants, and repairers that the hotel or motel needs. A staff of laundry room workers may also be needed. Small hotels and motels may send out their own laundry and that of the guests, but large ones find it cheaper to do their own work.

Since many housekeeping jobs require no previous training or experience, they can be a good way for beginners to get started and to learn how the hotel and motel business works. People who do well in these jobs can advance to the job of linen room supervisor or assistant housekeeper, or they can move to another job in the hotel or motel.

Resort hotels in ski areas need people who can teach guests how to ski. (*Courtesy Killington Ski Resort, Vermont*)

MAINTENANCE JOBS. Another large task in the hotel or motel is keeping the building itself and the mechanical things in it—such as the furnace, air-conditioning, plumbing, and television sets—in top condition. The chief engineer takes care of these jobs, with a staff that includes painters, plumbers, carpenters, electricians, engineers, and general repairers. If there are grounds and gardens, there also has to be a staff of yard workers and gardeners. The people who do these jobs generally need training or experience, or both, in their particular line of work. These jobs, like housekeeping jobs, are back-of-the-house jobs that don't require marketing skills. They can be very satisfying in themselves, or they can lead to other jobs in the business.

FOOD SERVICE JOBS. If the hotel or motel runs any kind of restaurant, the jobs in it are very important to the success of the hotel or motel itself. You have already read about the special jobs that are available in food service businesses. The large hotels and motels divide this part of their business into two departments: food preparation, run by the executive chef, and food service, run by the food service manager.

Besides feeding their overnight guests, large hotels and motels do a lot of banquet business. When people want to hold a large luncheon or dinner for business reasons or to raise money for charity, they need the kind of large dining rooms that the big hotels and motels have. Some of the really large hotels can seat more than 1,000 people at one time for dinner, which means that many people are needed to work in the kitchens and dining rooms. Hotels and motels also need people to work in the room service department, to take the trays of food up to the guests' rooms.

ENTERTAINMENT JOBS. Many hotels have jobs for musicians, singers, and people to assist the big-name entertainers who often perform at the hotel for a few weeks at a time. There may also be social directors to help the guests plan things to do. The large resort hotels also have jobs for people who can teach their guests to dance, swim, and play golf and tennis. There are caddy jobs at the golf courses. There may be lifeguard jobs not only at the resort hotels but also at any hotel or motel where there is a good-sized pool and a lot of activity. There are also jobs for baby-sitters.

PROTECTION JOBS. Guest staying in hotels and motels expect to be safe themselves, and they expect their belongings to be safe from theft. To guarantee safety, the hotel or motel hires house detectives, who quietly police the building and grounds to make sure that everything is in order. The people doing these jobs need physical strength, tact, and a concern for the guests' welfare. They answer to the chief of security.

SELLING, SALES PROMOTION, BUYING, AND STAFF SPECIALIST JOBS. Hotels and motels like to take care of conventions, which are meetings that go on for several days. For example, groups of business people, doctors, or teachers may have a convention to which members from a wide area will come. Attracting this business, as well as banquet business, is vital to the success of the large hotels and motels because they have such large staffs that they will lose money if the rooms are not filled most of the time.

This explains why the titles of sales manager, advertising director, and public relations director are common in this business. These people may work for large independent hotels or motels or in the central headquarters of corporate or franchised chains, where there are also jobs for purchasing agents. The chains also need specialists in real estate, management, law, and labor relations. To be hired for any of these jobs, you need specific training or experience, plus a strong interest in the hotel and motel business.

TOP MANAGEMENT JOBS. With so much going on in the hotel or motel, it is especially important to have people who can pull all the parts together. Large hotels and motels have several assistant managers, who may hold the top jobs in some of the departments we have discussed. For example, the front office manager or food service manager may also be one of the assistant managers of the hotel or motel. There may also be assistant managers who are in charge of such special jobs as personnel.

The job of the hotel manager is a very large one, requiring a broad base of knowledge and experience in the field of hotel management. This is true even for the people who manage very small hotels or motels because there are so many sides to the business. When the operation is a large one, the manager has enormous responsibilities.

This is why it is so important that the person who wants to be a manager learn as much as possible in special courses and on the job.

Assessing Hotels and Motels in Terms of Yourself

The most important thing for you to carry away from this discussion of the hotel and motel business is that this field does not call for one specific type of person. There is room in this field for people with very different personal characteristics. This means that you can work out the kind of career that suits you best. If you like doing your own job as well as you can, without being responsible for others, you will find that the career-level jobs in this field can be very rewarding. On the other hand, if supervisory jobs interest you, there are many opportunities for experienced managers both in this country and abroad.

It is also important to realize that the hotel and motel business does not lock you in. There are many lattice-type moves that you can make if you start in this field. The skills that you learn can easily be transferred to restaurants, hospitals, private clubs, college dormitories, nursing homes, and military installations. You might also move to one of the companies that sells supplies to hotels and motels. If your hotel and motel experience has taught you to deal with people, you can also move to many other areas of retailing.

- **UNDERSTANDING WHAT YOU HAVE READ**

    1. Customers in hotels and motels are always spoken of as "guests." What does this fact tell you about this business?
    2. Is it true that the only people who stay in motels are motorists? Explain your answer.
    3. What do budget motels offer their guests?
    4. Why are hotels and motels interested in hiring people who speak a second language?
    5. Why do hotels and motels like to handle banquets and conventions?

- **APPLYING WHAT YOU HAVE LEARNED**

    1. Participate in a class trip to a hotel or motel in your area and write a report on what you have seen.
    2. Choose one entry-level job discussed in this part and diagram the ladder- and lattice-type moves that a person could make from it.
    3. Participate in a class discussion based on the following statement: "The hotel and motel business has room for many different kinds of people." To prepare for the discussion, review Unit 2 and remind yourself of all the ways in which people can differ from each other. To summarize the class discussion, draw up lists on the following two subjects: (a) the ways in which hotel and motel workers may differ from each other and (b) the ways in which they must be alike.

part 31 Personal Services

After reading Part 31, you will be able—
- To identify and list six personal service businesses in the area where you live, giving the name of the company and the kind of service that it sells.
- To name a personal service job that could be done by each person described in a given list of personal characteristics.
- To identify one of your personal interests that could be the basis for a personal service job.

An area of retailing that has had tremendous growth in recent years is the business of selling consumers the personal services that make their lives more comfortable. There are many examples of these personal services that you are used to seeing right in your neighborhood shopping area—beauty salons, barbershops, laundries, dry cleaners, and shoe repair shops. There are other examples that you will perhaps learn about for the first time in this part. The important thing about all these services is that they represent a source of jobs that is widening every day.

One reason for this is that the population of the country is growing, but there are other reasons too. Many of these services have become part of the general standard of living. They have become things that people expect from life. For example, it is possible to clean woolen clothes at home by dipping them in a pail of cleaning fluid. But this is a difficult and quite dangerous thing to do, and most people don't even think of attempting it. They take it for granted that they should send their woolen clothes to the dry cleaner.

Another factor in the growth of personal services is that they offer a level of expertise that people can't reach by themselves. This is true of the dry cleaner, who is an expert at removing all kinds of stubborn stains and making garments look like new.

Personal services are also becoming more important because the pace of life is generally much faster today. Even though people work fewer hours than they did 100 years ago, they are always short of time. They have more active social lives and feel more strongly about having

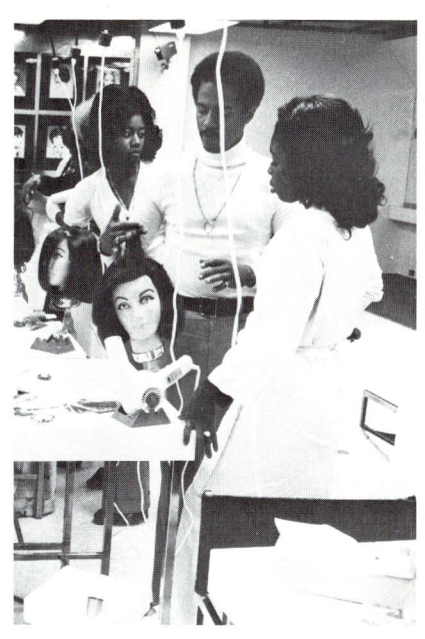

In recent years there has been a great increase in the number of personal service businesses that help people improve their appearance and tone up their bodies. (ABOVE LEFT *courtesy Harrison Conference Centers;* ABOVE RIGHT *courtesy Glemby International Hairdressing & Beauty Salons;* BELOW LEFT *courtesy Clairol;* BELOW RIGHT *courtesy The President's Committee on Employment of the Handicapped, The School of Visual Arts Public Advertising*)

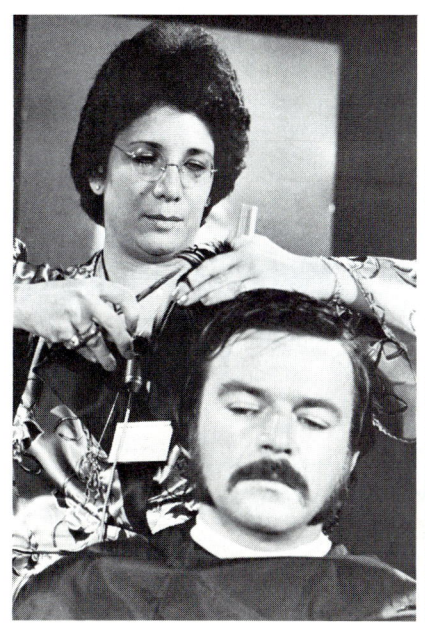

PART 31 • PERSONAL SERVICES • 363

time to pursue their favorite leisure-time activities. Thus they look to the personal service businesses to do many of their time-consuming chores for them. Also, more married women are working today than ever before, and those that aren't have many commitments outside the home. Even though many men are now sharing the burden of the household chores, most people still have a time problem—a problem that the personal service businesses can help to solve.

These factors help to explain why the personal service businesses have become an accepted part of life today and are thought of in many instances as necessities rather than luxuries. Because they are such an important part of the marketing picture, they should be considered by anyone who is interested in choosing a career.

THE KINDS OF PERSONAL SERVICE BUSINESSES

The personal service field is constantly changing as new businesses are opened up to answer new needs. An example of a business that grew out of an obvious need is the dog-walking service. Dog owners who

Personal service businesses are very important in households where both the husband and the wife have careers that take them out of the home.

live in apartment houses in cities find it hard to give their dogs enough exercise. To answer this need, there are businesses that provide "dog-walkers," who pick up the dogs at their homes, take them out for a specified amount of time, and then return them.

Now let's see what other kinds of personal service businesses have become important as a way of answering people's needs.

Services Connected With Appearance and Fitness

In our culture today, there is a great deal of pressure for people to look young and attractive and to be physically fit. There are many personal businesses that try to help people do this. These include beauty salons, which are now licensed in many states to care for men's hair as well as women's. Many barbershops also have both women and men customers, and the emphasis is often more on "styling" than on "cutting" hair. Many men now expect to get their hair colored, as women do, and to have hairpieces fitted. There are many businesses that are called "health clubs," "spas," or "reducing salons." These businesses offer people the chance to make their bodies stronger and more youthful with exercise classes, exercise machines, steam baths, and massages.

Laundry and Dry-cleaning Services

There are many different kinds of businesses that wash or dry-clean clothes or household linens and furnishings. There are small "hand" laundries, where the washing and ironing are done with careful attention to each individual piece. There are large laundries, where there is an assembly-line type of operation that makes use of the biggest and newest machines. There are also diaper service companies, which supply clean diapers every week for new babies.

The dry-cleaning business includes the small shops and large plants that dry-clean clothes or that specialize in the cleaning of leather, furs, rugs, or draperies. Often other services are combined with the dry cleaning. For example, there may be a tailor to mend or alter clothes, or the shop may offer a storage service for out-of-season clothes. There are also coin-operated self-service laundries and dry-cleaning businesses, where the customers can save money by doing their own washing and drying or dry cleaning.

Repair Services

Many repair services are run by retail stores. But there are also independent businesses that people can call on when they want such things as shoes, watches, jewelry, large and small appliances, tools, bicycles, typewriters, sound systems, and television sets put into good working order. Sometimes these businesses are run from a shop, and sometimes they are run from a truck. For example, a person who grinds scissors and knives to make them sharp again may have all the equipment in a truck. The truck is then driven to various areas on a definite schedule so people know when and where they can get service.

Rental Services

There are many times when people need something to wear or use for only a short time and therefore don't want to buy the item. For a small fee, these people can get what they need from one of the many rental services. For example, suppose that a young man is getting married. He and his ushers don't want to buy the formal clothing that they have decided to wear because they may never wear them again. So they go to a shop where they can rent everything they need.

There are other shops that rent furs and jewelry or tools and garden equipment. Some rental services specialize in the things that are needed in order to give a large party or hold a large meeting, such as chairs, tables, dishes, silverware, and linens. It is even possible to rent a whole houseful of furniture. Sometimes people are transferred to a new area but know they will not be there permanently. Rather than move their own furniture or move into a furnished house, they rent everything they need for as long as they need it.

Household Services

There are many businesses to which people can turn to get help in running their homes. Employment agencies find people to do full-time household work, and other businesses provide such temporary help as baby-sitters and serving help for parties. Homeowners can also call on one of the cleaning services to give their homes either a thorough one-time cleaning or a regular weekly or biweekly cleaning. There are also companies that just wash windows or just wax floors, and others that clean out gutters or chimneys. Other companies spray the house with chemicals to keep insects away.

Other Personal Services

There is a wide variety of other personal service businesses. There are companies that address Christmas cards or wedding invitations for people who are too busy to do their own. There are also businesses that will run weddings or large parties in their clients' homes, taking care of hiring the caterer, arranging for music, planning the seating arrangements, and handling all other details.

People can also go to photography studios to get their pictures taken. They can go to detective agencies to trace missing people or get protection for their homes. There are funeral homes that arrange for burials and cremations. There are auto-driving schools that teach people how to drive. There are also parking lots and garages that make it possible for people to leave their cars safely. These include places where attendants park the cars, as well as self-service facilities.

REVIEWING PERSONAL SERVICE JOBS

There are personal service businesses that are run by just one person, who takes care of all the different parts of the business single-handedly. Then there are the medium-sized businesses, where each employee handles several parts of the business. Finally there are the large businesses, where each employee has a very detailed and exact job. This means that there is room in this field, just as there is in the other areas of marketing, for people who like working for themselves and for those who prefer working for big organizations.

No matter how big the business is, there are certain jobs that have to be done. Let's see now what these jobs are.

Producing the Service

Because the personal service business must offer a service that is really worth buying, the job of producing whatever service is for sale is at the heart of every personal service business. Many of these jobs have very special requirements. For example, you can't just walk into a shop and apply for a job as a hairdresser or barber. You must go to special training schools to learn these trades. Then you have to take an examination to be licensed by the state in which you will work. Still another examination has to be taken if you want to open your own shop. Some people get this special training after high school, and others finish their high school years in technical schools, where they can learn their trade and get their high school diploma at the same time.

There are other jobs that don't have to be licensed but still have special requirements. For example, a photographer must have a talent for taking pictures and must know a great deal about cameras, lighting, and what makes a picture beautiful. A tailor has to know all about how to fit clothes and how to sew with various materials. A television repairer has to be very capable mechanically and must have had special training courses.

There are also many personal service jobs that can be learned without previous experience. When you are hired you are given a brief training course, and then taught the fine points of the job by working alongside an experienced worker. As you go along, you are given more and more opportunity to work on your own, until finally you are considered qualified. This is the way that you would start out in one of the

If you like working independently and owning your own business, the field of personal service businesses can offer you the opportunity to do just that. (*Daniel S. Brody/Editorial Photocolor Archives*)

housecleaning services, for example. You might think that anybody would know how to scrub a floor, but this isn't true. There is a right way to scrub a floor, which will please the customer and also save time.

In all these personal service businesses, it is vitally important to make the most of time, because the more services that can be done in a given time, the more money the business can make. But just working fast isn't the answer, because the service also has to be first class. This means that know-how is always important in any of these jobs, even those that seem the simplest.

If the idea of producing services appeals to you, use what you have read here as a springboard to discover more about what kinds of jobs you could do and how you can prepare yourself for them.

Selling the Service

Along with the problem of producing the service, there is also the problem of selling it. In many businesses, such as beauty salons and barbershops, for example, these two problems can't be separated, and the people who produce the services also sell them, possibly with the help of a receptionist at a front desk. In other businesses, the sales jobs may be separated from the production jobs. For example, in a large dry-cleaning shop, there will be a worker at the front desk who will do the selling for the business along with cashier duties.

If the business is run from an office instead of a shop, the person who answers the telephone may also be the salesworker. With such businesses as diaper services, the truck driver may also have many of the duties of a salesworker. In many of these cases, there will be some kind of a supervisor to back up these workers and be sure that the customers are getting what they want.

There are also some jobs that are strictly sales jobs. For example, a photographer may hire someone to interest new customers in the service. Also many personal services businesses sell merchandise for extra profits. For example, a beauty salon may sell such things as plastic rain hats, hair ornaments, and cosmetics. In this case, someone may be needed to handle the sales. Each of these selling jobs require an aptitude for getting along with people. Some also require the ability to handle money and fill out forms.

Maintaining the Place of Business and the Equipment

No one is going to believe that a first-rate service can be produced in a dirty, run-down place. Thus the manager of the personal service business must have definite plans for keeping the shop, office, or truck and all equipment clean and in good repair. In the small business, this may be a simple matter. But in large businesses, such as the health clubs, there may be a staff of maintenance workers. They need physical strength and the ability to handle things without breaking them. In the equipment rental businesses, people with a mechanical aptitude are needed to keep the things that the customers are going to rent in perfect condition.

Making Deliveries

Although the job of truck driver may be combined with that of salesworker or be part of the job of producing the service, there are also businesses that hire people just to make deliveries. For example, think of a company that rents things for parties. The customer's order is taken over the phone. Then the things that the customer wants are delivered before the party and picked up afterward. Another example is the driver who makes deliveries for the dry cleaner. Besides being very responsible, drivers for personal service businesses must have pleasant personalities so they can get along well with the customers.

Handling the Office Work

There is a lot of paper work to be done in every personal service business. The manager can handle these problems in the small business, but the large one needs cashiers, bookkeepers, accountants, and other office workers.

In many businesses, it is also very important to have someone who can schedule the work. For example, a photographer can't just take

Many personal service businesses require receptionists who greet customers, make appointments, and handle secretarial tasks. (*Courtesy AT&T*)

people's pictures as they come in off the street. Appointments must be made with the customers so there is enough time to work with each one. When this kind of scheduling is necessary, it is often done by a receptionist who doubles as a secretary and cashier. This kind of work requires careful attention to detail, since mistakes can be costly.

Managing the Business

Every personal service business needs someone who can pull all the sides of the business together and make sure that everything is being done correctly. In large businesses, where there are many jobs, there will be supervisors in the different areas of the business and a boss at the top. As this boss, you can work for yourself by owning the business outright or by having a franchising agreement that gives you the support of a parent company. Examples of such franchised chains are Edie Adams Cut & Curl and United Rent-All.

It is also possible for the manager of the personal service business to be employed by a corporate chain. Examples of corporate chains in this field are Sam the Shoe Doctor and the Airport Parking Company of America. The manager's job in many cases can be a stepping-stone to jobs in the central headquarters.

GETTING STARTED IN PERSONAL SERVICES

As you have seen, there are some personal service jobs for which you need very specific training. If you want to work in these special areas, you would have to plan to get this training. At the same time, this is a field that you can go into without getting a high school diploma. For example, as long as you have a driver's license, you can get a job as a parking lot attendant. You can also start out as a housecleaner without much education. However, not having a high school diploma will make it difficult for you to win promotions. This field is exactly like the other areas of marketing that you have learned about in that the less education you have, the longer and harder you have to work to move up.

While you are on your way to your diploma, it is easy to get a part-time job in one of these businesses. It may not be the exact kind of business you would eventually like to work in because not every business can be found in every locality. However, there is certainly some kind of personal service business, and probably more than one, right near your home. The job that you start out in will teach you the basic principle of every personal service business—the importance of pleasing the customer. This knowledge will help you to be successful in any other kind of personal service business or to move over to another area of marketing.

PLANNING A FUTURE IN PERSONAL SERVICES

Probably the most important fact about the personal service field from the point of view of someone who is trying to plan a career is its variety. As you have seen, there are many different kinds of businesses, each one offering something special that may match your own interests and abilities. But the opportunities for you to find the right career in this field go even beyond that, because there are so many differences even in the same kinds of businesses. For example, hairdressers can work in a wide variety of atmospheres, ranging all the way from the elegant to the psychodelic. Another example is the dry-cleaning business. You might work in a fast-paced large-volume business. Or you might work in a small business that emphasizes personal service for the customers who expect more and don't mind paying for it.

This variety gives you a special opportunity to find the kind of work which exactly suits your personal qualities and in which you can be successful.

• UNDERSTANDING WHAT YOU HAVE READ

1. Why have personal service businesses become such an important source of jobs?
2. Why is the job of producing whatever service is for sale at the heart of the personal service business?
3. Personal service businesses often charge the customer by the job, but pay their employees by the hour. In this case, what difference

does it make to the company if an employee (a) is a very slow worker or (b) works too fast to do a good job?
4. Tom Martinez has always liked the idea of having his own business someday, while Jean Evans would rather work for a big company. Which one of these people should rule out the idea of working in the personal service field? Explain your answer.
5. What does the variety that the personal service field offers mean to the person who is looking for a career?

- **APPLYING WHAT YOU HAVE LEARNED**

1. Identify and list six personal service businesses in the area where you live, giving the name of the company and the kind of service it sells.
2. The following are brief descriptions of five people. Name a personal service job that could be done by each one.
   a. A person who wants to be self-employed and has a mechanical aptitude
   b. A person who prefers sedentary work and has beautiful handwriting
   c. A person who likes outdoor work and knows how to handle dogs
   d. Someone with an aptitude for data and a interest in photography
   e. A responsible driver
3. Identify one of your personal interests that could be the basis for a personal service job. State what the interest is and how it could be used in this area of marketing. Then write a paragraph stating whether or not the job you have chosen would suit you in other ways.

part 32 Business Services

After reading Part 32, you will be able—
- To explain the difference between a business service and a personal service.
- To state whether each business service job in a given list requires an aptitude for people, data, or things.
- To choose one type of business service that interests you and write a paragraph explaining whether or not you think you have the right aptitudes for it.

The services that industrial consumers buy are spoken of as "business services" to distinguish them from the personal services that are bought by ultimate consumers. Just as personal services make people's lives more comfortable, so business services make it easier for industrial consumers to run their businesses. There are so many things that go into making a business profitable that industrial consumers often cannot cover them all satisfactorily by themselves. In many cases, they are glad to let the specialists that run business services take over some of their problems. This has always been true. But in recent years, business has become even more complex, calling for much more expertise. Because of this, spending for business services has increased even more than it has for personal services. When you have increased spending, you have also increased career opportunities. These opportunities are the subject of this part.

THE KINDS OF BUSINESS SERVICES
Industrial consumers have to watch expenses very carefully, as you know. So they must be sure that whatever services they buy are really worth the money they will cost. There are two tests for a service's value, and an industrial consumer will buy the service if it passes either or both of these tests.

The first test is whether the business service company can do the job for less money than the industrial consumer would have to spend doing the job alone. Having to hire full-time workers to do the specialized work that the service company does or paying overtime wages to the regular help often costs more money in the end, and the industrial consumer has all the headaches besides. The second test is whether the service being offered is so expert that the industrial consumer will make more money by using it. If the service will make the business run more efficiently, which in turn will mean lower costs, or if the service brings in more customers, the industrial consumer will come out ahead, even after paying for the service.

There are many different kinds of business service companies that have been able to meet these tests and have become a permanent and important part of the American business picture. Let's see now what services these companies offer.

Maintenance Services

Keeping the place of business clean and in good working order at all times is a necessary part of every business. This makes the customers think the business is well run, provides the employees with safe and comfortable surroundings, and increases the efficiency of the business. Many industrial consumers can handle this with their own crews of workers. But there are also many times when it is both less expensive and more efficient to hire one of the business service companies that specialize in this kind of work.

To handle the cleaning, there are cleaning and window-washing

Business service companies are hired by industrial consumers to keep their place of business clean and in good repair. (*Courtesy Kinney National Service, Inc.*)

companies and laundries. There are also companies that handle all maintenance problems. For example, an office building owned by a group of doctors may hire a company to take over all problems that come up with the heating and air-conditioning systems, as well as all repair and cleaning problems. There are other companies that are highly specialized, repairing just office machinery or just electric signs.

Security Services

The companies that sell security services specialize in helping industrial consumers safeguard their property. They supply uniformed guards or plainclothes detectives for such industrial consumers as factories, stores, offices, hospitals, schools, amusement parks, and theaters. They also supply electronic devices, such as closed-circuit TV, that help the guards and detectives do a better job. These companies also help industrial consumers to safeguard their property, customers, and employees by planning built-in security features for new buildings or those that are being remodeled.

    The industrial consumer can also use this kind of company to check on employees before they are hired to make sure that they are right for the job. This saves the industrial consumer the cost of training workers who would later prove to be undesirable. A security company may also study the operations of a business to see whether all the employees are doing the best possible job. By finding employees who are either stealing merchandise or giving out information that should be kept secret, the security company can save its customers a great deal of money. Still another service that the security company may offer is investigating insurance claims to make sure that they are honest.

Rental Services

In Part 31, you learned about the service businesses that rent things to ultimate consumers. There are many products that industrial consumers find it convenient to rent too. For example, a restaurant may rent the clean tablecloths, napkins, and uniforms for its workers that it needs each week from a linen supply company. Many other companies rent uniforms and linens too. Industrial consumers can also rent office equipment of all kinds, as well as office furniture. They can even rent green plants to be used as decorations.

Employment Services

If you read the "help wanted" ads in your local newspaper, you will see that many of the ads are placed by employment agencies. These employment agencies save industrial consumers time and money by

Stores often employ security service companies to protect their merchandise against shoplifters. (*Courtesy Pinkerton's, Inc.*)

acting as middlemen in bringing together the people who want jobs and the industrial consumers who have jobs to be filled. For these services, the agencies receive a fee.

Some employment companies specialize in supplying temporary or part-time help for industrial consumers when their regular help is on vacation or when they need a special job done. This may be anything from secretarial work to a mechanical problem. Some of these companies also act just as middlemen. But others hire and pay the workers themselves. Then they collect enough money from their customers to pay the workers' wages and still make a profit.

Secretarial and Printing Services

Many business service companies specialize in the work that secretaries, clerks, and typists would ordinarily do. They type letters, stuff envelopes, address mail, and make copies of material, either on mimeographing machines or on photocopiers. Industrial consumers are also good customers for the many printing companies that print to order such things as stationery, menus, order blanks, sales contracts, form letters, advertising material, and catalogs.

Telephone Answering Services

A service that is very popular with real estate agents, repairers who work from their trucks, doctors, and any other workers who are away from their telephones for part of the day is the telephone answering service. The telephone of each customer of this service is hooked up to a central switchboard in the office of the answering service. When a call comes in for the customer, the phone will ring in both the customer's office and the office of the answering service. The customers always let the answering service know when they are going to be out so the answering service operator can take the calls that come in during that time. Then the customers can call the answering service at their convenience and get all their messages. The answering service is well worth the small fee that it charges because it keeps its customers from losing business.

Accounting and Credit Services

The problem of keeping track of the money that comes in and goes out of the business and of watching the profits is such a large one that many industrial consumers have to get help with it. Industrial consumers may want help in preparing their taxes, or they may want to be relieved of all their accounting problems. Sometimes what they want is advice about how to improve the methods in their accounting departments.

There are also many times when an industrial consumer wants a periodic check of the books and records of the business to be sure that everything is in proper order. In fact, many corporations are required by law to have this periodic checkup by an independent accounting firm and to publish a report on their financial standing. There are many accounting companies, both large and small, that will provide these services for industrial consumers all over the country.

There are also business service companies that will help retailers with their credit problems by checking on the people who want to open charge accounts to see whether they can be trusted to pay their bills. Other companies will take over the industrial consumer's billing, often doing the billing by computer. Sometimes these companies also collect the money, and sometimes not. If industrial consumers have any unpaid bills, there are collection agencies that go after the money. Even though the collection agency gets a percentage of what it collects as its fee, the customers for this service are still further ahead than they would be if the money were not collected at all.

Still other companies will get information on the credit standing of various businesses. This makes it possible to know whether the business can be expected to pay its debts and whether it is a good company to deal with. This is one of the services of Dun & Bradstreet.

Advertising Services

Perhaps the most famous of all the companies that sell services to industrial consumers are the advertising agencies. The large agencies whose main offices are in New York City, such as Young & Rubicam

Advertising agencies plan advertisements for their customers. Here the plan for a television commercial is being plotted on a storyboard, which shows how each scene in the commercial will look and what the viewer will hear. (*Courtesy Cunningham & Walsh, Inc.*)

and Wells, Rich, Greene, are probably the best-known ones. But there are also thousands of other ad agencies, some of them quite small, spread out in cities across the country.

Advertising agencies plan advertisements for their customers, prepare the ads, and then place them on television or radio, in newspapers and magazines, or on billboards. These agencies also handle all kinds of promotional activities for their customers. For example, an agency may think up a new kind of contest with exciting prizes that will make people buy the product that is being promoted. Or it may design the promotional aids that will be given to storekeepers to help sell the product in the stores. Many agencies go even further and advise their customers on product or package design. They also help their customers plan a workable system for getting their products to the customers.

Sales Promotion Services

Besides advertising agencies, there are many other companies that help industrial consumers with their sales promotion problems. For example, there are companies that specialize in public relations. They help their customers create and maintain a favorable image. There are also businesses that will design whatever the customer needs, such as an identifying symbol, packages, stationery, shopping bags, boxes, and wrapping paper. Other companies supply either display materials or full displays to order. There are also companies that get together mailing lists for industrial consumers who want to send advertisements or samples through the mail.

Another kind of promotional service is the one that calls on newcomers to the community in their homes to advertise local businesses. Examples of this kind of service are Welcome Wagon International, Getting to Know You International, and Person to Person.

Management Consulting Services

When industrial consumers think their businesses are not running as well as they should, they can call on management consulting firms for help. These firms have experts in the various phases of business operations who study the industrial consumer's business methods and make suggestions for improving them. Management consulting firms may also set up new businesses or help several companies join together.

Some management consulting firms can cover any phase of their customers' businesses because they have many kinds of specialists on their staff. Other firms are highly specialized. For example, there are agencies that will just help industrial consumers solve their human relations problems. They specialize in courses that help the employees of the business, especially the managers, learn how to get along with other people more effectively. There are also management consulting firms that will study a business's employment policies with a view toward helping the business overcome those that represent any kind of prejudice.

Marketing Research Services

Since the final boss of so much business activity is the ultimate consumer, business people are becoming more and more aware of how important it is to discover the consumer's tastes, habits, likes, and dislikes. Many businesses have set up their own departments to find out all they can about these questions. However, there are many other businesses that prefer to buy their information from the companies that work full time in marketing research.

Some marketing research companies are so large that they can handle any problems connected with this field. Others just handle specific parts of the problem. For example, some companies specialize in conducting surveys and polls of people's opinions and attitudes. Others study what newspapers and magazines people read, what kinds of television shows they watch, and which radio shows are the most popular.

The reports that marketing research companies prepare help business people find out such things as what kinds of new products people would like and where to place their advertisements to get the most attention.

Other marketing research companies use what they find out about the public's buying habits to give advice on how to package new products or improve the packaging of products already on the market. There are also companies that will test a new product by placing it in stores in a selected area of the country to see how the public accepts it. If the people in that area don't like the product and don't buy it, then the manufacturer can save the expense of going into full-scale production of it.

An example of a marketing research company is the A.C. Nielsen Company, which sponsors a variety of marketing research services for more than 2,400 clients. This includes the famous Nielsen rating for television shows, which helps advertisers decide when to put their commercials on the air.

Other Business Services

There are many other services whose purpose is helping business people do a better job. For example, there are interior architects and space planners, whose job is to design offices, stores, and factories in the

Businesses often employ the services of data processing consultants to help them design computer systems. (*Courtesy The Ad Council*)

most efficient and attractive way possible. There are also interior decorators, who help to furnish and decorate their clients' places of business. There are other companies that lay carpets and floor coverings and repair appliances for home furnishing stores, or do the alterations for clothing stores.

CAREERS IN BUSINESS SERVICES

Business service companies come in all sizes, ranging from the small ones that can be run by the owner, with perhaps a few helpers, all the way to the huge firms that have branch offices all over the country. These large companies may even have branch offices in foreign countries or some connections with foreign companies that increase their own business. A good example of the kind of company that is spread out in this way is Pinkerton's, the famous security service company. Pinkerton's not only has 100 offices throughout the United States and Canada but also belongs to an international society of security companies that makes it possible for Pinkerton's customers to get service all over the world. Business services can also be franchised. Two examples of franchised business services are Safeguard Business Systems and General Business Services.

With this picture in mind of how business service companies are set up, let's see now what kinds of jobs have to be done.

Producing the Service

A business service company, like all the other marketing businesses you have read about, can only stay in business as long as it keeps its customers happy. This means that it has to sell them an expert service that completely satisfies their needs. So the jobs that have to be done to produce the service are at the heart of every business service company.

In some companies, these jobs can only be filled by highly creative people. The advertising agencies, for example, need artists, copywriters, and people to think up new ideas. All of these workers have to know a great deal about what makes people tick and about how they can be persuaded to buy things. When the advertising agencies hire beginning workers, they try to hire people who have a lot of promise along these lines. Thus they want people who have had college or art school training.

The jobs for the people who produce the services in accounting and management consulting firms also require college training and, even beyond that, training at special graduate schools for business. A person who wants to be a success in these fields should have the kind

The person with a special talent for plant care could find a satisfying career with a service company that rents and maintains plants for business customers. (*Courtesy Foliage Plant Systems, Inc.*)

of mind that can pinpoint a problem and then come up with an answer that is both logical and original.

At the other end of the scale are the jobs that require very little in the way of training—the beginning jobs in the cleaning services, for example, or some of the simple jobs with the linen supply companies. It is possible to get some of these jobs without even finishing high school. In the middle range, between the jobs that require a great deal of schooling and those that need relatively little schooling, are such jobs as telephone answering service operators, credit collectors, and bookkeepers. These are jobs for which high school graduates can be trained.

There are also many service-producing jobs in business service companies for people who bring special skills to their jobs, such as secretaries, printers, and mechanics. The extra time and effort that these people have to put into learning these special skills is bound to pay off. Because there is a real shortage of such workers, any young person who learns these skills can look forward to a high degree of job security.

The range of service-producing jobs shows that the business service field has room for people with many different qualifications.

Selling the Service

The most effective way for the business service companies to get new customers is by offering a superior service so its satisfied customers will pass the word along. But most business service companies also have to sell their services. They may do this by sending sales letters directly to business people, as well as by advertising in the magazines and newspapers that business people read.

Besides this nonpersonal selling, many business service companies also do some personal selling. For example, an advertising agency may go to the trouble of preparing a sample advertising campaign for a company that it thinks is interested in buying its services. Then it will try to sell this campaign to the company. Or a large cleaning service may have a salesworker who calls on business people to persuade them to buy the company's services. There are also jobs in some business service companies, such as linen supply companies, for route workers.

Selling for a business service is in many ways like selling in other areas of marketing. Although the same qualifications are required, selling in the business service field can be especially hard, because the customers are all business people. Their reasons for buying are not likely to be emotional ones. They want sales presentations that are weighted with facts and that explain very clearly why they should spend their money. This means that the people who do the selling jobs for business services have to be especially thorough in their preparation and especially businesslike in their manner.

Running the Business

A business service company couldn't provide a first-class service for its customers if there weren't a lot of people working behind the scenes to keep the business itself running. There must be people to keep the company's offices clean and in good repair. There must be other people to watch the profits of the business and to make sure that it is taking in more money than it is spending. There must also be people to buy the supplies that the company needs, and people to hire and train workers. Secretaries, typists, file clerks, and telephone operators are needed too. There must also, of course, be the top managers—the people who understand each part of the whole business and can make everything work together smoothly.

YOUR FUTURE IN BUSINESS SERVICES

Because the business service field is so vast and the job opportunities are so varied, it has only been possible to give you some small idea of the total picture. But the important thing is for you to start thinking about this field and to realize that it is one where you can get a very direct return on whatever you care to invest. If you are willing to put in the time and trouble that it takes to learn, you can expect to move up to jobs that involve more responsibility.

As an example of ladder-type movement, a person might start out as a guard in a security service company and then, by learning on the job, work up to the supervisory level. By taking extra courses, the person could move up even further in the company. This is true in marketing research too. Many of the jobs in marketing research companies have to be done by college-trained people. But high school graduates can start in an entry-level job, such as interviewing people. Then, if they are willing to take college-level courses as they go along, they can become research assistants, research supervisors, and research directors, for example. Also, the many franchise opportunities in this field make it possible for you to own your own company.

If moving up to management-level jobs is not what you want, you will find many opportunities in the business service field for career-level jobs that are satisfying. You will also find many opportunities to make lattice-type moves, moving over to other business service companies or to those companies that buy business services.

- **UNDERSTANDING WHAT YOU HAVE READ**

  1. Explain the difference between a business service and a personal service.
  2. What two questions does an industrial consumer consider when deciding if a service is worth buying?
  3. The receptionist in the Krause Company office is ill and won't be able to work for a week. What kind of business service could this company call on for help?
  4. Name five kinds of business service companies that help industrial consumers with sales promotion problems.
  5. Are all business service companies small operations? What does this mean in terms of jobs in this field?

- **APPLYING WHAT YOU HAVE LEARNED**

  1. Use the Yellow Pages to find one example in your area of each of the kinds of business services discussed in your text.
  2. Try to imagine what each of the following business service jobs is like. State whether each one requires an aptitude for people, data, or things, choosing more than one when necessary. Be prepared to defend your reasoning in a class discussion.
     a. A repairer of electric signs
     b. A telephone operator for a telephone answering service
     c. An accountant who keeps tax records for small businesses
     d. A display designer.
     e. An interviewer for a marketing research company.
  3. Choose one type of business service that interests you and write a paragraph explaining whether or not you think you have the right aptitudes for it.

part 33 Recreation Services and Tourism

After reading Part 33, you will be able—
- To take part in compiling a directory of the recreation services in your area.
- To explain why tourism is the world's single largest industry.
- To list ten of your personal characteristics and explain why you think each one would or would not qualify you for work in recreation services or in tourism.

Another kind of service that meets the consumer's needs is the recreation service. Recreation, which can be defined as "refreshment of strength and spirits after work," is very important to people in today's hectic world. People see their recreational activities as a way of making their lives fuller, richer, and more complete. There was a time in our history when "play" was considered to be somewhat sinful. But as the number of hours that people were expected to work decreased, it became necessary for people to learn how to fill their nonworking hours in a meaningful way. Because of this, the recreation services today are a multibillion-dollar-a-year business. In this part, you will have an opportunity to look at the various kinds of recreation services and to think about how a career can be built in this field. You will also be introduced to the traveling that people do for recreation, which is called **tourism.**

LOOKING AT THE KINDS OF RECREATION SERVICES

Recreation is considered to be so important that an allowance for it is usually included in the average person's personal budget, along with allowances for rent, clothing, and other necessities. In spending their recreation money and time, people have a wide variety of recreation services from which to choose. These services can be grouped under four main headings: (1) do-it-yourself sports facilities, (2) spectator entertainments, (3) amusement parks, and (4) other kinds of recreation services.

Do-It-Yourself Sports Facilities

In recent years, so much emphasis has been placed on staying physically fit that people have become sports-minded in a really big way. In Part 25, you learned that selling people the equipment they need for these sports is big business. There also have to be facilities where people can play these sports—golf courses, tennis courts, campgrounds, and so on. Sometimes these sports facilities are "public," meaning that they are owned by the federal, state, or local government, and sometimes they are privately owned by such organizations as country clubs. But many sports facilities are owned and run by people who are in business for themselves to make a profit. It is these businesses with which we are concerned here.

The growth of the opportunities in this field has been phenomenal. For example, 40 years ago skiing was a little-known sport. But today there are a total of 1,200 ski areas in the United States and Canada. Golf has become so popular that when people are not out on the golf courses, they are paying money to practice at one of the driving ranges or putting greens. Tennis has become a major interest for many people. It can now be played year-round in the many indoor tennis courts that have been built in response to the growing interest in the sport. There are also tennis "camps," where people can stay for a period of time to improve their game.

Bowling alleys are also enjoying a great upswing of interest. So are the campgrounds that provide space and services for the camper. Marinas are also bustling places these days. They rent dock space for privately owned boats and also repair and store boats during the winter. Other facilities that are popular today with active people are ice- and roller-skating rinks, billiard and table tennis parlors, dancing schools, and model car raceway centers.

Spectator Entertainments

There is another way to enjoy sports besides actively playing them yourself, and that is by watching others play them. There are huge ball parks and stadiums where people can watch their favorite teams play baseball, football, or soccer. There are also arenas where people can watch basketball and ice hockey games. Horse racing, car racing, and boxing are also popular spectator sports, as are the championship matches in golf, tennis, and track and field. People also enjoy going to the movies, plays, concerts, ballets, operas, rock festivals, puppet shows, and such spectaculars as rodeos, water shows, and circuses.

Amusement Parks

There are many varieties of amusement parks, ranging from the pocket-sized ones that are tucked into shopping areas to those that cover many acres. The traditional amusement park offers all kinds of

The increase in the number of sports and recreational facilities offers tremendous career opportunities for people who are interested in recreational activities and have acquired marketing skills. (ABOVE LEFT *courtesy Harrison Conference Centers;* ABOVE RIGHT *courtesy Kampgrounds of America;* BELOW *courtesy Killington Ski Resort, Vermont.*

PART 33 • RECREATION SERVICES AND TOURISM • 387

rides, from roller coasters to merry-go-rounds, fun houses, and games that you can play to win prizes. But even more popular today are the many "theme parks," which are built around a unifying idea. Probably the best-known examples of such parks are Disneyland in California and Disneyworld in Florida. Other well-known theme parks are the Land of Oz in North Carolina, King Island in Ohio, Santa's Village in New Hampshire, Astroworld in Texas, and Worlds of Fun in Kansas. These parks offer many imaginative things to do and see.

There are also companies that can create instant amusement parks. They have rides and games that either are on trucks or can be quickly set up. They travel around to fund-raising events put on by such charitable organizations as school PTAs, churches, and fraternal organizations. These instant parks can also be set up for company picnics and shopping center openings.

Other Kinds of Recreation Services

There are many other recreation services that don't fit into the above three categories. For example, you can buy a guided tour to a California movie studio or a New York television studio. You can take a ride on old trains, such as the Tweetsie Railroad in North Carolina.

In New York City you can take a guided tour of the United Nations Headquarters and learn about the purpose and work of the UN. (*Courtesy United Nations*)

You can see animals in their natural settings in the Jungle Habitat in New Jersey, which also offers rides and an animal show. In the Parrot Jungle in Florida, you can observe many kinds of tropical birds and plants and be entertained by trained parrots and marching flamingos. In many cities, there are wax museums. For example, in Gettysburg, Pennsylvania, there is one dedicated to Civil War history. In Gettysburg too, you can take a helicopter ride over the battlefield, just as you can take a boat ride under the falls at Niagara Falls. In New York City, you can buy a ticket and go to the top of the Empire State Building.

These are just a few specific examples of the many different kinds of recreation businesses that can be found all over the country. There are probably other recreation businesses in the area where you live that you could add to the list.

BUILDING A CAREER IN RECREATION SERVICES

The business of providing recreation services for the public is an extremely diverse one. Because recreation services range all the way from bowling alleys to concert halls, they are run by many different kinds of people, with different ideas about what they want to bring to and take from a career. There are recreation services all over the country, so it is not hard to find a job near your home. These businesses have to be open when people want to play, which means in the evenings and on weekends. Thus they need a lot of part-time workers. There are an especially large number of entry-level jobs in recreation services that don't need any previous experience or special training.

When you add these factors together, you can see that getting started in recreation services on a part-time basis while you are still in school may not be difficult. Now let's see what kinds of jobs you could do and what the future holds for recreation workers.

Reviewing the Kinds of Jobs

The main point of recreation services is to make it possible for people to enjoy themselves. When they do, they will advertise the business in one of the most effective ways possible, which is by **word of mouth.** This is an important term in marketing. It refers to the process whereby people give their opinions about something to their friends and acquaintances. A recreation service may have an exceptionally effective advertising campaign. But if you get bad reports about it from the people who have already gone to it, you probably won't go yourself. Every worker has to share the responsibility for making the recreation service enjoyable.

Because recreation services are so varied, it would be impossible to draw a really detailed picture of what the individual jobs are like. However, we can point out the kinds of things that have to be done in recreation businesses, in order to help you decide whether working in this field would be a good idea for you. When the recreation business is a small one, the jobs listed here can all be done by the owner or manager, either alone or with a few helpers. But there are also very large recreation businesses, where the jobs have to be divided up very specifically.

HANDLING THE BUYING. Every recreation service has the problem of buying the supplies and equipment that are needed to keep the business running. Many businesses sell merchandise for extra profit, and this merchandise must also be bought. For example, a roller-skating rink needs wax to keep the floor smooth. It also needs new brushes for its polishing machines, and the machines themselves sometimes need replacing. The skates that are rented to the customers have to be replaced if they wear out, and many customers want to buy skates.

In small businesses, the buying is handled by the management. In large businesses, such as the large theme parks, there are purchasing agents who do this work. These purchasing agents must be highly skilled in marketing. They must be able to analyze facts and figures so they know where, what, when, and how to buy in order to get the best possible terms. Buying in the field of recreation services is made easier because the suppliers are eager to provide help. Many purchases are made directly from the manufacturer. Others are made through wholesalers. But both manufacturers and wholesalers know that they will sell more goods if they help the recreation business manager do a better, more productive job. Thus their salesworkers are trained in all aspects of recreation business management.

MAINTAINING AND RUNNING THE EQUIPMENT. There are many jobs for maintenance workers, ranging from highly skilled mechanics to cleanup crews. As an example of how important maintenance is, think of an ice-skating rink, where the ice has to be kept satin smooth so the customers won't trip. This means keeping the ice at the right temperature and cleaning it off many times a day. Or suppose that no one knew how to fix the automatic pin-setting machines at a bowling alley when they broke down. You can imagine how angry you would be if you were the customer and couldn't finish your game.

When animals are part of the recreation business, there are jobs for people to take care of them on a day-to-day basis. In many recreation businesses, there must be people to run the equipment. This is true in the amusement park, where people are needed to run each ride. There must also be people to run the ski tows, pilot the planes for the sky divers, and run the projectors in the movie theaters.

For all of these jobs, some aptitude for handling things is required.

Some types of recreation businesses employ people to train and care for animals. (*Daniel S. Brody/Editorial Photocolor Archives*)

Many of them also demand a strong mechanical aptitude and a concern for safety.

SELLING THE SERVICE. The people who do the selling in recreation services include, first of all, ticket sellers. In some cases, the ticket is bought from a cashier by the customers when they are ready to use the recreation service, as in most movies and amusement parks, for example. The cashier might also sell you a ticket in advance so you could be sure there would be room for you. Many recreation businesses sell advance tickets through the mail, and they can also be sold through middlemen. For example, in New York City, there are companies that sell tickets to all the Broadway plays, the reserved-seat movies, and many sporting events. These jobs require the ability to deal with figures and to handle checks, cash, and credit cards.

Besides these ticket-selling jobs, there are also jobs that involve making the public want to buy the recreation service in the first place. Advertising and public relations are especially important in the recreation field, because people can't examine the product before they buy it, as they can in a store. In this case, they have to pay for the service before they even get it. Thus they want some assurance that they are buying something they are going to like. So it is up to the advertising workers to make the service sound enjoyable and to advertise it as widely as possible.

The public relations workers try to get good coverage from the

At Old Sturbridge Village in Massachusetts, costumed guides show tourists around and answer questions. (*Courtesy Old Sturbridge Village*)

media about the service. To do this, they try to think up newsworthy ideas that will attract attention. For example, a new movie may be shown for the first time in a very elaborate setting, and many stars in the entertainment field may be invited—and many reporters. The idea is to get the recreation service talked about as much as possible so people will not want to miss it.

The nonpersonal selling jobs in recreation services, as in many other marketing businesses, are often accompanied by a lot of pressure. But some people find that the constant search for new ideas is challenging and exciting, and they enjoy the fast-paced life that goes with it.

SERVING THE CUSTOMERS. Recreation businesses have a variety of jobs that involve working directly with the customers. In the entertainment businesses, there are ushers to help people find their seats and people to sell refreshments and souvenirs. Large amusement parks frequently hire people to work as guides or information clerks to help the customers find their way around, and other people drive minibuses to get the customers to the different parts of the park. Some of the sports businesses employ instructors to teach the customers how to get the most pleasure out of a sport. There also must be workers, such as lifeguards and detectives and security guards, to watch out for the customers' safety. There are also caddies on the golf courses to carry the players' heavy golf bags.

These jobs have various requirements. For example, golf caddies must have physical strength and know how to keep from disturbing the players. A minibus driver must have a driver's license and a high level of concern for the safety of the passengers and the pedestrians. A lifeguard at a swimming pool must be a strong swimmer and have a Red Cross lifesaving certificate. It isn't possible to list the requirements for each of the many kinds of jobs in this area. But their variety shows that this is a field where people can make the most of their aptitudes, abilities, and interests.

PERFORMING. There are many different kinds of performing jobs in recreation services. The major jobs are, of course, reserved for those people who have a well-developed, widely recognized talent in such skills as singing, dancing, or acting. There are also performing jobs for animal trainers, who can both train the animals and make them perform for the public. But there are also many performing jobs that are not so demanding. For example, an ice- or roller-skating rink might hire an organist to provide music for the skaters. In Disneyland, there are people acting as Mickey and Minnie Mouse, Pluto, and other Disney characters, who mingle with the guests.

HANDLING THE OFFICE WORK. Even the smallest recreation business needs someone to keep track of the money that comes in, pay the expenses, and make sure the business is earning a profit. In the large businesses, there may be a whole staff of secretaries, typists, clerks, telephone operators, bookkeepers, accountants, and business machine operators. These jobs provide a way for people who prefer sitting at a desk and working with data to enjoy the atmosphere of recreation services.

MANAGING THE BUSINESS. How many management jobs there are in a recreation business depends on the size of the business, of course. In the large businesses, there are several levels of middle management and top management jobs. There are also recreation chains, such as RKO and Loews movie theaters, which have management jobs in the individual units and in the corporate chain headquarters.

There are many people in management-level jobs who have worked their way up through the ranks. But the higher you want to go, the more you need courses in management. The odd hours in this business make it easy for you to study while you are working. These courses can also help you if you want to open your own business. An easy way of doing this is by becoming a franchisee of such companies as Kampgrounds of America, Putt-Putt Golf Courses of America, and United General Theatres.

Looking Toward the Future

When you take a job in a recreation service, you have many options for the future. One option is to settle into a career-level job that suits you in every way. Another option is to work your way up to the level of

Recreation services offer many different kinds of performing jobs. At Mystic Seaport in Connecticut, singers roam the grounds and sing sea chanteys to entertain the visitors. (*Mary Anne Stets/Mystic Seaport Photograph*)

management. You also have many options for lattice-type moves. You can move from one kind of recreation business to another. You can go to work for a manufacturer or a wholesaler who supplies recreation businesses. Or you can move to another area of retailing, where what you have learned about pleasing the customer will be important.

UNDERSTANDING TOURISM

Before World War II, international travel was reserved for the relatively few people in the upper income brackets. But since 1948, there has been a revolution in international tourism. Rather than being limited to the rich, tourism has become something to be enjoyed by a wide range of people. International tourism works in two ways. People from our country travel abroad, and people from abroad come here to travel. There is also a great deal of travel by Americans within the United States. In fact, traveling has reached such proportions that tourism has been the world's single largest industry for some years.

High prices have recently forced tourists from our country to rethink their travel plans. However, it seems that Americans have become too used to traveling to give it up altogether. They may not go as far or stay as long as they used to. But apparently they are not going to stop traveling. Meanwhile more and more tourists are coming here from abroad, so world tourism remains an extremely important industry. Let's see now what career possibilities there are in tourism.

The Work of the Travel Agent

A **travel agent** is a middleman who makes travel arrangements for consumers. As middlemen, travel agents bring together the people who are selling tourism services and the people who want to buy tourism services. In some cases, travel agents simply arrange for the customer's transportation. In other cases, they also arrange for hotels. For many customers, however, they provide a total service, making reservations for dinners, buying theater and concert tickets, and arranging for sight-seeing tours.

Most of the travel agent's services don't cost the traveler anything. The travel agent gets a commission on the price of the services from the tourism companies. They consider that the travel agent is acting as a salesworker for them and therefore deserves to be paid. This helps to explain why travel agents are used so extensively by the public. There are some travel agencies that are quite small and have just a few clerical workers and a few people who are well-informed about geography, as well as about transportation and hotel services all over the world. There are other travel agencies that are huge. They employ thousands of workers in offices all over the country and around the world. An example of such a company is the American Express Company.

Travel agents make arrangements for people to travel alone or in groups. Sometimes they arrange for their customers to join groups that have already been set up. In other cases, they organize trips for special groups. Many travel agencies hire salesworkers to seek out this kind of group business. In this case, the agency sends a **tour director** along on the trip. This is a person who travels along on a tour to see that all the arrangements actually work out.

Travel agents provide an item that most customers don't want to do without—expert advice. If this advice turns out to be poor and the customer's trip is unpleasant or full of snags, the travel agency will lose a customer. Thus travel agents have to know what they are talking about. This may involve doing a great deal of traveling personally, reading widely, and having contacts with people who travel. It is also important that travel agents know enough about people to be able to plan trips that the customers would like rather than those that the travel agents themselves would like.

Your Career in Tourism

In the tourism industry, there are many opportunities for glamorous and exciting experiences. One of the advantages of being a travel agent is that the transportation services offer you reduced fares and hotels give you bargain prices as a way of advertising their services. In some

Many people rely on travel agents to help them plan their trips and to arrange for their transportation and lodging.
(Jeremiah Bean)

cases, such as the opening of a new resort hotel, a group of travel agents may even be invited to be the guests of the management.

However, anyone who expects only glamour and excitement, day in and day out, wouldn't want to be a travel agent. This is a business that requires a precise attention to detail, in order to make things go smoothly for the customers. This means that travel agents must have a high aptitude for data. They must also be gifted in handling people. They need good memories, along with a willingness to recognize changes. They also have to be aware of current events, so that they know what is going on in the world that would affect tourism.

There is no special amount of education that is required to be a travel agent. But college-level training usually makes it easier to be hired. It is also common to move to the travel agent's job from an office job in the travel agency. In either case, the person who wants to be a travel agent has to attend special training sessions. But everyone in this business doesn't necessarily want to be a travel agent. Many people find that the office jobs in travel agencies are interesting career-level jobs in their own right. The very large travel agencies also offer satisfying jobs in office maintenance, advertising, public relations, and personnel.

Another exciting job in tourism is that of tour director. In many companies, the travel agents take turns doing this work. But there are also people who do this job full time. Tour directors must have an exceptionally high aptitude for getting along with all kinds of people. They have to be very patient and be able to cope when everything is going wrong. International tour directors usually have to know at least one foreign language, if not more. The disadvantage of being a full-time tour director is that you must be away from home a lot. The impact that this has on your personal life has to be balanced against the advantages of the job as you see them.

- ## BUILDING YOUR MARKETING VOCABULARY

    Define each of the following terms and then use each one in a sentence.

    tour director   travel agent
    tourism   word of mouth

- ## UNDERSTANDING WHAT YOU HAVE READ

    1. Have recreation services always been as important as they are today? Do you think they are going to be more or less important in the future? Explain your answers.
    2. Why are advertising and public relations so important in recreation services?
    3. What options do you have if you take an entry-level job in recreation services?
    4. Explain why tourism is the world's single largest industry.
    5. What are the requirements for being a travel agent?

- ## APPLYING WHAT YOU HAVE LEARNED

    1. With the rest of your class, compile a directory of the recreation services in your area by doing the following things:
        a. Using the Yellow Pages as a source, list the recreation businesses in your area.
        b. Assign teams of students to find out what kind of service each business sells, what its hours and prices are, how it can be reached, and whether food can be purchased there.
        c. Work with the class to compile this information into a booklet that could be given to visitors to your area.
    2. List ten of your personal characteristics and explain why you think each one would or would not qualify you for work in recreation services or in tourism.

part 34
Transportation Services

After reading Part 34, you will be able—
- To explain the interrelation between the quality of a country's transportation services and its standard of living.
- To list the transportation companies that serve your area.
- To state the transportation service or services that would be needed to get each product or passenger in a given list to a specific destination.

Every phase of business activity in a country is affected by how well its transportation services work. Mass production, mass distribution, and mass consumption are only possible when raw materials can be delivered and finished products can be moved along to wholesalers, retailers, and consumers. Also, people must be able to get to their daily jobs in factories, stores, and offices. Many people have to travel to distant places to sell their products or to supervise activities in companies that have offices in many locations. Transportation is also important for the many businesses that depend on people being able to travel for pleasure. For example, the hotel and food service businesses would suffer if people couldn't move about easily.

Dealing with the huge quantities of goods and numbers of people that have to be moved is an impressive job in itself. But the transportation service businesses are also expected to offer speed, convenience, and safety. They are expected to keep their costs down as much as possible, which is not an easy job when the economic situation is causing prices to be generally high.

The story of how transportation services meet the demands that are put upon them is one that excites the imagination. In this part, you are going to get a brief introduction to that story. You will also discover the kinds of marketing jobs that are connected with transportation and be able to think about the possibilities for working out a career in this challenging field.

THE KINDS OF CARRIERS

There are eight kinds of carriers that are used to transport either passengers or goods, or both: (1) ships and barges, (2) trains, (3) trucks, (4) intercity buses, (5) airplanes, (6) pipelines, (7) local transit vehicles, and (8) taxicabs and limousines. Those that carry goods may carry the mail for the U.S. Postal Service. They may also carry **express,** which are goods that are to be delivered in a hurry, or **freight,** which is the word used to describe goods that are shipped in fairly large quantities and do not require particularly rapid delivery.

Often both passengers and goods have to travel on more than one kind of carrier to get where they have to go. For example, goods may arrive from overseas on a ship, then be taken part way across the country by train, and then be moved directly to their destination by truck. Likewise, a passenger may arrive on the outskirts of a city by airplane and then take a bus to the heart of the city. It is because such combinations are possible that transportation services work so smoothly and effectively. Let's see now what each kind of carrier adds to the total transportation picture.

Ships and Barges

The first important business centers in this country were the cities that could be reached by water on the seacoasts, rivers, and lakes. This country was settled by people who came in ships, and ships were for many years the main lifeline of the country.

The ships and flat-bottomed river barges that are in use today are

For many kinds of shipments, water transportation is the most satisfactory. *(Courtesy The Port of New York Authority)*

PART 34 • TRANSPORTATION SERVICES • 399

far different from those used when the country was young. They have been improved in many dramatic ways. They now go faster, handle goods more safely, and can be loaded and unloaded more easily and quickly. The shipping companies make a constant effort to improve their services as a way of offsetting the fact that water travel is the slowest form of travel. Even though the ships and barges go much faster than they used to, they don't go as fast as the other carriers now in use. However, water travel is also the least expensive way of shipping goods. This fact is especially important for heavy or bulky goods, such as grain, ore, coal, sand, gravel, chemicals, petroleum, and machinery.

Because of the relative slowness of water travel, the number of passengers choosing this method has been steadily declining. There is still an active "cruise" business, where the large pleasure ships offer vacationing passengers a leisurely way of "getting away from it all." But most people today prefer to travel abroad on the much faster airplanes.

Trains

In the early days in this country, overland transportation, which was by horseback, stagecoach, or wagon, was slow and difficult. But then the locomotive was invented, and train tracks were laid in all directions across the country. People and businesses followed, because they knew they could count on the trains to bring in what they wanted to buy and carry away what they wanted to sell. The inland cities where the trains stopped became the kinds of business centers that the cities on the water had been.

Today trains carry about 40 percent of the freight that is moved between cities. This is more freight than any other kind of carrier handles. As for passengers, just a few years ago people were predicting that the railroads would go out of the passenger business entirely. But because Congress considered it essential to save railroad passenger service, it created a semipublic corporation called the National Railroad Passenger Corporation. Nicknamed Amtrak, this corporation is supported by public funds and by the various railroad companies that have joined the corporation. Because it operates most intercity railroad passenger service as a single system, it can operate more efficiently than the railroad companies can by themselves. An example of what Amtrak has accomplished is the popular, high-speed Metroliner and Turbotrain service between Boston, New York, and Washington. This is the kind of service that is drawing passengers back to the railroads. The energy crisis and the high cost of gasoline are also making railroad passenger service seem more attractive to many people.

Piggybacking combines the efficiency of trains and the flexibility of trucks. (*Courtesy Association of American Railroads*)

Trucks

The most important advantage of trucks is their flexibility. They are not dependent on water, railroad tracks, or airports. All they need are roads and service stations. Today there are excellent roads in almost every part of the country and a wide network of service stations. This means that small villages and towns are not cut off from the mainstream of business life. With trucks to carry goods back and forth from the bigger cities, this country has become one big marketplace.

Trucks are used mainly in two ways. They give **over-the-road service,** which is the long-distance hauling of merchandise, and they also handle **short-haul service,** which is the local delivery of merchandise. Trucks are a very important means of transportation on their own. They also represent a way of extending the usefulness of other carriers. A good example of how this works is **piggybacking,** which is a system for carrying loaded truck trailers on specially designed railroad flatcars. At the rail terminals, these trailers are hooked onto truck cabs and driven to their destination.

There is also a "fishyback" service, where the trailers are loaded on ships or barges. A similar idea is to pack merchandise into containers the size of truck trailers. These containers can be loaded on airplanes, as well as on trains, ships, and barges. Then they can be hauled away by truck. These ideas save the time, effort, and cost of unloading and reloading goods from one carrier to another. They also give the customer the convenience of door-to-door service, which would not be possible without trucks.

Intercity Buses

The large buses that carry passengers between towns and cities have the same kind of flexibility that trucks do. Often they are the only means of public transportation in rural areas. The main competition for the bus companies that serve such areas has been the private automobile. Thus the energy crisis has meant an increase in the number of passengers that the buses are carrying. There is a movement toward having the intercity buses carry express shipments in addition to passengers. For example, Greyhound Bus Lines runs a service for express packages. The packages, which must be taken to a Greyhound terminal and picked up from the terminal at their destination, are delivered quickly, safely, and inexpensively.

Airplanes

Because of their speed and convenience, airplanes have revolutionized people's thinking about distances. A two-week vacation used to mean a trip to the nearby mountains or seashore for most people. But now it may mean a trip across the country or to Europe or South America. The speed of planes has also opened up many new business opportunities, in overseas areas as well as in this country. In many cases, the problems of geography that used to limit what business people could do are now solved in a few hours' flying time.

Planes have become the most important carriers for passengers. More than three-quarters of the people in this country who buy transportation services to get from city to city choose to go by plane. (This figure excludes the people who use private means of transportation, such as automobiles.) For overseas travel, the figure is even higher, with nine out of ten passengers choosing to fly. The airlines are also important for express shipments, and many of them have started parcel delivery services. For example, with the American Airlines Priority Parcel Service, a package can be checked in on a given flight and then be picked up on the other end when the plane lands.

In the shipment of freight, the airlines still account for only a minute fraction of the total. But the amount of freight being carried by air is increasing every year. To win business, the airlines are stressing the idea of "total cost." It costs more to carry freight by air, if you count only the direct cost of the transportation. But the airlines are saying that if you add up all the costs, you may actually save money. For example, storage costs may be less if merchandise can be shipped as it is needed. Also, sales are not lost to competitors when quick delivery of the merchandise can be guaranteed.

Pipelines

In this country, there is a vast network of big steel pipelines that run underground. These pipelines are a very specialized but very important means of transportation. They carry much of this country's output of oil and all of its natural gas safely, cheaply, and for great distances. It is because oil and natural gas are essential products—products that industrial and ultimate consumers couldn't do without—that the pipelines are so important to the health of this country's economy.

Local Transit Vehicles

For people who live in or near cities, there are local transit companies to handle such everyday transportation needs as getting workers to their jobs, shoppers to the stores, and students to school. Local transit companies may run buses, trolleys, streetcars, or trackless trolleys. There are subway cars that run in tunnels under the ground and

The San Francisco cable cars are famous and well-loved local transit vehicles. (*Courtesy San Francisco Convention & Visitors Bureau*)

PART 34 • TRANSPORTATION SERVICES • 403

elevated cars that run above the regular roadway. A city may have just one kind of transit service or a combination of them. For instance, it may have both subways and buses. A city can become completely crippled when its transit services break down. Because transit services are so important, they are often run by the city government or other public authority instead of by private companies.

Local transit companies are very much in the news today. The energy crisis and the pollution problems that cities in general are having make it important that people drive their cars less and use local transit facilities more. But people will only be willing to do this if they can count on excellent service at a reasonable cost. After believing for many years that the best way to spend public money was on building bigger and better highways, this country is beginning to turn its attention toward improving public transit systems. Already some federal money is being made available to subsidize local transit, and many local communities are taking positive action to work out fast, efficient, low-cost systems. It is hoped that still more attention will be paid to this important problem in the future.

Taxicabs and Limousines

A transportation service that is very important in most communities is the service that taxicabs provide. Taxis take customers directly to where they want to go, from door to door. Some taxi drivers are "independents," meaning that they own their own cabs and are in business for themselves. Others work for large companies that own whole fleets of taxis. This is an expensive form of transportation, but people expect to pay more for the convenience that taxis offer.

Besides taxis, there are chauffeured limousines that can be hired for such special occasions as weddings. There are also limousines that carry about a dozen passengers at once. These limousines, which are frequently used for driving passengers to and from airports, pick up passengers at certain designated spots rather than going door-to-door.

MARKETING JOBS WITH THE COMMON CARRIERS

The transportation companies that sell their services to the public are called **common carriers.** This term is used in contrast to **private carriers,** which are transportation facilities owned and operated by individuals or businesses for their own use. For example, the oil tankers that are owned and operated by large oil companies to transport their own products are private carriers.

Common carriers come in all sizes, from those that consist of one person and a truck to those that have thousands of employees and own billions of dollars' worth of equipment. Some companies cover small local areas, and others go from coast to coast or have extensive overseas operations. This means that there is room in this field for the people who want to stay close to home and for those who want to travel. There is also room for people who prefer to work in small companies, where they are expected to be able to handle more than one aspect of the business, and for those who want to do one special job with a large corporation.

There are many different jobs that must be done to run common carriers. There have to be crew members who know how to run the ships, barges, trains, and planes. There are many jobs for skilled mechanics and for highly trained engineers, as well as jobs for relatively unskilled maintenance workers to keep the carriers and terminals clean. There are jobs in communications, signaling, and weather reporting. There are also jobs connected with getting the freight, express, mail, and baggage on and off the carriers and a wide variety of office jobs.

If any of the jobs we have mentioned so far interest you, you may want to find out more about them by talking to your guidance counselor, consulting the *Dictionary of Occupational Titles,* or contacting the carrier companies. Because our subject is marketing, we are going to concentrate here on those jobs in transportation that require marketing skills.

Jobs in Purchasing and Storing

Transportation companies have to buy many things in order to produce their services. These include new railroad freight cars, jet planes, tires, gasoline, machine parts, paper towels for the washrooms, plus thousands of other items, both large and small. The transportation companies also buy services. For example, airlines buy the services of food catering companies. The buying in small companies may be handled by the manager. But large companies employ purchasing agents, who must be well trained in the skills of buying. People who have had college-level training in marketing are generally preferred for these jobs. If purchasing agents buy highly technical equipment, they may have to be trained in engineering as well as in marketing.

Large transportation companies hire receiving clerks to receive and check incoming goods. There are many things that have to be stored until they are needed, so warehouse workers are also employed to store the goods in an orderly way and to distribute them as they are needed. These jobs require an aptitude for both data and things. They can be learned by high school graduates, who can advance to the supervisory level as they learn the necessary skills. If the people who do these jobs are willing to get the required college-level training in night school, they can also advance to the job of purchasing agent.

Jobs in Sales

Some transportation companies hire ticket agents, whose job is to sell tickets in situations where space doesn't have to be reserved. For example, tickets for commuter trains that take people from the suburbs into the cities are sold in this way. Ticket agents must know how to handle money and fill out daily reports. They are also expected to be friendly and polite to the customers and to be able to answer questions.

When space is limited and reservations must be made, reservations agents are needed. They must have an aptitude for people and enough aptitude for things to be able to learn how to work the computers that most companies now use for checking reservations on the spot. The airlines prefer people who have had community college or four-year college training to do this kind of work. It also helps to know a second language.

Another kind of sales job in transportation is done by freight agents. They have to be able to quote rates, figure out routes, and give advice on the best way to pack the freight. They need a strong aptitude for data, as well as an aptitude for getting along well with people. Many transportation companies also employ people who are highly skilled in personal selling to contact potential customers and to persuade them to buy freight service. Sometimes these salesworkers are called traffic

Airline reservation agents must have an aptitude for people and the ability to work quickly and efficiently.

agents. They must know what their companies offer, as well as what the competitors offer. They also have to understand the needs of the customers, which usually means knowing a great deal about the products the customers want to ship. This is a job to which reservations agents and freight agents can advance. The possibilities for advancement from this job include the job of regional sales manager and then sales manager for the whole company.

Besides jobs in personal selling, there are nonpersonal selling jobs in advertising and public relations. Because transportation is a fiercely competitive field, these jobs are very important. Often people who have had experience in direct selling move over to these jobs.

Jobs Serving the Passengers

If the transportation companies are going to get repeat business, it is very important that the passengers enjoy the service. This is why the airlines have flight attendants to make passengers as comfortable and relaxed as possible. Flight attendants are very carefully chosen. It is important that they be pleasant looking and well groomed. They have to be able to plan their activities, move fast, and keep their tempers when people are difficult.

Flight attendants are being asked more and more to know a second language, especially for overseas flights. Flight attendants usually have community college or four-year college training. If they have supervisory abilities, they can be put in charge of the other attendants on a flight. They can also be promoted to jobs where they teach newcomers in the special training programs that the airlines run.

The airlines also have workers called passenger service representatives, who help passengers while they are in the terminals, answering their questions and helping them to get checked in. These people can work up to the job of flight attendant or reservations agent. The system of flight attendants has worked out so well for the airlines that the railroads have copied the idea. There are passenger service representatives on some trains who perform many of the duties of flight attendants. Some cross-country buses also have people to watch out for the passengers' welfare.

The railroads need people to work in the dining cars. These are jobs that you have already learned about in Part 29. On the trains, there are also conductors to collect, or sometimes sell, tickets and answer the passengers' questions. On overnight trains, there are Pullman car conductors and porters, who try to make the passengers as comfortable as possible. The ships that carry passengers have a food service staff, as well as stewards to take care of the passengers' rooms. At the airports, railroad depots, bus stations, and docks, there are

Flight attendants serve meals and see to it that passengers are comfortable and enjoy their flight. (*Courtesy American Airlines*)

porters called "redcaps," who handle the passengers' baggage. None of these jobs requires any advanced training. However, they all require a strong aptitude for getting along with people.

Jobs in the Claims Department

Although the transportation services have an excellent safety record, there are times when freight and baggage are lost or damaged. When this happens, the customer's claim is investigated by a claims clerk. This job requires careful attention to detail, because the claims clerk must find out exactly what happened and why and fill out a number of papers. The claims clerk must also be able to handle people well and be sensitive to their feelings. Claims clerks can advance to supervisory positions in the claims department, including the job of claims department manager.

Driving Jobs

Driving jobs are generally considered to be marketing jobs because the driver must deal directly with the customers. For example, taxi drivers have to both produce and sell the service. Bus drivers have a definite public relations role to play. Many truck drivers also act as representatives of their companies when they deliver goods to customers.

To be hired for driving jobs, people must have commercial drivers' licenses, experience in driving, and safe driving records. They must also be exceptionally reliable. Once hired, the people who drive the large trucks and buses have to take special driving courses so they can learn to handle their vehicles under all conditions. Driving jobs, because of the responsibilities that they carry, can be very well paid. But over-the-road truck drivers have to spend a great deal of time away from home. This is a factor that has to be taken into consideration if these jobs interest you.

Drivers can advance to the job of dispatcher. In trucking, this calls for the ability to coordinate the movement of the trucks into and out of the terminals. The truck dispatcher has to make up delivery schedules and assign drivers to the trucks. Bus, taxi, and limousine companies also need dispatchers to make up the drivers' schedules and to act in a supervisory role. Dispatchers need an aptitude for data and must be able to plan and direct the work of others. They can advance to other management jobs in transportation.

TRANSPORTATION JOBS WITH MARKETERS

There are many marketing companies that offer transportation jobs. Many of these jobs are similar to jobs with the common carriers, except that no selling has to be done. A store may run its own delivery service, in which case the jobs would be similar to the jobs in an independent package delivery service. Also, a large corporation whose operation is very spread out may have its own small fleet of airplanes. This fleet has to have many of the same workers that regular airlines do. This gives the people who are interested in transportation careers an extra degree of flexibility. They can start with a private carrier and transfer to a common carrier, or vice versa. In either case, the skills that they have learned will be very welcome.

Marketers also have jobs for people who understand how the transportation service businesses work. Some large companies, for example, hire people to handle all the passenger reservations that have to be made for business purposes. These people must have an aptitude for data and for people. Marketers also need people who understand the various ways in which express and freight can be shipped by common carrier. Producers, wholesalers, and retailers have shipping departments, whose prime duty is to move merchandise in the best possible way. This may mean moving it by the cheapest way or by the fastest way. But usually it means striking a balance between the two.

Shipping departments have to work closely with freight agents. Thus they need people who talk the same language as freight agents and understand routes, rates, packing methods, and insurance. There are beginning jobs in shipping departments for clerks, who help the

Bus drivers must be exceptionally responsible and experienced drivers. And they should also be courteous to passengers and willing to answer questions and give directions. *(Bettye Lane)*

career-level shipping clerks by doing some of the routine jobs, such as preparing labels. A shipping clerk can become head shipping clerk and eventually traffic manager. This is a highly skilled, well-paid job that requires in-depth knowledge of transportation services. Usually the people who do this job have taken college-level courses in transportation along the way. Often they have had experience with the carrier companies.

FREIGHT FORWARDERS

The cheapest way to ship freight is in quantities sufficient enough to fill a whole truck trailer, railroad box car, or container. This is spoken of as "car lot shipments." But many marketers want to ship less than that at a time. To serve these marketers, there are companies called "freight forwarders." They are also referred to as "freight coordinators," which is a term that describes their work very well. They specialize in coordinating freight shipments so that the goods move as quickly, safely, and inexpensively as possible.

These companies will pick up and deliver the freight in their own trucks. Then they group the shipments according to where they are going and whether they are to be sent by ship, train, or truck, or by a combination of carriers. There are also air freight forwarders that specialize in shipments of freight by airplane.

By putting the individual shipments together, freight forwarders can get the savings that go with quantity shipping. Thus they can give the individual shippers a much cheaper rate than they would get alone. Even though they have to add on a charge for their services, the customer still saves money. Freight forwarders are performing a valuable middleman service.

Freight coordinators need truck drivers as well as workers for the terminals where the freight is sorted. They also need office workers. These are all jobs that can be learned by high school graduates. They need traffic managers to decide how the shipments should be sent and management experts to search for new ways of doing business that will cut costs. They also need a sales force and sales promotion workers to persuade people to buy their services.

THE LEASING COMPANIES

The leasing companies provide a service that can be a happy medium between public and private transportation. These are the companies that lease (rent) automobiles, trucks, railroad cars, and containers to customers as they are needed. The advantage of this system is that customers can use the equipment as if it were their own for as long as they need it, yet they are not stuck with it when they no longer need it.

Let's say, for example, that a toy manufacturing company has to make a lot of deliveries in the fall months for the Christmas market. If the company owned all the trucks needed during these months, they would be standing idle for most of the year. But it would be very expensive to ship all the toys by common carrier. To solve this problem, the toy company leases the trucks that it needs. This same toy company may also lease the cars that its salesworkers drive. Many companies find that it is more economical and convenient to lease cars for their salesworkers than to pay the salesworkers' expenses for using their own cars.

There are also companies that rent cars to individuals for short periods of time. For example, a family from the eastern part of the country may want to tour the western states. The family may fly to a western city and then rent a car to use until it is time to fly home. Business people also use the "fly and drive" idea to make the most of their time on business trips.

The leasing companies are big business and have many interesting job opportunities. They need some people to buy the equipment and others to maintain it. They need office workers plus customer service

Because sales representatives for car rental agencies handle reservations, they must have strong aptitudes for people and data. (*Courtesy Avis Rent A Car*)

representatives to deal with the customers. They also need sales promotion workers to tell people the advantages of leasing. Two well-known examples of leasing companies are The Hertz Corporation and Avis Rent A Car.

YOUR FUTURE IN TRANSPORTATION

Transportation is not an easy field for young people to sample on a part-time basis while they are still in school. Probably the best way to get early experience in the field is by working in the receiving or shipping department of a retail store. This will give you the chance to see what kinds of carriers are used to ship goods in and out of a store and to learn something about how the transportation companies operate. You can also see how goods are packed for shipment. This is the kind of experience that can help you to get a full-time job in transportation.

If you want to build a career in transportation, you must be the kind of person who is not upset by changes. The transportation picture is changing every day, as our scientific knowledge and engineering know-how increase. The people who work in this field must be able to adjust to these changes.

If you can meet this overall requirement, you will find that transportation offers you the chance to make the most of your own talents and interests. It also offers you many opportunities for ladder- and lattice-type moves on your way to building a career.

- **BUILDING YOUR MARKETING VOCABULARY**

  Define each of the following terms and then use each one in a sentence.

  common carrier
  express
  freight
  over-the-road service
  piggybacking
  private carrier
  short-haul service

- **UNDERSTANDING WHAT YOU HAVE READ**

  1. Explain the interrelation between the quality of a country's transportation services and its standard of living.
  2. What is Amtrak and how is it affecting railroad passenger service?
  3. What is the most important advantage of trucks?
  4. Why are the airlines stressing the idea of "total cost" to freight customers?
  5. Is it easy to get part-time jobs in transportation?

- **APPLYING WHAT YOU HAVE LEARNED**

  1. With the rest of your class, make a list of the transportation companies that serve your area. Obtain time and rate schedules for as many of them as possible.
  2. State the transportation service or services that would be needed to get each of the following products or passengers to their destination. Give the reasons for your choice.
     a. DE students from your school attending a meeting in the state capital
     b. A buyer for a local department store going to Paris, France
     c. A package too large to send by parcel post from your house to Chicago (If you live in Chicago, send it to San Antonio.)
     d. A repeat order for spring clothes to be sent from New York City to your area three weeks before Easter (If you live in New York City, make the shipping point San Francisco.)
     e. Lumber from a logging camp in the state of Washington to a wholesale lumberyard in your area
  3. Pretend that you are a family friend and write a letter of recommendation for yourself, pointing out why you should be hired for a specific transportation job that interests you. To do this, you have to think about the requirements for the job and your qualifications.

part 35 Finance and Credit

After reading Part 35, you will be able—
- To explain how credit cards are used.
- To give the name of a commercial bank that serves the area where you live and list five services that it offers.
- To list four requirements for each job in finance and credit in a given list.
- To write a paragraph explaining whether or not you would be interested in learning more about finance and credit.

Suppose for a minute that there were no financial and credit services—that is, no banks and no way for individuals and businesses to borrow money. This would mean that you would have to keep all your money at home, under the mattress or in some other equally unsafe place. Whenever you wanted to buy something, you would have to give the cash directly to the person you were buying from. If you wanted to buy a home, you would have to save all the money first. This might mean that you could never own a home of your own. You would also find it hard to open a business of your own. You would have to save up every penny that you needed for initial expenses, plus enough money to keep things going until the business started to earn a profit. Even if you managed to get the business started, you couldn't expand it without again saving all the money first.

These problems would be affecting not only you but also the whole economy. They would be slowing down the whole business process, and this, in turn, would mean many fewer jobs. For example, when people can't buy new homes, there are fewer jobs in the construction and home furnishings industries. Even the people who have homes cannot make as many home furnishings purchases if they have to pay cash for everything. There is also less business in a cash economy for automobile manufacturers and dealers and for all the companies that sell automotive products.

The examples we have mentioned are the ones that come to mind most readily. But the fact is that all businesses would suffer without financial and credit services. These are essential services. They make it

Commercial banks have to be as concerned with their image as other marketing businesses do. What do you think this bank's decor says to the customer? *(Courtesy MCA Inc.)*

possible for businesses to prosper and for individuals to enjoy more goods and services than they otherwise could and to enjoy them sooner. Let's see now how the financial and credit service businesses go about this important work and what kinds of careers they offer.

COMMERCIAL BANKS

Commercial banks got their name because they originally served just business people. But today commercial banks also take care of the needs of private individuals. Although these banks may have the words "state" or "national" in their names, this doesn't mean that they are owned by the government. It simply means that they have been chartered by either the state or the national government. They must follow a number of governmental regulations to get and keep their charters. But they are corporations, and they are owned by their stockholders.

There are commercial banks all across the country, wherever there are people and businesses to be served. Thus there are job opportunities in commercial banking near your home. However, there are far more opportunities in the heavily populated states, with 16 states employing over half the bank workers in the United States. To make

Getting him there takes money. Save at Mellon Bank.

Savings accounts that pay interest help people save money that they will need at a later time. (*Courtesy Institute of Outdoor Advertising*)

their services easily available to the public, the large commercial banks in most states have branches, just as department stores do. These branches can be found in suburban areas, especially near shopping centers. They are also spread around large cities. Some of the large commercial banks also have branches in foreign countries.

To see what the career picture is in commercial banks, we are going to look first at the services that they offer, then at the kinds of jobs that are available, and finally at what you could expect if you committed yourself to this field.

Services Offered by Commercial Banks

A bank is very much like a store. The main "product" that a bank sells is money. Like a store, the bank must first buy this "product." Then it must sell the money at a higher rate in order to cover the expenses of running the bank and make a profit. Commercial banks do this in so many different ways and offer so many other financial services that they are often called the "department stores of finance." In other words, you can shop for all your financial needs in a commercial bank, just as you can do all your personal shopping in a department store.

Commercial banks are also often called "full-service banks." The many services that they offer can be summarized under four main headings: (1) savings and checking accounts, (2) loan services, (3) special services for individuals, and (4) special business services.

SAVINGS AND CHECKING ACCOUNTS. When you have money that you don't need immediately, you can deposit it in a savings account. A savings account has two advantages for you. Your money is safe, and it also grows, since the bank will pay you interest on it.

Another kind of account that you can open in a commercial bank is a checking account. In this case, you can have a specific amount of the money that you have deposited paid out to a specific person by filling out a check. When the bank receives this check, it will pay the amount of money that is asked for and then subtract that amount from your account. Checking accounts are such a safe and convenient way of paying bills and keeping track of money spent that almost everyone, private individuals and businesses alike, uses them.

LOAN SERVICES. Commercial banks use the money that is deposited with them to make loans. This includes mortgage loans that allow people to buy houses. Loans are also made for any number of other reasons, such as adding on to a house, buying a car, or paying for a vacation. Some banks make agreements to give people small loans automatically, when they have drawn more money from their checking accounts than they have on deposit. Commercial banks also make loans to business people so they can start new businesses or expand existing ones.

The individual or business that borrows money from the bank has to pay the bank interest on the loan. This interest will be higher than the interest that the bank pays its savings account depositors. The interest that the bank pays can be considered the purchase price of the money. The interest that the bank charges is really the selling price. Like any other marketing business, the bank has to be sure that the difference between its selling price and its purchasing price is sufficient to allow it to make a profit.

SPECIAL SERVICES FOR INDIVIDUALS. There are many special services that commercial banks offer to individuals. They rent safe deposit boxes, where people can safely store such valuables as jewelry and important family papers. They sell travelers' checks for people who are planning trips and don't want to carry large amounts of cash with them. As another service, customers can deposit their stocks and bonds with the bank. The bank will collect the money that is due on the stocks and bonds and deposit it in the customer's account. The bank will also advise customers about buying and selling stocks. Commercial banks also help many of their customers to plan their personal finances for retirement or in case of death.

Commercial banks also work hard at offering their customers one of the most important services of all—convenience. In some cases, people can deposit and withdraw money without even getting out of their cars, by going to drive-up windows. They can also bank by mail or deposit money when the bank is closed. In many banks, customers can also withdraw money when the bank is closed, by inserting a special card in an electronic machine. In some cases, bank customers can have their charge accounts paid automatically, without even bothering to write a check. And many more conveniences are on the way.

Convenience is one of the most important services that banks offer their customers. This electronic machine allows people to withdraw cash from their accounts at any time of the day or night. *(Courtesy Chemical Bank)*

Banking, like all marketing businesses, is highly competitive. This means that banks are constantly looking for ways to improve their services and win new business.

SPECIAL BUSINESS SERVICES. Commercial banks also try to outdo each other in providing the most up-to-date services possible for businesses. They will set up and maintain pension trust funds. They will also manage profit-sharing plans, where employees share in the company's profits. They will help businesses make financial plans for the future. In fact, the very large commercial banks employ people who are specialists in the management of different kinds of businesses, so that they can give really expert advice. Banks with foreign branches are also in a good position to handle the financial problems of importers and exporters.

The services that commercial banks can provide have been greatly expanded in recent years by computers and other advanced business machines that can do difficult and complicated accounting jobs with amazing speed and accuracy. The banks that have these computers can send out bills for a company, collect the money, and then pay the bills that the same company owes, including its enti e payroll. They can analyze earnings for a company and predict futt re earnings. As more and more uses are found for computers, commercial banks will be able to offer even more kinds of services.

The Kinds of Jobs in Commercial Banks

Commercial banks come in all sizes. They range from the small single-office establishments that have around ten workers to the huge banks that have hundreds of domestic and foreign branches and employ thousands of workers. Because banking has become so complicated, many small banks are merging with large ones. This makes it possible for them to offer their customers a full range of services.

In small banks, workers have to double up on the specific tasks that have to be done, just as they do in small stores. There are fewer opportunities for advancement in these banks because there is less room at the top. However, you can be very close to the customers in small banks, which may be important to you. Also, what you have learned in a small bank can be useful if you decide to transfer to a larger bank at a future date. In the very large banks, each worker must have very specialized and exact duties. The jobs that have to be done in banks can be classified under four main headings: (1) clerical workers, (2) bank officers, (3) marketing specialists, and (4) maintenance workers.

CLERICAL WORKERS. Almost two-thirds of the workers in commercial banks are classified as clerical workers. This includes the kinds of office workers that are needed in other businesses, plus the skilled people who can run computers and advanced business machines. Banks also classify tellers as clerical workers. Tellers handle the deposits and withdrawals that customers make. They need a high aptitude for people along with an aptitude for data and things. They must be well groomed, pleasant, and courteous, even during rush hours, because they represent the bank to the customers.

Tellers must be high school graduates and must be able to use the machines that record each customer's business with the bank. Because of the large sums of money that they handle, they have to be "bonded." This means that the bank takes out an insurance policy that protects the bank from any losses caused by the tellers. In order to be bonded, a person has to have a record of honesty and reliability.

Small banks have tellers who can handle all the different kinds of transactions. But in large banks, tellers are assigned to more specific duties. For example, there are commercial tellers who cash checks and handle deposits and withdrawals. There are Christmas Club tellers, savings tellers, note tellers to handle loan repayments, and payroll

Commercial bank tellers cash checks and handle deposits and withdrawals made by bank customers. Tellers must be responsible and have a good record of honesty and reliability. (Jeremiah Bean)

tellers, as well as various other kinds of tellers. For tellers, the line of promotion leads first to the job of head teller.

BANK OFFICERS. The next largest group of commercial bank workers are bank officers, who account for about one out of every five employees. They have such titles as chairman of the board, president, vice-president, treasurer, and controller. There are also bank branch managers and assistant branch managers. In large banks, there are vice-presidents in charge of the various departments of the bank, such as the trust department or the loan department.

Working under the vice-presidents are other bank officers who have become specialists in the work of the particular department or even in a particular part of their work. For example, in the loan department, you will find officers who are experts in handling agricultural loans, business loans, home mortgages and other property loans, and consumer loans.

Bank officers have to be well informed about banking practices, business conditions, and people, as well as the particular area of banking that they work in. They must be able to make decisions on their own that are in line with the policies of the bank and that follow all the regulations set by law. In order to do this, they need both education and experience. The large banks have six-month to one-year management training programs that train college graduates and people who have degrees beyond college for these jobs.

But bank officers' jobs are not confined to the people who started out with at least a college degree. Banks are known for promoting from within. They encourage workers, such as clerks and tellers who have management ability, to get the advanced training that they need in order to move up to the jobs that involve greater responsibility. This encouragement is of the most practical kind. There are banks that will pay the full cost of the tuition. Besides studying at colleges and universities, bank employees can learn their way to better jobs by enrolling in courses offered by the American Institute of Banking in a number of cities around the country. The institute also offers correspondence courses, which can be completed at home.

Bank officers who are interested in international banking can be assigned to work in branches in foreign countries. The clerical workers and middle managers for foreign branches come from the country that the branch is in. But the top officers are generally sent out from the home bank. To work in this capacity, a bank officer must know the language, history, and geography of the country, as well as its political, economic, and social situation.

MARKETING SPECIALISTS. Large banks have a number of jobs for people who are experts in the field of marketing. There are jobs for purchasing agents, who buy the supplies that the bank and its branches use. There are jobs in marketing research and jobs for people to develop new kinds of services to offer to the public. Workers in advertising, public relations, and other kinds of sales promotion are needed too. There are also jobs for salesworkers, who sell the bank's services directly to prospective customers.

The people who do these jobs for banks must be well trained in marketing. They may come into these jobs directly from college courses in marketing. Or they may move over from similar jobs in other marketing businesses. They can move to management-level positions in the marketing area in which they work, such as marketing research director, advertising director, and sales manager. Because they have to learn so much about banking, they can also move to officer-level jobs in the bank.

MAINTENANCE WORKERS. The maintenance workers who take care of the bank building make up the last group of bank workers. This group includes cleaners, janitors, elevator operators, and cafeteria workers. It also includes guards, whose jobs are especially vital in banking. People expect to be able to transact their banking business in an atmosphere of safety. Also, each bank wants to be sure that the large amounts of cash that flow through the bank are safe. Bank guards are carefully chosen for their reliability and their ability to handle crisis situations.

It is sometimes possible to get maintenance jobs without a high

Some bank officers are experts in the area of home mortgages and are able to give financial advice to people who are planning to buy a home. (*Ed Lada*)

school diploma. Many banks encourage the people in this situation to finish high school so they can move up to more responsible jobs.

Your Future in Commercial Banks

Banks do have a need for part-time workers. For example, they employ many part-time tellers. But because most bank jobs require a high school education, it is almost impossible to sample this work while you are still in high school. However, if you want to start preparing for it, you can try to get a cashier's job in a supermarket, fast-food restaurant, movie theater, or other business that accepts high school students. This kind of experience is good to have on your résumé when you are ready to apply for a job as a clerk or teller.

Many commercial banks have summer employment programs for college students, where the students can find out whether they want to commit themselves to a banking career. If you are planning to go on with your education after high school, you may want to investigate these programs. If you feel now that you have a real talent for banking and that you would make a good bank officer, you would be wise to make definite plans for a college education. This is the fastest and surest way of getting to the officer level. With the many scholarships available, college may be a reasonable goal for you.

Because banking is an expanding business, it offers a high degree of job security. Usually when bank workers are displaced by new machines, they are retrained for other jobs in the bank. Some banks have evening hours, when the bank has to be staffed. Some clerical workers, especially machine operators, work on the evening or night shift.

The workweek in a bank is generally 40 hours or less, although overtime may be required at certain times, such as when the books don't balance. The fringe benefits that banks offer are generous, and the working conditions are generally pleasant. There is no doubt that commercial banks offer their employees many pluses. The question is whether they have what you are looking for.

SPECIALIZED BANKING INSTITUTIONS

Although the commercial banks are considered the department stores of finance, there are other institutions that specialize in certain banking functions rather than trying to offer them all. In some states, there are mutual savings banks, which do not have stockholders. They are organized and operated for the depositors and managed by professional bankers. They invest their money largely in home mortgages.

Another kind of specialized institution is the savings and loan association. Although these associations are called "cooperative banks" in some states, they are not actually banks. When people put savings into a savings and loan association, they are not "depositing" them. Rather, they are purchasing shares of the business, just as they do when they buy shares in a corporation. The income on their savings is called a **dividend,** instead of interest, which can be defined as a share of the profits. Savings and loan associations also invest almost all their money in home mortgages.

New banking laws that are just going into effect and some that are still in the process of being passed are changing the regulations for mutual savings banks and savings and loan associations to make it possible for them to offer more banking services. This will mean that they can be more competitive with commercial banks. If you are interested in banking, these specialized institutions offer you another road to a career.

CREDIT CARD COMPANIES

One of the most important inventions of the twentieth century as far as marketing is concerned is the **credit card.** This is a small metal or plastic card that is used to print the cardholder's name and identification number on sales checks. But a credit card is far more than that. It represents a way for cardholders to charge their purchases in a variety of places, even in other countries, without question and to receive one monthly bill. It also represents a way for many kinds of retailers to give a much broader range of customers the convenience of a charge account without the risks that would normally be involved.

Credit cards are now in such general use that many people never carry cash. Some marketers issue credit cards themselves. This is true of the oil and telephone companies, hotel and restaurant chains, airlines, car rental agencies, and some retail stores. In some cases, these company cards are honored by other marketers. For example, oil company cards can be used in some hotels and motels.

Credit cards that can be used in a variety of ways are issued by commercial banks. For example, BankAmericard was originated by the Bank of America in California and is now franchised to banks around the country. There are also all-purpose credit cards that are issued by such independent credit card companies as the American Express Company, Diners Club, and the Carte Blanche Corporation. For their services in acting as a collection agency, the banks and credit card companies charge each retailer a percentage of each bill. However, the retailer can count on being paid promptly and does not have the expenses that go with maintaining an independent charge account system.

There is a great deal of clerical work to be done in credit card

Using computers, customer service representatives for credit card companies can answer customers' questions and give them information about their accounts. *(Courtesy Bullock's)*

424 • UNIT 5 • CAREERS IN MARKETING SERVICES

companies, most of which is now being handled by computers. There are also jobs that involve working directly with the customers. For example, the American Express Company assigns a customer service representative to each cardholder. This is the person that the cardholder can contact if adjustments have to be made. These people must understand the systems and policies of the credit card company. They need an aptitude for data, since much of their work is with numbers. They also have to be able to deal reasonably and politely with people, even those that are angry.

There are jobs checking the credit of the people who are applying for cards to see whether they can be trusted to pay their bills. There are also jobs for people who try to collect overdue accounts. These jobs require tact and good judgment. Salesworkers are needed to persuade new retailers to accept the credit card as payment. Workers in advertising and public relations have to persuade retailers and the public of the advantages of the card. Top managers are also needed to set policy and see that it is carried out. The top managers are usually college graduates, but they may have gotten their education as they were gaining experience in the company.

SALES FINANCE AND CONSUMER FINANCE COMPANIES

In this country, such things as automobiles, refrigerators, and television sets are not considered to be luxuries that only the very rich can afford. They are part of what the average family expects from life. But not everyone who wants to make such major purchases has the cash on hand to pay for them in one lump sum. This explains why the sales finance and the consumer finance companies have such an important role to play in marketing. They provide a way for people to enjoy the use of goods and services right now, but to pay for them out of future earnings.

Sales finance companies do their work through those retailers who allow their customers to make major purchases "on time." This means that the customers can pay for their purchases gradually, or in "installments," over a period of months or even years. The agreement that a consumer has to sign to buy on time is called a **time-sales contract.** For most retailers who offer such contracts, it is a hardship not to be paid immediately. So they turn to the sales finance companies, who buy the time-sales contracts from the retailers, thus helping both the retailer and the consumer.

The consumer finance companies get their name because they make loans directly to the consumer. Formerly called small loan companies, consumer finance companies help people who have financial emergencies as well as those who need money for major purchases.

Jobs in the two kinds of companies are similar in many ways. Both kinds of companies need office workers and business machine operators. Both need people to make credit checks on would-be customers and people to try to collect unpaid installments. And both have a great need for people with management abilities, since both kinds of companies work from local offices that can be reached easily by the customers. In many cases, college graduates are hired directly for the special management-training programs that these companies run. But it is also possible for a promising employee who is a high school graduate to move into the management-training program. The managers' jobs can lead upward to the supervisory jobs in the home office of the company. They can also lead to jobs in banks and other kinds of finance and credit companies.

- **BUILDING YOUR MARKETING VOCABULARY**

    Define each of the following terms and then use each one in a sentence.

    credit card   dividend   time-sales contract

- **UNDERSTANDING WHAT YOU HAVE READ**

    1. Bank tellers are usually "bonded." What does this mean and why is it necessary?
    2. Are there many part-time jobs in banks for students still in high school?
    3. Explain how credit cards are used.
    4. How do sales finance companies help the consumer? How do they help the retailer?

- **APPLYING WHAT YOU HAVE LEARNED**

    1. Give the name of a commercial bank that serves the area where you live and list five services that it offers.
    2. List four requirements for each of the following jobs in finance and credit. Use your text to help you, but also add any requirements that you think would be part of the job.
        a. Bank teller
        b. Loan officer
        c. Bank guard
        d. Bank branch manager
        e. Customer service representative for credit card company
        f. Sales finance office manager
    3. Write a paragraph explaining whether or not you would be interested in learning more about finance and credit.

Insurance and Real Estate

After reading Part 36, you will be able—
- To explain how insurance companies earn a profit.
- To analyze an advertisement from an insurance company to see what buying motives it is appealing to.
- To list the seven main kinds of services that are part of the real estate business.
- To react in a personal way to talks by insurance and real estate workers in your classroom.

To complete your study of marketing services, we are going to look now at insurance and real estate. Like many of the other services you have learned about, these are essential services—services that are needed to keep the business cycle functioning smoothly. Besides being major employers themselves, insurance and real estate companies make it possible for other businesses to flourish. This means more jobs in the total economy. Insurance and real estate businesses also serve you directly as an individual by providing you with a way of building financial security. In this part, we are going to see how these two important services work and what career opportunities they offer.

CAREERS IN INSURANCE

Insurance is not something that can be used right away, like a new car or a vacation trip. When you buy insurance, you are buying the most intangible of all services. You are simply buying a *promise* that the insurance company will pay you *if* you have a loss in the future. In other words, what you are buying is protection. Providing this protection is such big business that the insurance field employs about 1½ million people. They work at a wide variety of jobs, some of which may be of interest to you.

Insurance: How It Works

The amount of money that the customer has to pay for insurance protection is called a **premium**. In return for this money, the customer receives a written contract, called a **policy**, that spells out exactly what the insurance company promises to do. There is nothing haphazard about either the premium or the terms of the policy. The insurance company figures out very carefully how much risk it is taking. It makes a study of what the chances for loss are in a given situation in a given amount of time. Then it sets the premium for each policy so that when all the premiums of all its customers are pooled together, the insurance company will have enough money to cover the losses that do occur, plus enough money to pay its expenses and make a profit.

To put this another way, the insurance company does not just gamble on how many policyholders it will have to pay off each year. It hires people called "actuaries" to make very exact studies of what has happened in the past in order to predict what will happen in the future. As an example of this, take the problem of automobile insurance. The company's actuaries study the number of accidents that occurred in past years and figure out how and when the accidents happened, how serious they were, and what kinds of people had the accidents. Then the company knows how to set its rates for different areas of the country and different kinds of people and how much protection to promise.

When the insurance company is planning its finances, it also counts on being able to earn additional money by investing part of the premiums that it collects. It puts this money to work by buying stocks and bonds and by lending money to build homes, apartments, commercial properties, hospitals, and so forth. The insurance companies invest so much money in this way that they have an important influence on the business health of the country.

The Kinds of Insurance

Insurance falls into three main categories: (1) life insurance, (2) property and liability insurance, and (3) health and accident insurance. Insurance can be sold on an individual basis, or it can be sold to groups, such as the employees of a large store. Group insurance has become very popular because it usually costs less than individual policies do. Because of the amount of business the insurance company is getting, it can afford to lower its rates. Many employers offer group insurance as a fringe benefit for their employees. Group insurance is also issued to labor unions, professional associations, and other groups.

LIFE INSURANCE. In its simplest form, life insurance provides financial protection in case of death. Individuals buy life insurance so their families will have enough money to live on if they die. A business may buy life insurance for a key person in the company, one whose ability is so great that the company would suffer if that person were to die suddenly. Many insurance policies also carry with them the opportunity to save money. They do this by providing those individuals who live to a certain age or who are disabled with a monthly income for the

People buy property insurance to protect their belongings against loss. (*Courtesy Allstate*)

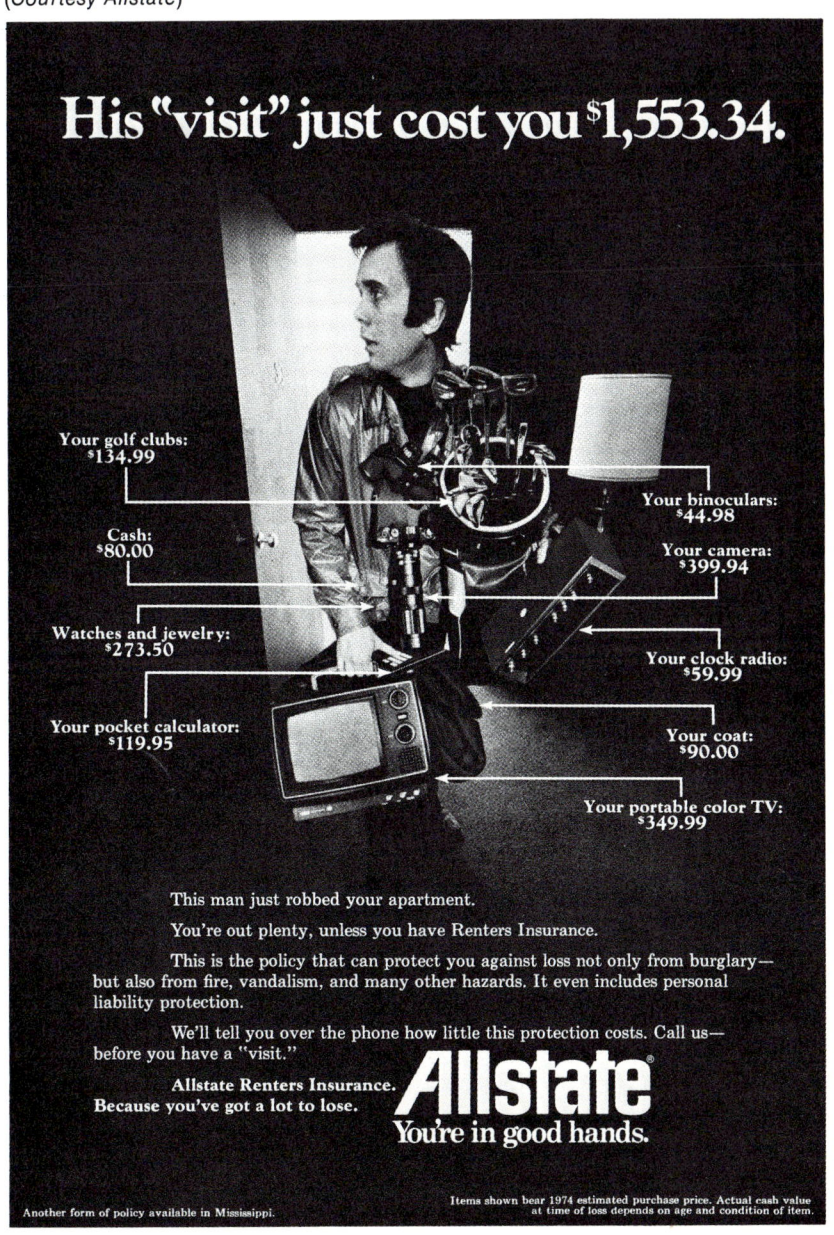

His "visit" just cost you $1,553.34.

Your golf clubs: $134.99

Cash: $80.00

Watches and jewelry: $273.50

Your pocket calculator: $119.95

Your binoculars: $44.98

Your camera: $399.94

Your clock radio: $59.99

Your coat: $90.00

Your portable color TV: $349.99

This man just robbed your apartment.

You're out plenty, unless you have Renters Insurance.

This is the policy that can protect you against loss not only from burglary—but also from fire, vandalism, and many other hazards. It even includes personal liability protection.

We'll tell you over the phone how little this protection costs. Call us—before you have a "visit."

Allstate Renters Insurance. Because you've got a lot to lose.

Allstate
You're in good hands.

Another form of policy available in Mississippi.

Items shown bear 1974 estimated purchase price. Actual cash value at time of loss depends on age and condition of item.

PART 36 • INSURANCE AND REAL ESTATE • 429

rest of their lives. These policies offer protection from financial worries when a person retires. This kind of policy is widely used by businesses to provide pension plans for their employees.

PROPERTY AND LIABILITY INSURANCE. Property insurance is bought by individuals and businesses. Individuals buy it to protect such things as houses, furniture, automobiles, boats, art works, clothing, furs, and jewelry. Businesses buy property insurance to protect buildings, equipment, and inventory. Goods can be insured while they are in transit, as well as while they are being stored. Property insurance can provide protection against fire, burglary, theft, floods, windstorms, falling aircraft, and other hazards.

Liability insurance takes many forms, but basically its purpose is to protect policyholders in case they are responsible for injuring anyone or damaging anyone's property. For example, suppose that your house has a loose floorboard on the front steps. If someone trips down the steps and is hurt, you are legally responsible and will have to pay "damages" to the injured person. If you don't have insurance, you have to pay the damages yourself. But if you do have insurance, the insurance company will handle the problem.

An especially important form of liability insurance is the kind that covers the owners of cars, buses, trucks, and other vehicles in case the vehicle causes injury to people or damage to property. Workmen's compensation is another important form of liability insurance that covers the obligations of employers to their employees. When employees are injured in work-connected accidents, workmen's compensation provides medical care and weekly payments. It also provides benefits for the workers' dependents in case of death.

HEALTH AND ACCIDENT INSURANCE. Because of the high cost of medical services today, health insurance is considered to be an essential form of insurance. It pays a major part of your hospital and doctor bills when you are sick. There are also insurance policies that give you certain extra benefits if you have an accident. For example, you may be paid a weekly income for the length of time that you are unable to work. Health plans that cover dental bills are also becoming popular.

Jobs in Insurance

Insurance companies may sell all three kinds of insurance—life, property and liability, and health and accident. Or they may specialize in just one or two kinds of insurance. The size of companies varies a great deal, with life insurance companies, some of which have thousands of employees, being the largest. Some insurance companies work in just one state, whereas some of the big ones cover all 50 states.

Every insurance company has a "home office," which is its main place of business. This is where many of the jobs that the public doesn't see are done. But like other marketing businesses, insurance companies have to make themselves easily accessible to the public. To do this, some of them have field offices in many locations throughout the geographic area that they cover. These field offices are run by their own managers.

In other cases, companies are represented by "general agents," who also run local offices. But general agents are in many ways self-employed, hiring their own office staff and salesworkers, who may be called "insurance agents." A general agent has a definite agreement to act as the representative of one insurance company or more in a certain community. There are also "insurance brokers," who don't have such a definite affiliation with a particular company. Brokers decide which insurance company will best meet their clients' special needs. Then they place the insurance with that company. Through field offices, agents, and brokers, insurance companies are able not only to sell new policies but also to provide a continuing service for their customers.

Let's look now at the kinds of jobs that have to be done in insurance companies. They fall into five main categories: (1) insurance salesworkers, (2) claims adjusters and examiners, (3) office workers, (4) specialists and top managers, and (5) maintenance jobs.

INSURANCE SALESWORKERS. The job of selling insurance is so important that it involves about one-third of all insurance workers. Because insurance is an intangible, insurance agents and brokers have to be exceptionally well trained for their jobs. They must know a great

Insurance agents must have excellent communication skills in order to explain clearly the terms of insurance policies to their clients. (*Courtesy Aetna Life & Casualty*)

deal about people and be able to win their confidence. They must have very detailed information about insurance in general and the particular policies of their own and competing companies. They must believe in what they are selling so they can show people how and why insurance can help them to be more secure financially. They also need a very high aptitude for data.

Insurance agents and brokers have to be highly skilled in the art of selling. They must have excellent communication skills, for they have to explain many of the technical points about insurance to their clients in everyday language. They have to be self-starters, who can go out and look for new prospects. They must also be self-disciplined, because they have to plan their own work. They must be able to take turndowns as part of the business rather than taking them personally. Frequently they have to see clients at night or on weekends, when the clients have free time. Thus their hours tend to be long.

With few exceptions, the people who sell insurance have to be licensed in the states where they work. In most cases, this means that the agent or broker must pass a written examination about insurance and the state laws concerning it. Also, insurance companies generally give their salesworkers a training course, plus on-the-job training with experienced salesworkers.

Because the requirements are so strict, insurance saleworkers consider themselves to be professionals. Frequently they give such a personalized kind of financial advice that they have much the same relationship to their clients as doctors and lawyers. This is the kind of job that can't be done by an uneducated person. It can be done by a high school graduate who is willing to learn. But high school graduates seldom go directly into this work. Usually they get some experience first, perhaps in an office job in an insurance company or perhaps selling in another field. It is much easier to be hired if you have a college education. Even then, however, you must go right on studying while you are working by attending courses and conferences sponsored by various insurance organizations.

Although selling insurance is demanding work, insurance is a field where the salesworkers' efforts are amply repaid. In fact, the job of selling insurance can be one of the best paid jobs in business. The earnings of agents and brokers are in the form of commissions. This means that their financial rewards are directly related to their own ability and drive. Insurance salesworkers also have the advantage of being able to work anywhere in the country, since selling is done from local offices. Insurance agents can advance to the job of general agent or to sales management jobs in district offices or the home office. Brokers and agents may also move up to jobs as officers of the insurance company. However, many insurance agents and brokers prefer to remain in sales work, where they can work directly with the public.

Insurance claims adjustors must examine damages with the keen eye of a detective in order to determine the extent of damage covered by the policy. (*Courtesy Aetna Life & Casualty*)

CLAIMS ADJUSTERS AND EXAMINERS. Two jobs that are unique to the insurance industry are those of claims adjuster and claims examiner. When a loss is reported to the insurance company, claims adjusters must decide whether the loss is covered by the policy and the extent of the loss. To do this, they have to go to the place where the loss has occurred—to see how much damage a fire has caused, for example, or to interview someone who has been hurt. The claims adjuster has to gather all the facts about what happened—how, when, where, and to whom. Thus the claims adjuster must have the same ability to notice details and add together information that a detective needs. The claims adjuster must be able to get along well with people in order to get information from them and to settle claims diplomatically.

Claims adjusters may have to work odd hours. They must be able to plan their time to the best advantage. Besides working for an insurance company, they are sometimes self-employed. In this case, an insurance company or the people who have had a loss may hire them to defend their interests. You don't need a college education to do this work. But a college degree makes it easier to be hired and shortens the time that it takes to advance to the job of chief adjuster in a field office or to managerial jobs in the home office. When they are hired, claims adjusters have to be specially trained through courses and on-the-job training. In many states, they have to pass an exam to earn a license.

Because claims adjusters often have to be specialists in one area of insurance, your special interests may help you to be hired. For example, suppose that you have always been interested in cars and have worked for a time as a mechanic. You could specialize in automobile damage claims. If you have an interest and perhaps some experience in the building trades, you could specialize in damage to buildings. Students who have studied premed can investigate claims of bodily injury.

Claims adjusters can also advance to the job of claims examiner. In many companies, this is the person who reviews the work of the adjusters to be sure that the claim is being settled fairly. High school graduates have to start out as clerks in the claims department and work their way up. But college graduates can often start out directly as junior claims examiners. Claims examiners must be well informed about the kinds of policies their company issues and the terms of those policies. This makes it possible for them to be sure that all company rules and regulations are being followed in settling claims. But they also have to make many independent judgments, because many new problems come up with individual claims.

Claims examining is a desk job. The person who does it has to be able to concentrate for long periods of time without moving around. New claims examiners must take a special course, and they are encouraged to go on studying afterward. They can move up to the job of claims approver, where the final approval for difficult claims is given. They can also move to other supervisory jobs in the home office.

OFFICE WORKERS. Because of the amount of paper work that has to be done, the insurance industry has an especially large need for office workers. There are many jobs for people to run the computers and other advanced business machines that can handle many clerical jobs today. Secretaries, typists, general clerks, file clerks, and bookkeepers are also needed, to work in the home office and in local offices. The people who do these jobs can move to other jobs in the insurance field, where their training in working with data is a distinct asset.

SPECIALISTS AND TOP MANAGERS. Among the many specialists that insurance companies need are the actuaries, who have already been mentioned. Actuaries need an exceptionally high aptitude for data, because their work is largely with numbers and statistics. Another kind of specialist is the "underwriter," whose main duty is to decide how much risk the company will accept by approving or rejecting new policies and outlining their terms. Underwriters must be precise about details and be able to relate facts to each other. They generally have to be college graduates and must take additional courses to learn the insurance business in detail. They can be promoted to the job of senior underwriter and then chief underwriter.

Insurance companies also hire accountants to analyze the financial records of the company to be sure it is operating in a sound way. Lawyers advise the company on its legal obligations and represent the company when very difficult claims have to be settled in court. People who are experts on investments look for new ways to invest money and watch over present investments. These people all need special training in their particular area of expertise. They usually have degrees beyond college, in law or some aspect of business. But they may have gotten these degrees after they started working, in night school.

Insurance companies also employ sales promotion specialists in advertising and public relations. Marketing experts are needed to help train agents and brokers and think up new marketing methods and systems. These are jobs to which agents and brokers can advance. Or people can move over from similar jobs in other marketing businesses.

Top officers of the insurance companies have very responsible jobs which demand people who have acquired "the broad view" through both education and experience.

MAINTENANCE JOBS. In the insurance business, about one out of every 50 workers holds a maintenance job in a local or home office. Some of these workers have not finished high school. Others have engineering backgrounds that allow them to take responsibility for the running of the large buildings that house the home offices of the large companies. Many people who work in maintenance jobs are doing the work they want to be doing. Others would like to get into other jobs in the insurance business. If they have a high school education, this is possible. If they do not, they must go back to school.

Your Future in Insurance

It is sometimes possible to get a part-time job in a local insurance office. Your best chance of doing this is if you have acquired some office skills, such as typing. If you can get this kind of job while you are still in school, you can begin to see whether the insurance business is right for you. If this kind of job is not available, you can try to get a job where an aptitude for data is required—perhaps as a cashier or office worker in a supermarket. This will help you find out whether you like working with details.

You can use your school time to prepare for an insurance career by taking bookkeeping courses together with DE. Insurance in general is a field for skilled workers, so your chances for success depend on your willingness to develop skills. The more willing you are to make the effort to learn, the more possible it will be for you to have a secure job with a promising future. Insurance offers material benefits and the chance to help people free themselves from financial worries.

CAREERS IN REAL ESTATE

The term **real estate** means property in the form of land and building. There are seven main kinds of services that the people who own property may need and that are also important to the people who want to buy or rent other people's property:

1. Arranging for the sale or lease of property.
2. Appraising property, which means establishing how much it is worth.
3. Managing large properties, such as apartment houses and shopping centers.
4. Giving advice when large tracts of land have to be developed for housing or for commercial or industrial use.
5. Helping to make the financial arrangements between buyers and sellers and finding sources of money.
6. Giving advice about how to get the most out of real estate.
7. Doing research to find the answers to present and long-range real estate problems.

The important thing about each of these seven kinds of services is that they must be done by people who have developed special skills and knowledge, which make them valuable middlemen. Let's see now what these middlemen do and what this field has to offer you.

Real Estate Agents

In real estate, the terms "agent" and "broker" are used somewhat differently than they are in insurance. "Real estate agent" is used in the broad sense to mean anyone who handles the exchange of real estate. "Real estate broker" is a more narrow term, meaning a real estate agent who is a principal member of a real estate firm. There are also salesworkers, who are not principals in a firm but are hired by the firm. These salesworkers are called agents, so when we say "real estate agent," we are including both brokers and salesworkers.

Still another term that you may hear is **realtor**. This is a real estate agent who is a member of the National Association of Realtors and abides by that organization's strict code of ethics. Some real estate agents deal in all kinds of properties, but most specialize in either the sale and rental of homes and apartments, farm property, commercial property, or industrial property.

THE SALE AND RENTAL OF HOMES AND APARTMENTS. When people want to buy or sell a home, they can do it on their own. Yet most people go to real estate agents, even though these agents must be paid for the work they do. This is because the expert advice and service that real estate agents give is well worth the price of their commission. They spend a lot of time developing "listings," so they know where the people are who want to sell. They also work hard at finding customers—that is, people who want to buy. Then they get the two sides together in a way that benefits them both.

To do this, real estate agents have to know all the details about each house that is listed with them, including the style of architecture, method of construction, heating and utility costs, taxes, and the possi-

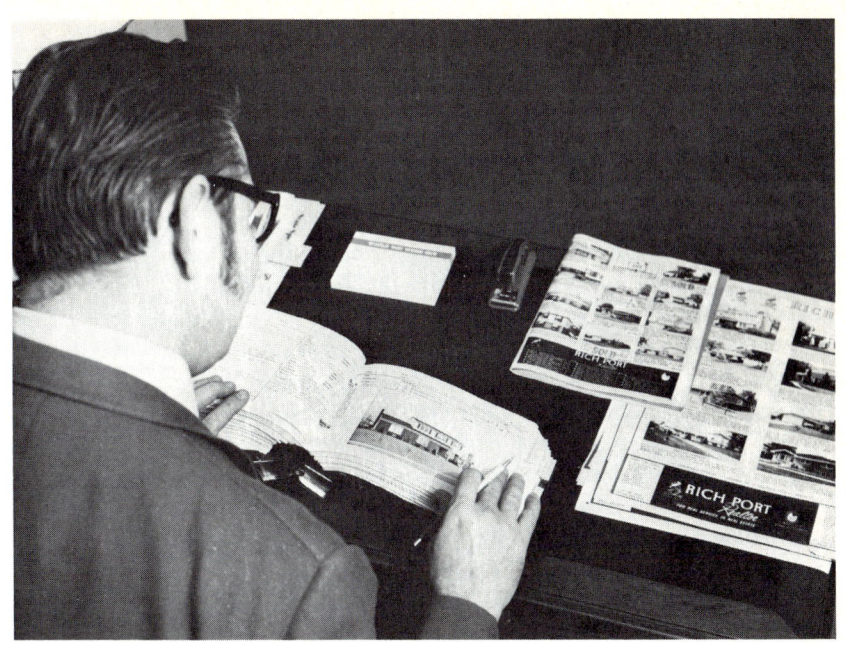

Real estate agents must study the houses listed with them so they can show the right house to the right buyer. (*Courtesy Rich Port Realtors*)

bilities for modernizing it or adding to it. For each house, they also have to know what the neighborhood is like, as well as where the schools, churches, and shopping areas are, and all the other things that matter to people when they are choosing a home. At the same time, real estate agents also have to be well informed about the people who want to buy. They have to know what size and kind of house each client wants and how much each client can spend. By gathering information on both sides like this, real estate agents can get the right buyer to the right seller with the least amount of effort for all concerned.

In addition to selling houses, real estate agents sell "cooperative apartments," the kind of apartments that are located in buildings owned by the tenants cooperatively. Real estate agents also handle the rental of homes and apartments. They need a high aptitude for data, for they must understand the terms of the sale or of the rental agreement, which is called a **lease**. They must be highly skilled in selling and must be able to get along well with all kinds of people. They have to be able to drive and are usually expected to provide their own car. They must plan their own time, much of which is spent showing clients around. They have to work at the clients' convenience, which often means on weekends. But the amount of money that they can earn is in direct proportion to their own drive and ability. Also, helping people to answer their basic need for shelter carries many satisfactions with it.

FARM PROPERTY TRANSACTIONS. There are real estate agents who specialize in the sale of farm property. They work in very much the same way as the agents that sell and rent houses and apartments do. They too must be very well informed about what they are selling. They have to know about soil conditions, water supply, drainage, erosion, and taxes. They must also know where the market centers are, what the transportation facilities are like, and whether the property is suited to the newest techniques for farming. They have to help the buyer to analyze what can be expected from the farm in terms of possible income. Because the real estate agents who handle the sale of farm property must have such specific and expert information, they need some kind of background in farming. This might be through agricultural courses in high school or college or through working on a farm.

COMMERCIAL PROPERTY TRANSACTIONS. A different kind of information is needed by the real estate agents who handle the sale of land for such commercial properties as office buildings and shopping centers. They may also sell the buildings or rent space in them. They have to understand commercial leasing practices. They must also be informed about the kinds of businesses their clients are in so they can advise them about where to locate. They have to know about taxes, insurance rates, and local zoning laws in order to know what business can be carried out in what area. They must also know what the community is like so they can help their clients figure out what their chances for success are.

The real estate agents who handle commercial properties have to be highly skilled. They must be able to talk the same language as their business clients. They need a great deal of experience in either real estate or business, or both. This kind of work demands a close attention to many kinds of details. It also requires the ability to talk to a group of people, since the facts may have to be presented to a committee or a board of directors.

INDUSTRIAL PROPERTY TRANSACTIONS. Another kind of real estate agent who often has to sell to a group of people at one time is one who specializes in the sale of industrial properties for factories and warehouses. This has become a very important part of real estate for many reasons. It has not been possible to adapt many older factory buildings to modern production methods, and these have had to be replaced. In many instances, this has meant a new location. Modern transportation facilities have opened up many rural and suburban areas that couldn't be used earlier for industrial purposes. Also, an increased concern for the comfort of the workers and the general interest in improving the environment have led to more carefully planned factories.

The real estate agents who deal in industrial properties have to be able to supply information and answer questions about transportation, taxes, and utility rates. They must know whether a supply of labor is

An important aspect of appraising is a careful examination of the property to determine whether it is structurally sound and in good condition. (*Courtesy National Institute of Real Estate Brokers*)

available in the area and what the general wage scale is. They must understand the needs of the particular manufacturer. They also have to know about the community so the people who will be moving with the factory into the area will know what it is like. This kind of work, like commercial real estate, demands a great deal of experience.

Appraisers

Appraisers have the job of giving property a dollar value. This is one of the most important jobs in real estate, for it protects both sellers and buyers from being cheated. It calls for the ability to figure out the value of the property on its own merits and then to balance this against other factors, such as the location of the property. A piece of land in the middle of the city, where land is badly needed, will be worth more than a comparable piece of land in a rural area.

To determine property values correctly, appraisers have to be experts in the real estate field, with an ability to deal with figures and to analyze facts. There is a large amount of technical knowledge that they must acquire by taking courses. The way to prepare for this work is by working first as a real estate agent and then with a qualified appraiser. Appraisers can work as specialists in large real estate firms, or they can be self-employed.

Jobs in Property Management

There are many times when the owners of buildings need help in managing them. For example, an individual or company may own a large apartment building, a group of houses, a shopping center, or an office building. In such cases, the owners frequently have too many other interests to be able to take care of their property themselves. They therefore hire professional real estate managers to take over all the management problems.

Managers are in charge of renting the space, which includes advertising for new tenants, preparing leases, collecting rents, and working out problems with the tenants. Managers hire and supervise the people who do the maintenance work, making sure that the work is done correctly. Managers have to be well informed about methods of construction and costs, because they are in charge of upkeep, redecoration, and repairs. Managers must be able to deal with many different kinds of people. They also have to be interested in details and be able to work with figures, since they must prepare many kinds of reports.

Large real estate firms in big cities have management departments where young people can begin to learn this part of the real estate business. After that, there are assistant manager jobs, which will eventually lead to the job of manager. People also come into this work from maintenance jobs, as well as from the job of real estate agent.

Jobs in Land Development

A real estate specialty that is often in the news today is land development. Because of the interest in ecology, people have become very concerned about how land is to be used. So today the land developer has to think about what is good for the community and the environment as well as what will be most profitable. Land development ranges from putting up a few houses to creating whole new towns. For example, Reston, Virginia, and Columbia, Maryland, were started "from scratch," with carefully planned shopping and recreational areas.

Land development takes a great deal of expertise. It is an area that real estate agents can move into. It is also done by construction companies, who either hire real estate agents to help them or have people trained in real estate on their own staffs. The real estate experts have to buy the land and then sell the completed houses or buildings.

Jobs in Real Estate Financing

The person who wants to develop a large tract of land and the person who wants to build a small house both have to borrow money. Also, there are people and companies, such as insurance companies, that have money to lend and want to invest it in mortgages for various kinds of real estate. What is needed here is a middleman to get the two sides together. There are some real estate firms called "mortgage companies" that specialize in this kind of work. Other firms do it as part of their total business. To help investors invest their money wisely, the mortgage expert must be highly skilled in all phases of real estate. This work is usually done by people who have had a great deal of real estate experience.

Jobs in Real Estate Counseling
Another area of real estate for people who have had very wide experience in the field is real estate counseling. The people who do this are called consultants. They may work for large firms or be self-employed. They advise people on how to use real estate to the best advantage. Their services are used by both sellers and buyers, as well as by property managers, land developers, and investors.

Jobs in Real Estate Research
Still another specialty is real estate research, which is especially important today. This is the area that makes long-range, intelligent planning for the future possible. There was a time when people were not very concerned about this. But today it is widely recognized that our resources are not unlimited, as we had once thought, and that planning is essential. Real estate researchers are interested in studying construction methods and materials in order to find new and better ways of putting up buildings. This work requires engineering training. Real estate researchers are also interested in figuring out what tomorrow's needs are going to be—how many and what kinds of houses, factories, stores, transportation terminals, schools, and other buildings will be needed. This work, which requires imagination as well as care in gathering information, is done by people who have degrees beyond college, often in city planning.

Your Future in Real Estate
It is not probable that you could sample the real estate business while you are still in school. There is a small chance that you could get a typing or office job in the field or a job where you would answer the phone on weekends in a small real estate office. But generally, this is a field for high school graduates. Many real estate agents are also college graduates, and some have majored in real estate. If you want to be an agent, you have to take a specific course that ends with a licensing examination. The licensing exam for brokers is more difficult than the exam for salesworkers. Many real estate agents go right on studying,

especially if they want to move to one of the specialized areas of real estate.

Real estate work is available all over the country, although there are more opportunities in large cities and fast-growing communities. You can work for a small company or for one of the huge companies, such as Cushman & Wakefield in New York City, which has many interests. Working for a large company gives you the opportunity to hold management jobs on various levels, such as sales manager and general manager. You can also work for yourself by opening your own office.

The financial rewards in real estate can be very high, depending on how hard you want to work and how good you are at your job. Real estate is a respected job in the community. In addition, it can lead to excellent jobs with other companies. For example, corporate and franchised chains have real estate experts on their staffs to help them find new locations and decide when to close existing facilities.

• BUILDING YOUR MARKETING VOCABULARY

Define each of the following terms and then use each one in a sentence.

lease   real estate
policy   realtor
premium

• UNDERSTANDING WHAT YOU HAVE READ

1. Explain how insurance companies earn a profit.
2. Why do insurance salesworkers consider themselves professionals?
3. How can you prepare now for a career in insurance?
4. Why don't people sell their homes on their own instead of going to real estate agents, who must receive a commission?
5. List the seven main kinds of services that are part of the real estate business.

• APPLYING WHAT YOU HAVE LEARNED

1. Bring to class an insurance company advertisement taken from a newspaper or magazine, or write a brief description of one that you have seen on television. Think about what buying motives the ad is appealing to. Have a class discussion on what the ads have in common and whether they seem to be successful.
2. Invite someone who works in the insurance field and someone who works in real estate to come to your classroom. Ask them to discuss their work and the opportunities for young people in their fields. After their talks, write a brief summary of how you reacted to what they said and to what you have read in this part.

EXPERIMENTS IN MARKETING

1. Make a list of eight ways in which the businesses that market goods and those that market services are alike. Use your list to help you participate in a class discussion and to draw up a master list that the class agrees upon. Here is an example to start your thinking: They all have to maintain the goodwill of their customers.
2. For each of the following service business workers, name a job in another service business or in a business that sells goods that the worker could make a lattice-type move into:
   a. Hostess/headwaiter in a restaurant
   b. Detective in a hotel
   c. Self-employed photographer
   d. Advertising director for a recreation business
   e. Route worker for a linen rental company
   f. Purchasing agent for a transportation company
   g. Bank teller
   h. Insurance claims adjuster
3. With the help of your teacher, choose a shopping center or district in your community. List the name of each business and state what kind of business it is, using what you learned in Units 4 and 5 to help you.
4. "A chain is only as strong as its weakest link." Write a paragraph explaining how you think this saying applies to the problems of hiring and firing workers in marketing businesses.

UNIT 6

After completing this unit, you will be able to make a major personal career decision by deciding whether or not to go on with your study of marketing.

The time has come for you to turn the spotlight squarely on yourself, so that you are the center of attention. In this unit, you are going to face the question of whether a career in marketing is right for you. You are also going to think about where you want to go from here and how you can get there.

Starting Your Education and Experience

part 37 Broadening Your Horizons

After reading Part 37, you will be able—
- To identify the personnel and facilities that your school provides to help you with career selection.
- To bring an account of a current event to class to demonstrate how newspapers can give you valuable career information.
- To assist in a class project to identify the scholarship and aid programs in your community.

It is hoped that this book has taught you that there are many different approaches to careers. But because this book has been written for students who live in a wide geographic area, it cannot give specific details about the actual marketing jobs and career possibilities that are available where you live. To make this book work for you in a personal way, you have to think of the conclusion of this book not as an end but as a beginning. You have to use it as a springboard from which you can broaden your view of what your own possibilities are for building a satisfying career. This means that on the basis of what you have learned in this book, you have to make the effort to learn more about the jobs in your area, yourself, and the resources available to you. When you have this information, you have the basis for making rational decisions about your future.

LEARNING MORE ABOUT JOBS

Let's suppose that you have been working at odd jobs and saving every penny that you can lay your hands on for more than a year. You finally have enough money to buy the sound system you have been dreaming of. You have no problem about which sound system to buy because while you were saving your money, you checked all the stores in your area. You already know the advantages and disadvantages of the various sound systems, and you have decided which one you want. You also know which stores carry it and how much money you are going to need. Since your money is so hard to come by, you wouldn't think of shopping in a careless and haphazard way.

Your high school years are a time for fun and good times with your friends. But they are also a time for making serious and responsible decisions about your future. (*Arthur Sirdofsky/Editorial Photocolor Archives*)

Because your future is so important, you will want to use the same kind of reasonable approach in finding your first job and starting your career. This is, of course, far more complicated than buying a sound system. But the principle is the same. You can find out ahead of time, before you are ready to "buy," where the jobs are, what their advantages and disadvantages are, and what you are going to need in terms of requirements. Let's look now at some of the ways in which you can get this information together.

Checking Your School Bulletin Boards

Many companies make a policy of sending notices about current job openings to the high schools in the area. These notices are usually posted on a bulletin board in your school's guidance or placement office. It is a good idea to make a habit of reading these notices on a regular basis. Even if you are not ready for a job yet or if you already have one, you can learn a lot about where the employers in your area are and what their needs and requirements are.

On these same bulletin boards, you will find notices of such special events as "career nights." These are evening meetings when various people from the community come to the school to discuss their careers with the students. A career night might be sponsored by the school or by a civic group. If it has not been tried yet in your community, perhaps you and your teacher can suggest it to the appropriate people. Some communities are also starting programs where young people can actually watch what different people do. For example, you might be allowed to sit in an advertising agency for a day to see what working there is really like.

The bigger your school, the more responsibility you have to take for staying informed about what job possibilities your guidance or placement offices are trying to make available to you.

Making the Most of Books on Careers

In your school guidance or placement office, you will also find a number of books and pamphlets that can be helpful to you in planning your career. These include a number of governmental publications. Among these are two musts: *The Dictionary of Occupational Titles* and *The Occupational Outlook Handbook*. These two books give very detailed information about specific jobs and the chances for success in various fields.

Because of the current interest in career education, many new books are now available. Besides checking your guidance or placement office, you should also check your school library to see what materials it has. Perhaps your school also has a career center where all the books and pamphlets on this subject are readily available for your use.

It is also important to check your community library to see what it has that applies to the field you are interested in. Community libraries now carry many more materials than they used to on the subject of careers. To make the most of the library, you have to know how to use

Libraries have many resources to help you learn about career opportunities in fields that interest you. *(Courtesy Fordham University)*

the card catalog. If you don't know how, ask the librarian to help you find the material that you want and to show you how to use the card catalog for the future.

Another book that you want to be sure to make full use of is the telephone directory. The advertisements for the Yellow Pages that say "Let your fingers do the walking" apply to the job hunter as well as the shopper. You can find out a great deal about where the employers are in your community by "walking" through the Yellow Pages.

Learning About Business Associations

When you are looking for a job, you want to find the job that is right for you. At the same time, the employer wants to find the person that is right for the job. This is very important to the employer because every worker who is hired has to be trained to some extent. This costs the employer time, effort, and money, all of which will be wasted if the employee quits or has to be fired. Also, the employer doesn't want the constant headache of looking for new employees instead of being able to count on people who are loyal because they are happy in their jobs.

To help them find the right employees, many employers count on help from the trade associations to which they belong. Examples of such **trade associations** are the National Association of Food Chains, the National Restaurant Association, and the National Ski Areas Association. These are groups of businesses that have joined together to protect and further their common interests. These associations have prepared materials that describe the job opportunities in their particular fields. You can obtain these materials by writing to the trade associations that you are interested in. *The Occupational Outlook Handbook* suggests the appropriate trade associations for various jobs and gives the addresses.

Another source of information about jobs is the **chamber of commerce** in your town or city. This group, to which the business people in the area belong, exists to promote the area as a good place to shop and do business. It may have public relations materials that will help you. It is also a source of speakers for your DE classes and DECA meetings. Other groups of business people—such as the Rotary, Kiwanis, and Lions Clubs—may also be able to help you get information.

Writing to Companies That Interest You

Many large companies are willing to send you their own public relations materials about jobs. So if you are interested not only in a particular field but also in a particular company, you should write to the company. Generally you can get the address of the company's main office from one of its local offices.

Learning About Labor Unions

Among the important labor unions in marketing are the Retail Clerks International Association; the Retail, Wholesale, & Department Store Union; and the Service Employees International Union. Labor unions also have public relations departments, whose job is to inform the public about the union and its activities. The unions provide another source of information to help you discover what the trends and possibilities are in the area that interests you.

Talking With People About What They Do

It is a good idea to make a practice of talking with the people you know about what they do. This is one of the most direct ways of finding out what jobs are like. Ask your parents, relatives, and friends what they do and how they feel about their jobs. If they are dissatisfied, see if you can figure out why. Did they have less chance of making good because they didn't have enough or the right kind of education? Are they unhappy because their jobs are not really good ones? Or is their problem that the job was never right for them in the first place? If they are pleased with their jobs, find out why this is the case.

By benefiting from other people's experiences in this way, you may be able to save yourself from making costly mistakes. However, you have to keep in mind that people can have very different reactions to the same situations. One person may especially like what another

You can learn many things that will help you in making career decisions by talking with people you know about the work they do. (*Courtesy Bauder School of Fashion*)

person is violently against. So when you are trying to learn from other people, remember to keep in mind the personal characteristics of the person you are talking to. Remember too that the same kind of job can be different in different companies. This will help you to keep a sense of balance when you are trying to judge what your own possibilities for success are.

Checking the News Sources

A very important source of information about jobs and careers is the daily newspaper. Reading the want ads regularly is an excellent way to keep your finger on the pulse of jobs in your area. The want ads placed by employers and employment agencies tell you what kinds of positions are open, what wages and salaries are being paid, and what qualifications are expected. There are also want ads placed by people who are looking for jobs. These too can teach you a great deal about the current job situation in your area.

The news columns of the newspaper also give you much-needed information about jobs. You will learn whether business is good or bad in general and what is happening in specific areas. You will learn about new governmental regulations that affect business, new labor contracts, and new businesses that are opening in your area. These are examples of the kinds of information you get from newspapers that help you make judgments about the job situation. You can get these same kinds of information from news magazines and radio and television news and talk shows.

LEARNING MORE ABOUT YOURSELF

One of the main aims of this book was to set you thinking about yourself in new ways so you could appreciate that you are a special person with much to offer. But what you have learned about yourself in this course should be only a beginning for you. One thing that is especially important for you to realize is that you are growing and changing all the time. In the plans that you make for yourself, you have to leave room for this growth. You want to make plans for the kind of person you are going to become as well as the person that you know yourself to be now.

One way to go on learning about yourself is to have the courage to try new things. Some people are very afraid of anything that is new, possibly because they fear failure or rejection. But the only way to expand your interests and abilities is to reach out beyond what you are already doing. You are your own main resource for building a career. It is just as important to know what you are not good at as what you excel at. This is what you can find out by stretching your horizons.

You can make sure that the time you spend in school isn't wasted by checking out the courses that are available and selecting a program that is right for you. (*National Education Association*)

LEARNING MORE ABOUT YOUR RESOURCES

Besides yourself, you have some other important resources to help you in building a career. However, these resources require two things from you. You have to know what they are, and you also have to know how to use them to the best advantage. The five areas that are important to you are (1) the course selection at your school, (2) your school personnel, (3) post-high school possibilities, (4) scholarship and aid programs, and (5) help from family, friends, and the community.

Understanding the Course Selection at Your School

Your high school is set up so that it offers certain courses. It is important for you to know not only what these courses are called but also what their content is. Then you can decide which courses are right for you. In most schools, you choose your courses by talking first with your guidance counselor and then with your parents. In some cases, this process of choosing a course of study is helped along by a printed listing of all the school's offerings. But even with such a list, you still have to be sure that you understand the facts about each course. When you do, you can make your choice on the basis of what you want and need. Then, when you graduate, you won't have any regrets about what you have missed.

Knowing Your School Personnel

There are a number of people in your school who are directly interested in helping you plan your future. These people include your teachers, particularly the DE teacher-coordinator, who has to be very well informed about the job opportunities in your area. Your guidance counselor is also there to help you and has the best chance of doing so when you make the effort to be informed. Many schools also have occupation specialists and placement counselors, who can see to it that you get the right information about the career area that interests you. They may also be able to place you in a job.

Checking Post-High School Possibilities

There are many young people who just assume that they will have to stop their formal schooling when they receive their high school diplomas. It is one thing to stop your schooling because you have decided on the basis of the facts, that this is the right thing for you to do. But is is another thing to stop your schooling because you don't know that there are other possibilities.

Your family's financial situation may make it impossible for you to consider going to a four-year college where you have to live at the school. But there are many ways of going to school that cost much less than that. There are colleges in many areas now where you can go to school without paying any tuition charges or by paying very little. You can go to these schools and live at home, which is much less expensive. You can get a part-time job in the evenings and on weekends to pay for your books, transportation, and other needs. There are co-op programs in some of these schools, where the idea of earning while learning is built into the curriculum.

Another possibility for continuing your education is to get a job during the day and go to school at night. There are many schools that have low-cost night school programs. In order to take advantage of any of these possibilities, you have to know exactly what is available in your community. What kinds of schools are there and what do they offer? Until you know this, you can't be sure whether or not you want to go further with school.

Researching Scholarship and Aid Programs

Your feelings about whether or not to get more schooling might be different if you understood all the possibilities for getting financial help. Many colleges award scholarships on the basis of financial need and academic promise. There are also many companies that offer scholarships so the daughters and sons of their employees can attend the

There are many possibilities for scholarships and financial aid. Before giving up the idea of going to college, look into the opportunities available to you. *(Courtesy Chemetron Corporation)*

schools of their own choice. Many civic organizations offer help to young people who want to go on to school. Sometimes this help is fairly modest, in the neighborhood of $100 to $200. But this can be enough to buy books and supplies in a school where there are no tuition fees.

The problem with scholarships and aid programs is that you must know about them in order to apply for them. The people who want to give these awards are generally in touch with the schools. If you are in touch with your school too and are making a point of reading the bulletin boards and talking regularly with your teachers and counselors, you will get the necessary information.

Assessing Help from Family, Friends, and the Community

In planning your future, whether you decide to go for more schooling or get a job immediately, you should plan to take advantage of any help that your family, friends, and the community can give you. Sometimes young people think that it is wrong to let anybody help them in any way. They think they must make it on their own or not at all. But there is nothing wrong with getting job leads or introductions from relatives, friends, or people that you know in the community. Sometimes companies don't want to advertise for help because they don't want to take the time to interview and screen all the people who apply. In this case, they may be counting on their employees to spread the word about job openings. But it is wise to remember that no matter whose friend you are, the company is not going to hire you or keep you once you are hired if you are not qualified.

Your family can also be an important plus for you if you want to continue your schooling. Sometimes families aren't able to give any financial help, but what they *can* give is encouragement. This is a simple but priceless resource.

- **BUILDING YOUR MARKETING VOCABULARY**

   Define each of the following terms and then use each one in a sentence.

   chamber of commerce   trade association

- **UNDERSTANDING WHAT YOU HAVE READ**

   1. Why is it a good idea to read the bulletin boards in your school's guidance or placement office regularly?
   2. What is a career night and how can it help you in planning your own career?
   3. What is your main resource for building a career?
   4. Why do companies sometimes not advertise when they need help?

- **APPLYING WHAT YOU HAVE LEARNED**

   1. With the other members of your class, prepare a directory of the personnel and facilities that your school provides to help you with career selection. Find out what hours each person or place can be visited, whether advance appointments are necessary, and what kind of assistance is offered.
   2. Write to one trade association or company that interests you, requesting career-related materials.
   3. In the newspaper, find an account of a current event that affects business or the general economic situation. Bring the news item to class and be prepared to discuss how newspapers can give you valuable career information.
   4. Assist in a class project to identify the scholarship and aid programs in your community. Your school guidance office can help you carry out this project.

part 38 Developing a Personal Career Plan

After reading Part 38, you will be able—
- To list five advantages of setting a long-range career goal at this point in your life.
- To list three advantages of eliminating from your thinking the jobs that are obviously wrong for you.
- To explain what the idea of painting yourself into a corner has to do with career selection.

Understanding what you have to work with is a necessary part of decision making, but it is, of course, only the beginning. Once you have the information that you need about jobs, yourself, and your other resources, your next step is to use this information to develop a personal career plan. The emphasis here is on the word "personal," because you don't want this to be anybody's plan but your own. This doesn't mean that you shouldn't seek advice from the people you trust, because good advice can be a valuable resource for you. But advice is only a recommendation. Your family, friends, and school personnel can recommend, but *you* are the one who actually has to make the decision and take the course of action.

In this part, we are going to look at some of the things that you have to think about in developing your own career plan.

TAKING RESPONSIBILITY FOR YOUR CHOICES

The right to make your own decisions carries an obligation with it. You have to be prepared to take the responsibility for whatever you decide. When things go right, taking the responsibility is no problem. Then your decision becomes a credit to you. It is much more difficult to accept responsibility when things go wrong. But there is a real advantage in doing so. Instead of wasting time and effort finding someone else to blame, you can get right to the point of figuring out what is wrong and why. Then you can spend your time where it counts, on working to make things right.

Your ability to accept responsibility is a measure of your maturity. You will find that the more responsibility you accept, the more you will

Accepting the responsibility for things you do, whether they turn out to be wrong or right, is a mark of maturity. (© 1962 United Feature Syndicate)

be given. Your family, teachers, and counselors will be much more willing to let you make your own decisions if they see that you understand what that means.

APPRECIATING THE VALUE OF A HEAD START

Some young people begin their search for a job and a career *after* they have finished school. This is just as true of college graduates as it is of high school graduates. They see themselves stopping school and starting a job, as though one had nothing to do with the other. Then they are surprised when they have to settle for any job that they can get instead of being able to choose the job that they want. This leads to the kind of worker dissatisfaction that is bad for both the employee and the employer and that infects the whole business community.

This is the kind of trap that you can avoid. You have already gotten a head start on building a satisfying career. You have recognized that it is possible to *choose* your career rather than relying on luck. It is interesting that people always speak of "dumb" luck, using an adjective that means "markedly lacking in intelligence." People also speak of "blind" chance and "fickle" fate. This points up that anyone who expects major problems to be solved by luck, chance, fate, or any other form of nonreason is taking a great deal of risk. Just recognizing that you don't have to take this risk is a major step in itself. But you now also have a head start on getting the facts about yourself and about careers so you can match the two in the most appropriate way.

The head start that you have gotten this year means that the rest of your high school years will be a time of preparing rather than just waiting. You can get ready in a quite specific way for whatever you want to do after high school. This puts you way ahead of the person who thinks that tomorrow is time enough to start planning.

MAKING A DECISION ABOUT MARKETING

When you are thinking about the direction you want to take, your first decision is whether or not to go on with the study of marketing. This book was designed to let you explore the idea of a marketing career by showing you what a broad field it is, how many different kinds of career opportunities it offers, and how DE can prepare you directly for it. But it has been assumed from the beginning of the course that you would use this information to reach *your own* decision.

If you do want to go on with your study of marketing, you can move directly into the DE program. There you will find that the broad picture of marketing you have gotten this year has given you a firm base on which to build future knowledge. You will be able to get down to the details of marketing much more quickly because of what you have learned this year. However, if you have decided that you would rather study something else, it is important for you to know that your time this year has not been wasted.

By exploring a field as broad as marketing and deciding against it, you are ahead of where you were when you started. When you are trying to plan for your career, it can be as important to know what you don't want to do as what you do want. Besides, what you have learned this year can help you in whatever career you choose. This is because there is some kind of marketing angle to most jobs. For example, doctors, lawyers, and other professional people have to market their services in many of the same ways that any service business does. Likewise, the school principal who wants to present a proposal to the Board of Education has to know how to sell it. And we all have to sell ourselves and our ideas in many social as well as business situations. Your study of marketing has also taught you to be a better-informed, more careful consumer, and that will help you for the rest of your life.

TRYING TO SET A LONG-RANGE GOAL

The only decision that you have to make at this point is whether or not to go on with the study of marketing. But it may be that you are now ready to take a major step beyond that. As you were working with

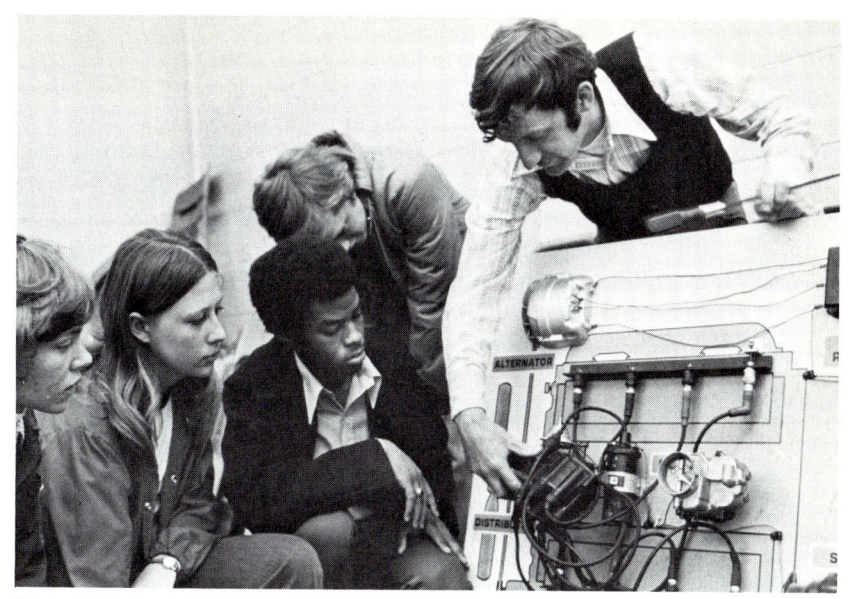

Knowing about the kinds of career opportunities in the field of marketing automotive products could help a person interested in mechanics to set a long-range career goal. (*National Education Association*)

Parts 20–36, where you learned about the different kinds of marketing businesses, you were encouraged to think about yourself in relation to the advantages and disadvantages of various kinds of jobs. These parts were planned to start you thinking about which jobs match your personal characteristics, your values, and the kind of life style you want for yourself.

By thinking about what the various kinds of jobs in marketing offer you and what they demand from you, you may have been able to make a fairly specific career choice within the field of marketing. Perhaps you have such a definite leaning in one direction that you know exactly what you want to do. For example, you may be so interested in high fashion and so talented along those lines that you know that you want to become a fashion coordinator for a department store. Or perhaps you don't know exactly what you want to do. But you do know that you would like to work in a particular kind of job, such as a selling, driving, or marketing research job, or in a particular area of marketing, such as food stores or floristry.

Making this kind of decision early gives you a long-range goal to work toward. This provides you with a way of directing your actions and turning your ideas about yourself into reality. The special value of long-range goals is that they make it much easier for you to set short-range and intermediate goals. For example, your immediate task is to make a decision about the courses you will take for the rest of your

PART 38 • DEVELOPING A PERSONAL CAREER PLAN • 459

high school years. Assuming that you have decided to take DE, you still have other choices to make. If you have a definite long-range goal, you will find that these choices are much easier to make.

For example, if you are interested in a job in the control area of marketing, you will want to take bookkeeping. Or perhaps you will want to supplement your DE program with art courses because you are interested in display or advertising. Home economics can help to prepare you for a career as an apparel buyer. Industrial arts can help you if you are interested in the automotive or hardware business.

Having a long-range goal will also help you get the most out of the DE program. When you have a choice of projects in your DE classes or in DECA, you can choose the one that fits in best with your long-range goal. Also, if your DE coordinator knows what you are trying to do, she or he will take this into consideration when assigning your cooperative work experience. You may not be able to work in the exact area you are interested in. But your assignment can be one that will be helpful to you in developing the skills you will need.

The often-difficult decision about whether or not to go on with your studies after high school will also be easier if you have a long-range career goal. By making this decision early, you can be sure you are meeting the requirements for the kind of school you hope to attend. Then you won't find, as a senior, that you are missing the credits that you need. If you are planning to go directly to work, an early decision is equally helpful in letting you plan the courses that will best prepare you for what you want to do.

NARROWING DOWN THE ALTERNATIVES

Although there is no doubt that setting long-range goals early has many advantages, don't worry if you are unable to make a career choice at this time. Making a specific choice is harder for some people than for others, so there is nothing wrong with being one of the people who needs more time. However, there is one thing that you almost certainly can do and that is to rule out the kinds of jobs that are obviously wrong for you. For example, if you are the kind of person who needs a lot of physical activity, you will want to eliminate the jobs where you have to sit at a desk for the entire working day. As another example, if you have only a limited aptitude for data, you can rule out many of the jobs in banking and insurance that call for an exceptionally high ability with figures.

Once you have scratched off the jobs that are out of the question for you, you will have a list that is much easier to deal with. You will also know which courses you don't want to take and which projects you don't want to work on. This does not mean that you can skip

If you cannot make a specific career choice now, you can narrow down the alternatives. For example, people who are extremely active might want to rule out jobs that require them to sit at a desk all day. (Edahl/ Editorial Photocolor Archives)

learning the basic skills or getting the broad base of knowledge that makes the difference between the ignorant person and the educated one. But it does mean that you have a sense of direction that will help you in your final career choice. By eliminating from your thinking the jobs for which you are not suited, you are narrowing down the possible alternatives and making your ultimate decision that much easier.

KEEPING YOUR OPTIONS OPEN

If you were painting a floor, you wouldn't be so careless as to paint yourself into a corner so you couldn't get out of the room. When you are preparing for a career, you don't want to paint yourself into a corner either. To put this another way, you want to be sure that you are not locking any doors behind you that you will someday wish you had left open.

If you go into the DE program, you will be opening doors rather than locking them. If you have not yet been able to make a career choice, you will find that DE will give you more information about what marketing jobs are like. It will also give you many opportunities to find out more about yourself by letting you try your hand at different marketing skills. Meanwhile, you can keep your options for your future completely open by choosing other courses that will give you the kind of broad background that can apply to anything you eventually want to do. An example of this kind of subject is personal selling, which can

If you take the time now to check out potential careers, when you graduate from high school you'll know exactly where you are going. *(Edahl/Editorial Photocolor Archives)*

help you in almost any marketing job that you choose, as well as in many jobs in other fields. Another example of a subject that is generally useful is economics, where you learn basic business principles. Such subjects as these give you a sound foundation on which to build many kinds of careers.

DE also leaves the door open for those people who already have definite ideas about their futures. Because you are still growing and changing, you may change your mind about what you want to do. If so, there will be many directions in which you can move. The more you study DE, the more you will see how closely the various parts of marketing are related to each other. This is not a field that has clear-cut distinctions. The skills that you learn in preparing for or doing one job are easily transferred to other jobs.

Knowing this may make it less frightening for you to make a career choice. You don't have to feel that you are making a once-in-a-lifetime decision that you will be stuck with for all your working days. If your needs, values, and goals change—as they probably will—you will find that marketing gives you the freedom to choose another direction without having to go back and start all over. Instead of finding yourself in the corner with no way to get out without ruining the paint job, you will be right by an open door.

- **UNDERSTANDING WHAT YOU HAVE READ**

    1. What obligation do you have to accept if you want the right to make your own decisions?
    2. List five advantages of setting a long-range career goal at this point in your life.
    3. List three advantages of eliminating from your thinking the jobs that are obviously wrong for you.
    4. Explain what the idea of painting yourself into a corner has to do with career selection.
    5. Suppose that you choose to study marketing at this point, and at some time in the future you find that your needs, values, and goals have changed. Will you have to start over? Explain your answer.

- **APPLYING WHAT YOU HAVE LEARNED**

    1. In Units 4 and 5, you thought about the requirements for the various kinds of marketing jobs. On the basis of what you have learned, list ten requirements that all marketing jobs share. Use your own list as a preparation for a class discussion that seeks to draw up a master list of requirements that the entire class agrees on. Here is an example to start your thinking: All marketing workers are expected to be interested in their jobs. As a conclusion to this project, the class should decide which of the requirements on the master list apply to all jobs, not just to marketing jobs.
    2. Copy the list of requirements that the class has drawn up. Put a line through the requirements that you don't meet now and don't care to meet. Put a check beside the requirements that you are already able to meet and a star beside the ones that you would be willing to work to fulfill.

EXPERIMENTS IN MARKETING

From the three projects suggested, choose the one that reflects your present thinking.

1. If you have decided not to continue your study of marketing, make a scrapbook of 25 nonmarketing jobs, using pictures that you have cut out of magazines and newspapers. For each job, think of one way in which a knowledge of marketing can help the worker to do a better job. Write your suggestions beneath each picture.
2. If you are interested in a particular job in marketing, do additional research on what the job is like. Ask your teacher or school librarian to help you look up the job in *The Dictionary of Occupational Titles,* and use other materials as recommended in Part 37. When you have finished your research, answer the following questions in detail:
   a. How does this job match your (1) physical characteristics, (2) aptitudes, (3) interests, (4) personality traits, (5) values, (6) goals, (7) standards, and (8) desired life style?
   b. What other advantages does this job offer that are important to you?
   c. Are you aware of the disadvantages of the job? What are they, and why are you willing to accept them?
   d. What are the requirements for the job? As you list each one, indicate where you are now in terms of the requirement and what you still must do to meet it.
   e. Once you get this job, where can you go from there?
3. You may want to go on with your study of DE but have not been able to settle on a particular part of marketing. In this case, write a report on how you arrived at your decision. List all the facts about marketing that made you decide that this was the right alternative for *you,* considering your own personal characteristics, values, and goals. Also, discuss any speakers or other experiences during the course that helped you make up your mind. As a conclusion for your report, state which areas of marketing you have been able to eliminate from your thinking.

INDEX

Accessories, apparel and, 239–254
Accounting services, 377, 381
Actuaries, 428, 434
Advertising:
 definition of, 23
 as expense, 159
 practice through DECA, 195
 truth in, 47–48
 (*See also* career discussion for each marketing area)
Advertising agencies, 377–378, 381, 383
Airplanes, 398, 402–403
Amusement parks, 386–387
Antique stores, 262–263
Apparel and accessories, 239–254
Appearance, 61, 88, 199, 250
Application for employment, 201
Appraisers, 439
Aptitude, 90–91, 121, 126, 195
Artists, 252, 270, 332, 381
As-is policy, 44
Assemblers, 13–14
Attitudes, 61, 93–94, 201
Auto-driving schools, 367
Automatic vending machines, 345
Automobile dealers, 304–306
Automotive products, 294–307
 automobile and truck dealers, 304–306
 oil products wholesalers, 302–303
 parts and accessories dealers, 306–307
 service stations, 295–302

Baggers, 218
Bank officers, 420–421
Banks, 25, 415–423
Barber shops, 164, 178, 277, 362, 365, 367, 368
Barges, 398–400
Basic skills, 144–151
Beauty dealers, 277
Beauty salons, 164, 178, 277, 362, 365, 367, 368
Bell captain, 358
Bellhop, 355, 357, 358
Boutiques, 242, 260, 319
Bowling alleys, 386
Branch offices, 381, 416, 418
Branch stores, 243, 261, 315, 326
Brand names, 27
Bridal consultant, 253
Brokers, 288
 insurance, 431–432
 real estate, 436
Budget, 184, 348, 385

Building supplies, hardware and, 322–334
Bulk breaking, 226
Bus drivers, 408–409
Buses, 398, 402
Business services, 373–384, 418–419
 (*See also* specific service)
Buyer training programs, 248, 268, 282, 291, 330
Buyers:
 definition of, 233–234
 (*See also* career discussion for each marketing area)
Buying:
 as area of concern, 183
 as business expense, 157
 importance in marketing, 20–21
 (*See also* career discussion for each marketing area)
Buying motives, 187–190, 192, 265
Buying offices, 247

Cafeteria service, 341, 346
Campgrounds, 386
Career:
 decisions concerning, 119–121
 defined and explained, 61–64
 marketing, 121–127, 458
Career ladders, 62–64
Career lattices, 64
Career-level jobs:
 definition of, 63
 (*See also* career discussion for each marketing area)
"Career nights," 447
Career plan, personal, 456
Carhops, 342, 347
Carryout clerks, 218
Cash-and-carry stores, 244
Cashier:
 lattice-type moves, 64
 (*See also* career discussion for each marketing area)
Catalog discount showrooms, 261–262
Catalog retailing, 244, 251, 261, 288, 312, 315, 326
Catering services, 339, 344–345
Chain department stores, national, 243, 261, 288, 306, 312, 326
Chamber of commerce, 449
Channels of distribution, 11–14
Charge accounts, 155, 417
Checking accounts, 416–417
Chefs, 346
Claims adjuster, 433
Claims approver, 433
Claims clerk, 270, 408
Claims examiner, 433
Cleaning services, 366, 374–375, 382, 383
Collection agencies, 377

INDEX • 465

Commission: 123, 249, 280, 302, 395, 432, 436
Common carriers, 404, 409
Communication skills, 144–148
Comparison shopping, 46, 251
Compartmentalization, 117
Competition:
  benefits for public, 33, 35–40
  definition of, 33
  effect on prices, 160–161
  government efforts to preserve, 34
Compromise, 117
Computerized cash register, 194, 220
Conductors, train, 407
Consensus, 117
Consumer affairs specialist, 237, 304
Consumer finance companies, 425–426
Consumer products, 16
Consumer resistance, 160–161
Consumerism, 43, 49–50, 215
Consumers:
  channels of distribution to, 10–14
  definition of, 4
  industrial, 16
  ultimate, 11
Containers, 401–402
Control division, 185, 252, 299
Controlled economy, 30
Controller, 237, 271, 357, 420
Convenience stores, 216, 221–223
Cooperative chains, 171, 217, 229, 234, 278
Cooperative education, 136–137, 197–205, 253, 300, 313, 453, 460
Cooperatives, 169, 312, 423
Copywriters, 252, 270, 381
Corporate chains:
  decentralization in, 230
  definition of, 170–172
  organizational plan, 185
  (*See also* career discussion for each marketing area)
Corporations, 167–168
Counter service, 342
Counter worker, 305, 347
Credit:
  careers in, 415–425
  cost of, to marketers, 157–158
  definition of, 47
  role in marketing, 414–415
Credit cards, 357, 423–424
Credit collectors, 382
Credit services, 377
Customer complaints, 183
Customer service representatives, 411–412, 425
Customers, differences in, 155, 177–181, 241, 340
Customs, 79–80

Dancing schools, 386
DE (*see* Distributive Education)
Dealer-owned wholesaler, 326
Debts, business, liability for, 165–167
Decision making:
  personal, 107–116
  social, 116–117
Delivery service:
  parcel, by airlines, 402
  by retail stores, 221, 409
  ways of paying for, 5–6
  workers, 270, 318, 369
Demand, supply and, laws of, 32–33
Department stores:
  apparel and accessories in, 242
  automotive products in, 306
  definition of, 185
  hardware and building supplies in, 326
  health and beauty products in, 276
  home furnishings in, 261
  leisure-time goods in, 288
  nursery and garden supplies in, 315
  organization of, 184–185
Departmentalized specialty stores, 242–243, 259, 261, 276
Designers, 332
Detail salesworkers, 281
Detective agencies, 366–367
Detectives, 360, 375, 392
Dictionary of Occupational Titles (DOT), 88, 405, 448
Direct marketing:
  by catalog, 12, 244
  definition of, 11–12
  direct to home, 12
  through producer-owned stores, 12, 17–18, 242
  by producers to industrial consumers, 278, 328, 334
Direct selling, 244–245, 263–264, 276, 280
Discount, 157
Discount drugstores, 275
Discount food stores, 215
Discount stores, 178–180, 244, 261, 276, 288, 306, 315, 326
Discretionary income, 188
Discrimination (*see* Prejudice)
Dispatchers, 237, 303, 409
Display:
  artist, 266, 268–269
  definition of, 23
  as expense, 159
  experts, 237, 251–252, 293
  jobs in, 292, 299, 304, 313, 332
  practice through DECA, 195
Disposable income, 188
Distribution, 11

466 · INDEX

Distributive Education (DE):
  definition of, 134
  emphasis on economic facts, 154
  getting the most out of the program, 460
  high school program, 135–137
  post-high school programs, 138, 233
  practice in basic skills, 145, 149
  practice in social skills, 151–152
  preparation for jobs, 205, 266, 329, 435
  preparation for marketing career, 458
  source of speakers for, 449
Distributive Education Clubs of America (DECA), 138–142
  Career Development Conference, 141
  competitions sponsored by, 141, 190, 192, 195
  getting the most out of the program, 460
  how organized, 138–139
  program of, 140–142
  source of speakers for, 449
  state conferences of, 141
Dividends, 423
Drive-in service, 37, 342, 417
Driving ranges, 386
Drugstores, 274–275, 278–280, 282
Dry cleaners, 164, 362, 365

Ecology, 309, 319, 440
Economy, 30
Employment services, 366, 375–376
Entertainment and performing jobs, 360, 393
Entry-level jobs:
  definition of, 61
  (*See also* career discussion for each marketing area)
Environment:
  influence on individual, 78–84
  preservation of, 50, 304
Equal employment opportunities, 127–129
Equal Employment Opportunity Commission (EEOC), 127
Exchange policy, 44, 157
Expenses, marketing, 155–160, 180
Exporters, 418
Express, 399, 402, 409

Factory outlet stores, 244
Farm supply stores, 311–312
Farmers, 11–12, 227, 310–313
Fashion, 240, 251, 253, 259, 289
Fashion coordinator, 185, 252, 459
Fast-food business, 341, 342
Field offices, 431
Field representatives, 235

Finance and credit:
  commercial banks, 415–423
  credit card companies, 423–425
  importance of, 414–415
  sales and consumer finance, 425–426
  specialized banking, 423
Financial records, 26, 184, 300, 348, 357
"Fishyback" service, 401
Five-and-ten-cent stores, 243, 263
Flight attendants, 407
Floral designers, 318
Floriculture, 319
Floristry, 309, 317–320
Food processors, 224, 227
Food services, 338–349
Food stores, 210–223
Food wholesaling:
  careers in, 232–237
  cooperative chains, 229
  corporate chain methods, 228, 230
  and food costs, 225–227
  rack jobbers, 231
  specialty wholesalers, 230–231
  truck jobbers, 231–232
  unaffiliated wholesalers, 230
  voluntary chains, 229
Foreign language, need for, 357, 397, 406, 407, 421
Franchised chain, 172, 217, 242, 271, 275, 348, 370, 381
Franchised dealers, 172–173, 288, 304, 311, 314
Franchising, 172, 298, 307, 327, 342, 351, 384, 393
Free enterprise, 30–31
Freight, 399, 400, 402, 409
Freight agent, 406
Freight forwarders, 411
Fringe benefits:
  in businesses, 217, 233, 349, 423
  considered as pay, 163
  cost of, 157
  definition of, 123
Frustration, 73–74
Full-service wholesalers, 227
Funeral homes, 367

Garden supplies and equipment, 314–317
Garden supply store, 315
General merchandise:
  in catalog discount showrooms, 262
  in food wholesaling, 229
General merchandise discount stores (*see* Discount stores)
General merchandise stores:
  apparel and accessories in, 242–243
  automotive products in, 306
  catalog discount showrooms, 261–262
  definition of, 243

INDEX • 467

General merchandise stores (Cont.)
  department stores (see Department stores)
  departmentalized specialty stores (see Departmentalized specialty stores)
  discount stores (see Discount stores)
  farm and garden supplies in, 312, 315
  food service in, 339
  hardware and building supplies in, 326
  health and beauty products in, 276
  home furnishings in, 261
  junior department stores, 243, 261, 288
  leisure-time goods in, 288
  variety drugstores, 275
  variety stores (see Variety stores)
General stores, 311
Generalizing, 108–109
Goals:
  definition of, 97
  influence on career choice, 121
  possible changes in, 462
  types of, 459–462
  ways of achieving, 102–105
Goods, 6–7, 20
  definition of, 5
  getting to ultimate consumer, 10–14
  planning what to sell, 178
  quantity buying for savings, 170–171, 217
  transporting, 400–403
Governmental publications, 448
Government's role in marketing:
  assistance to businesses, 34–35
  charters, 167, 169, 415
  differences of opinion over, 50–51
  licenses, 348, 367, 432, 433, 441
  regulation of businesses, 34–35, 43, 46, 48, 160
Grading, 26
Gross pay, 162
Guarantees, 43–45
Guards, 375, 383–384, 392, 421
Guidance counselors, 453, 447–448

Hardware and building supplies, 322–334
Hardware stores, 13, 16, 315, 324–325, 329–331
Headwaiter/hostess, 347
Health and beauty products, 273–283
Health care industry, 278
Health clubs, 365
Health habits, 88, 205
Heredity, 77–78
Home furnishings, 256–271
Home furnishings counselors, 268
Home study courses, 223, 329, 355, 421
Hostess/headwaiter, 347
Hotels and motels, 351–361
Household services, 366

Housekeeping jobs, 358–359
Housewares, 257, 324
Housing starts, definition of, 323
Human relations, 152

Ideals, 101
Image, 177–181, 204, 340, 378
Importers, 246, 265, 288, 418
Indirect marketing, 14
Industrial consumers, 16
Industrial distributors, 16, 277
Industrial products, 16
Industrial Revolution, 3–4
Insurance, 26, 427–435
Insurance agent, 18, 431–432
Insurance brokers, 431–432
Intangibles, 5, 431
Intelligence, 89, 121
Intelligence tests, 89–90
Interest on money, 157, 417
Interests, 91–92, 121, 126, 289, 371
Interior architects, 332, 380–381
Interior decorators, 262, 266, 268–269, 381
International banking, 418, 421
Interview, job, 198–202
Inventory, 183, 261, 326, 328

Job, 59–61
Job interview, 198–202
Jobber, 298, 315–316
Junior department store, 243, 261, 288

Kitchen helpers, 346

Labeling, 28, 46
Labor, cost of, 157, 161–162
Labor relations experts, 237, 360
Labor unions, 157, 428, 450
Laundries, 164, 362, 365, 375
Layout artist, 270
Layouts, 180–181
Lease, definition of, 437
Leisure-time goods, 284–293
Liability for business debts, 165–167
Life style, 84, 121, 234, 343, 356
Limited-line stores, 212, 242, 259–260, 286–287, 306
Limousines, 398, 404
Line and staff organization, 185–186
Line organization, 185–186
Linen supply companies, 375, 382, 383
Lines, manufacturers', 247, 264
Listings, real estate, 436
Lumberyards, 325, 332

Machines, marketing, 194
Mail, 193, 399
Mailing lists, 379

Maintenance jobs (*See also* career discussion for each marketing area)
Maintenance services, 374–375
Malls, 40
Management:
  definition of, 175
  dividing the responsibilities, 184–186
  five areas of businesses, 182–184
  planning image for business, 177–182
Management assistance to retailers:
  by cooperative chains, 171, 229
  by corporate chains, 170–171, 228
  by franchised chains, 172
  in franchised dealerships, 172–173
  by service wholesalers, 227, 277, 302–303
  by unaffiliated wholesalers, 230, 234–235
  by voluntary chains, 171–172, 229, 234–235
Management consulting services, 379, 381
Management experts, 237, 304, 360
Management-level jobs:
  definition of, 63
  (*See also* career discussion for each marketing area)
Management training programs, 250, 282, 290, 330, 420, 426
Managers (*see* Middle managers; Top managers)
Manufacturer's representatives, 246, 288
Market weeks, 246, 264
Marketing:
  advantages of careers in, 62–64, 121–126
  advantages of studying, 120
  angle to other jobs, 458
  benefits to public, 35–40
  definition of, 8
  disadvantages of careers in, 127
  government's role in (*see* Government's role in marketing)
  history of, 5–6
  honesty in, 42–48
  need for different people, 122
  personal responsibility for, 48–51
Marketing research, 28, 140, 195, 379–384
Marketing research workers, 185, 237, 384, 421
Marketing skills, 187–195, 461
Marts, 264
Masonry supply outlets, 332
Mass production, 4, 5, 341
Materials handling, 237
Mathematical skills, 149–151
Maturity, 107–111
Meat wrappers, 218, 220

Mechanics, 111, 292, 299, 305, 313, 382, 405, 433
Mechanization:
  of offices, 26, 236, 333, 434
  of routine marketing jobs, 125
  of warehouses, 232, 235, 246, 269, 331
Media, 82, 392
Merchandise (*see* Goods)
Merchandising, 183, 234, 299
Merchant wholesalers, 13
Middle-management trainees, 138
Middle managers, 59, 184, 223, 237, 393
Middlemen:
  definition of, 13
  food wholesalers as, 225
  identifying by customers, 14–16
  in sale of services, 18
Models, 251
Modified free enterprise, 31–35, 136
Monopoly, 35, 46–47
Mortgage companies, 440–441
Mortgages, 417, 440–441
Motels and hotels, 351–361
Multiunit independents, 170, 330
Mutual savings banks, 423

Needs:
  as buying motives, 187–188, 240, 256, 273, 274, 278, 437
  definition of, 67
  future changes in, 462
  how work can satisfy, 75
  influence on career choice, 121
  list of basic human, 67–71
  order of satisfaction, 71–73
  and reimbursement for work, 124
Nurseries and garden supply stores, 314–317

Occupation specialists, 453
Occupational Outlook Handbook, 448–449
Office jobs:
  classified as nonmarketing, 220
  (*See also* career discussion for each marketing area)
Operations, 183, 185, 252, 282, 299
Options, 84–85, 393, 461
Order assemblers, 235, 292
Order checkers, 332
Order pickers, 235, 332
Overtime, 123

Package design, 195, 378
Packaging, 29, 282
Packers, 235, 292, 332
Paraprofessional, definition of, 59
Parking lot attendants, 357–358
Parking lots and garages, 367

Parliamentary procedure, 141
Partnerships, 165–167
Parts and accessories retailers, 306–307
Parts and accessories wholesalers, 306–307
Party plan, 264
Passenger service representative, 407
Performing and entertainment jobs, 360, 393
Personal data sheet, 199–200
Personal service businesses, 362–372
Personality traits, 94, 121
Personnel, 183, 185, 252, 299, 360, 396
Petroleum bulk stations, 302, 304
Pharmacists, registered, 274, 276, 279
Photographers, 252, 270, 366, 367, 369
Photography studios, 366
Physical demands of jobs, 88
Piggybacking, 401
Pipelines, 398, 403
Placement counselors, 453
Placement office, school, 447–448
Policies, 44–45, 178, 202, 216
    fair price, 45–47
Policy, insurance, 427–428
Porters, 357–358
Prejudice, 80–81, 127–129, 379
Prescription department, 274, 276
Prices:
    differences in stores, 155
    fair price policies, 45–47
    fixing, 47
    how marketing keeps down, 37
    in low-overhead stores, 178–179, 244, 261, 275
    raising, to increase profits, 160–161
Printers, 382
Printing services, 376
Private carriers, 404
Producers:
    definition of, 4
    as store owners, 12, 17–18
    use of channels of distribution, 10–14
Product knowledge, 190, 191, 250, 265, 286, 305, 314, 316, 318, 329
Product planning, 28
Professional, definition of, 59
Professional drugstores, 274
Profit:
    definition of, 31
    division of, in business organizations, 165–169
    expenses that affect, 155–160
    how to increase, 160–162
    as a motive, 31–32
Program wholesaler, 326, 331
Projects in DE program, 136
Property insurance, 428–430
Property management, 440
Property transactions, 438

Protection jobs (see Guards; Security services)
Psychology, 151
Public relations:
    definition of, 24
    as expense, 159
    jobs, 251–252, 292, 391–392, 396, 407, 421, 435
    practice through DECA, 195
Public relations companies, 378–379
Purchasing agent, 345–346, 360, 390, 405, 421

Quality standards, 45, 51

Rack jobber, 231, 277, 281
Railroads, 398, 400
Real estate:
    careers in, 435–442
    jobs with other marketers, 237, 304, 360
    property management jobs, 440
Real estate agents, 436–439
Real estate brokers, 436
Real estate counseling, 441
Real estate financing, 440–441
Real estate research, 441
Realtor, definition of, 436
Receiving, 183
Receiving clerks, 235, 292, 332, 405
Receptionists, 368, 370
Recordkeeping, 26
Recreation services, 385–394
Redcaps, 407
Reducing salons, 365
Rental services, 366, 375
Repair services, 365–366
Repairers, 16–17, 146, 270, 288, 292, 358, 367
Reservations agents, 406
Resources, 103–104, 309, 446, 452–455
Restaurants, 338–343, 345–349, 352–359
Retailers:
    as middlemen, 12–13
    management assistance to (see Management assistance to retailers)
Retailing:
    apparel and accessories, 241–245
    as approach to wholesaling jobs, 237
    automotive products, 295–299, 304–307
    floristry, 317–319
    food products, 211–223
    food services, 338–345
    hardware and building supplies, 324–326
    health and beauty products, 274–277
    home furnishings, 259–264
    hotels and motels, 351–354
    leisure-time goods, 286–288

Retailing (*Cont.*)
  nursery and garden supplies, 314–316
  personal services, 362–364
  recreation services, 385–389
  tourism, 394–395
Retailing middlemen:
  customers for, 14
  definition of, 14
  in sale of services, 18
Roles, personal, 109, 112
Room service department, 359
Route workers, 235, 281, 302, 303, 383

Safe deposit boxes, 417
Salary, definition of, 123
Sales branches, 311
Sales engineers, 303, 332
Sales finance companies, 425–426
Sales promotion:
  centralized by corporate chains, 171
  as expense, 159
  importance in marketing, 22–24
  jobs in, 251, 282, 299, 313, 328, 348, 411, 412, 421
Sales promotion services, 378–379
Sales representatives, 302–303, 332
Salesclerks, 250, 266, 279, 288, 299, 313, 318
Salesworkers:
  commission earned by, 249, 280, 302, 395, 432, 436
  differences in, 122
  general qualifications for, 121–122, 146
  importance of product knowledge, 190
  need for, 158
  and personal selling, 190–192
  (*See also* career discussion for each marketing area)
Savings and loan association, 423
Savings accounts, 416–417
Scholarships, 140, 223, 313, 355, 422, 453
School store, 136, 154
Scrambled merchandising, 214, 229, 259, 286, 315
Secondhand stores, 262–263
Secretarial services, 376
Security services, 360, 375, 381
Self-actualization, 73, 75, 195, 240, 256
Self-service:
  definition of, 158
  in food stores, 215
  in health and beauty products, 275, 279
  in home furnishings, 266
  in leisure-time goods, 288, 291
  in parking lots, 367
  in service stations, 296
Selling, nonpersonal, 22–24, 383, 392, 407
Selling, personal:
  five steps in, 190–191
  honesty in, 48

Selling, personal (*Cont.*)
  importance of, in marketing, 22
  practice in DE and DECA, 190–192
  (*See also* career discussion for each marketing area)
Selling jobs (*see* Salesworkers)
Selling price, 154, 417
Semiskilled workers, 59
Service adviser, 306
Service departments, 305, 306, 357–358
Service station attendants, 299–302
Service station manager, 298–299, 302
Service stations, 286, 295–302, 315
Service stores, 212
Service wholesalers, 227, 277, 302–303, 326
Services:
  channels of distribution for, 16–18
  cost of, 157–158
  definition of, 6
  place in marketing, 5–6
  planning which ones to offer, 178–180
  ways of paying for, 5–6
Shipping charges, 157, 170, 226
Shipping clerks, 235, 292, 332, 410
Shipping department, 409–410
Ships, 398–400
Shoe repair shops, 164, 362, 365
Shoplifting, 159
Shopping centers, 39, 243
Showrooms:
  for apparel and accessories, 246–247
  for building supplies, 328, 331
  for home furnishings, 262, 264–265
  for leisure-time goods, 288
Ski areas, 386
Skilled workers, 59, 435
Skills:
  definition of, 92
  ease of transfer in marketing, 125
  influence on careers, 92–93, 121, 126
  practice in school, 204–205
Small loan companies (*see* Consumer finance companies)
Social skills, 151–152
Sole proprietorship, 164–165
Sorting, 26
Specialty food store, 214
Specialty wholesaler, 230–231, 327
Staff specialists:
  duties of, 185–186
  (*See also* career discussion for each marketing area)
Standard of living, 35–37, 259, 294
Standardizing, 27
Standards, 105, 121
Stock clerks, 218, 220, 221, 235, 250–251, 270, 292, 313
Stock work, 282, 292, 300, 313, 329
Stockholders, 167, 415

INDEX • 471

Storage, 24–25, 226–227
Store group, 247–248, 265
Superettes, 216, 221, 223
Supermarkets, 214–223, 276, 315
Superstores, 214
Supplier, service stations, 298–299
Supply and demand, laws of, 32–33

Tailors, 252, 365, 367
Take-home pay, 162–163, 349
Take-out service, 342
Tangible products, 5
Taxes, 123–124, 159–160, 162, 163, 168
Taxi drivers, 408–409
Taxicabs, 398, 404
Teacher-coordinator, DE, 137, 139, 197, 198, 202, 203, 205, 233, 453
Telephone answering services, 376–377
Telephone directory, Yellow Pages, 449
Telephone skills, 193–194, 198
Tellers, bank, 64, 419–420
Terms of the sale, 157
Ticket agents, 406
Ticket sellers, 391
Time and place value, 7, 38, 227
Time-sales contract, 425
Tips, 123, 349, 357
Top managers, 59, 184, 253, 333, 348–349, 360–361, 383, 393, 425, 435
Tour director, 395, 397
Tourism, 385, 394–397
Toy supermarkets, 287–288
Trade associations, 449
Trade-in, 304
Trade magazines, 328
Trade shows, 264–265, 289, 328, 331
Traffic agent, 406
Traffic manager, 270, 410, 411
Training agreement, 202
Training plan, 202
Training sponsor, 202, 203
Trains, 398, 400
Transit vehicles, local, 398, 403–404
Transportation clerks, 357–358
Transportation services, 398–413
  freight forwarders, 410–411
  future in, 412–413
  importance of, 24, 398
  jobs with common carriers, 404–410
  kinds of, 398–404
  leasing companies, 411–412
Travel agent, 395–397
Travelers' checks, 417
Truck dealers, 304–306
Truck drivers, 236, 271, 292, 319, 332, 408–409, 411
Truck jobber, 231–232
Trucks, 398, 401
Twigs, 243, 261

Ultimate consumers, 11
Underwriter, 434
Unemployment insurance, 163
Uniform Product Code, 232
Uniform supply companies, 375
Unions, 157, 428, 450
Unit pricing, 46
Unskilled workers, 59, 61, 232, 331

Value system, 98, 124
Values:
  definition of, 97–102
  influence on career choice, 121
  kinds of, 98–100
  living and working by, 102
  possible changes in, 462
  in relation to pay, 124
  weighing, 100–101
Variety drugstores, 275
Variety store, 243, 261, 276, 288, 315, 326
Voluntary chains, 171–172, 217, 229, 234, 326

Wages, 123
Waiters/waitresses, 122, 346–347
Waiter's assistants, 346–347
Want ads, 451
Wants, 67, 121, 124, 187–188
Warehouse showrooms, 261
Warehouses, 226–227, 232, 235, 246, 260, 269, 331
Warehousing jobs (*See also* career discussions for each marketing area)
Wholesale distributors (*see* Industrial distributors)
Wholesalers:
  as middlemen, 13
  rack jobbers, 231, 281
  specialty, 230–231, 327
  truck jobbers, 231
  (*See also* career discussion for each marketing area)
Wholesaling:
  by corporate chains, 228, 230, 277
  customers for, 14–16
  and food costs, 225–227
  (*See also* career discussion for each marketing area)
Wholesaling middlemen:
  customers for, 14–16
  definition of, 16
  place in marketing, 13–14
Window-washing companies, 374–375
Word of mouth, 389
Work ethic, 56
Work permit, 201
Working conditions, 88, 122, 355, 423
Workmen's compensation, 430

HF
5415
.B38
1976

MAF

HF
5415
.B38
1976